Sheridan: A Biography, Volume 2

William Fraser Rae

Sheridan
from a drawing in pastels by John Russell, R.A.
in the National Portrait Gallery.

SHERIDAN

A BIOGRAPHY

BY

W. FRASER RAE

With an Introduction

BY

SHERIDAN'S GREAT-GRANDSON

THE MARQUESS OF DUFFERIN AND AVA

WITH PORTRAITS

IN TWO VOLUMES
VOL. II.

LONDON
RICHARD BENTLEY AND SON
Publishers in Ordinary to Her Majesty
1896

SHERIDAN

A BIOGRAPHY

BY

W. FRASER RAE

With an Introduction

BY

SHERIDAN'S GREAT-GRANDSON

THE MARQUESS OF DUFFERIN AND AVA

WITH PORTRAITS

IN TWO VOLUMES

VOL. II.

LONDON

RICHARD BENTLEY AND SON

Publishers in Ordinary to Her Majesty

1896

" The dead are like the stars by day,
Withdrawn from mortal eyes ;
But not extinct : they hold their way
In glory through the skies."
JAMES MONTGOMERY.

CONTENTS OF VOL. II.

		PAGE
I. THEATRICAL AND DOMESTIC		I
II. ON THE TREADMILL IN OPPOSITION		39
III. "FIGHTING FOR THE CROWN"		80
IV. HOME JOYS AND SORROWS		111
V. BUFFETED BY FORTUNE		152
VI. THEATRE AND PARLIAMENT		172
VII. SECOND MARRIAGE AND AFTER YEARS		200
VIII. CALAMITOUS YEARS		236
IX. EYES CLOSED "IN ENDLESS NIGHT"		263
X. CHARACTERISTICS AS A DRAMATIST		298
XI. CHARACTERISTICS AS AN ORATOR		323
XII. THE VERDICT OF POSTERITY?		350
APPENDIX		383
INDEX		435

ILLUSTRATIONS

CONTAINED IN THE SECOND VOLUME.

PORTRAIT OF SHERIDAN, BY JOHN RUSSELL, R.A., REPRO-
DUCED BY PERMISSION FROM THE ORIGINAL IN THE
NATIONAL PORTRAIT GALLERY - - *Frontispiece*

FACSIMILE OF LETTER FROM MRS. SHERIDAN IN WHICH
HER " AVADAVATS SEND THEIR DUTY TO SHERIDAN "
to face page 121

FACSIMILE OF THE COVER OF THE LETTER ADDRESSED
TO SHERIDAN AT SPEAN HILL - *to face page* 148

FACSIMILE OF LETTER FROM MRS. SHERIDAN *to face page* 149

PORTRAIT OF MRS. SHERIDAN AND MRS. TICKELL, REPRO-
DUCED, BY PERMISSION OF THE GOVERNORS, FROM THE
ORIGINAL BY GAINSBOROUGH IN THE GALLERY OF
DULWICH COLLEGE - - - *to face page* 156

MURAL TABLET OVER THE REMAINS OF THOMAS LINLEY
AND HIS DAUGHTERS - - - *to face page* 168

PORTRAIT OF MRS. SHERIDAN AND HER SON CHARLES,
ENGRAVED ON STEEL BY G. J. STODART FROM THE
ORIGINAL BY JOHN HOPPNER, R.A. - *to face page* 200

FACSIMILE OF SHERIDAN'S LETTER REFERRING TO "WAVER-
LEY" - - - - - *to face page* 234

FACSIMILE OF LETTER FROM THE PRINCE REGENT TO
SHERIDAN   -   -   -   -   *to face page*   243

PORTRAIT OF SHERIDAN BY CLINT (THE LATEST PORTRAIT
EXTANT)   -   -   -   -   *to face page*   280

FACSIMILE OF LETTER FROM THE DUKE OF WELLINGTON
to face page   291

FACSIMILE OF LETTER FROM THE MARQUESS OF WELLES-
LEY   -   -   -   -   -   *to face page*   292

REPRODUCTION OF SHERIDAN'S NAME CUT ON A PANEL IN
THE FOURTH FORM ROOM AT HARROW   *to face page*   370

BIOGRAPHY OF SHERIDAN

I.

THEATRICAL AND DOMESTIC.

DESPITE the competing claims and exhausting duties of public life, Sheridan achieved remarkable success in maintaining the high reputation of Drury Lane Theatre, whence he derived his income and to which he owed much of his fame.[1] He plumed himself upon his management of it. Being a consummate judge of players and plays, he obtained the best of both. He strengthened the company by enlisting performers of inimitable talent, among whom were John Kemble, Mrs. Jordan and Mrs. Siddons, and he employed skilful and popular playwrights such as Frederic Reynolds and James Cobb, to supply pieces for the amusement of their contemporaries. The names of nearly all the comedies which then attracted playgoers have passed from the public memory as completely as the names of many comedies which fill theatres at present will have done a century hence. They had their day and served their purpose; the space of their existence

---

[1] "Sheridan's supreme ambition was to be thought the best possible manager of a theatre."—Charles Butler's "Reminiscences," vol. ii., p. 78.

being as comparatively brief as that of the flowers
which are in full bloom for a few hours only, or of
the butterflies which open their beautiful wings at
sunrise and fold them for ever at sunset. General
Burgoyne's *Heiress* was one of the few exceptions.
It is still known by name. However, the marvel
now is that it should ever have been put on a par
with the *School for Scandal*.[1]

Sheridan found it an easier and a less sorrowful
task to gratify playgoers than to soften the heart of
his eccentric father, who considered that his deserts
had not been duly recognized when he was appointed
stage manager of Drury Lane Theatre. He was unpopular there. Mrs. Linley nicknamed him "Old
Surly Boots." A nickname is not an argument.
Yet it is unquestionable that Mr. Thomas Sheridan
conducted himself in a very strange and rather discreditable fashion as a parent. On the 22nd of
June, 1780, he wrote to his son, Charles Francis:
"Never was anything so shocking as the behaviour
of that wretch," his younger son; and, on the 2nd of
December, in that year, he said: "You are the only
treasure I have on earth, and if that were gone, I know
nothing in this world worth living for," saying in the
same letter: "I begged in my last there should be

---

[1] A memorandum by Sheridan concerning, "Remuneration to
Authors for first prices, including copyright," may interest some
readers: "Dramas produced without any considerable expense,
or not exceeding a sum of £100, should be entitled to one-half
the receipts, *First Price* on the 3rd, 6th, 9th and 12th and 21st
nights. If with expense, 6th, 9th, 12th, 15th and 21st nights.
Entertainments without expense, half the second price on the 3rd,
6th, 9th, 12th and 21st nights "

no communication through that quarter," meaning Richard Brinsley. He characterized his daughters in the first of these letters as "two young women who are utterly unqualified to do anything for themselves," adding: "This would make me more unhappy, were it not entirely their own fault; for had they carried into execution the only plan it was in my power to lay down for them, they might at this day not only have been in a state of independence, but of affluence, instead of remaining a burden on their old father."

The truth is that his elder daughter, Alicia, had been happily married, with his consent, to Mr. Joseph Lefanu four years before he expressed himself in this strain, while Elizabeth, the younger one, devoted herself with the loving care of a true daughter and tender woman to cheer his loneliness, and to nurse him in his many hours of illness. She did not marry till after his death. Both of them are thus described in the same letter: "My eldest daughter resembles him [Richard Brinsley] so much in disposition, and in many parts of her character, that I verily believe had she been born of the other sex, she would have been much such another. The younger, who might have been made something of, has been rendered good for nothing, by her example."

On the 15th of April, 1783, Mr. Sheridan wrote to his elder son, whom he had styled "the only treasure I have on earth," and then said that his endeavour would be, "to remember that I have had two daughters, and, if possible, forget that I ever had a son. It may be of use to your peace of mind to forget

that you ever had such an affectionate father." This
letter contains a narrative of grievances during his
connexion with Drury Lane Theatre, while he was
stage manager, and his position is thus depicted :
" At length a scene opened which promised better
days. Garrick's retiring, whose jealousy had long shut
the London theatres against me, such an open[ing]
was made for me both as manager and actor as
might soon have retrieved my affairs, and in no
long space of time have placed me in easy circumstances.   But here a son of mine steps into possession, whose first step was to exclude me wholly from
having any share in it.   Afterwards when by extreme
ill conduct they were threatened with ruin, he agreed
to put the management into my hands upon condition
that I should not appear as a performer, and in this he
got his brother to join him with such earnestness, that
merely to gratify him I acquiesced. . . .   I desire to
know whether if the theatre of Drury Lane had fallen
into the hands of the worst enemy I had in the world,
determined upon ruining me and my family, he could
have taken more effectual means of doing it, than
those which have been pursued by my own son ?"

Elizabeth Sheridan kept a *Journal* during her
sojourn in England between 1784 and 1790, and she
wrote in it on the 5th of October, 1785 : " My father
declared himself much displeased with my conduct
in not having joined in his resentment to Richard
instead of proposing a reconciliation.   He then went
into his usual complaints of the ill conduct of both
his sons and even hints as if he may be driven to
appeal to the world if they persevere in denying

their assistance to his favourite plan." This plan
is thus described by one of his friends, the Rev.
Peter Peckard, Master of Magdalen College, Cambridge, in a letter to Archdeacon Blackburne: "There
is not upon this earth a man of more honour and
honesty [than] my old friend Sheridan. . . . He
thought all the evils of Ireland, civil, moral, and
religious, were owing to this cause, that the bakers,
tailors, and shoemakers, were not brought up
orators. I remonstrated as far as I could touch so
delicate a subject, considered it as folly. He called
me the croaking raven—I was always throwing cold
water on his most favourite scheme. Some of this
cold water at length fell on our correspondence."[1]

On the 11th of July, 1786, Elizabeth Sheridan
recorded: "In speaking of Dick now, my father is
the first to say what you [her sister, Mrs. Joseph
Lefanu] or I or any of his friends last year would have
wished to insinuate but in vain. He acknowledges
his neglect of him [Richard Brinsley] and that even
in the theatrical business that so severely hurt him, he
did not wonder at his [son's] conduct when he reflected
that [though] it was done to serve him and the other
patentees, he still so thwarted Dick's schemes and
wishes that he was not surprised he opposed him.
When I compare this with last year's violence and
execrations on this same son, who has since done
nothing to make him alter his opinion, I can only
wonder at the effects of passion, which could so far
blind a man of my father's understanding and morality

[1] Introductory memoir to "Reminiscences of Mrs. de Morgan,"
p. xxiv.

to the destruction of his own peace and that of his friends."[1]

Sheridan acquired a serviceable companion and most useful associate in his brother-in-law, Richard Tickell. They may have first met in Bath, where Tickell lived in earlier years and was on terms of intimacy with the Linley family. Both of their grandfathers were notable and worthy men, the grandfather of Tickell standing in the relation to Addison that Sheridan's did to Swift. Some pamphlets from Richard Tickell's pen being talked about and praised, he was appointed a Commissioner of Stamps through the influence of his friend Mr. Brummell, private secretary to Lord North. He produced plays and verses after entering the public service. He had a facile pen and a light touch. Moreover, he was, what Mr. Puff professed himself to be, " a practitioner in panegyric, or, to speak more plainly, a professor of the art of puffing." Several plays which the public flocked to see at Drury Lane Theatre owed much of their notoriety to Tickell's exertions in the newspapers.[2]

---

[1] Elizabeth Sheridan wrote her *Journal* for the information of her sister, Mrs. Lefanu, in Dublin. I am under a deep obligation to Mrs. Le Fanu, the widow of Mr. W. R. Le Fanu, the author of "Seventy Years of Irish Life," for allowing me to examine her family papers, of which the *Journal* is one, as well as to Miss Le Fanu for having made faithful copies of those which I desired to use.

[2] Sheridan was not unpractised in the art of puffing. I have found the following paragraph in his handwriting, headed for *The Public Advertiser :* " The manager has got it up in his usual style of liberality ; the performers highly merit the thanks of the author, the manager and the public. The performers were all at home

In 1780, Tickell became the husband of Mary Linley, who, after her eldest sister's union with Sheridan, had filled her place, without exercising her fascination, in the concert rooms at Bath. Maria, the third sister, died unmarried in 1784. Shortly before expiring, she raised her head from the pillow, and sang in a manner that thrilled the sympathetic bystanders, " I know that my Redeemer liveth," her gentle spirit passing away with the last note from her lips.

Most of Sheridan's connexions by marriage were associated with him in his theatrical venture. Mr. Linley, his father-in-law, had a share in the Patent which gave a partial monopoly to Drury Lane Theatre, and he was constantly engaged, in concert with his son Tom, till that son's death by drowning in 1778, either in composing music for new plays or in superintending the production of oratorios. Mrs. Linley had charge of the Wardrobe and she exercised her duties with a regard to economy which was almost over-scrupulous. Her daughter Mary called her " very stingy," and gave her sister examples of the failing. Elizabeth Sheridan met her at The Deepdene in 1788 and noted in her *Journal* that she was incurably vulgar and miserly, adding " though Mrs. Linley's avarice often leads her to do the meanest actions to save a trifle, yet her purse is freely opened to those she loves should any extra-

---

in their respective parts. Mr. Henderson was great beyond description, and if possible excelled his usual excellence. Miss Young and Charles Lewis shone with incomparable lustre, and received from a most crowded and brilliant audience, repeated bursts of applause."

ordinary occasion require her assistance." She lived to the age of 91, and her two sons, the Rev. Ozias Linley and his brother William, had a tablet placed near her grave in St. Paul's, Bloomsbury, "in grateful remembrance of an ever careful and indulgent mother."

Mrs. Sheridan was often assisted by her sister, Mrs. Tickell, in passing judgment upon the new pieces which were offered to the manager of Drury Lane Theatre, and Mrs. Sheridan wrote verses for some which were represented, one being Burgoyne's adaptation of Sedaine's *Richard, Cœur de Lion*. Tickell was not a general favourite : Elizabeth Sheridan wrote to her sister, "You know how I love him and I believe Mrs. Sheridan not much more partial, but these things cannot be helped." Yet he was a great help to Sheridan. He was always ready. His wife wrote to her sister that King, the stage manager at Drury Lane, applied to him for "some new strokes" to be introduced at the end of the first act of *The Critic*, whereupon Tickell at once struck off these references to the events of the day :—" Let me see—Oh! I must revive the Irish propositions in *The Morning Post* and overthrow the Austrian army in *The General Advertiser;* I shall then metamorphose the Minister [Pitt ?] to a spark at Brighthelmstone and conclude the day with a merry attack on the Commissioners at Guildhall and write down the shop tax with their own ink."[1]

The truth is that Sheridan exacted too much from others without delegating sufficient authority

[1] Unpublished Letters from Mrs. Tickell to her sister.

to them.   His father's complaint that he was too
much hampered was not wholly unfounded.   King,
who succeeded him as stage manager, resigned
because he was held responsible without being permitted to exercise sufficient power.   Though hindered by Parliamentary and social engagements from
giving unremitting attention to the theatre, Sheridan
was too jealous of his supremacy to permit a rival
near his chair ; while he had a confidence, which was
not wholly misplaced, in his own capacity for evolving
order out of chaos.   When things were at the worst
he interfered with advantage.   He would have displayed greater foresight and judgment if he had
acted so as to avert entanglements and confusion.

His cleverness rendered him overweening, and
his good fortune in often extricating himself from
difficulties misled him into thinking that he could
never fail.   He inspired others with a belief in himself as an organizer.   Mrs. Tickell gives evidence
of this in a letter which she wrote to her sister in
December, 1784 : "Sheridan seems full of business,
yet in good spirits, so I hope he hasn't many plagues,
tho' there's no judging by his manner.   For, like
Charles in *The School for Scandal*, his spirits and
distresses generally rise together, I think."

While Mrs. Tickell had a high opinion of her
brother-in-law, she was not reticent about his shortcomings, and her remarks are valuable both for their
acuteness and their sincerity.   Her admiration is
shown by writing to Mrs. Sheridan :—"I in particular am one who think you cannot ever be half
kind enough to Sheridan."   The following hint is

suggestive : " I hope you will beg Sheridan to open all his letters ;" and this one is equally so : " You know as well as I that Sheridan's days are generally weeks."

Thomas Linley was subject in middle life to violent headaches and to fits of depression ; in later years his mental faculties were entirely obscured ; while, after Sheridan married his daughter, he required to be cheered and comforted. His son-in-law appears to have done his best for him. Writing about her father, Mrs. Tickell says to her sister : —" What a comical letter Sheridan writ to him. Did you see it ? It was a very good-natured action in him and as such I put it down in my white book." Four years after Mrs. Tickell wrote these words, Elizabeth Sheridan gave her sister in Dublin the following account of Mr. Linley : "Mrs. Sheridan is very uneasy about her father who, ever since [having had a kind of paralytic attack] has suffered constant violent pain in his head. It is really distressing to see him, and [she] says she cannot divest herself of the horrid dread of seeing him fall dead before her ; loving him as she does, you may suppose what she suffers Her attentions to him are unremitting." She adds in a subsequent letter : " If Mr. Linley had no other cause of illness [than his wife's incessant prate] such constant teasing would be sufficient to account for his headaches."

During the fiery debates which succeeded the acceptance of the Premiership by William Pitt, when he was in a minority in the House of Commons, Mrs. Tickell wrote to her sister : " I send you *The Morning*

Chronicle of Tuesday, which only came out to-day, that you may read the debate. I suppose Sheridan has been modest about himself, but you will see by the papers what credit he got, and I assure you everybody says his was the next best speech to Fox's in the House."[1] While he was on a visit in the country, Mrs. Tickell wrote that her husband had told her : " Sheridan is expected in town every day, so it is to be hoped he will set matters in a little better train at Drury Lane ; for at present he [Tickell] says the receipts are dismal to a degree of ruin ; that my father, however, seems contented with the quiet of King's management."

Mrs. Tickell wrote daily to her sister when they were separated and commented on theatrical affairs in a way which was always shrewd and sometimes very happy. On the 2nd of January, 1784, she saw Mrs. Siddons play Lady Randolph in *Douglas*, and wrote :—" Mrs. Siddons is as much the rage as when she first appeared—this illness has given an amazing fillip to people's curiosity to see her—and I think she plays better than ever she did ; 'twas Lady Randolph last night and she exerted herself beyond anything I ever saw." When she played Margaret of Anjou in *The Earl of Warwick*, towards the close of the same year, Mrs. Tickell thus characterizes her performance :—" I may tell you Mrs. Siddons was charming and very different from what we had ever

---

[1] It is probable that the speech referred to was delivered on the 16th of January, 1784, in Committee on the State of the Nation. The report, which is imperfect, begins : " Mr. Sheridan very ably supported the motion."

seen of her.   If you remember the part, there is not only a great deal of ranting, that is in the style of *Zara*, but also a sort of irony and level speaking, or rather familiar conversation that placed her quite in a new light.   *I* thought she was very great indeed. Yet in your life you never saw anything so like Kemble in every look and word as her familiar tones. She had amazing applause, yet it was the *fashion* I found, after the play, to speak rather slightingly of her, for Mr. Fitzpatrick came into the box and gave his fiat rather against her."

Next to Mrs. Siddons, no more popular actress than Mrs. Jordan was engaged by Sheridan for Drury Lane Theatre.   Her first appearance there on the 18th of October, 1785, was chronicled by Mrs. Tickell :—" I went last night to see our new Country Girl, and I can assure you, if you have any reliance on *my* judgment, she has more genius in her little finger than Miss Brunton in her whole body.   I could not help looking back at past days, during the play, as, if you have recollection of the circumstances, it was in *this* play, altered purposely by Garrick, a certain friend of *yours* was to have made an honourable and delicate *entrée* into the world.[1] But to this little actress ; for little she is and yet not insignificant in her figure, which, though *short*, has a certain roundness and *embonpoint* which is very graceful.   Her voice is harmony itself, in level *quiet* speaking (we had an opportunity of judging this in

---

[1] The allusion here is probably to Mrs. Tickell herself, whom some have supposed to have been an actress, while her adopting the stage as a profession was contemplated, but not carried out.

a few lines she spoke in the way of epilogue like
Rosalind), and it has certain little breaks and unde-
scribable tones which in simple archness have a
wonderful effect, and I think (without exception
even of Mrs. Siddons) she has the most *distinct*
delivery of any actor or actress I ever heard.   Her
face I could not see, owing to the amazing bunch of
hair she had pulled over her forehead, but they tell
me it is expressive, but not very pretty ; her figure
is such as I have described, and uncommonly pretty
in boy's clothes, which she goes into in the 3rd act.
Her action is *odd ;* I think there is something foreign
in it, at least it is a little *outré*, which however was
probably affected for the character—for nothing
could suit it better.   Tickell was in raptures, and,
indeed, I think Sheridan would be almost tempted
to give us the poor *Forresters* if he saw what a
pretty boy Mrs. Jordan makes."[1]

Mrs. Tickell next saw Mrs. Jordan on the 11th of
November, when she played Viola in *Twelfth Night*,
and then she wrote :—" Now for Mrs. Jordan.   I dare
say I am wrong in my opinion, as everybody else
likes her very much indeed, but I own I do not

[1] Mrs. Inchbald records that, at this performance, Mrs. Jordan
" displayed such consummate art with such bewitching nature—
such excellent sense, and such innocent simplicity, that her
auditors were boundless in their plaudits, and so warm in their
praises, when they left the theatre, that their friends at home would
not give credit to the extent of their eulogiums."   Boaden writes
that when she appeared in male attire in the 3rd act, " the great
painter of the age pronounced her figure the neatest and most
perfect in symmetry that he had ever seen."—" Life of Mrs. Jordan,"
vol. i., pp. 69 and 72.

entirely approve of her Viola ; to me she was too
precise in her manner of delivery, too like tragedy,
and, by-the-bye, she (I am sure) would make a sweet
tragedian, for her voice in the pathetic is musical
and soft, and she has the Siddons' 'Oh !' in perfection. Her figure is very pretty and she has a
very elegant deportment, particularly in her breeches.
You can't conceive how she was applauded, and
really deserved it."

Ten days later, Mrs. Tickell saw Mrs. Jordan in two
parts, performed for the first time by her in Drury
Lane, that of Imogen in *Cymbeline* and Priscilla
Tomboy in *The Romp*, the latter proving to be a
favourite one, and she wrote to Mrs. Sheridan :—
"Well, ma'am, all I can say, now that I *have* seen her,
is that I think her by much the best comedian on
either stage, or that *I* ever saw, the Imogen was
but la la, that is, by way of anything great . . . the
Romp, however, made amends for all, and very great
applause indeed she very deservedly received. She
is not much of a singer, but her voice is by no means
disagreeable, and she sings very well in tune. The
Papers did not praise her half enough. . . . I saw
Mrs. Siddons after the play in Fosbrook's room.
She had been in Dr. Ford's box and was delighted
with Mrs. Jordan."[1]

[1] Windham was in Sheridan's box at Drury Lane on the 28th of
May, 1791, when Mrs. Jordan appeared as "Rosalind," and he
wrote: "I am still of opinion, there is more in her person and
natural manners than in her acting. Her merit lies out of her
part. The words set down by the author she does not repeat with
greater propriety of tone, emphasis or gesture than others. But
she has of these, certain peculiarities, which indicate dispositions,
such as take strong hold of the affections, at least of the male

In a letter written between those from which the last two extracts are taken, there is an interesting reference to Gainsborough's great painting in which Mrs. Sheridan and Mrs. Tickell are depicted to the life, and those who have admired it in the Gallery at Dulwich may be gratified when they read what was thought of it by those who were immediately concerned :—" When I came home last night [November 1st, 1785] I found *our* picture come home from Gainsbro's very much improved and freshened up. My father and mother are quite in raptures with it : indeed, it is in *my* opinion, the *best* and *handsomest* of *you* that I have ever seen."

The following letter was probably addressed by Mrs. Sheridan to her sister-in-law in Dublin, Mrs. Lefanu, about the same time as those from which I have given extracts : " I would say something by way of excuse for my long silence, only that you must confess the fault has been mutual. The fact is, we are both lazy correspondents and, while we believe we are both happy and well, are not too anxious to trouble one another with long letters. I am sincerely rejoiced to hear that you are in a better state of health and hope that you will not be prevented by *any* cause from paying your visit to this land of beef and pudding as you intended this winter.

part of her audience ; and therefore, when the part is of a sort to admit a large portion of these, she produces a great effect. The true acting of the part may, in many instances, not require what she throws into it, but it may admit it ; and if the expression so thrown in is of the sort described, the effect of the whole will be improved, though the part is neither better nor worse acted."— " Diary " of William Windham, pp. 227, 228.

"I am sorry you have not seen Mrs. Canning.[1] She is the woman I love best out of my own family and I was anxious that you should be acquainted, because I am sure you would like one another. She complained to me in her letter of having called on you often in vain. I hope by this time all mistakes are cleared up, and that you have met. . . .

"I heard of Mrs. C. Sheridan's happy advancement some time ago, and expected to hear she had been delivered. Charles wrote Dick a letter of ten sheets on your Irish politics. Dick offered me the perusal, but I declined it as you may suppose, being fully satisfied at hearing that *he* thought *all* parties *perfectly in the wrong*, and that all the speeches that had been made in the English House of Commons were perfect *nonsense*, tho' he allowed Dick's to be the best and nearest to common sense. I don't trouble my head much on the subject, as I see no prospect of our gaining any advantage from Pitt's

[1] Her maiden name was Mehetabel Patrick. She was the mother of Lord Stratford de Redcliffe. In a letter from Mrs. Sheridan to Mrs. Canning, during Mrs. Canning's visit to what Mrs. Sheridan styles "the land of saints and potatoes," she says : "I have at last the satisfaction of knowing that your silence has not been occasioned by anything more disagreeable than your eternal dinner parties of fourteen. The description of the life you lead has given me the horrors, and I think I had rather submit to any confinement, than *suffer* your *Irish hospitality* for a month together. My head aches at the thought of the endless bustle, and fatigue of body and mind you must endure. Never complain of weak nerves, or call me a little wiry woman again, I entreat you, for if you return safe and sound after this ordeal, I am sure it will be affectation in you to pretend not to be able to keep up with me in the gentle dissipation of a London life."

disgrace, tho' to be sure it is not unpleasant to have him so completely odious and unpopular as he has continued to make himself everywhere. He has been burnt in effigy in most of the great towns in England and I fancy you think burning too good for him with you.

"I have been leading a very quiet life lately at Putney in Mrs. [Stratford] Canning's cottage, which she kindly lent me during her absence. I came to Town last week, and have been detained from day to day by the Duchess of Devonshire, who expects to lie in every hour, and consequently never goes out. And the Town is so extremely empty that every person is of consequence to her, as she has a little party every night. I am afraid tho' this must be the last I can afford her, for I have just heard from my sister, who returns from her excursion to the sea to-night, and means to go directly to her children at Hampton Court, where I shall be impatient to see and embrace her.

"I have had the care of her little ones in her absence, and anxious enough I have been about them, as you may suppose. They are beautiful and engaging creatures. Her girl makes me such a fool that I am sometimes persuaded I never loved Tom [my own son] so much. He is very well and at home for the holidays. He is a fine boy with great talents for everything, but he has been sadly neglected and a little spoilt, but we are making amends now, and I hope in a few years he will be no dishonour to his house. God bless you. Give my compliments to Mr. Lefanu and kiss [for] me *my* nephew. Dick sends his kindest love to you."

She wrote to her father from Hampton Court, during a visit to her sister at the Palace, on the 5th of September [1785 ?]: "I have just been scolding Sheridan well for depriving me of the satisfaction I should have felt at receiving a cheerful letter from you, but he says in his defence that he kept it from me purposely, as he was sure it would not have had the effect on me you perhaps intended. As he wrote to you himself, I hope he told you of this trick, otherwise I fear I must have appeared very unkind and neglectful towards you, when in reality I was suffering a great deal of uneasiness at your silence.   I am afraid I shall not see you [for] some time, as we leave Town [on] Wednesday morning, but I am rejoiced to hear you intend going to the sea.   Brighthelmstone is the nearest place to London and you will probably find it the more agreeable as Mr. and Mrs. Birch are going there, who will save you the trouble of seeking society among new faces, which I know you are not fond of.

"You will find that theatrical affairs are going on very well.   Sheridan has had a great many consultations with Mr. King, and the pantomime promises to be very successful.   By Sheridan's desire, too, Mr. Cobb has been some time engaged in writing an Opera,[1] which is finished and which Mr. King thinks very highly of.

"Sheridan has promised to correct and improve it, and proposes that you should take it with you to the sea-side, where the setting it will, I trust, be no

---

[1] This was *The Strangers at Home*, performed at Drury Lane Theatre on the 8th of December, 1785.   The piece had a run of fourteen nights.

unprofitable amusement to you.   Sheridan has a
great opinion of Cobb as a comic writer, and means
to give him every assistance in his power, but he
has been particularly anxious to have this Opera
finished on your account, as he thinks (with me) that
such an employment will occupy your thoughts, and
assist the sea air to dissipate all your glooms and
bring you back to us as well and happy as we wish
you to be.

"There is no doubt but we shall have a better
season this year than we have ever had.   Sheridan
thinks the pantomime will do great things.   It is to
be a speaking one.   Cobb writes the dialogue and
there are to be two harlequins, a talking one and a
dumb one, which we think will have a very good
effect.   Then there is Mrs. Cowley's comedy and
General Burgoyne's (to say nothing of Dr. Delap)[1],
and the Opera to conclude with as a *bonne bouche*, if
it is not ready before, so you see, my dear father, the
theatre has a good prospect.

"And now I have some good news too for you,
that concerns you more particularly, which is that
the scheme of the Oratorios at the Pantheon is
entirely given up, so that they are still open to you,
and depend on it, if you will but exert yourself and
engage good performers, the King will still come to
them.   I shall see Sir Watkin [Williams Wynn]

[1] The first of these three is *A School for Greybeards, or The
Mourning Bride* which was produced on the 25th of November,
1786; the second is *The Heiress*, the first representation of which
was on the 14th of January, 1786, and the third, *The Captives*, was
put on the stage on the 9th of March, 1786.   Kemble wrote to
Malone after the third representation of the last piece: "The
Captives were set at liberty last night amidst roars of laughter."

very soon and will talk the matter over with him the first opportunity. . . . Would it not be advisable for you to see Cramer again now, as I am convinced if you could fix him as your partner, he would not let the Queen rest till he had gained a promise of protection. You may depend on the truth of the Pantheon scheme being given up, as Sheridan had it from Simpson himself. They could not agree among themselves, and he was afraid of the expense, as the King would only promise to come six times. I daresay you might retain them with credit, by a little spirit, which I hope you will exert directly. I am only anxious for this, as it will amuse and occupy you ; for the profit is not an object, I insist upon it, to affect your happiness or comforts, for as I told you before, I'm sure we shall be all Crœsuses very soon.

" Mr. Pitt will be routed next sessions, and then we shall get something *substantial*, that cannot be lost again. In the meantime, Sheridan is settling all his affairs very comfortably, and he has interested himself a great deal about the theatre, in order that you may have the less to prevent your going to the sea and taking care of your health, which is as dear to him as anybody in the world. He has bargained with a very clever Frenchman too, to get over all the new French little pieces as they come out, if they succeed. Beaumarchais is going to bring one out soon which is expected to be better liked than *Figaro* and we are to have it certainly.[1]

[1] The work referred to may have been Beaumarchais' Opera *Tarare*, which disappointed the expectations expressed above ; not succeeding in Paris, and not being represented in London after translation into English by C. James.

"I have written you a long dull, matter of fact letter, but I hope you will find it more entertaining than my flights of the imagination, and that the prospect of everything succeeding so well will give you as much satisfaction as it does me to be able to assure you of the truth of all I have told you. I have only to add that we are all in good health and spirits here, and beg our joint loves and affection to all at Bath."

The pantomime, about which Mrs. Sheridan expressed herself sanguine of success, was called *Hurly Burly, or the Fairy of the Well.* She was at Bath on the night of its production during the Christmas holidays of 1785, and her sister informed her of the result : " ' When the Hurly Burly's done, When the battle's lost or won ';—this was not a very inapt quotation you'll say, for last night before the play began ; but alas! my dear friend, to our unspeakable dismay, and most particularly my mother's, there was no Hurly Burly but *on* the stage ; pit, box and gallery were as *orderly* as our enemies could wish. However, the night was *dreadful*, which was a back door for your vanity to creep out at. . . . I must refer you to the newspapers for a critique, as they were more just than favourable, but upon my word, I think upon the whole the pantomime was by no means a bad one tho' there is not that entire novelty announced in the bills, for in the first place, you know, the idea of a speaking and dumb harlequin was brought forward at Colman's theatre [in the Haymarket] in the summer, and the power of a ring changing persons etc. certainly takes root from harlequin Touchstone."

She said in a subsequent letter :—" The fact is, between ourselves, the pantomime totally failed, that is so far failed in *never* bringing a good house, which I take it is of worse consequence to the Treasury, tho' perhaps not so *disgraceful* as if it had been fairly damned the first night."

Mrs. Sheridan's hope that William Pitt would soon resign, was as fallacious as her expectation that the pantomime would succeed, and the flattering tale of the family becoming "Crœsuses," with which she comforted her father, displayed greater liveliness of imagination and buoyancy of disposition than capacity for coolly calculating chances. However, she may have felt compensated for other disappointments by the success of General Burgoyne's *Heiress*. Her sister had read that comedy in manuscript, and she wrote concerning it :—" I must scribble my critique on *The Heiress* (which perhaps is a name you may not know the new comedy by). I think your applause much too cold for it, and I'm sure I can find the hand of the *Master* in several tints—eh ? Is it not so ?" This comedy was first performed on the 14th of January, 1786. Mrs. Tickell's letter about it, dated, with customary vagueness, " The very middle of the night," informed her sister :—"We have *all* just been roused from the leaden arms of sleep by your express, and I scribble this from bed with only one eye open. The play went off with the most brilliant and satisfactory applause, epilogue and all, which poor Burgoyne had prepared in a hurry, in case of an emergency.[1]

[1] Sheridan had forgotten his promise to write the epilogue.

"They have had a meeting at King's [room] to-day, (or I believe rather yesterday) to make a few necessary curtailments which the whole house was of opinion was the only thing to be done to it, to render it the most finished performance since the comedy *The School for Scandal.*"

Horace Walpole informed Lady Ossory, on the 16th of January, 1786, he had heard that *The Heiress* "succeeded extremely well and was, besides, excellently acted ;" nearly a year later, Walpole said that General Burgoyne had written "the best modern comedy, because he moved in good society."

Debrett, the publisher, gave two hundred pounds for the copyright of *The Heiress*, this being the largest sum which had then been paid for such a work ; yet his liberality did not empty his purse, as ten editions of the comedy were sold within a year. It was translated into French, German, Italian, and Spanish. Despite its success on the stage and in print, and Walpole's exaggerated praise, Burgoyne's blundering at Saratoga will preserve his memory longer than his triumph on the stage of Drury Lane. To put *The Heiress* on a par with *The School for Scandal* is as ridiculous as to rank Dryden's version of *The Tempest* with Shakespeare's. Not a character in it is a familiar name to any except the few who are careful students of dramatic literature, nor does one of them deserve lasting remembrance. Lady Sneerwell and Sir Peter Teazle, Charles and Joseph Surface, Lady Teazle and Sir Benjamin Backbite are as well known names as those of the popular novelists and statesmen of the day ; but who is there

that knows, or, being acquainted with them, cares anything about the principal personages in *The Heiress*,
such as Lady Emily Flint and Mr. Clifford, Lord Gay-
ville and Mr. Blandish, Miss Alscrip the vulgar heiress
and Mr. Alscrip her still more vulgar father, Mrs.
Blandish the fawning friend and Tiffany the pert lady's
maid, Chignon, the caricature of a French servant,
and Prompt, the caricature of an English one? The
best point in the piece may have been borrowed
from, or inserted by, Sheridan. Clifford having said,
" Words are wanting, Lady Emily," she interrupts
him with the phrase :—" I wish they may be, with all
my heart ; but it is generally remarked, that ' wanting
words ' is the beginning of a florid set speech."

A play by Burgoyne, which had as great success
as *The Heiress* and deserved it better, was *Richard,
Cœur de Lion*, adapted from the French of Sedaine.
In the French version the music was by Grétry ; the
words and air of the song : " *O Richard, O mon Roi*,"
were long in favour with royalist Frenchmen; Linley
supplied the music for the English adaptation. Eight
days before the performance of the piece at Drury
Lane, another version by Leonard MacNally had
been put on the stage at Covent Garden Theatre,
and Mrs. Tickell wrote a depreciatory account of
it, being quite right in her censure, as MacNally's
rendering failed to attract. After seeing Burgoyne's
adaptation on the 24th of October, 1786, she said :
—" Richard's himself again ; in plain matter of fact
prose, never were the most sanguine expectations of
success so completely gratified last night as at our
Richard, and what delighted us all more than any-

thing was that the carpenters exerted themselves so
much that there was not the least degree of im-
patience shown by the audience before the 2nd act
opened with such a wonderful alteration of beautiful
scenery that it seemed quite the effect of magic to
have had it there so soon." She wrote again :—
"We ladies went to Mrs. Garrick's box, and there
for the *third* time we were charmed with *Richard*.
It went so much better than either of the preceding
nights, and the applause if possible was much
warmer." The acting of Mrs. Jordan and Kemble
produced a strong impression. Nothing had been
omitted that could bring about the desired result.
Mr. Tickell, as his wife told her sister, "was very
busy in preparing his *cleveralities* for the Papers, so
look for the hand of a master in *The Herald*."[1]

Mrs. Tickell's letters resemble sprightly conversation. Though less beautiful and accomplished than
her eldest sister, she was greatly admired and deservedly beloved.[2] Her death at the early age of

[1] Sir Gilbert Elliot saw the piece on the 13th of February, 1787,
and wrote : "Never in my life was [I] more highly entertained and
delighted than by *Richard, Cœur de Lion*. It is a most interesting
story from our history made into a little opera at Paris, and translated now into English. Mrs. Jordan is quite divine in it."—
"Life and Letters," vol. i., p. 128.

[2] Elizabeth Sheridan wrote in her *Journal* for the 30th of
September, 1784 : "When dinner was over Mrs. Sheridan and I
went to Drury Lane. We found Mrs. Tickell seated in the box ;
she came up to me with the warmth of an old friend and I was
really happy to see her. She has grown a complete little matron.
She looks I think much older than Mrs. S. and has more completely lost her beauty than I thought possible for so young a
woman."

twenty-eight was as truly mourned by her sister as by her husband.   The story of her closing years is succinctly and pathetically recorded by Mrs. Sheridan, on the 24th of August, 1791, in a paper enclosing the letters which she treasured almost as carefully as she did her sister's three children :—" In February, 1787, my dear sister came to Town in a bad state of health.   On the 15th of May, she returned to Hampton Court without having received any benefit from the various remedies prescribed for her.   The three last letters were written between the 15th and 25th, when she was once more brought to Town dangerously ill of a fever which turned to a hectic that never afterwards left her.   On the 15th of June she was carried back to Hampton Court, where I remained with her, and on the 19th we went by slow stages to Clifton Hill near the Hot Wells with a faint hope that the air and waters might restore her ; but after struggling with this most dreadful of all diseases [consumption], and bearing with gentlest patience and resignation the various pains and horrors which mark its fatal progress, on the 27th of July she ceased to suffer, and I for ever lost the friend and companion of my youth, the beloved sister of my heart, whose loss never can be repaired, whose sweet and amiable qualities endeared her to all who were so happy [as] to know her.   She died in the 29th year of her age, universally regretted and lamented, and was buried in the Cathedral at Wells, where she spent her infancy, and where she enjoyed happiness and poverty the first year of her marriage.   In less than two years afterwards Mr. Tickell married again a beautiful young woman of 18!!!   The dear children remained with me till that time.   The [two] boys were then taken home by their father.   The girl, the dying legacy of her ever dear and lamented mother, is still mine and constitutes all my happiness."[1]

Mrs. Sheridan wrote some lines on her sister which have been printed.   She wrote an epitaph which, if published, is not widely known :

" You who have mourned the sister of your heart,
   The dear companion of your youthful years,
Pass not regardless, drop ere you depart
On this sad spot your tributary tears.
For here the truest friend for ever lies.
The best, the kindliest, loveliest, most beloved,
Whose cheerful spirit brightened in her eyes
And graced the virtues which her life approved.
Modestly wise and innocently gay,
She lived—to my grieved heart a blessing given,
Till God approving, from its beauteous clay,
Called the pure spirit to its native Heaven."

Twelve months after Mrs. Tickell's death, Sheridan mourned the loss of his father.   In the summer of 1788, the impaired state of Mr. Sheridan's health made him resolve to make a voyage to Lisbon, as Henry Fielding had done thirty-four years earlier.   The brutal treatment to which Fielding was subjected on board ship contributed to his death two months after reaching the city where he hoped

[1] Richard Tickell died on the 4th of November, 1793, owing to a fall, which may have been an accident, from the parapet outside the rooms at Hampton Court where he was in the habit of reading.   His spirits had been greatly depressed before his death. Sheridan made provision for his two sons, obtaining a writership in India for the one and a commission in the Navy for the other.

to regain strength.   Mr. Sheridan's daughter, Elizabeth, accompanied him on his journey from Dublin
to Margate.   When resting in London on the way,
she records a visit received on the 27th of July,
"from Dick and his wife.   All passed off very well.
My father a little stately at first but soon thoroughly
cordial with his son, who staid till near six but could
not dine with us."   On the following day, after returning from a walk, she says that she : "found
Mrs. Sheridan with my father, as kind and attentive
to him as possible, strongly pressing him to spend
some time at [The] Deepdene, offering to be his
nurse, to play with him [at cards], in short everything
that could flatter him or induce him to comply, but
he keeps to his own intentions."

Disregarding his physician's advice, Mr. Sheridan
took a hot salt-water bath at Margate and was
attacked with a violent fever.   After learning that he
was dangerously ill, his younger son hastened to his
bed-side, and wrote to his brother, Charles Francis,
two days before the end came : "It is to no purpose
to use many words in communicating tò you the
melancholy situation in which I have found my father
at this place [Margate].   He is I fear past all hope.
I have requested Dr. Morris to write you a more particular account ; but be prepared every hour to hear
the worst.   No view of sickness or decay while death
is at a distance gives an idea of the frightful scene
of being present at the last moments of such a person
and so circumstanced.   You will prepare and inform
my sister in the properest manner.   Poor Betsy [his
sister] is almost laid up."

Mr. Sheridan died in the afternoon of the 14th of August, 1788, and Dr. Morris, who was his friend as well as his physician, sent particulars of the event to Charles Francis in Dublin. Mr. Jarvis, a surgeon in Margate who attended Mr. Sheridan before the arrival of Dr. Morris, informed Moore that he was present when the younger son arrived, " and witnessed an interview in which the father showed himself to be strongly impressed by his son's attention, saying, with considerable emotion, ' Oh! Dick, I give you a great deal of trouble,' and seeming to imply by his manner that his son had been less to blame than himself, for any want of cordiality between them."

No special merit is due to Sheridan for displaying filial piety towards a parent who had thwarted and vilified him.[1] Mrs. Sheridan, however, acted in a way which not many daughters-in-law have done, when they have been hated and reviled. On the 17th of August, 1788, she wrote as follows to Mrs. Lefanu, the elder daughter of Mr. Sheridan :

" By the time you receive this, I hope your reason and religion have brought your mind to submit with duty and resignation to the severe affliction it has pleased God to visit you with. On such occasions,

---

[1] " Rogers mentioned that Sheridan's father said : ' Talk of the merit of Dick's comedy ! [*The School for Scandal.*] There's nothing in it. He had but to dip the pencil in his own heart, and he'd find there the characters of both Joseph and Charles.' " " Lord Lansdowne told me in the evening that old Sheridan once gave a very bad character of Richard Brinsley to his father Lord Shelburne ; said he was a person not to be trusted." Moore's *Diary*, vol. iv., pp. 226-230.

I, by woeful experience, well know how idle all attempts at consolation are by argument or eloquence.

"Your own reflection, my dear Lissy, must, and I hope has afforded you the greatest of all possible comforts, the consciousness of having done your duty, and promoted, to the best of your ability, the happiness and welfare of your father through life. You will likewise reflect, and be grateful that he was not taken from his family prematurely, that he lived to see his children established in the world with honour and reputation, and to be himself the object of universal respect and esteem, as well for his public talents as private virtues. Had he lived longer, it would have been only a prolongation of pain both of body and mind, and we have every reason to be assured that he has exchanged this life for a better. The principles of our religion which I know you profess and believe, teach us to hope that the greatest sinners may receive mercy from a being whose first attribute it is. But your father, my dear Lissy, was a *good* man, he had no vices to repent of, his foibles were as few as most men's, and in him more constitutional than habitual.

"These are all motives of comfort; to use any arguments to persuade you to make use of that reason which God has blest you with, would be affronting both to your understanding and the goodness of your heart. You have ties to endear life, and your affection and duty to those dear objects which surround you will, I have no doubt, restore your mind to the tranquility and happiness which, with such blessings, you ought to enjoy with gratitude.

" My dear Dick and poor Betsy came here from
Margate last night, both, I thank God, perfectly
well, and more resigned and comforted than I could
have hoped. My Dick had the delight of seeing his
poor father sensible of and grateful for the dutiful
attention and affectionate tenderness shown to him,
and though he acknowledged the worth of such a
son too late, I thank God he *did* at last look on him
with tenderness, and appeared touched with the
anxiety he expressed about him.

" Betsy has not yet quite recovered her fatigue
and affliction, but I trust in a few days she will feel
more comfortable and at her ease in a strange place,
which this, at present, must appear to her. I have
endeavoured to convince her, that her future happiness will be an object very interesting to me, that
my house shall always be a home, and my heart a
refuge for her, that my dear husband's sister is *mine*
in every sense of the word, and that nothing in my
power will be wanting to make her easy and happy.
There are some occasions where excess of feeling
deprives one of the power to express it, and my
great anxiety to make poor Bess feel at her ease, and
consider herself with me, as with a sister who loves
and esteems her, will probably prevent my expressing
myself as warmly as I feel. Do you then, my dear
Lissy, assure her of my sincerity and tell her how
happy she will make me by appearing easy in her present situation, and confident of my affection for her.

" Dick desires me to say all that is kind and affectionate to you, and to assure you (but I am sure I
need not assure *you*) that he will do everything in

his power to make poor Bess comfortable and *in-dependent*, which wherever she resides *must* be necessary to her enjoyment of any kindness. I hope to hear from you soon. God bless and comfort you, my dear woman."

Sheridan returned to Margate, without resting a night at The Deepdene, and his brother-in-law, Tickell, and his friend Richardson were present with him at his father's funeral in the church at St. Peter's, being the parish adjoining that in which Margate is situated.[1]

The *Journal* kept by Elizabeth Sheridan contains a graphic picture of the life led at The Deepdene by her brother and his wife. A week after her father's death she wrote for the information of her sister in Dublin : "Since my brother's leaving us to go to Margate, I have sat at times with Mrs. Sheridan, who is kind and considerate ; so that I have entire liberty. Her poor sister's children [Mrs. Tickell's] are all with her. The girl gives her constant employment, and seems to profit by being under so good an instructor. She is a little affected but as that is not encouraged by her Aunt it will wear off, of course, and she will probably be a very fine girl. Their father was here for some days, but I did not see him. Last night Mrs. Sheridan showed me the picture of Mrs. Tickell which she wears round her

---

[1] Mr. Sheridan enjoined in his Will, which was executed at Richmond in Yorkshire in 1774, that he was to be buried in the parish next to that in which he died. He made provision for a sister, for his son Charles Francis, and for his two daughters ; but he did not even mention the son who soothed his last hours, whose purse was at his service and who was chief mourner at his funeral.

neck. The thing was misrepresented to you :—it was not done after her death, but a short time before it. The sketch was taken while she slept, by a painter at Bristol. This, Mrs. Sheridan got copied by Cosway, who has softened down the traces of illness in such a way that the picture conveys no gloomy idea. It represents her in a sweet sleep; which must have been soothing to her friend, after seeing her for a length of time in a state of constant suffering. . . .

" Last night Tom [Sheridan] who came home for the holidays brought yours of the 16th [of August] enclosing Harry's note. I cannot answer any letter at present till I hear from you and Mr. Lefanu. I shall not have a minute's ease. It will be a fortnight Tuesday since I sent the first alarming intelligence to Mr. Lefanu. Dick is still in Town and we do not expect him for some time. Mrs. Sheridan seems now quite reconciled to these little absences which she knows are unavoidable.

" I never saw anyone so constant in employing every moment of time, and to that I attribute in great measure the recovery of her health and spirits. The education of her niece, her music, books, and work occupy every minute of the day. After dinner the children (who call her Mama-aunt) spend some time with us and her manner to them is truly delightful. The girl you know is the eldest. The eldest boy is about 5 years old, very like his father but extremely gentle in his manners. The youngest is past three. The whole set then retire to the music room. As yet I cannot enjoy their parties. A song from Mrs. Sheridan affected me last night in a most painful manner. I shall not try the experiment soon again. But at least here I am at liberty in every respect. Mrs. Sheridan blamed herself for putting me to the trial, and after tea got a book which she read to us till supper. This I find is their general way of spending the evening."

About six weeks later she wrote : " Yesterday our little circle was broke up. Mrs. S. and I had walked and had just agreed that we would save ourselves the trouble of a second toilette when a note from Dick changed our whole plan. He announced his return to dinner and also a visit from the Duke of Norfolk [who had lent him The Deepdene] who has been expected here for some days past. . . . About six he made his appearance. Dick not yet arrived and what was worse some fish and game which he had promised to bring was expected for dinner. Mrs. S. put the best face on the matter and ordered up dinner such as it was. Some time after the cloth was removed, arrived our Brother who had been detained by a variety of cross accidents. . . . In the evening we had music. Miss [Jane] Linley's voice goes charmingly with her sister's in duets. Mrs. Sheridan's voice I think as perfect as ever I remember it. That same peculiar tone that I believe is hardly to be equalled in the world as every one is struck with it in the same way. We had no cards.

" The Duke in appearance gives one the idea of a good honest gentleman farmer, dressed in a plain grey frock, and brown curly head ; his face is handsome but his person very large and unwieldy. He is very civil, very good humoured seemingly, and perfectly unaffected. . . .

"This morning our visitor left us. Yesterday the dinner made up for the plain fare of the day before. Turtle, venison &c., and he did such honour to it as showed he must have been punished the first day. To see him eat, his bulk is at once accounted for, as any four reasonable men might be satisfied with what he takes in a day. In the evening Cribbage was proposed which I play ill but as there was one absolutely wanted and the Duke was my partner I ran no risk in playing as Dick and I were to settle together so I lost without being any the poorer. . . . Mrs. Sheridan is now working hard at some music they were preparing for Drury Lane Theatre to save him [her father] the labour as much as possible. Indeed I think she exerts herself rather too much, for upon the idea of keeping herself constantly employed I think she exhausts her spirits."

In her records of conversation, she gives Mrs. Sheridan's experiences in "animal magnetism" which excited as much wonder and empty speculation then as wonders of an analogous character do at the present day. Mrs. Sheridan placed herself under the influence of Dr. Marmaduke[1] and "was thrown into a state which she describes as very distressing. It was a kind of fainting without absolute insensibility. She could hear and feel but had no power to speak or move." When she told her

[1] Sir Gilbert Elliot spells the name Mainaduc and says that Dr. Bell was another "of the magnetising quacks." He adds that "Lady Palmerston, Mrs. Crewe, Mrs. Sheridan and Miss Crewe have been twice at Mainaduc's. . . . The next time, Mrs. Sheridan and Miss Crewe were both magnetised, and both had what is called a crisis."—"Life and Letters," vol. i., p. 111.

husband what had happened, " he blamed her very much and made her give him a solemn promise never to try the experiment again." Miss Sheridan adds that when Dr. Marmaduke exercised his power, " the Duchess of Devonshire was thrown into hysterics, Lady Salisbury put to sleep the same morning, and the Prince of Wales so near fainting that he turned quite pale and was forced to be supported. To what good purpose this amazing power can be turned I cannot at present conceive."[1]

Many entries in Miss Sheridan's *Journal* show that her brother lived in a whirl of theatrical and political business. She makes it clear that he was a most good-natured man. Such an one, however, is often an untrustworthy friend. She observed daily that her brother promised what he was wholly unable to perform ; but in her own case he kept his generous undertakings to the letter. He was ready, also, to make appointments which he could not keep, and in this way he gave offence to strangers who interpreted his forgetfulness or inability to mean a deliberate slight. His sister-in-law, Mrs. Tickell, wrote a bantering letter on this subject to her sister : " *You* have no doubt by this time been honoured with the sight of one of the brightest ornaments of the age, R. B. Sheridan, Esqre., an honour and pleasure, for some wise purpose of fate, I suppose, reserved for me to some future time. Indeed I deserve my disappointment for so arrogant a presumption as that of imagining

---

[1] Miss Sheridan notes in her *Journal* that: "There is a kind of influenza in the house, almost all the servants are laid up, and poor Tom [her nephew] as bad as anyone."

that anything so insignificant as myself could attract him one day from his business and pleasure. . . . Time was indeed ; but time is *past*, a truism I feel the force of more and more every day I live."

Mrs. Tickell bears witness to Sheridan's recklessness in money matters ; but in his case it took a unique form. Other men have dealt meanly with their creditors ; he treated his own in a fashion which I should style princely, were it not utterly foolish. There is abundant evidence of an occurrence chronicled by Mrs. Tickell not being exceptional. Having given Mr. Taylor his note of hand for £100 and repaid him that sum, Mr. Taylor, who was as unscrupulous as most of Sheridan's creditors, called for and received a second payment because Sheridan had omitted to ask for the return or cancellation of the note of hand !

The affairs of the nation and his theatre jostled each other in his thoughts. He was always planning a hit in either. His relatives as well as his friends were startled when they heard that he had bought Dr. Ford's share in Drury Lane. His sister wrote from Dublin to inquire whether the report were well founded, and Elizabeth Sheridan replied as follows from The Deepdene : " It is true that he is the purchaser of Dr. Ford's share but he does not choose to have it generally known. The Duke of Norfolk did not lend him the money but who did is, I believe, equally a secret to Mrs. S. and myself. She declares she is often astonished at the points apparently almost impossible which he accomplishes. He now says his great object is to make as much money as he can and she is certain he will succeed. His time has latterly been entirely engrossed by the theatre which he has been putting into the best possible train he could, Mr. King having (luckily I think) deserted them at the eve of opening the house."

By way of contrast to this record of Sheridan's engrossment in the affairs of the theatre, I may add a statement by his sister-in-law of his being equally engrossed at another time with the affairs of the nation. Mrs. Tickell wrote to her sister : " I saw Sheridan at the play last night. Poor fellow! he is monstrously fagged with their consultations [on political questions]. I made him swear last night to go home directly and go to bed, for it's beyond credibility the hours he has kept lately. He said he had a crow to pluck with me about writing a bad account of him to you and complaining of never see-ing him. This I don't recollect.[1] However, you may assure yourself, his time has been entirely devoted to politics except when he has been writing to you."

The truth is, to use a common but expressive phrase, Sheridan had too many irons in the fire. He frittered away much time which, if concentrated on a single object, might have been profitably spent. This is to be regretted. Yet it is really wonderful, and almost incomprehensible how he should have succeeded, as he did beyond dispute, in doing so many things infinitely better than any of his con-temporaries, and how he should have avoided, as it was also his good fortune to do, ever failing in a manner which would have entailed illimitable dis-grace upon himself or his associates.

[1] Mrs. Tickell's complaint about his neglect of her is printed on p. 36.

II.

ON THE TREADMILL IN OPPOSITION.

THE emphatic approval of the country, in 1784, of William Pitt's appointment and policy as Prime Minister was a turning point in its history. For the first time since his accession, George the Third's choice of Ministers had been sanctioned by a large and unbought majority outside the walls of Parliament. During the first twenty years of his reign, George the Third had conferred the office of Premier upon eight men. During the succeeding eighteen years, the Prime Minister was William Pitt. This was as little anticipated by the King as by the leaders of the Opposition. The King never fancied that he would find a master in Pitt as well as an efficient head of the Government. The leaders of the Opposition underestimated Pitt's capacity. They thought him too young, yet some of them lived to see France prostrate at the feet of a ruler and Europe under the heel of a conqueror whose years did not number many more than Pitt's when he was greeted by his followers as a Heaven-sent Minister.[1]

[1] Pitt had then an opportunity of which, unhappily for the country, he had not the courage to avail himself, and to which his

Fox, Sheridan and Burke continued to oppose Pitt with all their might after 1784, yet they generally wasted their strength in vain. The majority in both Houses of Parliament was on his side, and the Premier who can count upon the unswerving support of a preponderating number of Peers and Commoners is as absolute a ruler, within constitutional limits, as any Eastern potentate whose unbridled will stands in the stead of law.

Sheridan was as shrewd and unsparing a critic as Fox of Government measures, and his speeches were often more effective and stinging than Burke's. On two subjects he held and expressed strong personal opinions. The one was the immorality of gaming ; the other, the iniquity of the Game Laws. His denunciation of them gave great offence to the country gentlemen who, in his day, were powerful in Parliament. On the 23rd of July, 1784, he said that these Laws constituted " a system of oppression and tyranny," that they were a disgrace to a free nation, and that " the Game Laws made the poachers." Pitt declared himself to be " as little a friend to the arbitrary spirit of the Game Laws as the honourable gentleman " but that he was not prepared to modify them, " without giving due notice to those country gentlemen for whose benefit and convenience the Game Laws were originally provided." A few weeks later, Sheridan declared that " there never had passed an Act relative

---

friend Wilberforce thus refers : " He was then able, if he had duly estimated his position, to have cast off the corrupt machinery of influence, and formed his Government on the basis of independent principle."—" Life " of Wilberforce, vol. i., p. 64.

to game, and he was convinced there never would pass one, that was not irreconcilable to common sense or common justice."

When a tax on race horses was proposed by Pitt, the Earl of Surrey moved that a heavier tax ought to be imposed on the owner of the winning horses. Pitt agreed with him, whereupon Sheridan made a few remarks which, though not reported, are said to have amused the House, and they must have been both apt and entertaining to have elicited the following comment from the haughty and unimpressionable Chancellor of the Exchequer: "He believed that this was the first time that so dull a business as a Committee of Ways and Means, employed all day in proposing taxes, was ever concluded with so lively an epilogue as had just been delivered by the honourable gentleman opposite to him."[1]

Sheridan took an active part in the debates on Fox's India Bill, and he shewed himself a vigorous and lively critic of the Bills on the same subject which were introduced to Parliament by Pitt's Administration. The first of them was considered and rejected during the desperate struggle between Pitt and the banded followers of Fox and North, and Sheridan did not criticize it. An incident connected with the measure on the same subject introduced by Pitt in 1784 and passed into law, is thus recorded in a letter from Mrs. Tickell to her sister :—
" I had sealed my letter and given it to Will for the Post when Sheridan came in to dinner about six

[1] The "Parliamentary History," vol. xxiv., pp. 1247, 1248, 1251, 1252.

and, in the course of Tickell's chat with him, there came out a piece of news which I thought curious enough to break open my letter for. . . . This piece of news may be none to you after all, it is only that Burke, Mr. Edmund Burke, the great co-patriot of your Charles [Fox], is gone over to Pitt!!! Now could I swear that Mrs. Bouverie [of Delapré Abbey, where Mrs. Sheridan was on a visit] dropped her cards, or dish of tea, or anything else she might have had in her hands :—but resume part of your tranquillity sweet ladies—'tis not so bad for the cause of virtue and honour. The real fact is that both Windham and he have been with Pitt, closeted with him, and to give him advice about his India Bill. Don't you think this very absurd ? Sheridan was in amaze when Tickell told him of it, for 'tis a fact."[1]

Sheridan often spoke during the debates on Pitt's second India Bill and on one occasion, during the absence of Fox, he was twitted by Pitt with acting as his proxy. Sheridan's criticisms were usually telling and just, and he tried to get the Bill re-committed in order to amend such a clause as that "wherein a dead person was to give an account of how he came by certain papers." He added :—" The East India Company remonstrated against the first Bill, because

[1] Mrs. Tickell adds that she thinks there is "a little wrongheadedness all through this great family, for there is a strange sort of story about young Dick [Burke] going into St. Paul's church with his hat on and persisting in keeping it so in spite of the verger, minor Canons and all the solemn people of the Church. Nay, they say a clergyman will absolutely commence a lawsuit against him for giving him the lie. This is a part of a very long story my father told."

orders were to be transmitted to India without their consent, and insisted on the right of some of their Directors being acquainted with all matters before they were despatched. To please them, the Right Hon. gentleman [Pitt] had suffered them to have a secret committee of three Directors; but the Company were not a bit nearer; for those three directors were sworn not to divulge anything done in council; of course they must cut a ridiculous figure; for they might be present at a Court of Directors and see and hear measures carrying on, and regulations making, diametrically opposite to what they knew had been determined on in council, and by their oaths were debarred from giving any other information than a nod or a wink across the table, or a grave shake of the head, to intimate they knew something which they dare not divulge."

He happily ridiculed the extent to which the Bill had been amended, saying, " by the references it was plain that twenty-one new clauses were added, which were to be known by the letters A. B. C. D. E. F. G. H. I. K. L. M. N. O. P. Q. R. S. T. V. W., therefore it was to be hoped some gentleman would add three more clauses for X. Y. Z., to make the alphabet complete; which would then serve as a horn-book for the present Ministry. The old clauses, now left out, were referred to, and known by being in black letter at the bottom of the column; where, to be sure, they stood in mourning for the folly of their parents, and pointed out the slovenly manner in which the Bill was originally drawn."[1]

[1] "Speeches," vol. i., pp. 86, 87.

The elaborateness of Sheridan's speeches on finance was a terror to reporters and one of them, who was probably William Woodfall, said in the report of a speech concerning the Civil List, which was made on the 19th of August, 1784: "Mr. Sheridan entered into a long train of arguments founded upon figures, through which it was impossible to follow him in detail from memory." His criticisms were treated with marked respect by the Chancellor of the Exchequer, and several of the suggestions which he long urged in vain were eventually approved and adopted. It is almost incredible now that Sheridan should have had to address the House on the 3rd of June, 1791, in these terms :—" Revenue regulations and tax bills they appeared to consider as things which they were to vote on confidence in the Minister ; notwithstanding the multitude of provisions which they generally contained, by almost every one of which the liberty of the subject was more or less affected.

" In consequence of this confidential carelessness, he had never been able to get a tax bill printed, though he had often attempted it—an attempt in which he was persuaded he must at length succeed ; for it was not to be believed that the House would agree in passing bills, containing a great variety of important and complicated clauses, without taking the ordinary means to comprehend and understand them."[1]

After the Chancellor of the Exchequer had opened his budget on the 11th of March, 1793, Sheridan

[1] "Speeches," vol. ii., p. 68.

remarked:—"The Right Honourable gentleman had, however, called on the House to watch the whole of the business with vigilance, and even with jealousy. The call was not necessary to him, for he had uniformly acted on that principle upon all revenue questions, and, without apologizing for an essential act of duty, he would always continue to do so."

Sheridan's strictures were practical and often amusing, as when he said of the Horse, Stamp, and Window Bills: "that the wording of some [clauses] conveyed the idea of the horses not only inhabiting the houses, but the extraordinary circumstance of their looking out of the windows." He had not, however, mastered the science of finance, neither was he, like Pitt, a disciple of Adam Smith, while he was quite as unversed as Fox in the principles of Political Economy. All the heresies against social wellbeing and national progress which are concentrated in the cry of protection to native industry were treasured and treated by him as sacred precepts which it was unpatriotic to dispute, and cruel, as well as almost criminal, to disregard. The followers of Pitt who voted blindly for his measures were as ignorant as their opponents in Opposition of the economic doctrines expounded by Adam Smith. Sheridan's merits as a financier may not have been great, yet his grossest shortcomings can be paralleled by the utterances and action of Presidents of the United States and of the French Republic, of Prime Ministers of the Dominion of Canada and of the great Colonies in Australasia, all of whom share the delusion, under which he laboured, that a nation's wealth consists in the stock of gold which it has accumulated, and that any nation can enjoy substantial prosperity without freely exchanging commodities with all other nations.

He was an incisive critic of a scheme for fortifying the dockyards which, though plausible, and possibly patriotic, had its weak and ridiculous side. He spoke with regard to it in so masterly a fashion on the 27th of February, 1786, that Fox alleged there was no reason for doing more than express his concurrence. The Duke of Richmond, who was Master-General of the Ordnance, devised the scheme which Pitt advocated and of which Sheridan said:—"The noble Duke deserved the warmest panegyrics for the striking proofs he had given of his genius as an engineer, which appeared even in the planning and construction of the paper in his hand. The professional ability of the Master-General shone as conspicuously there as it could upon our coasts. He had made it an argument of posts; and conducted his reasoning upon principles of trigonometry as well as logic. There were certain detached data, like advanced works, to keep the enemy at a distance from the main object in debate. Strong provisions covered the flanks of his assertions. His very queries were in casemates. No impression, therefore, was to be made on this fortress of sophistry by desultory observations; and it was necessary to sit down before it, and assail it by regular approaches. It was fortunate, however, to observe, that notwithstanding all the skill employed

by the noble and literary engineer, his mode of
defence on paper was open to the same objection
which had been urged against his other fortifications;
that if his adversary got possession of one of his
posts, it became strength against him, and the means
of subduing the whole line of his argument."[1]

It was admitted that Sheridan's speech killed the
Duke's scheme. The numbers were equal on a
division and the Speaker felt himself compelled to
put the Government in a minority by giving his
casting vote to the Opposition.[2]

No member on the side of the Opposition, with
the exception of its leader, was more alert and
impressive than Sheridan when the proceedings connected with the Westminster Scrutiny were debated in
the House of Commons. It was a gross blunder in
tactics on Pitt's part to oppose the return of Fox to Parliament; yet, while the blunder cannot be defended,
the defence of which his conduct is susceptible has
not yet been set forth. Pitt was astute enough to
perceive, from the moment that the King implored
his services as Premier, that he could not obtain the
King's entire confidence unless he ministered to
some of the King's prejudices. George the Third
hated Fox even more than he did Lord North, who,
after long acting as his instrument, betrayed him, as

---

[1] "Speeches," vol. i., p. 170. The critical reader will not
require to be told how closely Sheridan's rhetorical method, as
exemplified in this speech, corresponds to his dramatic method
as exemplified by the remarks of Dr. Rosy in the farce of *St.
Patrick's Day*.

[2] In proposing the motion Pitt spoke of "South Britain" when
he meant England.

he phrased it, by forming a coalition with Fox. One of his most unfortunate aberrations was to attribute to the example and influence of Fox all the shameful actions of his eldest son.[1]　Hence the savage animosity displayed by Pitt to his rival caused the King to think still more highly of Pitt.

Both the Ministry and the Court strained every nerve and the law to hinder the re-election of Fox for the City of Westminster.　Sir Cecil Wray was the favoured candidate and not only were "gold pills," as the King termed them, freely administered on his behalf to the electors, but 280 of the Guards were ordered to record their votes for him.　Horace Walpole wrote that, though this was legal, yet it was an act which his father, "in the most quiet seasons, would not have dared to do."[2]　At the close of the

---

[1] The King consulted Lord Chancellor Thurlow and Lord Ashburton as to "what redress he could have against a man who alienated from him the affection of his son," and the Chancellor's reply is said to have been that, "he would have no peace till his son and Fox were secured in the Tower."—"Last Journals" of Horace Walpole, vol. ii., p. 599.

[2] "Letters," vol. viii., p. 469.　Walpole records and deprecates with unwonted feeling an act of fiendish cruelty which has only to be stated to be abominated: "Me nothing has shocked so much as what I heard this morning : at Dover they roasted a poor *fox* alive by the most diabolic allegory!—a savage meanness that an Iroquois would not have committed.　Base, cowardly wretches ! how much nobler to have hurried to London and torn Mr. Fox himself piecemeal !"

Pitt disgraced himself in a minor fashion by writing to Wilberforce: "Westminster goes on well, in spite of the Duchess of Devonshire, and the other *women of the people*."—"Life" of Wilberforce, vol. i., p. 63.

poll, Fox's majority was 236. Thomas Corbett, the High Bailiff and returning officer, a furious partisan and rabid hater of Fox, proclaimed that he had conscientious scruples against declaring him duly elected, and he consented to a scrutiny being held which it was calculated would last for three years and prove ruinous to its object.

Fox was elected for the Kirkwall Boroughs, without his knowledge or wish, by sympathetic friends, and the Government endeavoured to prevent him from taking his seat as their representative without, however, succeeding in the ungracious attempt. Consequently, he was able to argue in person the question of the Westminster Scrutiny and to make the best speech that he ever delivered. Sir Lloyd Kenyon, the Master of the Rolls, sank the Judge in the partisan and supported the High Bailiff. Pitt staked his credit as a member of the Bar, and his reputation as a statesman, in defence of the unprecedented and illegal action which the High Bailiff's sensitive and political conscience had compelled him to take, and which was in singular and complete accord with the desire of the Government. Pitt wrote to the Duke of Rutland that, whatever course was followed, " I have no doubt of Fox being thrown out."[1]

Pitt's reply to Fox's great speech on the Westminster Scrutiny was alike weak and unworthy. Sheridan said of it : " If the impression made by his Right Honourable friend's speech could be effaced by hard words and lofty sounds, its effects would be to the full as slight and trifling even as the effect of

---

[1] Stanhope's "Life of Pitt," vol. i., p. 213.

the Right Honourable gentleman's own speech. If severity of epithet, if redundancy of egotism, if pomp of panegyric upon Administration could refute the arguments of the most convincing speech he had ever the good fortune to hear, undoubtedly it was very completely refuted. But, if the people of England looked for the defence of the High Bailiff of Westminster, and of his Majesty's Ministers (who were in this case synonymous) upon principles of law, justice, good sense or equity, beyond all doubt they were disappointed."[1]

The ludicrous farce of the scrutiny, which Lord North ironically said was designed to relieve "the unsettled and embarrassed state of the High Bailiff's mind," lasted for nearly a year, during which majorities in the House of Commons approved of his mind remaining "unsettled and embarrassed," and the costs, which Fox had reckoned would be £18,000, were mounting up to that figure with the result of his large majority being lessened by two votes only. In a debate on the 9th of February, 1785, some of Pitt's supporters, who were members of the Bar, indulged in legal quibbles to defend the false position of their chief. Sheridan then said, "they had that day been honoured with the counsels of a complete gradation of lawyers ; they had received the opinion of a judge [Sir Lloyd Kenyon, Master of the Rolls], of an Attorney-General in petto [M. A. Taylor], of an ex-Attorney-General [Lee], and of a practising barrister [Bearcroft]. The encomiums passed on his Right Honourable friend [Fox] by one learned

---

[1] The "Parliamentary History," vol. xxiv., p. 938.

gentleman [Bearcroft] were so applicable, that when
the learned gentleman added that, besides his other
great and shining talents, his Right Honourable
friend stood distinguished for his boldness and
candour, for his quickness of discernment and good
sense, everybody who knew his Right Honourable
friend thought the learned gentleman had really
been successful in his description and had drawn a
just portrait ; but when the learned gentleman afterwards stated, that at the time his Right Honourable
friend professed most candour he was then most
dangerous, and that he was to be the least trusted
when he wished to thrown himself into the arms of
the House, the learned gentleman completely did
away the resemblance, and proved that he was
wholly unacquainted with the true character of his
Right Honourable friend, who was not more remarkable for his splendid abilities than for the genuine
liberality and unaffected candour of his mind, and
the manly, direct and open conduct that he had ever
pursued.

" Had the learned gentleman's statement been
correct, his panegyric would have proved a satire ;
and it must have been understood that, when he
talked of his Right Honourable friend's boldness, he
meant his craft, and when he mentioned his candour,
he designed to charge him with hypocrisy.   It was
not from such men as his Right Honourable friend
that danger was to be dreaded.   If the wolf was to
be feared, the learned gentleman might rest assured
it would be the wolf in sheep's clothing, the masked
pretender to patriotism."

Twelve days later the subject was again brought before the House, when Fox effectively quoted a remark made in the Court of King's Bench by Mr. Bearcroft to the effect that "the Scrutiny was the confusion of all law and common sense." Mr. Bearcroft said with reference to Sheridan's amendment to a motion which had been made, that Sheridan "had the quickest penetration and the liveliest and readiest wit he ever knew a man possess; his amendment was ingenious, and well calculated to throw ridicule on that of the noble Lord ; however, he would adhere to the latter, and support it with his voice." On the 3rd of March, 1785, Alderman Sawbridge moved that the High Bailiff make a return of the members chosen for Westminster. Pitt thereupon moved the adjournment of the House. So many Ministerialists deserted him that he was placed in a minority of 38, and Sawbridge's motion was agreed to unanimously.

The result of this motion was almost miraculous. For nearly a year the conservative conscience of the High Bailiff had resented acknowledging the fact that Fox had been chosen for Westminster. The Attorney General [Pepper Arden] affirmed in the House that "cavillers might talk of law and of statutes, but there was neither law nor statute that could compel a man to do what in his conscience he could not do."[1] Pitt had declared that "it was impossible" for the High Bailiff to make a return before his supersensitive conscience had been pacified and pleased. Nevertheless, this political conscience

---

[1] "Parliamentary History," vol. xxiv., p. 828.

proved to be as responsive to a vote of the House
of Commons as the needle is to the Pole, and on the
day after Sawbridge's motion was carried, the High
Bailiff returned Lord Hood and Fox as the duly
elected members for Westminster. Despite the
Attorney-General's dictum that " neither law nor
statute " could prevail against the High Bailiff, this
sticker for the right to hinder Fox representing the
majority of voters in Westminster, was condemned
by a Court of Justice to pay £2000 damages to Fox,
the sum being afterwards distributed among the Westminster charities, to the great advantage of Fox's
popularity. It has never been alleged that Pitt
suffered the High Bailiff to be the poorer for acting
on his conscientious convictions. Pitt had a victory,
however, which was more deplorable than his defeat.
He successfully opposed Fox's motion to erase the
record of these discreditable proceedings from the
Journals of the House. The King sincerely con-
doled with Pitt on some of his recognized supporters
voting against him when he was entirely in the wrong,
and characteristically added, that Fox had " hurt his
cause by taking so strong a step as proposing to
expunge from the Journals the several Resolutions
which have been made relative to the Scrutiny."[1]

It is noteworthy, and necessary to bear in mind
that Sheridan never let an opportunity slip for pro-
claiming his personal independence on all the questions which he discussed. He was charged in his
later parliamentary life with disregarding or despising

[1] Letters from the King in appendix to vol. i. of Stanhope's
" Life of Pitt," pp. xv, xvi.

party claims and connexions; but those who affirmed this were ignorant alike of his temper and career. When the Irish Propositions were under consideration on the 30th of May, 1785, he was taunted by Pitt with being the mouth-piece of a party which supported inconsistent measures and was composed of inconsistent men. Sheridan protested, and said : " that he was the mouth-piece of no party, as the Right Honourable gentleman had been pleased to call him, nor was he the tool of any party. He had as strong party feelings as any man ; but he had those feelings, because those he was attached to. neither expected from him servility of judgment, nor pliancy of principle."

Not being swayed in his political action by petty motives or personal aims, Sheridan's high and strong position in the House of Commons was conspicuous when he united with others in impeaching Warren Hastings of high crimes and misdemeanours. The impressions which he had formed were due to information supplied by Philip Francis to Burke and communicated by Burke to him. Neither Burke nor he can have fully apprehended and been rightly informed of the spite and malice on the part of Francis of which Hastings was the victim. That Hastings was often high-handed is indisputable; but his conduct as Governor-General materially benefited the people of India. It was then supposed that India was a very rich country, the truth being that many persons had accumulated much gold and many precious stones there, and that the mass of the people had to work hard for daily bread. The well-

being of a nation is not to be measured by the wealth
of a few. Where millionaires abound, the struggle
for subsistence is the most severe. Warren Hastings
undoubtedly exercised pressure, which may have
been undue, to force rich Indians to hand over to his
master, the East India Company, some of their
hoarded treasures ; but he was not sordid in his
action, neither did he seek his own aggrandizement.
He could boast, after ceasing to be Governor-General
that he had found the resources of the Indian Government equal to three millions and had left them equal
to five millions sterling annually and, moreover, that
he had left the people " happy and contented." If
Warren Hastings had been in advance of his age he
could have drawn many more millions from Indian
coffers, for executing profitable public works, and
thus enriching both the Company which he served
and the land over which he ruled.

The generous breast of Burke boiled with indignation at the tales of rapacity and cruelty attributed
to Hastings, and he felt most keenly for the victims
who were Princes or Princesses. Having inspired
Sheridan with the feelings which animated him,
Sheridan took an active part in the parliamentary
investigation which preceded the impeachment of
Hastings. Burke bore witness to this when he
wrote to Mrs. Sheridan : " I am sure you will have
the goodness to excuse the liberty I take with you,
when you consider the interest which I have and
which the public have (the said public being, at least,
half an inch a taller person than I am) in the use of
Mr. Sheridan's abilities. I know that his mind is

seldom unemployed ; but then, like all such great and vigorous minds, it takes an eagle flight by itself, and we can hardly bring it to rustle along the ground, with us birds of mean wing, in coveys.   I only beg, that you will prevail on Mr. Sheridan to be with us *this day*, at half after three, in the Committee.   Mr. Wombell, the Paymaster of *Oude*, is to be examined there *to-day*.   Oude is Mr. Sheridan's particular province ; and I do most seriously ask that he would favour us with his assistance.   What will come of the examination I know not ; but, without him, I do not expect a great deal from it ; with him I fancy we may get out something material.   Once more let me entreat your interest with Mr. Sheridan and your forgiveness for being troublesome to you, and to do me the justice to believe me, Madam, your most obedient and faithful humble servant."

A few days later Burke wrote to Sheridan : " Well, all will turn out right,—and half of you, or a quarter, is worth five other men.   I think that this cause, which was originally yours, will be recognized by you, and that you will again possess yourself of it. The owner's mark is on it, and all our docking and cropping cannot hinder its being known and cherished by its original master."

An unpublished letter sent from Beaconsfield by Burke to Sheridan on the 18th of April, 1786, gives a glimpse behind the scenes while the arrangements for the projected impeachment were in progress : " As I came along I reflected on the subject of our last hurried conversation.   It is but mercy to bring off this young man decently : It is but prudence to

take care of all Indians ; especially if they are young,
dashing, and not yet provided for. I think, and
indeed am persuaded, that if the Clerk, or any one
else, has mentioned the newspaper to him at the
right or the left, he ought, without seeming aware of
any exception, to converse with him again, merely
as to ascertain and arrange his evidence and then to
leave the matter wholly to himself.

"There is no evil turn that they will not give to
our most innocent actions. I trust this will get to
you time enough possibly to prevent any mention of
it to him at all. This would be the best—the other
will require some delicacy in the management as all
patchwork does.

"I think Edward's evidence ought to be arranged.
I mean by this that all the matters of which it is
composed should be placed by themselves. We got
into some confusion, by the disorder in which Holt's
was entered. What does very well for the Minister,
and indeed is unavoidable there, will not do as a
Brief. As to the rest I take it for granted all is in
order. We had best have nothing to do with Jaques
or perhaps Gilpin. Surely we ought to meet on
Monday evening. It may be at your house, or
Foxes, [*sic*] or mine as you think best. Let me
know by a note at my house, that I may get on my
return to Town, how you settle this—and I hope to
find, that nothing has been advised as to the paper,
or that it has been set to rights in some proper
mode."[1]

[1] Sheridan's aid was highly esteemed; but the difficulty of
securing his presence, which made Burke appeal to Mrs. Sheridan,

The confidence felt by Hastings and his friends as to the rejection of the threatened impeachment was heightened after Burke had failed, despite a powerful speech by Fox, to obtain the sanction of the House on the 1st of June, 1786, to the Rohilla charge,[1] the supporters numbering 67 and the opponents 119. When, however, on the 13th of June, Fox brought forward the charge relative to Cheit Singh, it was supported by Pitt and approved by 119 to 79. On the 7th of February, 1787, the case of the Begums of Oude was presented by Sheridan in a speech, occupying five hours and a half, of which an imperfect outline has been preserved. Contemporaries who heard the

---

is further exemplified by this unpublished letter which Fox wrote to him in the House of Commons relative to a motion made by Lord Hood and seconded by John Wilkes on the 9th of May, 1787: "I am defending you for not being here on the ground of Mrs. Sheridan not being very well, which I hope I am grounded [in]; but if it is possible for you to leave her, you really ought to be here. Lord Hood has moved to put off the second reading of the Report on the articles of Impeachment, and Wilkes, who is seconding him, puts it chiefly on the ground of the Begum's rebellion. But even if this were not so, upon such a question as the impeachment itself, it would not have a good appearance that you should be absent.

"Mind I defend you to others."

John Wilkes in his speech referred to Sheridan and avowed himself to have been "dazzled with the brilliant eloquence and captivated with the beauty and variety of the honourable gentleman's wit on the fourth charge."

[1] Dr. Watkins writes that this charge related to the injustice of the war "against the inhabitants of the Rohillas," which would be paralleled in absurdity if a bookmaker were to write now that the Japanese recently waged war against "the inhabitants of the Chinese."—"Memoirs" of Sheridan, vol. i., p. 348.

speech exhausted the language for epithets wherewith to eulogize it.   Burke declared it unequalled by
anything of which there was a record or tradition.
Pitt, who was a sterner and less friendly critic,
acknowledged that "an abler speech had, perhaps,
never been delivered."   Wraxall voted against
Sheridan's motion, yet he styled his speech "the most
splendid display of eloquence and talent which has
been exhibited in the House of Commons during the
present reign," and added that Sheridan "neither lost
his temper, his memory, nor his judgment throughout
the whole performance, blending the legal accuracy
of the Bar when stating facts or depositions of witnesses with the most impassioned appeals to justice,
pity and humanity."[1]

Sir Gilbert Elliot, another member of Parliament,
wrote to his wife on the day following Sheridan's
speech : "This last night, though the House was up
soon after one, and I was in bed before two, I have
not slept *one wink*.   Nothing whatever was the
matter with me, except the impression of what had
been passing still vibrating on my brain. . . . Sheridan
spoke exactly five hours and a half, with such fluency
and rapidity that I think his speech could not be read
in double the time.   You may imagine the quantity
of matter it contained.[1]   It was by many degrees the
most excellent and astonishing performance I ever

---

[1] "Posthumous Memoirs," vol. iii., pp. 385, 386.

[2] Daniel Pultney informed the Duke of Rutland that Sheridan
had told him "at the Bar [of the House] a day or two before, that
he could not take less time than seven hours."—Report on Rutland
Manuscripts, vol. iii., p. 370.

heard, and surpasses all I ever imagined possible in eloquence and ability. This is the *universal* sense of all who heard it. You will conceive how admirable it was when I tell you that he surpassed, I think, Pitt, Fox and even Burke, in his finest and most brilliant orations. . . . It is impossible to describe the feelings he excited. The *bone* rose repeatedly in my throat and tears in my eyes—not of grief, but merely of strongly excited sensibility ; so they were in Dudley Long's, who is not, I should think, particularly tearful. The conclusion, in which the whole force of the case was collected, and where his whole powers were employed to their utmost stretch, and indeed his own feelings wound to the utmost pitch, worked the House up into such a paroxysm of passionate enthusiasm on the subject, and of admiration for him, that the moment he sat down there was a universal shout, nay even clapping for half a second ; every man was on the floor, and all his friends throwing themselves on his neck in raptures of joy and exultation. This account is not at all exaggerated, and hardly does justice to, I daresay, the most remarkable scene ever exhibited, either there or in any other popular assembly."[1]

Sir Gilbert Elliot did not exaggerate. On the day he wrote to his wife, the Earl of Chatham wrote to the Duke of Rutland and said : " Everybody is full of Sheridan's speech on Mr. Hastings' business. I really think it, without any exception, one of the most wonderful performances I ever heard, and

[1] " Life and Letters of Sir Gilbert Elliot, first Earl of Minto," vol. i., pp. 123, 124.

almost the greatest imaginable exertion of the human mind."[1]

Sheridan's oratory was acknowledged to be supreme; but Sheridan's personal triumph was even greater than his speech. Great orators have always abounded in the House of Commons, and its record is emblazoned with their names during the eighteenth century. That of William Pitt is radiant among them. He was a self-possessed statesman, as well as a consummate master of speech; he was impervious to appeals based on sentiment and unsupported by reason and his mind was proof against sophistry however skilful and however cunning. Yet he admitted his inability to vote with perfect calmness on the question before the House while his intellect was swayed by Sheridan's oration. The majority naturally followed his lead, and the debate was adjourned till the following day in order that members on both sides of the House might recover their self-possession. An adjournment in these circumstances and for such reasons is a unique event in the annals of Parliament. When the debate was concluded on the following day, Sheridan's motion was carried by 175 votes against 68, and the impeachment of Warren Hastings became inevitable.[2]

[1] "Manuscripts of the Duke of Rutland"; fourteenth Report of the Historical Manuscripts Commission, Appendix, p. 369.

[2] The adjourned debate was resumed by Philip Francis, who did not like Sheridan and was not liked by him, and whose words have the greater value on that account: "He said he had wished to pay his tribute of applause to that wonderful performance at the moment when the impression of it was strong upon him; that

While the results are historical, the speech which produced them has passed into an oblivion as absolute and deplorable as that which has engulphed the speeches of Bolingbroke and Chatham.   Fragments of what Sheridan said are extant and they differ so much as to be unworthy of acceptance, the version in *The Parliamentary History* being, perhaps, the worst and most absurd.

A copy of *The London Chronicle*, which I have found among Sheridan's papers, may have been

---

he doubted much whether he should have been able to do it even then, in the instant of feeling, nor should he be able to do it now, after many hours of reflection.   That to do justice to the ability, to the industry, to the arguments, and to the astonishing eloquence of his honourable friend, would require a power of ability and eloquence approaching to his own ; that he should leave that task to others : that he himself looked higher—to the moral mind, that created and directed the intellectual power; to the honourable, generous and virtuous heart, which was the true source of all those efforts and brilliant operations of intellect, which the House had only admired as acts of the understanding ; to that he attached himself.   That he had always considered the human heart as the true source of human wisdom and folly, as well as of virtue and vice ; that therefore the Book of Wisdom, to express the extremity of all folly, had declared, 'The fool had said in his heart.'   If this were true, the world would measure the virtues of his honourable friend by his abilities ; they would judge of the pure and copious fountain by the magnificence of the stream, and give him a higher and more honourable place than ever among the greatest of mankind.   That his virtues, and, of course, his abilities, swelled and expanded, according to the occasion that brought them into action, and spontaneously rose to a level with the new office which they were called upon to execute.   To him, indeed, that day had decreed a glorious triumph ; a triumph independent of victory ; and if defeat were possible, victorious in defeat."—" Parliamentary History," vol. xxv., p. 309.

preserved because it contained the best report of the speech, and the concluding sentences are less nonsensical than those in the other reports.[1] Towards the end, the reporter wrote that Sheridan "came now to his conclusion and it was burning and rhetorical," and added: "He said he knew of factions and parties in that House. There was scarcely a subject on which they were not broken and divided into sects [sections ?]. The Prerogative of the Crown found its advocates even among the Representatives of the people. The privileges of the people met [had ?] their opponents. The measures of every Minister were supported by one body of men and thwarted by another. But when inhumanity presented itself, it found no division among them. They set upon it as their common enemy, as if the character of the land were involved; in their zeal for its ruin they left it not till it was completely overthrown. It was not given to that House, as it was to the officers who relieved (to behold the objects of their compassion and benevolence) and

[1] Sir Nathaniel Wraxall gave this version of a simile: "A crooked, circuitous policy regulates all his actions. He can no more go straight forward to his object than a snake can proceed without writhing in curves, or can imitate the undeviating swiftness of the arrow."

In *The Parliamentary History* the reptile's part is thus represented: "As well might the writhing obliquity of the serpent be compared to the swift directness of the arrow, as the duplicity of Mr. Hastings' ambition to the simple steadiness of genuine magnanimity."

In *The London Chronicle* it is thus referred to: "The serpent could as well assume the direct flight of an arrow, as Hastings could pursue his object by a direct course."

who so feelingly describe the ecstatic emotions of
gratitude in the instant of deliverance.   They could
not behold the workings of the hearts, the quivering
lips, the trickling tears, the loud and yet tremendous
[tremulous ?] joys of the millions whom their vote of
this night would snatch or save from the tyranny of
corrupt favour.

"But, though they could not perceive this, was
not the true enjoyment of the passion of benevolence
increased by the blessing being conferred unseen!
Would not the omnipotence of the Parliament of
Britain be demonstrated to the wonder of nations,
by stretching its mighty arm across the deep, and
saving by its *fiat* millions from destruction?   And
would the blessings of the people thus saved dissipate in empty air?   No!   If I may dare to use the
figure, Heaven itself shall become the agent to
receive the blessings of their pious gratitude, and to
waft them to your bosoms."[1]

If the vainest of men, he ought to have been sur-
feited with praise.   But his affections were stronger
than his vanity and his heart beat highest to the
applause of his domestic hearth and family circle.
He waited in vain, however, for a letter of congratu-
lation from his father, though his brother wrote one
in which there is more heart than in any other from
his pen, while his elder sister gave open and true
expression to her feelings of love and admiration.

[1] In *The Parliamentary History*, the version of the concluding
sentence is nonsensical: "If I may use the figure, we shall con-
stitute Heaven itself our proxy, to receive for us the blessings of
their pious gratitude, and the prayers of their thanksgiving."

They both felt that his family had been intellectually ennobled by him.

Charles Francis wrote on the 13th of February, 1787, from Dublin Castle : "Could I for a moment forget you were my brother, I should, merely as an Irishman, think myself bound to thank you, for the high credit you have done your country. You may be assured therefore that the sense of national pride, which I in common with all your countrymen on this side of the water must feel on this splendid occasion, acquires no small increase of personal satisfaction, when I reflect to whom Ireland is indebted for a display of ability, so unequalled, that the honour derived from it seems too extensive to be concentred in an individual, but ought to give, and I am persuaded will give, a new respect for the name of Irishman. I have heard and read the accounts of your speech, and of the astonishing impression it made, with tears of exultation—but what will flatter you more—I can solemnly declare to be a fact, that I have, since the news reached us, seen good honest *Irish* pride, national pride I mean, bring tears into the eyes of many persons, on this occasion, who never saw you. I need not, after what I have stated, assure you, that it is with the most heartfelt satisfaction that I offer you my warmest congratulations. . . . Give my love to Mrs. Sheridan and let me congratulate her too."

His elder sister Alicia wrote on the 16th of February, 1787: "The day before yesterday I received the account of your glorious speech. Mr. Crawford was so good as to write a more particular and satisfactory one to Mr. Lefanu than we could have received from the papers. I have snatched the first interval of ease from a cruel and almost incessant headache to give vent to my feelings, and tell you how much I rejoice in your success. May the God who fashioned you, and gave you power to sway the hearts of men and control their wayward wills, be equally favourable to you in all your undertakings, and make your reward here and hereafter! Amen, from the bottom of my soul! My affection for you has been ever 'passing the love of women.' Adverse circumstances have deprived me of the pleasure of your society, but have had no effect in weakening my regard for you. I know your heart too well to suppose that regard is indifferent to you, and soothingly sweet to me is the idea that in some pause of thought from the important matters that occupy your mind, your earliest friend is sometimes recollected by you.

"I know you are much above the little vanity that seeks its gratification in the praise of the million, but you must be pleased with the applause of the discerning, with the tribute I may say of affection paid to the goodness of your heart. People love your character as much as they admire your talents. My father is, in a degree that I did not expect, gratified with the general attention you have excited here : he seems truly pleased that men should say, 'There goes the father of Gaul.' If your fame has shed a ray of brightness over all so distinguished as to be connected with you, I am sure it has infused a ray of gladness into my heart, deprest as it has been with ill-health and long confinement."

She wrote at the same time to Mrs. Sheridan :

" Nothing but death could keep me silent on such an occasion as this. I wish you joy—I am sure you feel it: 'O moments worth all ages past, and all that are to come.' You may laugh at my enthusiasm if you please—I glory in it."

Till the delivery of Sheridan's great speech in the House of Commons concerning the Begums of Oude there was little public interest in the charges brought against Warren Hastings; but the speech itself set the world of fashion talking and wondering, and rendered its members ardent to hear Sheridan address the High Court of Parliament before which Hastings was impeached. Fifty pounds were paid for a ticket of admission. Though the Court did not sit in Westminster Hall till noon, on the 3rd of June, 1788, all the approaches to it were crowded at 6 o'clock in the morning with ladies and gentlemen in full dress. Two-thirds of the peerage were present. Sheridan spoke for several hours during three days and, though some who heard his speech in the House of Commons preferred it to that in Westminster Hall, yet those who heard him for the first time felt themselves in the presence of a commanding orator who moved their hearts, fired their imaginations and surpassed in force, splendour and pathos their loftiest anticipations. Sir Nathaniel Wraxall, who was present when both speeches were delivered, and whose bias against Sheridan was shown by voting against him and writing in his dispraise, has recorded that: "never perhaps was expectation raised so high as on his appearance, and never, I believe, in the history of modern ages, was it so completely gratified. . . .

Many of Sheridan's pictures were likewise so highly coloured, and so magically wrought up, as to produce an almost electric shock. . . . His success placed him on an eminence which no public man in either house of Parliament has attained in my time. The most ardent admirers of Burke, of Fox and of Pitt allowed that they had been outdone as orators by Sheridan."[1]

The general opinion was far higher and more complimentary than that of the cynical Horace Walpole, who was then in his seventy-second year, and who wrote on the day following the delivery of the first part of Sheridan's speech, that he did not quite satisfy all the passionate expectation which had been raised and that it was impossible he should, adding: "Well! we are sunk and deplorable in many points, yet not absolutely gone when history and eloquence throw out such shoots! I thought I had outlived my country; I am glad not to leave it desperate."[2] Gibbon, to whose grand historical work Walpole referred, has chronicled in his stately and Gallic fashion what he felt when he heard Sheridan mention "his luminous page" and couple his name with that of Tacitus: "Mr. Sheridan's eloquence commanded my applause, nor could I hear without emotion the personal compliment which he paid me in the person of the British nation."[3] In a

---

[1] "Posthumous Memoirs," vol. v., pp. 131, 132.

[2] "Walpole's Letters," vol. ix., p. 127.

[3] Moore quotes Gibbon's words on p. 510 of the 1st volume of his "Memoirs" of Sheridan, and adds on p. 511 the following words which have often been repeated: "On being asked by some honest brother Whig, at the conclusion of the speech, how he came to compliment Gibbon with the epithet 'luminous,' Sheridan

letter from him to Lord Sheffield, further details are given : " Yesterday the august scene was closed for this year. Sheridan surpassed himself; and though I am far from considering him as a perfect orator, there were many beautiful passages in his speech, on justice, filial love, etc. ; one of the closest chains of argument I ever heard, to prove that Hastings was responsible for the acts of Middleton ; and a compliment, much admired, to a certain Historian of your acquaintance. Sheridan at the close of his speech sank into Burke's arms ;—a good actor ; but I called this morning, he is perfectly well."[1]

Sir Gilbert Elliot, like Wraxall, heard both speeches. When writing to his wife an account of what passed on the first day in Westminster Hall, he began by admitting that the inordinate curiosity which had been excited might not have been fully gratified, adding that the speech was "a very great exertion of talent, understanding, and skill in composition and was the work of a man of very extraordinary genius. There was not one sentence in which you did not perceive the exercise of a most ingenious, acute, penetrating and lively mind ; and it was strewed very thick

---

answered, in a half whisper, 'I said *vo*luminous.'" Need I say that Sheridan never uttered these words? Gibbon was seated next to Dudley Long and asked him to repeat what Sheridan had actually said about him. "Oh," replied Dudley Long, "he said something about your *voluminous* pages." Lord Russell was told this "by Dudley Long himself."—Sir Gilbert Elliot's " Life and Letters," vol. i., p. 219. It is improbable that Gibbon did not see the joke, or would have recorded, with satisfaction, a compliment which he had neither heard nor understood.

[1] Gibbon's " Miscellaneous Works," vol. ii., pp. 421, 422.

with more brilliant periods of eloquence and poetical imagination, and more lively sallies of wit, than could be produced probably by more than one other man in the world [Burke], with whom, however, they spring up and shoot out with all the luxuriance and grace of spontaneous nature. . . . I thought also that Sheridan starved his present argument a little by avoiding his former speech, which he was unwilling to repeat. . . . I must assure you that, though I have observed these imperfections and drawbacks, I admire this speech as one of the very finest and surprising exertions of genius I ever witnessed."

The letter in which these words occur was penned on the 5th of June ; on the 7th, Sir Gilbert wrote : " My prediction has been fully accomplished, and Sheridan displayed powers yesterday hardly to be conceived, and perhaps never equalled in their kind. . . . The character of his speech yesterday was the same as that of the day before, and indeed of all his great appearances—that is to say, acute and forcible and close reasoning, delivered in easy but perfectly lucid language, and relieved and enlivened by epigrammatic points, and by sallies of wit, both of the higher and the more familiar kind. This is the ground, as it were, and there is no part of the work which is less excellent than that I have described. But on this ground are added innumerable beautiful ornaments, and the principal of these are so splendid, so rich, and so exquisitely finished, as to excel the most extravagant notions of perfection. These splendid passages are all most elaborately composed but they are composed by a person warm with his subject, and inspired by the occasion and the audience for which they are intended, and therefore do not partake in any degree of the coldness generally belonging to this artificial fire. He rises on these occasions to a pitch above any specimens we have of oratory, and soars fairly into the highest regions of poetry. . . . I am now convinced that his powers in this kind are far beyond any other man's, and that nobody living could execute what he did yesterday."

Sir Gilbert wrote after the third and concluding day of Sheridan's speech, when the trial was adjourned till the following session of Parliament: " He was finer yesterday than ever. I believe there were few dry eyes in the assembly ; and as for myself, I never remember to have cried so heartily and so copiously on any public occasion. . . . My admiration of his last day is without any abatement or qualification whatever. Burke caught him in his arms as he sat down, which was not the least affecting part of the day to my feelings, and could not be the least grateful testimony of his merit received by Sheridan. I have myself enjoyed that embrace on such an occasion, and know its value."[1]

[1] "Life and Letters," vol. i., pp. 206 to 219. The concluding sentences in this extract from Sir Gilbert Elliot's pen may be read with surprise by those who have trusted to Macaulay's essay on Warren Hastings for their knowledge of the facts. Macaulay wrote: "Sheridan, when he concluded, contrived, with a knowledge of stage-effect which his father might have envied, to sink back, as if exhausted, into the arms of Burke, who hugged him with energy of generous admiration." The only authority for this assertion is Gibbon's statement to Lord Sheffield quoted at p. 69.

Though the praise had been pitched in a high key, yet it is one of Burke's many distinctions to have alone struck the highest note. On the evening of the second day that Sheridan spoke in Westminster Hall, the House of Commons met and Mr. Burges, one of the obtuse and respectable men who represent the inferior moods of the House, was impatient to learn what authority existed for paying counsel to assist the Managers of the Impeachment. Then Burke in his finest manner and naturally adopting that grand style which Matthew Arnold both admired and styled the criterion of excellence, rose before Mr. Burges had got a seconder and said that "he did not mean either to second or resist the present proposition, but simply to congratulate the mover on his having

---

Sir Gilbert Elliot who was in the Managers' box and next to Sheridan may be accepted as a better witness in this case than the Historian of the Roman Empire who was seated at a distance. Sir Gilbert has recorded that Sheridan, whose constitution was not strong, had suffered physically while he was delivering his speeches in Westminster Hall. On the 7th of June he wrote to his wife that Sheridan "had been extremely ill the night before and had strained himself by vomiting so severely as to make it doubtful whether he would be able to speak at all." The letters of Sir Gilbert from which I have quoted were not written for publication and they were not printed till 1874. He was impressed with the part which Sheridan played in the proceedings against Warren Hastings and he was minute in his account, not with a view of giving it to the world, but for the homelier reason that it might serve "as a memorial to recur to hereafter when we gossip of these things as belonging to old times." A man who writes to his wife in this strain and with such an object deserves a confidence which cannot be accorded to him who writes for the public of his own or a future day.

selected this glorious day, after the splendid exhibition which we have recently witnessed, when thousands hung with raptures on my honourable friend's accents, for examining the items of a solicitor's bill. Instead of resolving ourselves into a committee of miserable accounts, let us, like the Romans after Scipio's victories, go and thank the gods for this day's triumph in Westminster Hall. As to myself, I have been too highly strained, and my mind is not sufficiently relaxed after the sublime repast of which I have just partaken, to sink my thoughts to the level of such an inquiry."[1]

While the marvels of Sheridan's oratory were the theme of talk and eulogy in Parliament and throughout the land, the impression in his domestic circle was quite as congenial to his mind as the warmest praise of the greatest statesmen. His wife had helped him in the mechanical labour of copying documents and arranging them. She took a keen interest in the proceedings. Mrs. Siddons and she sat together when Burke formally impeached Warren Hastings, and his speech is said to have melted Mrs. Siddons into tears and caused Mrs. Sheridan to faint away.[2] What she felt when her own husband had

[1] Wraxall's "Posthumous Memoirs," vol. v., pp. 133, 134. While the ill-timed motion of Mr. Burges gave Burke an opportunity to display his grandeur as an orator, he owed it to him that a subsequent rhetorical effect was a failure. He received from Mr. Burges the dagger which he threw down on the floor of the House of Commons with the view of emphasizing his remarks and with the result of rendering them ridiculous.

[2] Lord Auckland's "Journal and Correspondence," vol. i., p. 469.

moved his audience to irrepressible emotion and had been hailed as an incomparable orator may be sur- mised from the tenour of a letter to her sister-in-law in Dublin, written four days after the conclusion of her husband's speech : " I have delayed writing till I could gratify myself and you by sending you the news of our dear Dick's triumph !—of our triumph, I may call it ; for, surely, no one in the slightest degree connected with him, but must feel proud and happy. It is impossible, my dear woman, to convey to you the delight, the astonishment, the adoration, he has excited in the breasts of every class of people ! Even party prejudice has been overcome by a display of genius, eloquence and goodness which no one with anything like a heart about them, could have listened to, without being the wiser and the better for the rest of their lives. What must *my* feelings be !—you can only imagine. To tell you the truth, it is with some difficulty that I can 'let down my mind,' as Mr. Burke said after- wards, to talk or think on any other subject. But pleasure, too exquisite, becomes pain, and I am at this moment suffering for the delightful anxieties of last week. . . . I hope by next week we shall be quietly settled in the country, and suffered to *repose*, in every sense of the word ; for indeed we have both of us been in a constant state of agitation, of one kind or another, for some time back."

The trial lasted seven years. At its conclusion on the 23rd of April, 1795, Warren Hastings was acquitted upon each of the charges brought against him. He was then suffered to go free after having paid the sum of £76,000 for his successful defence. Sheridan had to reply, as one of the Managers of the Impeachment, to the points raised by the counsel employed to defend Hastings. That reply has received less attention than it deserves ; I purpose dealing with it in another chapter. Meanwhile, I shall give a long extract from a letter from his younger sister Elizabeth to her sister at Dublin, wherein she narrates her experiences, during a sojourn with her brother, in May, 1789, while the trial was in progress, and her impressions after being present in Westminster Hall : " To-night they [the Sheridans and Mrs. Crewe] are all going to a ball given by the Duke of Clarence. . . . I will tell you a *fact* that sets our amiable Queen's character in a true light. Friday last the Duke of York went to Kew for the first time since his duel [with Colonel Lenox at Wimbledon]. He found the King sitting in an outward room with a door of communication open to that where the Queen was. The minute he saw the Duke he went softly to shut the door, then running to him embraced him most affectionately and with tears congratulated him on his safety — in short in his whole manner was quite the father. On the Queen's entering, he drew back and fell into the reserved manner he has assumed latterly. She took no other notice of her son than with a cold and distant air asking whether he had been amused at Bootle's Ball, which was the evening of the day he fought.

" It is no wonder that all her sons are disgusted with a conduct so truly unfeminine. They showed their displeasure by leaving the Ambassador's grand

entertainment before supper, and this step of course
has given great offence. Our brother is much with
them all, and when a head is wanted they have
recourse *to his*. He has great influence and will no
doubt rise one day as high as his utmost ambition
could wish. Mrs. Sheridan told me a little circumstance that happened at Bootle's that shews the
footing he is on. The Prince [of Wales] in the
fulness of his joy for his brother's safety had taken
rather too many bumpers to his health. Some one
told our brother, that they feared he was setting in for
drinking and desired he would try to get him away.
He accordingly went up to him but finding that he
did not readily yield to persuasion, he pushed the
bottle from him, saying, '*You shall not* drink any
more.' The Prince fired at the idea of control and
said, 'Sheridan I love you better than any one, but
shall not is what I can't put up with.'

"However with the help of one of the Conways,
they got him away, and no doubt his Royal Highness was thankful next morning for having been prevented from giving a handle to his enemies for
increasing their abuse. . . .

"Just as I received your letter yesterday I was
setting out for the trial with Mrs. Crewe and Mrs.
Dixon. I was fortunate in my day as I heard all
the principal speakers. Mr. Burke I admired the
least, Mr. Fox very much indeed. The subject in
itself was not particularly interesting as the debate
turned merely on a point of law, but the earnestness
of his manner and the amazing precision with which
he conveys his ideas is truly delightful. And last,

not least, I heard my brother. I cannot express to you the sensation of pleasure and pride that filled my heart at the moment he rose Had I never seen him or heard his name before, I should have conceived him the first among them at once. There is a dignity and grace in his countenance and deportment very striking,—at the same time that one cannot trace the smallest degree of conscious superiority in his manner. His voice, too, appeared to me extremely fine. The speech itself was not much calculated to display the talents of an orator as of course it related only to dry matter. You may suppose that I am not so lavish of praises before indifferent persons, but you, I can assume, will acquit me of partiality in what I have said.

"When they left the Hall we walked about some time and were joined by several of the Managers, among the rest Mr. Burke whom we set down at his own house : they seem now to have better hopes of the business than they have had for some time, as the point urged with so much force and apparent success relates to very material evidence which the Lords have refused to hear, but which, once produced, must prove strongly against Mr. Hastings. And from what passed yesterday they think their Lordships must yield.

"We sat in the King's box by which means we had a full view of these noble personages as they went out, and I do think them as ugly a collection as ever I beheld."

Before the protracted trial of Warren Hastings had ended in his acquittal, it was generally acknowledged that his impeachment had been a blunder. Public sentiment, which is unstable as water, was against him at the beginning and in his favour long before the close. He was regarded at first as a malefactor of the deepest dye and afterwards as a martyr of the purest water. The reaction in the minds of his contemporaries was largely due to the length of the proceedings ; his guilt became doubtful when it was seen how much time was required to set forth his alleged criminalities. Subsequent investigation has made it clear that he was partly the victim of circumstances and not the monster of wickedness which the Managers of the Impeachment pourtrayed. He emerged from a fiery ordeal unscathed in reputation, jubilant and penniless.

If those who had played leading parts in the Impeachment could review their conduct in the light of history, several of them would bitterly regret that they had been induced to regard as a criminal the man who was a benefactor to India. Burke is one of those who might feel no remorse and whose prepossession could not be modified by indisputable facts. He never admitted that he had been betrayed through misdirected passion into errors which his critical faculty, if allowed full scope, would have reprobated. Francis hated Hastings after becoming his colleague. He inoculated Burke with some of his feverish detestation. Yet Francis would have been pacified by becoming Governor-General of India. Among those who distinguished themselves as Managers of the Impeachment, three played leading parts and made names for themselves, yet they have lost nothing in the esteem of their fellows by their mistake of labouring to convict an illustrious man of atrocious crimes.

No one thinks the worse of Fox for his efforts on behalf of the people of India when he honestly believed that they had been the victims of tyrannical and remorseless power.   Mr. Grey, better known to posterity as the great Earl who presided over the Government which reformed the representation of the people more effectually than Pitt would have done if his views had prevailed, was as much in error as Fox and, like him, he was guiltless of any wanton exaggeration or of an unworthy disposition to assume the guilt of Hastings.   It cannot be denied that Sheridan had assuredly laboured to ascertain the truth.   His examination of witnesses was thorough. His sifting of evidence was masterly.   He may unconsciously have kept his eyes fixed too closely upon one set of facts and he may have hearkened too credulously to the sinister prompting of Francis and the lurid conclusions of Burke.   It is certain, however, that while the proceedings connected with the Impeachment were in progress, no Manager of it was a more notable figure than he.   Now that the details of what then passed are familiar to students only, the speeches of Sheridan are still read and admired by many who care little for history.   If they had not been delivered, the proceedings against Warren Hastings would have passed out of public memory as quickly and completely as the preceding impeachment of Lord Macclesfield and the subsequent trial of Lord Melville.

III.

"FIGHTING FOR THE CROWN."

SHERIDAN'S irreparable misfortune was to have been honoured with the friendship of the Prince of Wales. He served the Prince with unswerving and true Celtic devotion, and was calumniated by him after death had sealed his lips. That Prince never realized the greatness of the honour which he received when Sheridan and Sir Walter Scott acknowledged him as their superior. Sheridan was envied when he ought to have been commiserated. He suffered both in fortune and reputation through enjoying the Prince's favour.

How or when the intimacy began is not clear. William Earle, writing as " An Octogenarian," narrates that Sheridan told his son Tom he had been introduced to the Prince of Wales at Devonshire House. Their acquaintance must have been formed before 1781, while Mr. Earle, on his own showing, was not personally known to Sheridan before 1788.[1] A letter from the Prince to Mrs. Sheridan, which is dated with the punctiliousness of George the Third: " Windsor Castle, October 12th, 1781, Saturday evening ½ past five o'Clock," proves that he had met her

---

[1] "Sheridan and his Times," vol. ii., p. 164.

before 1788 and that he had been guilty of impoliteness: "Dear Madam, If it is not inconvenient to you I should be excessively happy if you would allow me to call upon you early to-morrow morning, soon after 9 o'Clock, in order to explain to you my reasons for yᵉ apparent indifference with which I behaved to you some little time back. Believe me nothing could be farther from yᵉ sentiments of my heart. I should be very unhappy could I suppose I meant to treat you ill, or indeed anybody in a manner unlike a gentleman. I am dear Madam most affectionately yours, G. P.

" My footman brings this and will bring me your answer immediately, as soon as you have written it."

The Prince of Wales was then as much adored in the fashionable circle of fair women as any millionaire is at the present day. The tongue of scandal did not always lie when coupling his name as a lover with those of high-born or highly-accomplished beauties. Mrs. Sheridan, however, was deservedly spared the indignity of becoming the subject of dishonouring gossip. She never lost the self-respect which others, less beautiful than she, had lightly and shamelessly parted with, when marriage ties were stronger in law than in fact, and marriage vows were often pronounced in view of the pleasure of breaking them. Her spotless life, as well as her exquisite features and form, caused the Bishop of Meath to style her "the connecting link between woman and angel."

As the Prince's friend, Sheridan was expected to defend him in the public Press and praise him in the House of Commons. In his earlier years, the Prince was a patron of the Turf and his horses were prizewinners at Newmarket. Improper conduct was alleged against Sam Whitney, who was his jockey. A long and able defence of the Prince was written by Sheridan. The Prince's innocence may have been complete, yet no man or woman relied upon his word, and the public regarded his retirement from Newmarket as perfectly befitting. He had the good sense not to return, even when obsequiously entreated to do so.

He had his own trials in the abode of his parents and these were sometimes acute. Mrs. Tickell supplies a piece of private history in a letter written to her sister in 1785, and she does so on the authority of her husband, who was in a position to learn what his wife called "a great secret," which was that "the Prince a few mornings ago went to the Queen's House [now Buckingham Palace] to pay a visit to his Mama and was denied. The next morning he went again and found the King and Queen together, the former standing with his face to the fire. The Queen made the handsomest apology for not admitting him the morning before, alleging as an excuse that she was undressed, upon which his Majesty, without deigning to look at the Prince, said 'unwelcome guests are best denied.' This is a fact because it came directly from the Prince."

The Prince's training had not been good. Education can do much; indeed, as Rivarol said, it can make bears dance. Yet inherited tendencies can scarcely be exorcised or counteracted, and George, Prince of Wales, was an almost hopeless subject for a schoolmaster, while the treatment which

he underwent developed the worst side of his nature.
His father's feelings when the Prince was irreclaim-
able were pathetically expressed in a letter to Lord
North concerning the payment of £5,000 for the
recovery of letters written by the Prince, under the
name of "Florizel," to Mrs. Robinson, whose assumed
name was "Perdita," when he said the matter had
pained him so much that he preferred to treat it in
writing rather than in conversation, and that, though
the sum demanded appeared enormous, yet he had
elected to pay it as his wish was to extricate the Prince
from "the shameful scrape." He added, with a touch
of complacency : " I am happy at being able to say
that I never was personally engaged in such a transaction, which perhaps makes me feel this the stronger."[1]

The Prince's entanglement with " Perdita " was
but one scrape among several into which he volun-
tarily fell and out of which he counted upon being
extricated at the expense of the nation. So long as
he got money he was as indifferent as Charles the
Second as to the source whence it came, and he was
quite as ready as Charles to become a pensioner of
France. Indeed, he was thwarted in an endeavour
to obtain a loan from the notorious Duke of Orleans
on terms that would have put him in a degraded
position which he would have occupied, perhaps,
without shame or remorse. Whether Pitt and the
King were cognizant of the intrigue is not known, yet
it is improbable that they had not been informed of it.
The Duke of Portland heard about it, and he invoked
Sheridan's help to avert an arrangement which, when

[1] George the Third's "Letters" to Lord North, vol. ii., p. 382.

completed and made public, would have aroused a
storm of indignation throughout the land from which
the Whig party would have suffered to an extent far
more than it did in 1784 for mere political blundering. A letter from the Duke of Portland to Sheridan
contains all the particulars of the infamous transaction which have been preserved : " Since I saw you
I have received a confirmation of the intelligence
which was the subject of our conversation. The
particulars varied in no respect from those I related
to you, except in the addition of a pension which is
to take place immediately on the event which entitles
the creditors to payment and is to be granted for life
to a nominee of the Duke of O——s. The Loan
was mentioned in a mixed company by two of the
French Women and a Frenchman (none of whose
names I know) in *Calonnes'* presence, who interrupted
them, by asking, how they came to know anything
of the matter, then set them right in two or three
particulars which they had mis-stated, and afterwards
begged them for God's sake not to talk of it, because
it might be their complete ruin.

"I am going to Bulstrode—but will return at a
moment's notice, if I can be of the least use in
getting rid of this odious engagement, or preventing
its being entered into, if it should not be yet completed. Yours ever, P."

Sheridan's intervention and representations proved
immediately effectual, for the Duke wrote to him on
the following day from Bulstrode : " I think myself
much obliged to you for what you have done. I
hope I am not too sanguine in looking to a good

conclusion of this bad Business. I will certainly be in Town by two o'clock. Yours ever, P."

The Prince expected his political friends to act as parliamentary advocates for replenishing his purse. Pitt was a rigid and conscientious guardian of the public treasure and one who maintained, moreover, that he had no right to sanction and satisfy the Prince's extravagance without the King's express command. The King rejoiced at the Prime Minister's attitude. The Prince had contracted, not only debts without scruple, but also a marriage in defiance of the law; and some persons thought he had forfeited his title to succeed to the Crown. I shall not discuss the conditions under which the Royal Marriage Act was passed, nor determine whether the Act of Settlement, which forbids the heir to the throne marrying a Papist under the penalty of exclusion from it, was worthy of the wisdom ascribed to our ancestors, or justifiable in the circumstances. The experience and apprehensions which prompted that prohibition may have become ridiculous when the Prince of Wales went through the ceremony of marriage with Mrs. Fitzherbert, which she understood to be valid and the Church of Rome, to which she belonged, held to be binding. The Royal Marriage Act disgraces the Statute Book as much as the Prince did the name of gentleman.

He was guilty of other conduct which was also indefensible when he authorized Charles James Fox to declare in the House of Commons that it was untrue he had married Mrs. Fitzherbert. She was

indignant.   Her husband protessed amazement, exclaiming, "Only conceive, Maria, what Fox did
yesterday! He went down to the House and denied
that you and I were man and wife."

Fox was informed, by a person who was present,
that the ceremony of marriage had been performed
between Mrs. Fitzherbert and the Prince, and Fox's
regret in having been the agent of imposing upon
the House of Commons was naturally most poignant,
and for a time he shunned the Prince's society, whose
duplicity had the result of placing himself in the
dilemma of satisfying at once the public whom he
had caused to be misled and Mrs. Fitzherbert whom
he had wronged.   He summoned Mr. Grey, and
confessed that the marriage had taken place, and
entreated him to say something which should take
the edge off Fox's declaration and pacify his own
wife.   Writing on the subject afterwards Lord Grey
said, "He put an end to the conversation abruptly by
saying, 'Well, if nobody else will, Sheridan must.'"[1]

While this subject was under discussion the King
was highly incensed against the Prince, yet he felt
it indispensable to make terms with regard to his
debts.   He sent a message requesting the House of
Commons to vote £161,000 in payment of them and
£24,000 towards furnishing Carlton House, and he
promised to add from the Civil List an annual sum
of £10,000 in addition to that of £50,500 which he

[1] "Correspondence" of C. J. Fox, vol. ii., p. 288.   Lord
Holland's version of what Lord Grey told him is: "Well, then,
Sheridan must say something."—"Memoirs of the Whig Party,"
vol. ii., p. 140.

had paid to him. It was added that the Prince had assured the King he would never run into debt again. In the debate on the 4th of May, 1787, most of the speakers expressed their pleasure that father and son had been reconciled, and Sheridan spoke in the same strain, concluding his remarks, as the reporter states, " with paying a delicate and judicious compliment to the lady to whom it was supposed some late parliamentary allusions had been pointed, affirming that ignorance and vulgar folly alone could have persevered in attempting to detract from a character, upon which truth could fix no just reproach, and which was in reality entitled to the truest and most general respect." These complimentary yet pointless phrases appear to have had the effect of gratifying Mrs. Fitzherbert and of closing the mouths of curious inquirers. Sheridan's part in the matter cannot be praised or envied, and he forfeited more than he gained in playing it.

He was employed in a worthier fashion during the political crisis which was caused by George the Third temporarily losing his reason. Fox being then absent in Italy, Sheridan acted in his stead. When the incapacity of the King was indisputable and the appointment of a Regent was mooted, the prevailing belief was that, if the Prince of Wales became Regent, the Whigs would return to power. The presence and counsel of Fox being desired by all his followers, the Duke of Portland despatched a special messenger to Bologna urging his immediate return to England. Fox had travelled through Switzerland, where he spent two most enjoyable days with Gibbon at

Lausanne ; he read many books during his travels ; but, as he seldom glanced at a newspaper, his mind was undisturbed by anxiety about current affairs and uninfluenced by false intelligence. When he learned, however, that the King's mind was unhinged and his life in danger, he travelled home with a speed which seriously injured his own health. On the 24th of November he arrived in London.

Fox was not satisfied with the results of Sheridan's activity and he specially objected to the overtures which had been made to Thurlow to continue Lord Chancellor in a Whig Administration, that office having been reserved for Loughborough. He gave expression to his feelings in the following note to Sheridan : " I have swallowed the Pill, a most bitter one it was, and have written to Lord Loughborough, whose answer of course must be consent. What is to be done next ? Should the Prince himself, you, or I, or Warren [Physician to the King] be the person to speak to the Chancellor ? The objection to the last is that he must probably wait for an opportunity, and that no time is to be lost. Pray tell me what is to be done. I am convinced after all the negociation will not succeed, and am not sure that I am not sorry for it. I do not remember ever feeling so uneasy about any political thing I ever did in my life. Call if you can."

Sheridan's contemporaries marvelled at his activity and his ambition. He was understood to covet the office of Chancellor of the Exchequer. The Archbishop of Canterbury did not disdain to circulate the unauthenticated gossip of the day, and he wrote to

Mr. Eden, afterwards Lord Auckland, that " Sheridan is on all hands understood to be the prime favourite, and to be so sensible of it as modestly to pretend to a Cabinet place, which is hitherto firmly resisted by the Duke of Portland, who says they cannot both be in the same Cabinet. He would willingly submit to be Chancellor of the Exchequer; but it is thought things are not ripe enough for the manager of Drury Lane to be the manager of the House of Commons." The Archbishop wrote with greater smartness than accuracy. The manager or leader of the House, in the event of the Whigs returning to office, would of course have been Fox. It was unnecessary to tell Sheridan that he could not become Chancellor of the Exchequer and remain manager of Drury Lane Theatre. Indeed, neither could the Governor of the Bank of England have occupied that office and acted as custodian of the national purse contemporaneously. Another letter in this Correspondence contains this incorrect statement : " The Duke of Portland has declared to the Prince his determination not to act with Mr. Sheridan in council, who is just now Prime Minister at Carlton House. . . . Charles Fox, besides ill-health, is plagued all day long, dissatisfied with Mr. Sheridan's supremacy."[1]

There are few periods in English history during

[1] " Correspondence" of Lord Auckland, vol. ii., pp. 267, 279. " Edmund Malone wrote to Lord Charlemont on the 2nd December, 1788, that he supposed Sheridan would be Chancellor of the Exchequer in the projected Administration," and added at the end of his letter : " I have this moment heard that Lord John Cavendish will accept his former place and Sheridan be Treasurer

which party warfare was conducted with greater
virulence and discredit than that which intervenes
between the 5th of November, 1788, when George
the Third "burst into positive delirium" at his
dinner-table,[1] and the 23rd April, 1789, when Pitt
had an interview and found him clothed and in
his right mind. Political passion raged, while the
unhappy monarch was struggling to regain his
senses and his eldest son was labouring to obtain
his place. A new sovereign and a new system of
government were anticipated with hope by many,
and by as many with well-founded apprehension.
George the Third had failings ; but his eldest son
had no virtues. To have substituted the Prince of
Wales for George the Third in the eighteenth century
would have been as idiotic as to have replaced at an
earlier day Charles the Second by the Duke of York.

Yet the Prince of Wales felt confident of assuming
the reins of power with the hearty sanction of Parliament. In the Upper House he had on his side
the Duke of Portland, Lord Loughborough, who
was Chief Justice, and their followers, while Lord

---

of the Navy."—" Historical Manuscripts Commission." Thirteenth
Report. Appendix, part 8, p. 82.

The amateur Cabinet makers of that time were often as greatly
mistaken as those of later days. Not one then guessed that Fox
had resolved to take the office of President of the Board of Control. I have a letter from him to Thomas Grenville in which he
makes a statement to that effect and expresses the hope that
Grenville would serve under him. Grenville's own wish was to go
as Ambassador to Paris. Fox's letter was written at Bath on the
3rd of February, 1789.

[1] Madame D'Arblay's "Diary," vol. iv., p. 284.

Thurlow, then Lord Chancellor, had allowed the Prince to understand that he was eager to serve him. His most enthusiastic supporters in the House of Commons were Fox and Sheridan, Burke and Lord North. If a man of lesser capacity and less determined to remain in office than Pitt had been Prime Minister, the Prince and his friends would have triumphed over the Government and the Constitution. Pitt had underestimated his own strength. Many of his followers turned, with the instinct and baseness of courtiers, to the quarter in which the sun was expected to rise; but the majority remained staunch and true.[1] The country was with him then as in 1784 and, if he had proposed, as he ought to have done, that Queen Charlotte should act as Regent till the King's incapacity had ceased to be temporary, he would have beaten his opponents. However, he trampled them under his feet in argument, and showed himself a great Minister in a great crisis. Fox made the inexcusable blunder of asserting the natural right of the Prince of Wales to exercise the sovereign functions which his father was incapable of doing. Sheridan capped this blunder by warning Pitt of the danger which he ran in provoking the Prince to assert his claim to the Regency. Lord Loughborough spoke as foolishly in the House of

---

[1] Wraxall relates that James Macpherson: "ever since Pitt came into power, down to that time, [the 12th of December, 1788] had generally supported Administration, but like many other members of Parliament, he now went over to the party of the Heir-apparent." Perhaps, Macpherson had an eye to the Laureateship! It became vacant in 1790. — "Posthumous Memoirs," vol. v., p. 218.

Lords as Fox had done in the Commons, while Burke did not display greater wisdom, in this matter, than Sheridan. The Duke of York informed his brother Peers: "no such claim of right had been made on the part of the Prince [of Wales], and he was confident that his Royal Highness understood too well the sacred principles which seated the -House of Brunswick on the throne of Great Britain, ever to assume or exercise any power, not derived from the will of the people, expressed by their representatives, and their Lordships in Parliament assembled." Earl Stanhope, who spoke later, expressed his regret that the Duke's words were not in writing; happily, however, they are on record in the twenty-seventh volume of *The Parliamentary History.*

Yet Pitt was the statesman whose firm and valiant hands upheld the ark of the Constitution when it was imperilled to a more grievous extent than in subsequent years. No praise can be too high, however, for the vigour with which he maintained and the success which he had in the defence of the absolute power of Parliament, acting on behalf of the people, to determine how, and by whom, the office of first Magistrate should be filled.[1]

[1] The words of Lord Shelburne in the House of Lords are as worthy of respect and remembrance as those of Pitt in the Commons: "I contend, therefore, that the hereditary succession cannot be considered as a right. It is a mere political expedient, capable of being altered by the two Houses. In cases of exigence, they [the two Houses] had always been termed the Legislature, in order to prevent the greatest of all possible evils, a disputed succession."—Wraxall's "Posthumous Memoirs," vol. v., p. 239.

Sheridan was untiring while the crisis lasted.[1] He confidentially advised the Prince of Wales ; he negociated with members of his own party and he intrigued with members of the Ministry. His younger sister then communicated to the elder one in Dublin what passed before her eyes. Her letters give a vivid picture of life in the Sheridan household and of public feeling as understood there. She said on the 16th of November, 1788 : "I am here in the midst of news and politics. Ever since breakfast Mrs. Sheridan has had a constant *levée* and the present situation of the King of course the only topic of conversation. I have been, as you may suppose, chiefly a listener. I have been a good deal amused

---

[1] It was affirmed without authority that the Duke of Portland would not assent to Sheridan being associated with him in Cabinet office. He was a gentleman in the true and full sense of the term, and such a man would not act confidentially with Sheridan and yet refuse to become his colleague. I have quoted a letter from him wherein he relies upon Sheridan's influence with the Prince of Wales. He wrote again to him while the Regency was pending in terms which are not commonly used by one man to another unless he is on very intimate terms with him : " Dear Sheridan, Lord Loughborough has left me this moment; it is extremely material that you should see him before you go to your appointment, which astonishes us, as we had the strongest reason to believe that the Chancellor had gone to Windsor. Take no notice of our surprise to your company ; but it is not five minutes since the Duke of York told Lord Loughborough that he had come up to consult the Chancellor on the degree of force that might be used, and had pressed him to go in the chaise with him [the Duke of York] immediately to Windsor, which the Chancellor declined but promised to follow him instantly in his own carriage. Yours ever. P.

" I will meet you at Lord Loughborough's a little after eight, unless, which I don't know or think can otherwise happen, you receive an excuse from the Chancellor."

with their various conjectures and opinions which were all suited to their different interests.[1]

"Among the last group came Mr. [afterwards Lord] Erskine, to me the most pleasing man of any I had seen. There is so much fire and sense in his manner that it is impossible for the moment not to be entirely of his opinion. What might perhaps influence me in his favour is the knowledge of his being a respectable and amiable private character. The fact is that the reports of the King's amendment relate wholly to his health. His mind continues in the same state it has been for some time past."

On the 21st of November, she continued her narrative: "We are as unsettled and uncomfortable as you can conceive. Ever talking of going to the country and the house all confusion so that I literally can sometimes hardly find a place to sit down and write a line to tell you of this to account for the brevity and confusion of my latter journals. Tuesday, we dined at home and alone. In the evening Tickell and Richardson as usual. Wednesday, dined at home. Dick with us but so engaged in thought

---

[1] Lord Sydney had written to the Marquess of Buckingham in these terms three days before: "As you may easily imagine, there are not wanting those who are thinking of extracting *good* to *themselves* out of this misfortune; nor are they over-anxious to conceal their eagerness to accomplish their ends. I am old enough to have been in the scene on a demise of the Crown, an event which does not bring the virtues of men more into light than the contrary qualities. I do not promise myself a more agreeable picture of mankind than one which I have never thought of but with disgust and detestation." — "Courts and Cabinets" of George III., vol. i., p. 447.

he hardly seemed to hear or see us, and so went to the play,—*Confederacy* and *Sultan*, Mrs. Jordan delightful in both. The usual intimates came home to eat oysters. I now have got the method of going to bed as I could not hold out a month of Mrs. Sheridan's town life. . . . This morning I was just reading yours of the 17th when Sir Watkin [W. Wynn] and T. Grenville were announced. He recollected me almost immediately and I think I should have known him anywhere, just the same pleasing ingenuous countenance you remember.

"The news just the same. But certainly something will soon be settled and according to our wishes. I scribbled a few lines to you on the subject yesterday which you in your wisdom will reflect on. I also wrote to Harry [Henry Lefanu, who afterwards became her husband] some of my ideas which he will communicate to you. I wish to God you were on the spot. As I am certain that once he [Sheridan] has the power there is nothing he wishes more than to serve you by employing his interest for Mr. Lefanu.

"*Cher frère* has been gone since four o'clock this morning to a private conference. He is the head they all apply to now, and he will be, if things turn out as we have reason to expect, just what he chooses. . . . Among the numbers that drop in we hear a variety of anecdotes relative to the King's situation. One I heard yesterday shocked me very much. It seems he had been very anxious to go to the Queen but they were obliged to prevent him. This he complained of bitterly, repeating frequently,

I am eight and twenty years married and now have no wife at all, is not that very hard? And then said looking at the Duke of York, 'I love you Frederick, but I love the Queen better, she is my best friend.' These sort of ideas have however seldom troubled him. He is generally very busy about some particular object. Latterly he has been making commentaries on the Bible and Cervantes which he dictates to the pages in waiting. They have not been able to prevail on him to get up or to be shaved. Nor has he lately liked to see the Prince, who however is constant in his attendance at Windsor. Some nights ago he went softly into the room and put his eye to a hole there was in a large screen that stood between the bed and the door. While he looked at the bed the King happened to look up and immediately perceived the eye. The Prince withdrew at the instant but the King called to one of the pages and said 'I have seen my son.' They assured him he had not, however he persisted and when he found they still denied it he gave no other answer but a most significant glance at the screen."[1]

Parliament met on the 4th of December. The day before, Elizabeth Sheridan wrote in her *Journal* what was doubtless the prevailing view in her

[1] The conduct of the Prince was not so blameworthy in this case as in that related by Mr. W. W. Grenville to his brother the Marquess of Buckingham : "Think of the Prince of Wales introducing Lord Lothian into the King's room when it was darkened, in order that he might hear his ravings at the time that they were at the worst."—"Courts and Cabinets" of George III., vol. ii., p. 12.

brother's household: "Pitt has sent impertinent
restrictions to the Prince and in an impertinent
manner—by a common servant. But the Prince,
in compassion to the unsettled state of the nation,
does accept the Regency even on these terms and
has informed the Cabinet of his intentions in a letter
sent last night to them. For he did not choose to
address his answer to Mr. Pitt in particular. Nothing
can be better than what he says on this occasion.
The most perfect moderation blended with a strong
sense of the unworthy manner in which he is treated
by the Minister.[1] . . . The King continues the same.
Their new word 'comfortable' meaning nothing more
than his not being outrageous. Wm. Grenville [after-

---

[1] The document to which Elizabeth Sheridan refers is doubtless
the following which I have found in her brother's handwriting,
addressed to the Lord Chancellor. A copy made by Mrs. Sheridan
was forwarded : "The Prince conceives the *pressing a decision* on
a *question of right* to be personally injurious and insulting to him,
and any opportunity taken of discountenancing that proceeding
will be considered as a decisive act of friendship to the Prince.

"The Prince most cordially acquiesces in any measure that is
necessary to secure the King's re-possession of the Government
on the return of his health, as he conceives that as absolutely
necessary, but hopes that no measures not necessary to that
object, but which may tend to weaken and distract his Government at a crisis when every support is necessary, will be framed
by anyone who professes not to have a personal distrust of him
but expects at least that no limitations or restrictions whatever will
be exacted as the conditions of Parliament consenting to his being
placed in the Regency.

"The custody of the King's person, and the power of making
the most liberal and respectful appointments for attendance on his
Majesty is an object which the Prince expressly wishes to be in the
hands of others."

wards Lord Grenville] is talked of very positively as Speaker.[1]

"He is just nine and twenty. I have already told you that I saw Mr. Fox. His manners are certainly plain and unaffected to the greatest degree. If one did not know he was a great man, the idea one would take up would be merely that he was good-natured and good-humoured to the greatest degree."

She wrote again from The Deepdene, on the 7th of December, when she believed that her brother would soon be in office, as Fox did also and said about the same time: "Whether we are [beaten] or not, I think it certain that in about a fortnight we shall come in. If we carry our questions, we shall come in in a more creditable and

---

[1] W. Wyndham Grenville succeeded Charles Wolfran Cornwall, who died in office as Speaker, on the 2nd of January, 1789. Grenville was Speaker for a few months only; his successor being Addington, afterwards Lord Sidmouth.

Among the many papers which Sheridan left there is one containing some lines on the death on the same day of the Speaker and his predecessor in the Chair, lines which show that if he had elected to write satires, he would have rivalled Donne, Hall, Overbury and Churchill: "On the death of Lord Grantley and the Rt. Hon. C. W. Cornwall, who had both been Speakers of the House of Commons, both Chief Justices in Eyre, died at the same time and were equally eminent for political integrity and personal veracity.

> "Mourn, mourn St. Stephen's choir with ceaseless grieving
> Two kindred spirits from the Senate fled !
> In the same chair we heard them lie when living,
> On the same day we see them both lie dead !

> "Sure in one grave they ought to lie together,
> Then in their praise should fiction's self be loth ;
> The stone that says a civil thing of either,
> May praise impartially and lie for both."

triumphant way, but at any rate the Prince must be Regent, and of consequence the Ministry must be changed,"[1] and then she told her sister : "Now that I am informed of your ideas relative to employment, I shall be better qualified to speak to my brother when I can find an opportunity which, from my letters of late, you must have perceived has been hitherto impossible. We go to Town for certain to-morrow and I shall make it my object to watch the first leisure moment he can command. They are very few, for the whole party seems to trust to his head and lately he has added to his other cares, a great deal of anxiety about Charles Fox, who has been most alarmingly ill. This day he [Sheridan] writes word that he [Fox] is mending fast and the note is dated from his sick friend's room." Five days later, she wrote from Bruton Street : "Dick came home to dinner yesterday at seven. He seemed much harassed, for added to the trouble that naturally falls to him, every difficult negotiation, every mistake to be rectified is put upon him."

A few words from Elizabeth Sheridan's pen reveal the methods practised in her day for the manufacture and management of public opinion, methods which seem crude when compared with those of the party managers now who, through the medium of picked deputations to Ministers and packed public meetings, can plausibly represent the great heart of the Sovereign People as beating in response to their piping : "Yesterday," [the 19th of December] she notes, "Tickell and Richardson were here all day

[1] Memorials of C. J. Fox, vol. ii., p. 29.

preparing an address to come from different parts of the country to counteract Mr. Pitt. . . . George Canning dropt in at night." An entry made in her *Journal* on the 22nd of December, displays the difficulties under which Sheridan laboured : " Dick meant to have the day to himself to read over precedents and prepare for this day's business. Before he was up, comes a message from the Prince [of Wales] to beg to see him immediately ; he sent word that he was not very well and had taken a medicine that made it necessary to keep house. In less than half an hour the Duke of York was in Bruton Street, and shortly after him the Prince himself, both boring him and preventing him reading said papers. And to complete all they begged him to see another person who idled him two hours more in the evening. . . .

" The accounts from Kew are worse and worse. For several days past he [the King] has had the strait-waistcoat and has been obliged to be lashed down in bed besides. . . . Willis certainly acted a strange part on Tuesday last [16th December]. In the course of the debate a note from him was delivered to Mr. Pitt informing him that the K — had had a very great and sudden change for the better and that he had continued some hours in that state of amendment and that he (Dr. Willis) had now the strongest hopes of recovery in a very short time. The note was circulated through the House and 'tis not a very unreasonable supposition that many might be influenced in their vote by such a prospect being held out to them. Dr. Warren who had been at Kew in

the morning and had not perceived these violent
symptoms of approaching amendment set off immediately to inquire into the matter and found the
K— in the state I have already described, and
on questioning all the attendants was informed by
them that he had never been worse than during the
precise point of time that Dr. Willis had marked as
the period of amendment."[1]

The spectacle is as ridiculous as it is unedifying
of rival politicians professing to put their trust in the
decisions of rival doctors who had prostituted their
professional duties to party considerations ; of a Lord
Chancellor speculating whether to side with Pitt who
was in power, or with Fox who might displace him ;
of a Prince of Wales whose chief concern was to secure
as much as possible of his father's authority during
his father's lifetime, and of the absence of real and
immeasurable sorrow for the unhappy monarch in
a strait-waistcoat and strapped to his bed at Kew.
Several weeks after the last passage which I have
quoted was written. a change for the better in the
King's health had occurred and dashed the hopes of
those who never thought that he would be himself
again. Elizabeth Sheridan notes on the 28th of
February, 1789, that Willis is to leave the King,

---

[1] Musk was one of the medicines which Dr. Willis prescribed for
his patient : "The scent was very objectionable to the King, and
he begged that it might be discontinued. Dr. Willis explained
that he could not obey or attend to his Majesty's wish, as he so
depended upon its efficacy. Everybody seemed to suffer from the
power of it, and poor Mr. Papendiek was almost in a stupor from
it."—"Court and Private Life" in Mrs. Papendiek's Journals,
vol. ii., p. 54.

but that " he has instructed the Queen how to control him which he does very completely. His own pages are removed and four of Willis's men appointed his constant attendants. . . . Suspense being over for the present we go on much better than we did. *Le cher frère* is quite himself and Mrs. Sheridan infinitely more cheerful than for many weeks past. The most disappointed faces are those who had the least right to be sanguine." On the 2nd of March she added : " To-day the K— parted with his four pages and as a farewell gift gave each a pair of razors. Willis's men have taken their places. The Windsor apothecary who attended him got a fall lately which confines him, so his Majesty walked to Richmond, where he is, yesterday and sat two hours with him, saying often you took care of [me in] my illness, it's my turn to nurse you now. He has a plan in his head of going publicly to St. Paul's Church to return thanks for his recovery. All these [things] are facts."[1]

[1] The stories recorded by Elizabeth Sheridan represent, as I have said, the opinions prevailing in her brother's household, and her brother had special opportunities for getting accurate information. If she believed certain things to be " facts " which were not entitled to the name, she did not err more than the Archbishop of Canterbury who wrote to Mr. Eden on the 16th of January, 1789, that " Sheridan is actually an inmate of Mrs. Fitzherbert's [house] now, with his wife. They took refuge there on being driven out of their own house by the bailiffs who are now in it."—" Auckland Correspondence," vol. ii., p. 267. Elizabeth Sheridan was unconscious of her brother and his wife having been driven out of their house, as she chronicles nightly parties in it, and remarks how difficult it was to get the use of the carriage, owing to her brother requiring it for the greater part of each day.

Mrs. Crewe called on the Sheridans' in Bruton Street and told them, as Elizabeth Sheridan chronicled on the 9th of March: "That the K— has been quiet now for some time but not one whit more rational. His present fancy is to think himself a Quaker and he is dressed like one from head to foot. He carries the Queen of Hearts in his pocket, and calls it Lady Pembroke's picture, for she is the object of his affections ever since his mind has been disordered. So much for his amendment!" This curious statement is authenticated by another in the "Journals" of Mrs. Papendiek, whose husband was in attendance upon the King, to the effect that, when the King was supposed to be able to resume his duties, "he absolutely refused to see the Queen! He said that he had always respected her and had paid her every attention, but when she should have screened his malady from the public she had deserted him, and left him to the care of those who had used him ill, inasmuch that they had forgotten him to be their sovereign; that he had always felt a great partiality for Queen Esther (Lady Pembroke), and with her, upon a proper agreement, he would end his days."[1]

As late as the 12th of March, it was Elizabeth Sheridan's expectation that the Prince of Wales would be Regent and exercise sovereign control in Ireland in accordance with the resolutions of the Irish Parliament; she informed her sister that she hoped their brother would obtain a "Patent Place" there, and that she had discussed the matter with Mrs.

[1] "Court and Private Life" by Mrs. Papendiek, vol. ii., pp. 62, 63.

Sheridan, with the result of writing : "Such is our brother's shyness of applying for any personal favour that though she knows the Regent would rejoice in the opportunity of providing for him, she sees no hope of his taking one step in the business." When there was an end of any likelihood that the Government would be changed, she wrote : "Tickell came in the evening as dismal as a prospect of disappointment could make a man possessed of a good share of both vanity and ambition. Dick came to us between 12 and 1 and we did not break up till past 2. He confirmed the news [of the King's recovery] we had heard, but he has a spirit unacquainted with despondence, and though fatigue was added to the anxiety he must feel, yet there was something cheering in his manner that in a great measure conquered the glooms that hung over us before his return."[1]

Sheridan's conduct during the protracted episode concerning the Regency was less praiseworthy than

---

[1] Moore was probably unacquainted with what Elizabeth Sheridan had written, and his statement, made on the authority of one who was present, confirms and gives further interest to it. When Sheridan arrived at his house with the news of the King's recovery: "there were present—besides Mrs. Sheridan and her sister, Tickell, who, on the change of Administration, was to have been immediately brought into Parliament, Joseph Richardson, who was to have had Tickell's place of Commissioner of the Stamp Office, Mr. Reid and others. Not one of the company but had cherished expectations from the approaching change, not one of them, however, had lost so much as Mr. Sheridan. With his wonted equanimity he announced the sudden turn affairs had taken, and looking round him cheerfully, as he filled a large glass, said, 'Let us all join in drinking His Majesty's speedy recovery.'"—"Memoirs" of Sheridan, quarto edition, pp. 427, 428.

his fortitude and good humour under the disappointment with which it closed.   He wrote many papers
for the Prince, some of which have been published and
others may still remain, without loss, in their manuscript form, and he delivered many speeches which
excited admiration, but did not influence a division.
On the 16th of January, 1789, he said in a speech
which the reporter characterized as "pointed, witty
and argumentative," "When he heard Dr. Willis
attribute his Majesty's illness to seven-and-twenty
years of extreme study, abstinence and labour, and
declare that his Majesty was recovering, assigning
as a reason, that the physic which he had that day
given him had produced the desired effect, what
must he think of Dr. Willis when he heard him
assert that his physic could in one day overcome the
effects of seven-and-twenty years' hard exercise,
seven-and-twenty years' study, and seven-and-twenty
years' abstinence? It was impossible for him to maintain that gravity which the subject demanded. Such
assertions reminded him of those nostrums, which
were to cure this and that malady, and also disappointments in love and long sea voyages."

In this speech he referred to Pitt's taunt about
the Opposition being a political party and said :
"The Right Honourable gentleman had more than
once wantonly attacked that side of the House as
containing a political party. As for himself, he
made no scruple to declare that he thought it the
glory and honour of his life to belong to that party.
He who knew the character of that party, knew that
it was an honour any man might covet to belong to

it. Was it a disgrace to have been formed under
the Marquess of Rockingham, and under his banners
to have combated on behalf of the people with success? Was it a disgrace to be connected with the
Duke of Portland, a nobleman who, swayed by no
mean motives of interest, nor influenced by any
ambitious designs to grasp at power, nor with a
view to any other purpose than the welfare of the
country, devoted his days unremittingly to the promotion of the public good? He could not advert to
his Right Honourable friend [Mr. Fox] without declaring that it was the characteristic distinction of
his heart to compel the most submissive devotion of
mind and affection from all those who came under
the observation of it, and force them, by the most
powerful and amiable of all influence, to become the
inseparable associates of his fortune. With respect
of his talents, he would not speak of them; they
would derive no support from any man's attestation,
nor from the most sanguine panegyric of the most
enlightened of his friends. This much he would
only observe, with regard to the abilities of his Right
Honourable friend, that it was the utmost effort of
any other man's talents and the best proof of their
existence, that he was able to understand the extent,
and comprehend the superiority, of those of his Right
Honourable friend. It was the pride and glory of
his life, to enjoy the happiness and honour of his
friendship."[1]

[1] Mr. Drake, one of Pitt's declared partisans, avowed that
"he felt himself so much agitated by the eloquent oration of
Mr. Sheridan, that it was with the greatest difficulty he could

The Whigs played the party game in a blundering fashion when George the Third, who hated and had despitefully used them, was incapacitated by illness from acting as sovereign. If the resolutions proposed by Pitt had been adopted without needless dispute and discussion, the Prince of Wales would have been Regent for two months at least before his father's recovery, and he might have been advised by a Whig Ministry. That he would have called for Pitt's resignation is not certain. His affirmation that he would do so justifies a doubt whether he could resist the pleasure of breaking his word and the lesser temptation of showing his father how dutifully he had acted.

George the Third's popularity was greater than that of anyone in the country, and the rejoicing on his recovery was truly national. Fox and Sheridan were as great losers by their conduct during the debates on the Regency, as they had been by coalescing with Lord North. When they hailed in just and glowing terms the advent of Constitutional Government in France their course excited suspicion

restrain the emotions of his soul when that honourable gentleman sat down." At the outset of this speech Sheridan took notice of a quotation from Demosthenes with which Lord Belgrave, who preceded him, had closed his speech, and he showed that Lord Belgrave had misapplied the words. Later in the debate Colonel Fullarton remarked that "Philip of Macedon seemed to be an intimate acquaintance of a noble Lord." Colonel Fullarton's reference has escaped remark ; but Sheridan's has been distorted into the statement that he quoted sham Greek to mystify the House of Commons. Those who believe this have been hoaxed. —"Sheridania" contains many stories as silly as this, p. 290.

among those who had been dissatisfied before, and the country at large rallied to the side of Pitt, who was far more narrow-minded in his views and was entirely wrong, at the outset, in his foreign policy. Even when Fox and Sheridan averted their gaze from the horrors which were perpetrated throughout France in the name of liberty, and execrated the policy of pillage and massacre which was rampant, they did not receive credit for being in earnest.

Both of them, however, were as greatly shocked as Burke at the maltreatment of the King and Queen of France, though they avoided the blunder which Burke made of censuring a whole people panting and struggling for freedom because some of them were chargeable with atrocious crimes. The majority in France outraged liberty, as the Puritans in England had done before them, by taking the life of the Sovereign after a trial which was a farce. The case of Marie Antoinette would have melted a harder heart than Sheridan's. No excuse that is worth a straw can be offered for the inhumanity with which she was treated. A letter preserved in Devonshire House which the Duke of Leeds wrote to the Duchess of Devonshire contains the following passage : "An odd piece of confidence was made to me by Argus [Sheridan][1] whom I accidentally met in the street on Wednesday, and he told me he would go to St. Anne's Hill that night and prevail on the owner [C. J. Fox] to write to Barnave and inform him in what a detestable light they would appear to all Europe and to this country in particular

---

[1] In the manuscript, "Sheridan" is inserted beside "Argus."

if the Queen's person was insulted or violently used by the people."

When the execution of Louis the Sixteenth was impending it must have been denounced by Sheridan in private, and possibly he may have expressed his desire to make an appeal on the King's behalf.   M. Pellenc, who had been Mirabeau's private secretary, was present when he spoke in this strain, and imperfectly understanding his intentions, he may have written as follows, from London on the 28th of December, 1792, to Count de Mercy-Argenteau at Wesel: "Even the party of the Opposition here desires that the King's life should be spared. . . . I am of opinion that the members of the Opposition might personally appeal to the Assembly and make the safety of the King an indispensable condition for the recognition of the new Government; and as I have learned that Sheridan had prepared a speech in defence of the King which he wished to deliver at Paris, I shall do my utmost to persuade him, or anyone else, to make the journey."[1]

Obloquy was the lot of Fox and Sheridan for giving sage advice when the first French Revolution had thrown most of their countrymen off their balance.   They perceived, as a few of the Whig party did also, that the French had a perfect right to choose whatever form of Government they pleased, and that a Republican form of Government was not necessarily one with which it was impossible to live in amity.   Their wisdom is a commonplace now ; but

[1] · " *Correspondance entre Comte de Mirabeau et le Comte de la Marck,*" iii., p. 362.

their stand was a bold one at the time. They were maligned and misjudged ; yet they kept their heads cool and their armour bright, knowing that they were fighting for the cause of freedom which, though often imperilled, has always prevailed. They were denounced as Republicans, and in their day a Republican was regarded throughout Great Britain as either a lunatic or a traitor. They may have perceived, what their calumniators could not do, that a Republic can be constituted so as to give scope for the most senseless forms and the most tyrannical action of despotic power, and that a monarchy, wherein the will of the people is really supreme, has a superiority over any Republic which has yet been established, that of Switzerland alone excepted, since Rome was in its glory and Athens in its golden prime. Popularity was dear to Sheridan. He gloried in the applause of his fellows. Yet, when neither popular nor applauded, he bore himself with firmness and dignity.

IV.

HOME JOYS AND SORROWS.

IN 1773, *The Gentleman's Magazine* informed the public that Mr. Sheridan of the Middle Temple had married " the celebrated Miss Linley of Bath." After a few years, this lady was equally famous as the wife of the celebrated Mr. Sheridan. She never courted nor cared for celebrity whether as maid or matron, the family hearth being always her favourite sphere of influence.[1] She delighted as sincerely as Cowper did in watching the panorama of existence from some " loophole of retreat"; yet there was nothing morbid in her disposition, nor any unworthy shrinking from doing her duty in all circumstances. On the contrary, she entered the world of fashion with a grace which was a second nature, and she shone in it with a beauty which was unrivalled and a brilliancy nearly as remarkable. Her love for her husband was akin to worship ; he was attached to her with all the romantic jealousy and devotion of a lover. Being justly proud

[1] She wrote to her friend Mrs. Stratford Canning from Delapré Abbey and said that she had felt more truly happy in a cottage at Putney, "with an interesting book close to the fire than in the midst of all the gaiety and magnificence of Chatsworth."

of her he strove, not unsuccessfully on the whole, to act in the spirit of Burns's lines in his *Epistle to Dr. Blacklock :*

> " To make a happy fireside clime
>   To weans and wife ;
> That's the true pathos and sublime
>   Of human life."

Fifteen years after marriage, Mrs. Sheridan wrote to her husband in a strain which proves she had enjoyed a happy domestic atmosphere :—" I write to you my dearest love because I know you will like to have a line from me every day and I am willing to set you a good example, but I have nothing to say but that I love you dearer than my life and miss you ever so bad."   She proceeded to state that she had suffered from headache and that she had thought, if her " poor Dick " had been in the room, " he would speak to me and comfort me up and I should be well presently ; but it is very well to-day Sir, so don't frighten yourself and think I am ill."

From the beginning to the end of her married life she was ailing at short intervals, and her husband was always nervously anxious about her.   Even when concerned about her health, he penned lines that expressed more love than apprehension, and the following, which I have found in his handwriting, are worthy of being printed :

SPRING. A SONG.

1.

" From yonder Copse, yet poor in Shade,
    And faintly clad with Green,
Why burst such Notes to cheer the Glade,
    And praise the Season's Queen ?

2.

" Each Breeze, each Flow'r that glads the sense,
    To us new Raptures bring,
But do these Warblers learn from thence
    To hail the coming Spring.

3.

"Ah! No. They little mark the
Flow'r,
They little heed the breeze,
Nor early Beam, nor genial Show'r
Can call such Strains as these.

4.

"But with their annual Passion mov'd
'Tis Love that bids them sing;
And still to Love and to be loved
Is all they feel of Spring.

5.

"Shall I then Life's chill winter fear,
Whose bliss no Seasons bound?
Shall I, who love throughout the
Year,
One Hour in Grief be found?

6.

"A Life of Love is endless May:
Fortune I brave thy Sting!
For tho' thou should'st o'ercast my
Day,
Each Night shall still be Spring."

Sheridan always looked back upon the days which he spent at East Burnham as superlatively happy ones. I have already given examples of the profound and pleasing impression made upon his father-in-law during his visit there. I now add that he wrote after returning to Bath: "From my account of East Burnham to Mr. Adams, he will say Paradise was but a kitchen garden to it." The happy pair wrote many other verses during their honeymoon than those which have been printed. The verses by Sheridan beginning, "Teach me, fond Hymen," are well known. Others I shall now reproduce for the first time from copies made by Mrs. Sheridan:

I.

"Shall my Eliza to the birds, and
trees,
Alone communicate her tuneful
lays;
Still breathe her rhyme to the unmindful breeze,
And be content with Echo's idle
praise?

II.

"Oh! let your Sylvio share, my
gentlest love,
Let Sylvio share each line that
you rehearse,
Or he will hate flowers, elms, sweet
bird and grove,
Which shall inspire the too un-
social verse."[1]

[1] The manuscript volume from which I quote these and other lines, was bequeathed to Mrs. Canning by Mrs. Sheridan when on her death-bed, and it has remained in the Canning family's pos-

The lines to " Hymen," wherein Sheridan deplores being absent from his wife, appear to have drawn forth from her the following reply :

I.

" How dull and heavy are the hours !
   How slowly wastes the day !
Those once loved scenes, those
   favourite bowers
Appear no longer gay.

II.

" How oft, with pleasure have I stood
   To hear the gentle dove
Pour her soft murmurs from the
   wood,
And mourn her absent love.

III.

" Pleased I've beheld the woodbines
   grow
And yon tall oak entwine ;
Beheld the opening roses blow,
   With pearly dew-drops fine.

IV.

" But now forlorn how sad I stray,
   No longer these delight ;
With joy I see the setting ray,
   Yet dread the approach of night.

V.

·'Ah, Sylvio, dost thou now bestow
   A thought on Laura's pain !
Will thy fond heart in transport
   glow
When here we meet again ?

VI.

" Then shall thy kindness ease my
   heart
And soothe my cares to rest.
Wilt thou, when I my doubts im-
   part,
Remove them from my breast ?

VII.

" To-morrow's dawn shall see each
   flower
Melting in dewy tears,
Shall see them droop till that glad
   hour,
When the bright sun appears ;

VIII.

" Which, smiling on their breathing
   beds
Sends the soft cheering ray,
While thus they hang their blushing
   heads,
To kiss their tears away ;

IX.

" Thus will my Sylvio come to cheer
   His Laura's drooping heart,
Thus, he'll dispel the clouds of fear
   And bid each care depart ;

X.

" Then will each sense again delight,
   Again, she'll court the shade,
And wonder she could ever slight
   The grove, or fertile glade ;

session.   It was the favourite reading of the late Lord Stratford de Redcliffe.   I owe hearty thanks to his daughter, the Honourable Louisa Canning, for being allowed to reproduce such of the contents of the volume as may be suitable for this biography. On the second page there is this entry in Mrs. Sheridan's handwriting : " E. A. Sheridan, Harrow, Novbr 27th 1782."

XI.

"Then will she find the turtle dove
  No more in grief to moan,
But fly to meet her constant
  love,
And greet his wished return;

XII.

"For then each anxious care shall
  cease,
All jealous doubts remove;
And virtue shall detain sweet peace
  To dwell in Burnham Grove."

In after years he thus addressed his wife :

I.

"If fortune to thee treasures gave
  Each debt of mine thou'dst gladly
    pay?
And nothing for thyself would'st
    save,
Nor deem thy bounty thrown
    away?

II.

"Cruel Eliza! would this ease
  My burdens, or make me more
    free,
When the wish only does in·
    crease
The debt of love I owe to
    thee!"

Mrs. Sheridan was as much beloved by Garrick as her very clever mother-in-law had been. He commonly spoke of her as "the Saint," and she had for him a great and sincere admiration. They exchanged pretty compliments in rhyme. Garrick wrote and sent to her these "Verses on a Lady singing":

I.

"Whence are those sounds that raise
  the soul,
And tears of joy and grief draw
  forth;
A cherub sure has hither stole,
  That we may taste of heaven on
  earth?

II.

"What! is it rosy, winged and
  sleek
The being that so sweetly sings?
Oh no! 'tis thin, and fair and
  meek
And with a covering hides its
  wings.

III.

"Tho' through the air the magic floats,
  To fascinate our ears and sight,
Yet still we fear; for with such notes,
  She seems prepared to take her flight!"

This was Mrs. Sheridan's "Answer to the preceding Verses":

I.

"What dost thou say, a cherub,
   Garrick? no.
  Nor sounds divine, nor wings
   concealed have I,
'Tis true I'm thin, and meek, for
   aught you know,
  But though I still may sing, I
   cannot fly;

II.

"And though a shadowy form I now
   appear,
  With your sweet wife much longer
   should I stay,
So kind is she, that had I wings, I
   fear
  I soon should be too plump to
   fly away;

III.

"But if to animate some other
   breast
  My spirit is recalled by fate's
   decree;
Perhaps, though changed I still
   shall be your guest,
  My *wings revealed*—a Robin I
   may be;

IV.

"Then in the *walnut tree*, I'd build
   my nest,
  Again '*pick up my crumbs*' in
   Hampton Grove,
And still my cheerful song should
   be addressed
  To those whom Garrick, and
   the muses love;

V.

"Nor think when many years are past away,
  Sweet Hampton's shades shall e'er forgotten be,
Still shall the bards with joy attune the lay
  To Shakespeare's *mulb'rry*, Garrick's *Walnut Tree*."

Another set of verses addressed by him to Mrs.
Sheridan, is entitled: "What is my thought like?
Why is Mrs. Sheridan like a cat?":

"The simile is plain and pat;
Why is Cecilia like a cat?
Whene'er she pleases to be purring,
All's silent, not a mouse is stirring;
Whene'er both with love are smitten,
They both produce a *pussy-kitten*;[1]

"And more to make the likeness sure,
They're playful both, with looks demure,
We warmly wish this best of wives,
More like a *cat*—to have *nine lives*.'

---

[1] "Mrs. Sheridan's little boy, called so by Mr. Garrick."
Footnote by Mrs. Sheridan.

Mrs. Sheridan's pen was often active to please her friends or acquaintance, and her husband in particular; but she never imagined, as less admirable writers have done, that what might suit and charm the domestic circle deserved publication. If her good sense had not been equal to her modesty, she could have given to the world a volume of stories in verse, and of tales after the manner of Ossian, which might have been lauded by friendly or foolish critics, read with pleasure by an undiscerning public and recalled in after days by the compilers of biographical dictionaries.

The verses from her pen which have been printed and others still in manuscript are pretty, and, though not additions to the stock of poetry, they possess the extrinsic value of clearly indicating the cast and character of her mind and taste. Her letters are without literary finish, yet they have the merit of being lively and womanly and convey the impression that she wrote as she must have spoken; their special charm is the air of good humour which pervades them. When visiting Lady Watkin Williams Wynn at Winnstay, Mrs. Crewe at Crewe Hall, Mrs. Bouverie at Delapré Abbey or the Duchess of Devonshire at Chatsworth she wrote what she called Journal letters to her sister and these went the round of her family and friends. The praise given by contemporaries renders my regret the keener that no trace of them can be found and that they have probably been destroyed.

I repeat what I said earlier in this work that, with many titles to esteem and praise, Mrs. Sheridan was as lacking as most of her contemporaries in the minor virtue of dating her letters. The covers of most are lost. The following one was written by her at "near eight." She says: "I am writing in my bed half asleep, Sir. I did not know Edwards [the man servant] was going to Town till I was quite undressed going to bed, when he knocked at my dressing-room door to know if I had any commands He might have told you that I was angry with him for not telling me before. My poor Dick! I am grieved to hear that you should be vexed and disappointed, and wish to my soul that I could remove the difficulties which tire you. I still hope to see you for I have such faith in your conquering all obstacles which oppose you in any way, that I think nothing impossible for you. God bless thee my dear Dick. I am half blind with sleep."

Mrs. Sheridan was probably visiting her sister at Hampton Court when she wrote to her husband: "My dearest love, nothing can equal my disappointment on receiving your note. We expected you last night, and sat up till two this morning, and waited dinner till five to-day. I wish, that instead of Ned that you had sent the horses that we might have come to you, for I almost despair of seeing you to-morrow at Heston. Do you *really* long to see me? And has nothing but *business* detained you from me? *Dear, dear* Sheri don't be angry. I cannot love you and be perfectly satisfied at such a distance from you. I depended upon your coming to-night, and shall not recover my spirits till we meet. Pray send the horses to-night that I may be able to set off early to-morrow. The weather has been so bad we have not been able to stir out of the house, so that you may suppose we have been comfortably dull, and this additional mortification has made both Mary [Mrs. Tickell] and myself so cross that I believe nobody would envy us our *tête-à-tête* to-night.

" I wish I could share your vexations with you my poor love ; but indeed I do so in imagination, though I am afraid that will not lighten your burdens. But don't fret my dearest, for let what will happen we must be happy if I may believe your constant assurances of affection. I could draw such a picture of happiness with you that it would almost make me wish the overthrow of all our present scenes of future affluence and grandeur."[1]

When lovers in Bath, they exchanged notes between the intervals of their daily meetings. Possibly the desire of lovers for furtive meetings and to interchange letters grows less keen when they have been rendered happier by marriage. It may be inferred, then, that there was something exceptional when Mrs. Sheridan wrote as follows to him who had been her attached husband during ten years :—" My dearest love, I shall call at the office [of the Theatre] for the chance of seeing you, though I am afraid it will be in vain ; but I write again to beg you will come to us in the evening, for indeed my dear Sheri I am never so happy as when you partake my amusements and when I see you cheerful and contented with me. Your note had a tinge of melancholy in it that has vexed me because I know my own heart and that it

---

[1] The other half of this letter has been mutilated.

has not a thought or wish that would displease you, could you see it. I shall not therefore enjoy this party to-night unless you are of it. We shall not go from Mrs. Nugent's till half past ten, I daresay. The girls are to come in the coach to me there by ten to go with us and I shall direct them to call at the House of Commons for you; if it should be up before, leave word where you are to be and they shall call for you anywhere else. I don't suppose it is necessary to be drest, but if the House sits late and you cannot come at all, at least send me one little kind line by them to make me feel happy for the rest of the night. If by accident the coach should miss you, Mrs. N. lives in Portman Square. God thee bless, my dear one; believe that I love thee and will love thee for ever."

A paragraph from another note is couched in the same terms of devoted and unfeigned tenderness: the signature is an endearing nickname which he had given her and which she frequently uses: "Dear Sheri, let me see you soon to-night— good-natured and happy—for upon my soul and life, I love you, dearest, better than my soul and could be happier with you in some little cottage under the Alps, than with the whole world beside. Dear Sheri, believe me and love me; may I never see God if ever I had even a thought that could give you a moment's uneasiness. Your own true Poush."

In a few lines written at Putney in 1786, she says "my avadavats[1] are very well and send their duty

---

[1] This bird is defined in Dr. Murray's Dictionary as an Indian songbird, brown in colour with white spots. It is mentioned in

LETTER FROM MRS. SHERIDAN MENTIONING HER AVADAVATS.

to you." Keats refers to an Avadavat in his fragment "*The Eve of St. Mark*," and describes how, on the screen in Bertha's room were depicted :—

> " Macaw, and tender Avadavat,
>   And silken-furr'd Angora cat."

Some lines by Sheridan on the death of an Avadavat are as neat as any which proceeded from his pen, and the last verse contains a finely turned compliment to his wife. The copy which she made of the verses is headed : " Elegy on the lamented death of an Avadavat ":—

I.

" Why trickles the tear from Elizabeth's eye,
    Why thus interrupted her elegant chat ?
Ah ! bootless that tear, and bootless that sigh,
    They cannot recall your poor *Avadavat !*

II.

" Each bird that is born of an egg has its date,
    No power can lengthen its days beyond that :
Then let us submit to the dictates of fate,
    And no longer lament the poor *Avadavat.*

III.

" Some comfort it is that no violent death
    Assailed it, from shooter, from bird-lime or cat,
But a common disorder arrested its breath :
    'Twas the *husk* served its writ on the *Avadavat.*

The School for Scandal. Joseph Surface says that all his uncle Oliver had sent from India was " china, shawls, congou tea, avadavats and Indian crackers." His uncle remarks in an aside, " Here's gratitude for twelve thousand pounds ! Avadavats and Indian crackers !" In a letter from Mrs. Sheridan to Mrs. Stratford Canning it is said : " Your boy [afterwards Lord Stratford de Redcliffe], and I are got a little better acquainted ; but I have not vanity enough to suppose that any merit of mine has procured me the honour of a visit now and then. I am afraid the attraction lies in a pair of very pretty avadavats which his godfather sent me as a present last week."

IV.

"The prisoner insolvent who dies in
  the Fleet
    From death gets his *Habeas*, as
    Wilkes did from Pratt.[1]
When caged up for life no joys
  could be sweet,
    And this was the case with the
    Avadavat.

V.

"And now it has flown to new scenes
  of delight,
    Where Venus's pigeons, long
    cooing have sat,

While Lesbia's famed sparrow,
  with envy moults white,
    And the Muses all chirp to the
    Avadavat.

VI.

"Astonished they list to its musical
  throat,
    And Euterpe in vain tries a sharp
    or a flat ;
In vain ! for from *Her* the sweet
  bird caught its note,
    Who excels every Muse, as her
    Avadavat."

Both Sheridan and his wife once contemplated, in
sentimental fashion, retiring to live in the country.
He had purposed making Gresford in Flintshire his
abode, and his wife, who was in favour of the project,
went to examine the house while a visitor at Crewe
Hall.   After stating the advantages and drawbacks
attendant on his becoming half country gentleman
and half farmer, she adds :—" My idea originally you
know was to give up our house in Town entirely,
and then the money we should get for our furniture
there would pay for what we should want here, and
when you were obliged to be in Town, a ready
furnished house would do as well as another for us
and would be trifling expense in comparison with
Bruton Street.   I wish to God you would reconcile
yourself to this.   Suppose people should say you
could not live in so large a house, where would be
the disgrace and what *can* they say more than they
do at present ?

[1] Pratt, Chief Justice of the Common Pleas, is better known
now as Lord Camden.

"You never will persuade people you are very rich, if you were to spend twice as much as you do, and the world in general, so far from condemning you for retrenching, would applaud you for it. Do think of this my dearest Dick and let me have a little quiet *home* here that I can enjoy with comfort. I am now going to bed. God bless you. Goodnight." She kept the letter open till the following day when, as the result of further inquiries about Gresford, she adds,—"I am afraid we must give up all thoughts of it," and continues, "I am impatient to be at Crewe Hall because I hope to find another fat packet from you. Tell me all about your affairs my dearest Dick and tell me honestly whether we ought in *prudence* to indulge our inclinations for a country life. Have you done anything in regard to the Prince of Wales which you said you would? If you could but get a friend to relieve you from these ruinous annuities at legal interest, it would make us quite happy."

Being as good a daughter as a wife, and feeling aggrieved when her husband neglected calling upon her parents, she wrote : "I do think it is very odd, my dear Dick, that you never say a word of my poor father and mother. Surely you and my father have had no quarrel in settling your affairs! I really begin to be uneasy at your silence for 'tis very odd if you have been so often with Wallis without calling on them. You have not said a word about Stafford, or whether you meant to see the cub [Tom] or no. I wrote him word that it was possible you might call on him in your way down and I hope that

will be very soon. God bless thee my dear soul.
Thank you for all the good news of politics. I hope
it is all really good, but you are such a sanguine pig
there's no knowing. We go on here very quietly.
We are reading *Constance*[1] aloud and that is some
little amusement to us of an evening. Make haste
my own love and write to the last minute that I may
know for certain when to expect you."

In a subsequent letter from Crewe Hall she says :
" Well! I have got a nice letter from you this morning, Sir, but no positive time fixed for seeing you. . . .
You say nobody ever asks you to dinner, and then
you dine at Westley's, as if my poor father and
mother did not exist. It seems to me as if you
had not seen them since that first night at the
play,[2] for you don't say a word about them nor
Mary, [Mrs. Tickell], nor Mrs. Canning, nor the
theatre, nor if you have spoke to T[ickell] about
returning with you, and all these subjects are
more interesting to me than anything except
politics, which seem to be in a delightful train
if you are not too sanguine about them ; but they
say here you are and that people in general approve
of this commercial treaty [with France] very much.
Oh ! Sir, I shall be very glad indeed if what you say
is true and that we shall be so comfortable this
winter, and I hope you wont forget to give orders
for the house to be made so, too, before we return

---

[1] *Constance*, a novel by "A Young Lady," was published in
1785.

[2] Probably Burgoyne's *Heiress*, which was first performed on
the 14th of January, 1786.

to it, and that I may have my music home and the pictures up, etc., etc.

' Mr. C[rewe] is gone yesterday and Mrs. C[rewe] reads *Humphrey Clinker* to us at night whilst Mrs. L[ane] and I twist our bobbins about and this is all our amusement, Sir, and I miss my Cribbage very much indeed."

The opening sentence in another letter written at Crewe Hall in the autumn of 1786, is evidence that Sheridan was not always a bad correspondent :—
" You are a dear good boy my Dick to think of me so regularly when you have so much to do ; but if you knew how happy it makes me to get a fiff[1] from you every day you would not grudge the trouble. . . . Oh ! my own, you can't think how they beat me every night. If it goes on I shall soon be on the debtor's side of Mr. C[rewe's] book, and I am the more provoked at my illfortune as I was in hopes this little card purse of mine would have been particularly useful to us at this time. It is the abominable Whist they make me play, Mr. C[rewe] and Mr. Jenkinson against Mrs. Lane and me, and they beat us every game. I lost one and twenty guineas last night and fifteen the night before. I tell you this that you may provide accordingly, for I very much fear you will find no little hoard when you come."

Yet Sheridan did not always write as often as his

---

[1] I have not found the word " fiff " in any English dictionary. It was often used by Mrs. Sheridan and Mrs. Tickell, and sometimes by Sheridan himself, and the meaning intended to be conveyed is that of " a short note." Probably it was fabricated, and exclusively employed in the family circle.

wife desired :—" So Mr. Dick you have got into a trick of forgetting me every other day. No letter again this morning, and indeed if you knew how it disappoints me you would contrive to write a few lines before you go to bed of a night, for I know if you leave it undone till the day comes you would never be in time for the post. . . .

" Mary [Mrs. Tickell] writes me that Tom has written her a very clever letter which you have seen but which Tickell has contrived to lose for her. Pray tell me a little about it. A little rogue! I have never got one line from him though I have written both to him and Mrs. Parr since you went away. However it is a great comfort to me to hear he is well. Mary seems very much hurt at the thought of your leaving Town without seeing her and the children, but I still think you will contrive to do it yet, as I should be very sorry not to know how she looks and the dear little minikins. It is so wet under foot there is no walking, so Mrs. C[rewe] and I are going to get a little air in the open chaise. God bless thee my dear one. Love me dearly, and come very soon to your own Poush."

Few of Sheridan's letters to his first wife have been preserved ; indeed, he took greater care of her letters than she did of his, which is the more to be regretted, because she characterizes the long epistles which he sent her, " as ever so entertaining and comical." But it may be inferred, from what I am about to quote, that he had once written to her in a very jealous mood : " Thank you my dearest love for your nice comfortable letter. I did not sleep all night for thinking about it, and should have been quite miserable if I had been disappointed again to-day. I did not mean to lecture you my soul in my first letter, I was only vexed that you should ever fret yourself or be unhappy without a shadow of a cause, and indeed, indeed my heart's own one, you never shall have any, and I will do, or not do anything to make you happy, but if you have confidence in me, you will not wish to make me to do anything remarkable or studiously avoid every person whose society happens to be more agreeable to me than Mr. R. Wilbraham's or such people. I am delighted that you are settling all your affairs so comfortably, but you don't say a word of returning. . . . God bless you my dear soul. Remember me kindly to them all. Won't you see dear Mary [Mrs. Tickell] and sister Christian [Mrs. Stratford Canning]. I am more interested in their good looks etc., than all the Duchesses and Ladys in the World. . . .

"I forgot to tell you how delighted everybody here was at the parts of your letter that I read to them, and how I was envied by them all for having such a kind good attentive little badge of a husband ; but I told them you didn't love me a bit better than I deserved, for that I cared for nothing in the world but you."

What Mrs. Sheridan thought of her husband has already been shown ; but the fragment of a letter to her sister-in-law and friend, Mrs. Lefanu, contains a passage that has a special interest when read in connexion with those which precede it : " Perhaps I might check the effusions of my vanity on this

subject, but you, I know, can be partial enough to
his abilities to believe I do not flatter him when I
assure you he stands second to none but Charles
Fox in the House of Commons in the opinion of all
parties.   This is a pleasing subject and would lead
me to take up more of your time, if the clock did
not remind me that I must leave you to prepare for
an engagement to Ranelagh to-night with Mrs.
Crewe." It may be supposed, then, how pleased she
was to write to him in her usual playful vein from
Delapré Abbey: "There was a Mr. Thursby here
yesterday.   I did not see him, but Mrs. B[ouverie]
said he was very warm in his politics and in talking
of *you*, he said 'Oh! a leading man, Ma'am, a leading
man, solid, quick, lively, nobody like him Ma'am—a
leading man!' There's for you, Sir.   We laughed
for an hour, Mrs. B. and I at him—not for saying
you was a *leading man*, Sir, but at his manner."

Mrs. Sheridan did not shrink, however, from giving
him good advice, and she did so most emphatically
and properly in a letter from Crewe Hall written
about 1790: "Thank you, Sir, for your fiff [that is
note] and Ozy's letter, [Ozias Linley, her brother]
this morning and still more for the journal you
promise me to-morrow.   I see you are ever so
affronted with me, but upon my life without the
least cause.   I have never had one *cross* feel towards
you since you left Crewe, but I must say whatever
is in my mind to say on all subjects, you know, and
when you tell me how vexed and grieved you was
at not being able to speak that Monday, on account
of your making yourself so ill on Sunday, would you

have me say drinking to that excess is *not an abominable habit?* And where I see *idletons* as Jack Townshend can overcome all your good, and strong resolutions, mustn't I think that London and its inhabitants and their ways *do* alter people whether they will or no?

" These are the expressions you seem to take so ill, and upon my life I don't see how I can retract them, only that I protest I never had an idea of being cross or giving you a moment's vexation by them ; for indeed, my soul, you have been the dear good one ever since you left me, and so far from thinking, or saying, you neglected me, I have often wondered at your attention, and particularly, knowing how much you have to do ;. but yet, I should be very sorry if you were less so, and when you have missed your days [for writing], I have been disappointed and grieved, and of course my letters must have shown it, but I'll be hanged if they were cross, or if I have ever felt the least so since the first week. Your letters, my heart, are all the comfort and amusement I have. I have lost all pleasure in cribbage, for Mr. C[rewe] beats me so constantly and so unmercifully, that it is quite disgusting. . . .

" God love thee as well as I do and you will sit upon the finest cloud in Heaven and be better than all his cherubims. So good-night." The letter is continued on the following day, when the receipt of one is acknowledged with thanks for Sheridan's goodness and punctuality, and it is added : " I am very glad *The Rivals* is to be got up at Drury Lane. I dare say it will bring very good houses especially

if you alter Lydia Languish for Mrs. Jordan.[1] Is
that to be done or how? But I can't bear you
should be wasting your time, and your pretty
thoughts, on foolish epilogues when, if you are to
write, you might write something that would be of
real service to yourself. . . .

"I have anticipated your wishes, as you will see,
about the Duke of Bedford. *Great Wits jump?*
as the proverb says. I hope you will reap some
advantage from being bored with his horses and
bets. If he would but do what I mentioned in my
last letter, it would make our fortunes I'm sure, and
what would it do to him? Why don't you talk with
Charles [Fox] on the subject, and get him to propose
it as a good thing to the Duke of Bedford. Do, my
dear Dick, sacrifice a little of your *false delicacy*
(which nobody has to you) to our future happiness,
and manage this matter. I am sure it could be done
if you would. I can't make out what business you
are settling with Harris. Is it good or bad plagues?
I have no opinion of Mr. H. nor ever had. He is
selfish, that is, quite a man of the world. Of course
you are no match for him; but I trust you do not
deceive me when you say you shall settle things
well, though (as the poor sailor said) I'll be hanged
if I see how, for you seem all poor and pennyless, I
think, not able to play Whist when the fine ladies
wanted you, nor nothing."[2]

[1] The comedy of *The Rivals* was performed at Drury Lane on
the 16th of April, 1790, when Mrs. Jordan played the part of
Lydia Languish for the first time, as Miss Farren did that of Julia,
and Kemble that of Faulkland.

[2] Mrs. Sheridan's anticipation with regard to Mr. Harris was

Sheridan appears to have been a rather captious husband, while his wife's readiness to humour him, even when he was most whimsical, is displayed in her letters and was doubtless shown in her conduct. She, too, sometimes expresses fears about his constancy; but she does so in a playful and loving fashion, as in the following extract from a letter written at Delapré Abbey: "Heaven bless thee once again, and think of me always if ever you should be tempted by the wicked ones and that I love thee better than all the world besides and ever will."

The preceding extracts are taken from unpublished letters; a few more may be added which have appeared in print, but merit reproduction. In 1790, she wrote: "And now for my journal, Sir, which I suppose you expect. Saturday, I was at home all day busy for you, kept Mrs. Reid to dinner, went to the Opera, afterwards to Mrs. St. John's where I lost my money sadly, Sir, eat strawberries and cream for supper—sat between Lord Salisbury and Mrs. Meynell (hope you approve of that, Sir,) overheard Lord Salisbury advise Miss Boyle by no means to subscribe to Taylor's Opera,[1] as O'Reilly's would certainly have the patent,—confess I did not come home till past two. Sunday, called on Lady Julia, father and Mr. Reid to dinner,—in the evening at Lady Hampden's, lost my money again, Sir, and came home by one o'clock.

---

confirmed by the event. Sheridan and he engaged in a theatrical venture which failed. Mr. Harris went to Boulogne, leaving Sheridan to discharge all the liabilities.

[1] Sheridan entered into partnership with Taylor and was a loser.

"'Tis now near one o'clock, my father is established in my boudoir, and, when I have finished this, I am going with him to hear Abbé Vogler play on the Stafford organ.   I have promised to dine with Mrs. Crewe, who is to have a female party only,—no objection to that, I hope, Sir.   Whatever the party do, I shall do of course,—I suppose it will end in Mrs. Hobart's. . . .

" I am more than ever convinced we must look to other resources for wealth and independence, and consider politics merely as an amusement,—and in that light it is best to be in opposition, which I am afraid we are likely to be for some years again."[1]

Mrs. Sheridan watched the course of the General Election in 1790 with intense interest and with no little dread as to her husband's fate.   She wrote to him at Stafford :—" My dearest Dick, I am full of anxiety and fright about you.   I cannot but think your letters are very alarming. . . .   If you were not so worried, I should scold you for the conclusion of your letter to-day.   Might not I as well accuse you of coldness, for not filling your letter with professions, at a time when your head must be full of business?   I think of nothing all day long but how to do good, some how or other, for you.   I have given you a regular Journal of my time, and all to please you,—so don't, dear Dick, lay so much stress on words.   I should use them oftener, perhaps, but I feel as if it would look like deceit.   You know me

---

[1] Mrs. Sheridan's fear was justified.   Nearly sixteen years elapsed from the date of her letter before the Whig party returned to power.

well enough to be sure that I never do what I am bid, Sir ; but, pray, don't think I meant to send you a cold letter, for indeed nothing was ever farther from my heart. . . . Do, my dearest love, if you have possibly time, write me a few more particulars for your letters are very unsatisfactory and I am full of anxiety. Make Richardson write,—what has he better to do ? God bless thee, my dear, dear Dick, —would it were over and all well ! I am afraid, at any rate, it will be ruinous work."

Two days later, she wrote again : " My poor Dick, how you are worried ! This is the day [Friday, 18 June] you will easily guess how anxious I shall be ; but you seem pretty sanguine yourself, which is my only comfort, for Richardson's letter is rather croaking. You have never said a word of little Monckton [his colleague] has he any chance, or none ? I ask questions without considering that, before you receive this, everything will be decided. I hope triumphantly for you. What a sad set of venal rascals your favourites the Blacks must be, to turn so suddenly from their professions and promises. . . . We had a very pleasant musical party last night at Erskine's where I supped. I am asked to dine to-day with Lady Palmerston, at Sheen ; but I can't go unless Mrs. Crewe will carry me, as the coach is gone to have its new lining. . . . the Duke of Portland has just left me ; he is full of anxiety about you. This is the second time he has called to inquire."[1]

---

[1] In 1790, as in 1784 and 1780, "little Monckton" headed the poll at Stafford, Sheridan being elected also.

I have said that Sheridan, as a husband, was extremely sensitive, or, as would be said in common speech, absurdly touchy. He insisted not only that his wife should write daily when he was separated from her, but also that she should fill her letters with repeated protestations of affection. I have given some of her replies to complaints which were founded on a jealousy that was alike unjust and undignified. The following letter which ought not to have been withheld by Moore, does her infinite credit and places her character in a true as well as a charming light :—" My dear Dick, though I do not yet despair of seeing you to-night, I write for fear you should be unavoidably detained again, for I fretted very much last night that I had not done so, as I thought you would have liked to have received a fiff from me this morning when it was too late to send you one. Your note from Sevenoaks found me alone in very bad spirits indeed. It comforted me a little ; but I cannot be happy while you are otherwise, whatever you may think to the contrary. Whilst I live in the world and among people of the world, I own to you I have not courage to act differently from them. I mean no harm. I do none. My vanity is flattered, perhaps, by the attentions and preference which some men show towards me ; but that is all. They *know* I care for nothing but *you*, and that I *laugh to scorn* anything that looks like sentiment or love. I feel naturally inclined to prefer the society of those who I think are partial to me. Lord F. and H. Greville both appear to like me, that is to say as far as laughing and talking goes. As to anything serious, even if they were inclined to think of it, they know me too well to risk being turned into ridicule for the attempt. I never miss an opportunity of declaring my sentiments on the subject and I am perfectly convinced they have no other views in seeking my society than that of amusing and being amused.[1]

" However, I am not sorry, as you are so foolish about them, that they are gone. They went Monday morning meaning to return to the Prince's ball Thursday for two days, when Lord F. goes to Scotland.

" I trust my dear Dick that matters are going better than you expected in Town ; but let what will happen, do not despair. It is in times of trouble and distress that the real feelings of the heart are known. You, who think me given up to folly and dissipation, put me to the proof. Say, ' Betsy I am ruined ; will you prefer going with me to the farthest part of the globe and to share with me there the misery of solitude and poverty, to staying in the world and to be still flattered and admired ?' and see if I hesitate a moment. Believe me, my dear Dick, you *have* a

---

[1] The sentiments here expressed are set forth by Mrs. Sheridan in the following lines, which I have found among her papers, and were intended, probably, for some one who had importuned her with unwelcome addresses :

> " Go—still thy fluttering heart to rest
> And brood o'er calm delights ;
> Forsake not halcyon's peaceful nest
> For passion's evil flights.

> " No more, too near the solar beam
> On vent'rous pinions rove,
> Risk not Eliza's *sure esteem*
> To catch at *doubtful love*."

resource if you really love *me* better than your ambition.   Take me out of the whirl of the world, place me in the quiet and simple scenes of life I was born for, and you will see that I shall be once more in my element, and if I saw you content I should be happy. . . .[1]   God bless you, my dear Dick, and depend on it I should not say all I have done in this letter if I did not feel it."

While Sheridan was jealous of his wife without any reason,[2] she had good cause for complaining about his conduct.   He was not a pattern of unbending morality, neither was he " the reckless and careless man of pleasure " of Mrs. Oliphant's imagination. Some of his contemporaries were more ascetic, and Pitt was irrationally ridiculed for having no other

---

[1] These words really expressed the desire of her heart.   In 1788, she wrote to her sister-in-law, Mrs. Lefanu :—" I hope in a very short time now to get into the country.   The Duke of Norfolk has lent us a house within twenty miles of London [The Deepdene in Surrey] ; and I am impatient to be once more out of this noisy, dissipated town, where I do nothing that I really like, and am forced to appear pleased with everything odious to me."

[2] In Moore's note-book, there is the following memorandum : " From some letters of Mrs. S. to Mrs. Lefanu, the Duke of Clarence seems to have been pursuing her at one time, very seriously—she speaks of the necessity of being ' stout ' and putting an end to his pursuit at once."

Sir Gilbert Elliot wrote to his wife on the 2nd of April, 1787 : " Mrs. Sheridan is really nearer one's notion of a muse, or an angel, or some such preter-natural or semi-divine personage, than anything I have ever seen alive, and it is therefore not surprising that Mr. Mundy should be very much in love with her.   Sheridan it seems has taken notice of it ; but there has never been the slightest suspicion of Mrs. S. having listened to Mundy, or to anybody else."—" Life and Letters," vol. i., p. 148.

failing than over-indulgence in port wine. Dundas, who was his boon companion, held a place to which Pitt never aspired in the annals of vulgar gallantry. In an age less moral than the present, it might be possible to make allowances for the short-comings of public men who, being married, found any happiness apart from the society of their wives, and for this reason no other defence needs be made of Sheridan than that he was nearly as censurable as many of his most notable contemporaries.

A story has been printed which has made some uncritical writers depict him as Charles Surface. It is to the effect that he lost some love letters and regained possession of them in a forcible and illegal manner, and the narrator of the story, which is given at second hand, moralizes about his "vanity and passions too often leading him to yield to the temptations by which he was surrounded."[1] I have read the letters which he is said to have lost and recovered, and the impression left on my mind is that the fair writers were very indiscreet and that Sheridan was deaf to their prayers.

Another writer less trustworthy and less charitable than Moore, has gloried in showing, as he thinks he has done, that Sheridan was unworthy of his first wife, and in exploding, as he assumes he has also done, "yet one more of the Sheridan legends."[2]

[1] Moore's "Diary," vol. ii., 355, and his "Memoirs" of Sheridan, vol. ii., p. 143.

[2] "Lives of the Sheridans," by Mr. Percy Fitzgerald, vol. i., p. 370. Mr. Fitzgerald says that Sheridan began to neglect his wife for "metal more attractive," his meaning not being clear, as he uses the same phrase, at p. 73, to describe Sheridan's conduct

Elizabeth Sheridan has recorded in her *Journal* a lapse from virtue on her brother's part, and her story explains why Mrs. Sheridan bemoaned her lot and, after her injured feelings were appeased, copied the verses into the volume which she began to keep on the 27th of November, 1782, when at Harrow, along with others by her relatives and friends, and in which many of her husband's verses are preserved. If the sore had remained open, these verses would not have been inscribed in the album to which her friends had access. Like many others in it, they are headed " To ——"[1]

1.	**2.**

" Ah ! why when anguish rends the breast
Dost thou avoid with studious art
  To meet thy Laura's eye ?
Alas no angry glance is there,
A mute and unreproachful tear
  Perhaps may claim a sigh.
	" When first the cruel truth I found,
	Nor thou the wish to change dis-
	  owned
	Fierce madness seized my brain,
	But happier now my milder grief
	Affords a sad, but dear relief.
	  I weep—and can complain ;

when at Bath in 1772. He quotes moreover "some pathetic verses" from "one of the MS. books which came into Mrs. Canning's possession"; the same verses having already been printed in Professor Smyth's small work on Sheridan. A single book in manuscript was bequeathed by Mrs. Sheridan to Mrs. Stratford Canning and it is now before me.

[1] Professor Smyth quotes the two opening stanzas, not being able to remember the whole. Mr. Fitzgerald gives the second and makes a change in one of the lines. I subjoin Smyth's version in order that the reader may see how greatly it differs from the original :

> " Ah ! why, while anguish rends her heart,
>   Avoid'st thou thus with curious art,
>   To meet thy Laura's eye ?
>   No frown resentful sure is there,
>   A meek and a forgiving tear
>   Would rather claim thy sigh.

3.

" Too confident my love to hide,
It was my wish my only pride,
    My passion to avow ;
Could I have used my sex's art
I might have still possessed thy
    heart
    Nor mourned thy absence now.

4.

" But I believed this caution vain,
Nor wished by any jealous pain
    Thy constancy to prove,
Let others study how to tease
My only care was still to please,
    My only bliss—thy love.

5.

" Too well my boding heart foretold
A lover blest would soon grow
    cold,
    And disregard my woe ;
Pleasure indeed may swiftly fly
With its own transient blushes die
    But love — no change should
    know.

6.

" Ingrate ! that now has fled these
    arms,
Disdaining all those boasted
    charms
    That once had power to bless ;
Are then these sighs, these endless
    tears,
The sad reward for all *her* cares
    Who gave thee happiness ?

7.

" Say ! thou inconstant ! hast thou
    found
Those joys in dissipation's round,
    Thy fickleness requires ?
Hast thou yet seen the happy fair,
Designed thy softer hours to share
    And fix thy wild desires ?

8.

" Oh ! may her charms, her kindness
    claim
A bright and far more lasting flame
    Than ever glowed for me ;
My silent grief, I may endure
Nor murmur, if it can ensure
    A life of bliss to thee.

9.

" Yet, when my fancy calls to mind
Thy tender looks, thy words so kind
    Hope, through my tears shall
    shine,
And whispers, though the love of
    power
And conquest, claims the present
    hour
    A future will be mine.

10.

" Nature that formed thy generous
    heart
Meant not it ever should impart
    A grief it did not own ;
She formed it tender, fond, and true
Though fairer objects tempt thy view
    That heart is *mine* alone.

" When first the cruel truth I found,
Nor thou thy love of change disowned,
    Fierce madness seized my brain ;
But happier now, a milder grief,
A softer thought can bring relief,
    I weep and can complain."

" Memoir of Mr. Sheridan," p. 26.

11.

"When these illusions charm no more,
And memory shall those days re-
    store,
    When every hour was blest,
Unbidden sighs will then reprove
Thy cold neglect of Laura's love,
    And wound thy conscious breast.

12.

"When that dear moment comes at
    last
To recompense my sorrows past
    And new-born joys impart,
To Laura haste, thy faults forget,
She waits but for one kind re-
    gret,
    To fold thee to her heart.

13.

"When I behold thy softened eyes,
Thinkst thou a jealous thought will
    rise
    To darken such an hour?
Ah! fear not one reproachful frown
Smiles of delight thy days shall
    crown,
    And love resume its power.

14.

"That constant truth that love so pure
Which thy unkindness could not
    cure
    Shall still unchanged remain,
In pardoning thee I shall receive
A transport greater than I give,
    And every wish obtain."

That Mrs. Sheridan had reason to lament her
husband's infidelity is unquestionable, while it can be
shown that his backsliding did not last long and that
his repentance was sincere and lasting. Elizabeth
Sheridan has preserved the facts and it is better
to publish them than suffer conjecture to run riot.
She wrote to Mrs. Lefanu as follows, on the 27th of
November, 1788, from her brother's house in Bruton
Street : "As to your questions concerning Mrs. Crewe
and Mrs. Bouverie, I cannot entirely satisfy you as
I do not know the cause of their difference. That
Mrs. Crewe hates Mrs. B. is certain, and to such a
degree as to be distressed if they accidentally meet.
Mrs. B. neither seeks nor avoids her and from what
has dropped from Mrs. Sheridan I fancy she is the
injured person of the two. Some love affair I believe
to be the origin of the quarrel. As to Mrs. Crewe's
coldness with regard to Mrs. S. it is partly jealousy
of Mrs. B. to whom Mrs. S. certainly gives the

preference. You must also know that Mrs. Crewe among other lovers, (favoured ones I mean) has had our brother in her train. As his fame and consequence in life have increased, her charms have diminished, and passion no longer the tie between them, his affection, esteem and attentions returned to their proper channel, and he never has seemed or I believe never was in truth so much attached to his wife as of late, and this her *dear friend* cannot bear, and Mrs. S. tells me that while they were at Crewe Hall, she took little pains to conceal her jealousy."

Mrs. Sheridan was fonder of entertaining company than of being the guest of others, and her sister-in-law marvelled at the frequency with which she gave parties. Even the theatre did not act as a loadstone to draw her from home. Elizabeth Sheridan records in 1789 : "This evening I go to the play, for the first time these four weeks, to the utter astonishment of Mrs. Sheridan, who cannot conceive what pleasure we can find in it, while my wonder is no less that a woman of her taste and understanding can be amused by drudging night after night at cribbage." Yet she was fond of going to the Opera and she often went to the houses of the great because she thought it her duty to accept invitations from noble and royal personages. On one occasion she was present at a ball at Devonshire House, when in very delicate health, to end the campaign of defamation which venomous journalists had opened against her husband. Her sister-in-law writes : "Mrs. Sheridan has a reason for appearing in public of a curious nature. Among other infamous falsehoods propagated against our brother, it is now said that he locks her up and uses her in every respect ill, even to beating and starving her; how such ridiculous falsehoods can ever gain credit! and yet the eagerness for scandal makes them welcome." It is certain that Mrs. Sheridan's fragile frame was often overtaxed, and that her spirit was greater than her stamina. "A momentary return of strength," it is said, "always tempts her out;" and her sister-in-law judiciously adds: "I cannot help fearing she will at last exceed her strength." She had recorded a few weeks before that Mrs. Sheridan had suffered from "an ugly cough and spitting of blood in a slight degree these two days." In the summer of 1789 she had a miscarriage. She appears to have indulged in excessive gaiety in 1790; for her sister-in-law writes: "Mrs. S. is giving great parties and making up for last year's moderation. I am sorry to see the Faro table always makes a part of the entertainments."

Mrs. Sheridan's delicacy of health increased early in 1792, when a special reason again existed for her husband's uneasiness about her. It was her custom, even when suffering, "to be cheerful, if not lively in his presence,"[1] and to make light of her ailments when writing to him. Sheridan had taken a house at Isleworth, and when stopping there with her son Tom, she wrote to her husband: "I hope you received the letter I sent by the coach Friday night which would prevent your anxiety about me and hinder you from leaving Town perhaps at a very inconvenient time. I write this on that suppo-

---

[1] "Sheridan and his Times," vol. ii., p. 177.

sition that I have been better these last days than I
have been a great while.   My cough is still troublesome, but unattended by those dreadful heart-burns
and indigestions which tormented me so when you
were here. . . .   However I suffer, and I certainly
do and must continue to do so, there is nothing to
be alarmed at.   It is natural for my spirits to be
weakened by it at times, but since the cause is
known it ought not to frighten you or make you
unhappy.   I have been particular in my account
that you may be easy on the subject.

" Don't send any more papers if there is a risque
in it ; but tell me how it is to be, because on that
depends my ordering *The Morning Post.*   I see
Mrs. Siddons is announced.   Have you brought
her to reasonable terms ?   I want to know, too, why
Cymon is withdrawn and how you have managed
with the Duke of B[edford] about the Opera.

" Tom is very well—shoots gulls all the morning
and has read aloud to us every evening, but indeed
it is not the life he ought to lead, and I am very
uneasy about him at times."[1]

In the April number of *The Gentleman's Magazine*

---

[1] This letter is headed "Sunday morning."   It must have
been written in January, 1792, and probably on the 16th of that
month.   *Cymon* was performed at Drury Lane Theatre on the
31st of December, 1791, and on the 21st of January, 1792, Mrs.
Siddons appeared for the first time that season as Isabel in *The
Fatal Marriage.*   One of the characters in *Cymon* was Cupid,
represented by a little boy whom Michael Kelly had chosen out
of many candidates on account of his deep black hair.   He
was afterwards renowned as the tragedian, Edmund Kean.—
"Reminiscences" of Michael Kelly, vol. ii., p. 21.

for 1792, this announcement appeared : " At Crom-
well House, Brompton, Mrs. Sheridan of a daughter,"
the birth having taken place on the 30th of March.
The child was named Mary.   As the mother's
strength did not return and the symptoms of consumption which had appeared previously grew more
intense and menacing, she returned to the house at
Isleworth and wrote, probably after a visit from
him : " I have little to say so soon of myself.   I am
not worse than when you left me, better certainly
than I was yesterday.   I eat my boiled turkey with
an appetite which indeed I never want.   It has not
disagreed with me yet. . . .   Tom is to read to us
to-night, if I continue well, *Vaillant's Travels into
Africa*.[1]   God bless you.   I hope this will find you
well and safe arrived [at Nerot's Hotel, King Street,
St. James's], and pray, get rid of Brompton House
before Sunday, and don't pay another week for
nothing."   Two days later she wrote again and
said : " I have been so engaged with M. Vaillant's
travels into Africa to-night I quite forgot the hour,
and now it is too late for the post and to-morrow
there is none and I am afraid you will be frightened
so I send this by the coach to tell you that I had a
better night last night than I have had a great while
and have been fairly well to-day, so don't neglect
business of consequence to come sooner than you
intended."

[1] A translation from the French of Le Vaillant appeared in
1790, the title of the English version being "Travels into the
interior parts of Africa by way of the Cape of Good Hope.
1780-5."

She continued so ill that her husband resolved to take her to Hotwells, Bristol,[1] which had a reputation then analogous to that of Montpellier and Nice on the Continent, and to that of Madeira and Mentone, Davos and St. Moritz, Egypt, Teneriffe, and South Africa, at the present day, as a sanatorium for sufferers from one of the saddest and most hopeless of all the maladies to which the young, the good and the beautiful so often and sadly fall a prey. At Hotwells, however, it was supposed that health could be regained by drinking mineral water; whereas breathing the air of the mountain, the desert, or "summer isles of Eden," is now accounted a remedy for an incurable disease.

Mrs. Stratford Canning accompanied Mrs. Sheridan; no other friend's companionship could have been so welcome.[2] The letters have been preserved

---

[1] "It is worthy of remembrance, that probably no water was used so excessively for medical purposes all over England, as the Bristol Water, and that it was especially sent in large quantities to the West Indies. It is also an interesting fact, that at the time of the Lisbon Earthquake of 1755, these waters turned red."—Dr. Macpherson, "Our Baths and Wells," p. 67.

[2] Mr. Stanley Lane-Poole, in his "Life" of Mrs. Canning's youngest son, Lord Stratford de Redcliffe, is not accurate in stating at p. 13 of the first volume that "Mrs. Canning had long been intimate with Miss Linley, and did not at all approve of her marriage with Sheridan," seeing that there is no evidence of "Miss Linley" making Mrs. Canning's acquaintance till after she had been, for seven years, Mrs. Sheridan.

Mrs. Canning was a widow when she accompanied her friend to Hotwells. Her husband was a banker and merchant in the City, and highly esteemed by the leading Whigs. He died in May, 1787, and Windham made this entry in his *Diary* on the which Mrs. Canning wrote every day to her daughter while she was tending Mrs. Sheridan with loving care, and they supply an authentic narrative of the light fading from Sheridan's life and of his good angel passing from his home.

The party reached Hotwells on the 7th of May; Dr. Bain, a skilled physician there, examined Mrs. Sheridan and pronounced her lungs to be ulcerated; but he re-assured her husband by saying that he had known cures to have been effected in like cases, and ordered her to drink the mineral water. Mrs. Canning recounted this to her daughter in a letter written on the 8th from Ferry's Hotel, and added: "To-morrow we go into a charming house, the white bow-windowed one that looks over the strawberry garden."[1] On the 13th she wrote that Dr. Bain says "it really is *a lost case* and that she

---

23rd of May: "I learnt for the first time, from Sheridan at the House, of the death of poor Canning, the news of which shocked me less in consequence of the account I had heard before—and which shocked me a good deal—that he was past recovery. He was a very friendly, and seemingly a very honourable man, and one so linked with us by political sentiments and by other ties to those whom I am likely frequently to see, that his death makes a void in the prospect of life which will continue to be for some time perceived."

[1] Mr. A. J. Butler, who is the great-grandson of Mr. Stratford Canning, has done me the service of putting the letters at my disposal from which I quote, and others which I shall use hereafter. My thanks are the more cordially due to him because he did this unsolicited and before I had the pleasure of making his personal acquaintance, the announcement of my biography of Sheridan having met his eye and moved him to perform this act of considerate kindness.

could not live for six months." The sad truth was withheld from Sheridan, of whom Mrs. Canning says : " It is impossible for anyone to behave with greater tenderness and attention than he does. His whole time is devoted to her ; he reads us a sermon every evening and does everything in his power to soothe and comfort her, keeps up his spirits wonderfully before her, but when she goes to bed then he is low and dejected. He does not say much, but grief is pictured in his countenance."

On the 15th of May, the Doctor reported that Mrs. Sheridan's pulse was not above 90° : " This elated poor Sheridan very much, who being ignorant of the Doctor's real opinion, lays a great stress on the abatement of the pulse. . . . Mrs. Sheridan wrote a whole sheet of paper yesterday of directions which she sealed up and gave to me, having written on the outside 'To be opened after my death, and to be considered as my *last will*.' She gave it to me with great composure, and smiling said, she hoped there would be no reason to open it, but as her disorder was of a very deceitful nature, she thought it best to be prepared for whatever might happen. She read sometimes to herself, and after dinner sat down to the piano. She taught Betty [Tickell] a little while, and played several slow movements out of her own head, with her usual expression, but with a very trembling hand. . . . It was so like the last efforts of an expiring genius and brought such a train of tender and melancholy ideas to my imagination, that I thought my poor heart would have burst in the conflict. It did not strike Mr. S. in the same

light; he was pleased to see her able to amuse herself, and augured everything that was good from
such favourable appearances. To me it seemed like
the warnings of death and I thought, perhaps this is
the last time I shall hear that admirable creature
play!"

When he considered his wife to be slightly better,
Sheridan left her in order to bring back his son
Tom, who was under the care of Dr. Parr. She
wrote to him when expecting his return, addressing
her letter "to be left at the Castle, Spean Hill."
Having left the hotel for Hotwells before the
letter arrived, he received it there, because it had
been re-addressed and forwarded by post to Bristol.
It has a mournful interest, being the last letter
which she ever wrote; the substitute for a date is
"Wednesday," which was probably the 21st of
June: "Dearest Dick, I had a better night than
usual last night, and Dr. Bain, who has this moment
left me, says my pulse is better than it has been
these ten days. He confessed at last it was but 94°.
He was unwilling to tell me, because he thought it
might make me too bold; but you may depend on
my prudence. God bless you. I am happy to send
you this good account and shall be still happier to
see you and my dear cub [Tom] to-morrow. It tires
me sadly to write. God bless you." An irregular
line marks the place where her initials would have
appeared, if the pen had not dropt from her wasted
and weary fingers.

Mrs. Stratford Canning beheld other sufferers
seeking at Hotwells a cure which they would

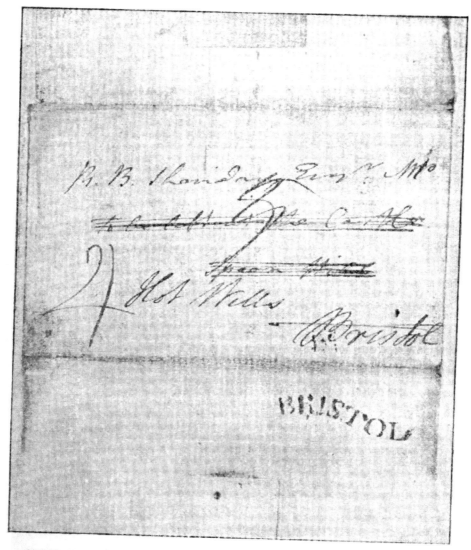

COVER OF THE LETTER ADDRESSED TO SHERIDAN AT SPEAN HILL.

Vol. ii. To face p. 148.

LETTER FROM MRS. SHERIDAN.

never get, and the lamentable spectacle made her write: "This place is as dismal as ever; there are as usual a great many invalids and most of them past recovery." Perhaps Mrs. Sheridan cherished less illusion than those who hoped that she would be cured by drinking water which could not benefit her. When Mrs. Canning bade her good-night on the 9th of June, "she desired me to pray to God to release her soon and to grant that she may not suffer much; all other hope she said was vain." Even in her sad plight, her beauty did not wane: "You never saw anything so interesting as her countenance" was Mrs. Canning's comment, who added, "even with death depicted in it, it is still lovely." In another letter she wrote: "If she feels herself free from pain and in tolerable spirits, she sends for me and Mr. Sheridan to chat a little by way of shortening the night."[1]

On the 27th of May, Mrs. Sheridan did not quit her bed. She wrote a paper committing her infant daughter to the custody and care of Mrs. Canning

---

[1] A story of Mrs. Sheridan's last weeks on earth is told by William Earle in "Sheridan and his Times," vol. ii., pp. 178, 187, professedly from personal observation. He romanced on details taken at second-hand, yet his fiction is not worse than that of Dr. Watkins who, at p. 124, of the 2nd volume of his "Memoirs" of Sheridan ascribes Mrs. Sheridan's death to shock caused by the horses and carriage in which she was about to take an airing on Clifton Downs, being "taken in execution by an unfeeling creditor." Dr. Watkins is a dull writer and, perhaps, a very stupid man, yet it is almost impossible to believe that he was so irresponsible for his thoughts as to be unaware that this story was as much a fabrication as many others.

and made both her friend and her husband sign it. She then bade farewell to her father, mother, sister, husband and son, being herself, as Mrs. Canning stated, "calm and composed, preaching patience and resignation. She is indeed an angel, and I trust the Almighty will receive her purified soul into the mansions of everlasting peace and happiness." It might then have been said of her, in the words which Keats used to pourtray Madeline in *The Eve of St. Agnes*:

> "She seemed a splendid angel, newly drest,
>   Save wings, for Heaven."

During the night between Wednesday the 27th and Thursday the 28th of June, Mrs. Canning and Sheridan watched by her bedside, and, observing a great change at four in the morning, they summoned Dr. Bain. When he came, Mrs. Sheridan requested to be left alone with him and she asked whether he thought her hours were numbered. He replied in the affirmative, and advised her to take some laudanum with the view of enabling her to support the final parting with her husband, her boy and the little orphan niece for whom she had manifested the tenderness and affection of a mother.[1]

---

[1] Moore in his "Memoirs" of Sheridan writes in a footnote to p. 163 of the second volume, that Dr. Bain finding she was dying said: "I recommend you to take some laudanum," upon which she replied, "I understand you : then give it me." These words convey the notion of the laudanum being given to deaden consciousness. In his *Diary* the whole of his conversation with Dr. Bain is recorded by Moore and there he adds to the words I have quoted: "Said (in telling me this) that the laudanum, he

Having taken "a most affectionate leave" of those dearest to her, the vital spark fled at five o'clock in the morning of the 28th June, and then Mrs. Canning "kissed her cold, pale cheek, beautiful even in death."

Mrs. Sheridan had once been the pupil of Jackson, the skilful composer and musician at Exeter, who said that when she sang, "you might think you were looking into the face of an angel." When the moment came for her passing through the deep, dark river over which there is no bridge, those who witnessed her departure with aching and saddened hearts, might have taken comfort in the fancy :

> " Hark ! they whisper ; angels say,
> Sister Spirit, come away."

knew, would prolong her life a little, and enable her better to go through the scene that was before her in taking leave of her family."—Moore's *Diary*, vol. iv., p. 280.

V.

BUFFETED BY FORTUNE.

SHERIDAN did not believe that his wife's recovery was hopeless till she had but a few days to live. He had often seen her seriously ill and rejoiced as often at the restoration of her health, and counted upon doing so again. Mrs. Stratford Canning said of him when writing to his sister, Mrs. Lefanu, on the 1st of June: "Poor man! he cannot bear to think her in danger himself, or that any one else should; though he is as attentive and watchful as if he expected every moment to be her last. It is impossible for any man to behave with greater tenderness, or to feel more on such an occasion than he does."

The wife whom he had loved and lost, knew better than anyone how keenly he was affected by the sufferings of those who were dear to him. She was the first to be informed of the illness to which his father succumbed, and she kept back the intelligence for a time in the hope that more cheerful tidings would reach her, affirming that she could not bear to give him the pain which she was certain the bad news would occasion, and adding in a letter to Mrs.

Lefanu: "I trust your next may remove my apprehensions and make it unnecessary to wound his
sensitive heart by the intelligence." In thus thinking and writing, she displayed a delicacy and depth
of feeling as marked and admirable as her husband's.

On Sunday, the first of July, Mrs. Stratford
Canning informed her daughter: "I am extremely
comforted by finding myself of such essential service
to poor Mr. S. whose behaviour is the most amiable
and proper that can be imagined. . . . Your God-
mother has left you her gold watch[1] and chain, her
best gold ear-rings and necklace, a ring and half her
wearing apparel; to me a ring and her dear picture
and to Bess P[atrick] a ring; but no remembrances
to any one of her fine acquaintance. She doated on
you."[2]

The greatness of Sheridan's loss could be measured

---

[1] This watch, which had been put in a cabinet for safety, was
abstracted and carried off by a burglar, who was unconscious that
its value consisted in precious associations which no gold could
replace.

[2] A letter from James Hare, an esteemed member of the Whig
party in the House of Commons, which is preserved in Devonshire House, makes it clear that Mrs. Sheridan's titled friends
were not wholly unmindful of her when she was stricken down
with mortal sickness. Writing to the Duchess of Devonshire on
the 17th of July, 1792, he says: "If I say nothing about poor
Mrs. Sheridan, I hope you will not think it is from not feeling for
her unfortunate fate; she did not suffer latterly, and her mind was
so wholly taken up with thoughts of another world, and so free
from apprehensions of her lot in it, that her death was less afflict-
ing than it might have been, both to herself and those who were
near her. I have not seen him [Sheridan] since."

and felt by none but himself. His writings before marriage were clever; while they were something more afterwards. His talent received a stimulus from his wife, and associating with her brought to him that inspiration which others have sought from the Muses of history and poetry. On the other hand, she profited after marriage by entering a world far more cultured and refined than that in which her own family had moved. Her early letters betray an imperfect education; her later ones are excellent specimens of familiar and finished prose. She was happily endowed with good taste, and its presence in all her writings is a mark of distinction which is as estimable as the good manners which were displayed by her in society.

Mrs. Sheridan's lack of pretension, her invincible modesty and her grace of speech and disposition must have been the reasons for John Wilkes styling her, even in youthful years, "a most pleasing, delicate flower." The charm of her features and her voice was the theme of constant eulogy, yet she was but one among many beauties of her day. Mrs. Crewe, Mrs. Bouverie, the Ladies Waldegrave, the Duchess of Rutland, the Duchess of Devonshire remain on the canvas of Reynolds as specimens of female loveliness, yet their good looks have alone survived. Many, who were not half so attractive, were praised for the brilliancy of their writing and conversation, while Mrs. Sheridan, without posing as a wit or a learned lady, gave delight by her talk wherever she moved; and this was heightened by the amiability for which she was noteworthy.

She was conscious, but not vain of her beauty. She wrote from Tunbridge Wells in 1790 to her sister-in-law, Mrs. Lefanu : " I feel that I am in very good health, and I am told I am in high beauty, two circumstances which ought [to] put me in high good humour." A passage in another letter is charmingly conceived and worded : " I don't believe what you say of Charles Francis not having been glad to have seen me in Dublin. You are very flattering in the reasons you give, but I rather think his vanity would have been more gratified by showing everybody how much prettier and younger his wife was than the Mrs. Sheridan in whose favour they had been prejudiced by your good-natured partiality. If I could have persuaded myself to trust the treacherous ocean, the pleasure of seeing you and your nursery would have compensated for all the fame I should have lost by a comparison. But my guardian sylph, vainer of my beauty, perhaps, than myself, would not suffer me to destroy the flattering illusion *you* have so often displayed to your Irish friends. No, —I shall stay till I am past all pretensions, and then you may excuse your want of taste by saying, ' Oh, if you had seen her when she was young !' "

Flattery had not spoilt her, even when it came in the sweetest and most seductive form. A woman is quite as susceptible to it as a man when skilfully administered ; but she expects praise and homage from a man as a matter of course, and the staid and comely matron bears with greater equanimity the unhallowed glances of the wicked, than their averted eyes or frigid looks. Yet, when a woman's beauty is

eulogized by one of her own sex with perfect sincerity, then she has good cause to feel vain and to
be highly elated, and when Mrs. Tickell wrote to
her sister that her likeness in the painting by Gainsborough, wherein they both figured, was "the best
and handsomest of her that had been painted,"
Mrs. Sheridan would have been unwomanly if she
had not been proud. The same sister, whose own
beauty was greatly admired, wrote on another
occasion that Mrs. Leigh, a common friend,
"thinks with the rest of the world there was never
so complete a creature" as Mrs. Sheridan. Her
brother-in-law, Tickell, was not addicted to making
fine speeches, yet he styled her "the tenth Muse
and the fourth Grace." Sheridan, who knew her
best, doubtless felt, to use the fine phrase of James
Russell Lowell, that she was, "Earth's noblest thing,
a woman perfected."

She was a thoroughly practical lady, which a great
beauty seldom is, being an excellent housekeeper
and a most sensible mother. She could bear dis-
comforts without thinking herself aggrieved for
having to submit to them. An illustration of this
is contained in a letter to Mrs. Stratford Canning,
written from Plymouth Dock on the 26th of August,
1786: "The truth is I am so bewildered with the
variety and multitude of subjects I have to write
upon, I am at a loss which to choose, whether I
shall exalt you on mountains, or place you (more
congenial to your feelings) by the purling rill in the
valley, whether I shall stick you up on a slippery
rock in the midst of a rapid river, having first led you

... by one of her own sex with perfe...
... then she had good cause to feel ...
... highly ... ... when Mrs. Tickell ...
... sister ... ... likeness in the painting ...
borough, ... both figured, was ...
and her ... ... that had been ...
Mrs. S... ... would have been unwomanly ...
had n... ... ... The same sister, whose
beaut... ... ... admired, wrote on an ...
occasion ... ... Leigh, a common fri...
... ... of th... ... there was ...
so ... ... Mrs. Sheridan.
... ... Tickell was ... addicted to ...
... ... "the tent...
... ... by ... ...dan, who ...
... ... fine phrase
... ... "Earth's ...
a woman p...

She was ... ... practical lad...
beauty s... ... ... being an excel...
and a m... ... ... mother. S...
comforts ... ... thinking ...
having to ... ...mit to them. ...
is contained in a lett... ... ...
written from Plym... ... on the ...
1786: "The tru... ... ... so bewild...
variety and m... ... ... of subjects I ...
upon, I am at a loss which to cho...
shall exalt you on mountains, or ...
congenial to your feelings) by the ...
valley, whether I shall stick yo...
rock in the midst of a rapid riv...

Walker & Boutall Ph. Sc.

Mrs Sheridan & Mrs Tickell.
from the picture by Gainsborough.
in the Dulwich Gallery.

through swampy ground up to your knees to get to it, or run you aground half a mile from any assistance at nine o'Clock at night, there leave you to contemplate the stars, converse with the echo's of the surrounding hills and bear with patience the hooting of owls, and braying of asses insulting your distress, till by the assistance of six men and a basket, at the end of three hours you are carried on shore though not without repeated sousings in mud which was in many places ten feet deep, and which sunk the poor bearers up to the middle at every step—these are the agreeable situations you must expect if you follow us through our western tour, which notwithstanding has been hitherto most delightful, and the more so (to my whimsical fancy) for these little *misadventures*."

While occupying Mrs. Stratford Canning's cottage at Putney during her absence in Ireland, Mrs. Sheridan sent her this lively account of an escapade by her son : " I suppose you have heard what a trick our young gentleman played us. You have no notion what confusion it caused, for to screen himself at first he said that many of the boys were come away from school at the same time. There was poor Mrs. Bouverie sending down an express to inquire after her little John. There was your nurse in agonies about 'poor Master Willy'; she was sure he could not walk so far &c. ; but it seems the spark was single in his elopement and was discovered by Mr. Cotton's man up to his middle in the water at Cranford Bridge trying to catch the fish. He would not go back to school, and the man was obliged to

follow at humble distance till they got on this side
Brentford, when (being heartily tired I suppose
having eat nothing but a halfpenny roll which he
bought at Colnbrook) he consented to go with the
man in an empty coach which was passing by and
which carried them to Knightsbridge, from whence
they walked home [to Bruton Street]. You will
easily guess how alarmed we must have been on
hearing this pretty exploit. S[heridan] set off
directly to Town at twelve o'Clock. I did not go
till the next day, when we packed off the young
squire again to school where he made proper submission and is at present in favour again."[1]

Mrs. Sheridan's good sense as a mother is shown
in what she wrote respecting her boy from Wynn-
stay to Dr. Parr, on the 27th of December, 1786:
" I am infinitely obliged to you for the very comfortable and satisfactory accounts you give me of my
dear boy. I trust and hope he will not disappoint
the hopes and expectations formed of him. . . . I
forgot to mention that Tom, in his letters, complains
of poverty, and requests a little money to be sent
him under the seal of my letter. This I have
refused, as I do not like to encourage such secret
negotiations; but I have directed him to apply
always to you on such occasions, openly and fairly,
as I presume he does not want it for an improper

---

[1] This boy must have been able to make his peace easily. His
Aunt Elizabeth wrote about him in 1788: "Tom leaves us in a
day or two and I shall really regret him as it is impossible to conceive a more amiable disposition than his united to spirits that
makes it impossible to be entirely sad in his company."

use. Will you therefore, my dear Sir, be so obliging
as to let him have any allowance you may judge
proper for him, and encourage him to make you his
friend and confidant on such occasions ?   Too much
money is very bad indeed for children ; but a little I
think quite necessary, to prevent their being betrayed into little pilfering meannesses ; and I dare
say you agree with me."[1]

I have adduced much contemporary testimony in
praise of Mrs. Sheridan's singing.   Before ending
my characterization of her, I shall add what Wilberforce wrote in his Diary for 1783 after supping at
Burlington House : " Mrs. Sheridan sang old English
songs angelically."   Sir Gilbert Elliot informed his
wife on the 24th of February, 1787, that he had
supped at Mrs. Crewe's where " Mrs. Sheridan and
[Mrs.] Tickell sang like angels, nothing can be more
enchanting."[2]

Many women, before and after Mrs. Sheridan,
have been endowed with divine voices.   They
have been idols of the public.   None of them,
however, ever devoted themselves, like her, while
still in the prime of beauty and power, to delight
private friends and acquaintance with the music
which thousands would cheerfully have paid large
sums to hear.   Nearly every one is easily intoxicated
with the applause of the multitude, and an artist who
has once experienced it is never happier than when
the sensation is renewed.   Mrs. Sheridan took no

---

[1] " The Works of Samuel Parr," vol. viii., pp. 468, 469.
[2] " Life " of Wilberforce, vol. i., p. 48.   " Letters " of Sir
Gilbert Elliot, vol. i., p. 130.

pleasure in it.   Her nature, as well as her beauty
and talent, had in it something unique.

Arrangements were made for laying her mortal
remains in Wells Cathedral near to those of Mary,
her beloved sister.   The day appointed for the
funeral was Saturday, the 7th of July.   Mrs. Stratford Canning sent the following detailed and pathetic
account to her daughter: " The sad scene is closed
at last, and I have seen my beloved friend laid in
the dark and silent grave.   Saturday was a day of
sorrow, and of continual and painful agitation.   We
were dressed before six o'clock in the morning ; but
did not leave the Wells till half past seven. . . . At
the end of two miles we stopped, and spent five
hours in a very uncomfortable inn, where we had
nothing to divert our attention from the melancholy
object in view.   In the evening we again set forward,
and about seven o'clock arrived within view of the
Cathedral at Wells.   We stopped about a quarter
of an hour in the road to adjust the ceremonials, and
then proceeded in slow and solemn procession to the
church, the whole scenery of which was to a great
degree beautiful and affecting and greatly heightened
by the recollection of its being the spot where her
early life was spent, and to which she was always
particularly attached.   The concourse of people whom
curiosity and affection had brought together on the
occasion was quite astonishing, and very much interrupted the luxury of our feelings.   The choir chaunted
the first part of the service, meeting the corpse at
the entrance of the Cathedral, and accompanying it
along the great aisle.

"Mr. S[heridan] and his son walked first as chief mourners ; Mr. Linley and Ozias [Linley] next, then Jane Linley and Mr. Richardson and last Mr. Leigh and myself, with poor little Betty [Tickell] between us. Faddy and Annette, with faithful George and Edwards, followed us. At the end of the aisle the coffin was set down and [the Rev.] Mr. Leigh read the Psalms and Lessons ; but the buzz and tumult were so great that although he exerted his voice to the utmost, we could hardly hear him. The coffin was then carried before us to the grave with singing as before. I thought I should have fainted with the heat, and terror and agitation altogether. The crowd pressed upon us so at the grave that poor Mr. Leigh was really afraid of being thrown into it. The dear remains were then let down into the last mansion and the service was concluded.

" Sheridan behaved the whole time with the most astonishing resolution ; at the last moment I perceived a wildness in his look, which terrified me, but it soon passed away, and we retired from the sacred spot immediately."[1]

[1] An account of the ceremony appeared in *The Bath Chronicle* in which it was stated that the congregation was large and that there were many among it who had known "the amiable qualities of the deceased from her infancy. In this accomplished woman it might be said, the Graces and Muses fondly resided." Four lines were added to and ended the report. I reproduce them, not because they are poetical, but because the sentiment expressed was doubtless the prevailing one :

"But though endued with seraph's face
    And syren's voice to charm mankind,
'Twas virtue's path she trod with grace,
    And heavenly truths adorned her mind."

No one can realize what Sheridan felt in his bereavement; it is impossible to measure or understand a purely personal grief. Yet the tenor of his thoughts was indicated by these words in his handwriting: "The loss of the breath from a beloved object, long suffering in pain and certain to die, is not so great a privation as the loss of her beautiful remains, if they remain so. The victory of the grave is sharper than the sting of death."

His son Tom was a comfort to him, penning the letters which he had not the heart to do. Mrs. Stratford Canning told Sheridan's sister that: "Tom behaves with constant and tender affection to his father; he laments his dear mother sincerely. . . . He is in all respects truly amiable, and in many respects so like his dear, charming mother, that I am sure that he will be ever dear to my heart."

Dr. Parr wrote on the 6th of July in reply to an intimation from Tom of his loss: "From your long silence I foreboded the worst. But I thank you for your letter, which was a very proper one, and though you have sustained a very heavy and irreparable loss in the death of a most accomplished and affectionate mother, still my friend, you must be happy in remembering that she was delivered from a lingering illness, and you will consider seriously that all these events are under the disposal of a wise and good being by whose mercy I hope, that you, my dear Tom, will meet your beloved mother in a better world, where separation will be dreaded no more.

"My good boy I entreat you from the affection I bear you to make good use of the calamity which has befallen you and so to conduct yourself from a pious regard to the memory of your mother as would have made her happy, if it had pleased God to extend her life.

"I am very anxious to hear about your father. He has a tender and a generous heart and, though very much engaged in the bustle of this world, he had those virtuous principles and he saw in his own mother that excellent example which, to my knowledge, have preserved him from all that weakness and all that wickedness which too many people fall into upon subjects of religion. The very best of us stand in need of these awful warnings and indeed, Tom, indeed it is a most painful reflection that in this world we shall not again behold those whom we love the most.

"Pray tell me how your father supports his spirits, and give him my most friendly wishes and tell him that a man of his wisdom needs not the common aids of consolation which friends are accustomed to furnish."

In the hours of gloomy depression which follow deep affliction a trifling attention is doubly valued, while neglect causes tenfold pain. Few men were more intimate with Sheridan than his brother-in-law, Richard Tickell; they had married sisters; they had many things in common, and the grief of the one should not have left the other indifferent. Weeks passed after Tickell had received a letter from his nephew Tom informing him of his mother's death, and no reply was sent by him. Having learnt that Sheridan wondered at this, he wrote from Tun-

bridge Wells and said : " I was shocked to find that
my long silence had offended you. Could you doubt,
my dear Sheridan, the keen sufferings of my heart
on such a subject? Who in the world, next yourself, had known so long, so entirely, her goodness,
her tenderness to my children! I am sure my heart
bleeds for your sufferings under this heaviest affliction, nor can I think of words to justify my thoughts,
or in any way express my sympathy. . . . Yet still
I should have written, and have only now to entreat
you to forgive my silence, and to believe that I
partake your affliction not as a brother only, but as
a friend. more and more attached to you by increasing
esteem for your worth that every new occasion proves
and establishes, and devoted to the restoration of your
peace and to your service by every tie of gratitude
and love. . . . It would indeed be presumption to
give counsel to a mind correct and manly as yours,
yet let me express to you that I rely upon every
exertion of your understanding to constrain the
imagination from dwelling with fond indulgence on
a calamity too heavy for almost reason to submit to,
unless sustained by principle. My dear Sheridan
let this dreadful affliction cement our friendship more
closely than ever."[1]

[1] A letter of condolence from Tickell is printed in Moore's
"Memoirs" of Sheridan at p. 158, vol. ii., and it is represented as
referring to Mrs. Sheridan's death. It had been sent to Sheridan
in 1788, after the death of his father!

Elizabeth Sheridan did not like Tickell; her father detested
him; but he was so comprehensive and irrational a hater that his
bad opinion deserves less attention than what she wrote when at
The Deepdene in 1788: "Tickell is here on terms of the greatest

Sheridan's elder sister hastened to condole with him immediately after hearing, as she said, from Charles Francis[1]: "That the fatal, the dreaded event has taken place. On my knees I implore the Almighty to look upon you in your affliction, to strengthen your noble, your feeling heart to bear it. Oh! my beloved brother, these are sad, sad trials of fortitude. One consolation, at least, in mitigation of your sorrow, I am sure you possess, the consciousness of having done all you could to preserve the dear angel you have lost, and to soften the last painful days of her mortal existence. Mrs. Canning wrote to me that she was in a resigned and happy frame of mind : she is assuredly among the blest ; and I feel and I think she looks down with benignity at my feeble efforts to soothe that anguish I participate. Let me then conjure you, my dear brother, to suffer me to endeavour to be of use to you. Could I have done it, I should have been with you from the time of your arrival at Bristol. The impossibility of my going has made me miserable, and

---

intimacy and friendship. He certainly can be pleasing, but a vein of satire in his conversation and a degree of captiousness in his temper do not make him, in my mind, an agreeable intimate. As to other points of his character I do not pretend to give judgment."

[1] A few weeks before Mrs. Sheridan's death, Charles Francis wrote from Dublin to his brother saying that his cousin Dick Sheridan had gone to Bristol to drink the water at Hotwells and asking his brother to lend him the money he wanted, as he himself found it inconvenient to do so. The list of Sheridans who called upon Richard Brinsley for pecuniary help and received it is a very long one. His elder brother found it convenient to make him the perpetual proxy for his charities.

injured my health, already in a very bad state. It would give value to my life could I be of that service I might be of, if I were near you; and as I cannot come to you, and as there is every reason for your quitting the scene and objects before you, perhaps you may let us have the happiness of having you here, and my dear Tom: I will write to him when my spirits are quieter. I entreat you, my dear brother, try what change of place can do for you: your character and talents are here held in the highest estimation; and you have here some who love you beyond the affection any in England can feel for you."

Perhaps it was as well that the affairs of Drury Lane theatre gave Sheridan much concern and occupation at a time when he required to be diverted from vain sorrowing for his departed wife. His mind was also occupied with planning how best to prepare his clever son for going to Cambridge and rear the infant daughter to whom her mother's death was a loss for which there was no compensation. At first, as Mrs. Canning writes, "he could not bear to be a moment without the child"; but he arranged to carry out his wife's wishes that it should be nursed and reared under Mrs. Canning's supervision.

He returned for a time to the furnished house which he had taken at Isleworth, and invited Mrs. Canning, her family and the Leighs to keep him company.[1]   Mrs. Canning wrote to his younger

[1] Horace Walpole told Miss Berry on the 26th of July, 1791, that "Mrs. Keppel has let her house at Isleworth to Sheridan for £400 a year—an immense rate, yet far from a wise bargain."— "Miss Berry's Journals and Correspondence," vol. i., p. 319.

sister : " I could hardly believe him to be the same man.   In fact, we never saw him do the honours of his house before ; that, you know, he always left to the dear, elegant creature, who never failed to charm anyone who came within the sphere of her notice. Nobody could have filled her place so well ; he seemed to have pleasure in making much of those whom she loved, and who, he knew, sincerely loved her.   We all thought he never appeared to such advantage.   He was attentive to everybody and everything, though grave and thoughtful ; his feelings, poor fellow, often ready to break forth in spite of his efforts to suppress them."[1]

Mrs. Sheridan's father felt and mourned for her as deeply and sincerely as her husband, and Mrs. Canning wrote of him when his grief was still fresh and keen : " Poor Mr. Linley is very much broke, but is still an interesting and agreeable companion. I do not know anyone more to be pitied than he is. It is evident that the recollection of past misfortunes preys on his mind, and he has no comfort in the surviving part of his family, they being all scattered abroad.   Mr. Sheridan seems more his child than anyone of his own, and I believe he likes being near him and his grandchildren."   His trials had indeed been many and grievous.   His eldest son, Thomas, after giving promise of extraordinary excellence as a musician and a composer, was drowned in 1778.

[1] A noble friend of Sheridan said that "happening about this time to sleep in a room next to him, he could plainly hear him sobbing throughout the greater part of the night."—Moore's " Memoirs " of Sheridan, vol. ii., p. 171.

A brain fever carried off his daughter Maria in 1785, when she was rivalling as a sweet singer her sisters, Mrs. Sheridan and Mrs. Tickell. These married daughters were, however, most attentive to him and fondly strove to rouse him out of "the coal black glooms" in which, as Mrs. Tickell wrote to Mrs. Sheridan, he was often sunk. Mrs. Tickell's death in 1787 afflicted him greatly; but that of Mrs. Sheridan was a severer blow, for she had always been his favourite. He never recovered from the shock and he gradually sank into imbecility, dying three years after Mrs. Sheridan and being laid beside her in the grave.[1]

The term for which Sheridan had taken the house at Isleworth expiring in the autumn of 1792, he then took one at Wanstead where Mrs. Canning had settled with her children. He engaged an experienced nurse for his infant daughter and paid what was considered "an extraordinary salary." His son Tom lived in this house under the charge of Mr. Smyth, a tutor to whom Sheridan paid the ample salary of three hundred pounds.[2]

[1] Mr. Percy Fitzgerald writes at p. 81 of the 2nd vol. of his "Lives of the Sheridans," that Mr. Linley, "reduced to ruin by his son-in-law sank into imbecility." On the 27th of November, 1788, Elizabeth Sheridan, who saw much of the Linleys, wrote in her *Journal*, that they "are really in affluent circumstances." Mrs. Linley, who survived her husband for a quarter of a century, had an income from money in the Funds and from house property in Bath.

[2] Mr. Smyth was in the habit of narrating his experiences as private tutor to Tom Sheridan and in 1840 he printed his recollections for private circulation. It is charitable to suppose that, after the lapse of forty-five years, he inadvertently made the grave

Near this place are deposited
the Remains of THOMAS LINLEY Esqr.
who departed this Life November 19th, 1795, Aged 63
together with those of two of his Daughters,
and his Grand Daughter
ELIZABETH ANN, Wife of R. B. SHERIDAN Esqr.
MARY, Wife of RICHARD TICKELL Esqr. and
MARY, the Infant Daughter of the former.

In this bless'd Pile, amid whose favoring gloom
Fancy still loves to guard her Votary's Tomb,
Shall I withhold what all the Virtues claim
The sacred tribute to a Father's name ?
And yet, bless'd Saint, The skill alone was thine
To breathe with truth the tributary line ;
The Mem'ry of departed worth to save,
And snatch the fading laurel from the grave.
And oh ! my Sisters, peaceful be your Rest
Once more reposing on a Father's breast,
You whom he lov'd, whose notes so soft, so clear,
Would sometimes wildly float upon his Ear,
As the soft Lyre he touch'd with mournful grace
And recollection's tear bedew'd his face.
Yes, most belov'd, If every grateful Care
To sooth his hours, his every wish to share,
If the fond Mother, and the tender Wife,
Could add fresh comfort to his Eve of Life ;
If Youth, if Beauty, Eloquence could charm,
Genius delight him, or Affection warm,
Yours was the pleasing task from day to day
Whilst Heav'n approv'd and Virtue led the way.
                                        Wm. Linley.

MURAL TABLET OVER THE REMAINS OF THOMAS LINLEY AND
HIS DAUGHTERS IN WELLS CATHEDRAL.

Writing from Wanstead, Mrs. Stratford Canning says: "It is impossible for anyone to be more devoted to his children than Sheridan is, and I hope they will be a comfort and a blessing to him when the world loses its charms." His son's tutor has recorded that his baby daughter was "beautiful and refined looking." Mr. Smyth also wrote in a jeering tone about Sheridan being so nervous lest any accident should befall his son, that he forbade him to skate. The son could not understand his father's morbid anxiety about him, being unaware, perhaps, that he had inherited the seeds of his mother's malady and would die from it in his prime. He had a young man's aversion to be treated as a hothouse plant and he doubtless saw the comic side of the advice which Mr. Grey is said to have given Sheridan: "Have a glass case constructed for your son at once."[1]

Sheridan invited a party of young people to his

mistakes with which he is chargeable. Mr. Percy Fitzgerald has repeated, without endeavouring to sift his allegations, all that is unfavourable to Sheridan. Mr. Smyth was a fellow of Peterhouse, Cambridge. He was appointed Professor of History in his University in 1807, and held that office till his death. Some of his statements about Sheridan are as authentic as those of Mr. Fitzgerald about him. According to Mr. Fitzgerald, he was "a young fellow at Oxford," on the look-out for a tutorship, who was "afterwards Professor of Poetry at Oxford."—"Lives of the Sheridans," vol. i., p. 399.

[1] Sheridan's parental feeling may have been excessive, yet it scarcely deserves the discreditable sneer of Mr. Percy Fitzgerald: "No one could call this real affection; it was no more than an unreasoning selfishness which could not bear a moment's uneasiness or to be disturbed about anything."—"Lives of the Sheridans," vol. i., p. 402.

house at Wanstead on the 23rd of October, 1793.
Dancing was about to begin, when Mrs. Canning
startled the company by rushing in and exclaiming :
" The child is dying !"   A doctor was summoned
and came without delay ; but he could not prolong
little Mary's life.   The grief of Sheridan was irrepressible, till he was convinced by the reiterated
assurances of Mrs. Canning that his little daughter
had neither been neglected nor mismanaged.   The
extraordinary resemblance of the child to its mother
intensified his affliction in parting with it.   He determined that the funeral should be at Wells and
when remonstrated with on account of the distance,
he exclaimed : " But where ought the child to be
laid but in the bosom of its mother ?" so the tomb
in the Cathedral at Wells was reopened to receive a
tiny coffin.   Mrs. Canning wrote at the time : " However Sheridan may assume the appearance of cheerfulness, his heart is not of a nature to be quickly
reconciled to the loss of anything he loves.   He
suffers deeply and secretly, and I daresay he will
long and bitterly lament both mother and child."[1]

He experienced the irony of existence as fully and
painfully as anyone on whom fortune alternately
frowns and smiles, with as little reason or warning
for the smile as for the frown.   He had overcome
great obstacles before marrying the idol of his heart.
He rose to the highest eminence as a dramatist.   He
achieved undying fame as an orator.   His life might
have glided happily and serenely to its close if she
whom he had loved from youth upwards had remained
by his side till the end.   If his little daughter had

[1] " Memoirs " of Frances Sheridan, p. 429.

survived, the feelings of earlier days might have been revivified in her society and he might have acquired more from her than he could impart.

The misery of his lot unhinged Sheridan for a time. He entered into reckless contracts concerning Drury Lane theatre ; he made as reckless bets at Brooks's Club. He took houses which he could not occupy and kept horses which never left the stable. Many years of a life which, though chequered, was brightened by several happy hours, were in store for him. He was the hero of fresh triumphs as an orator in Westminster Hall and the House of Commons. A second marriage was followed by the birth of another son who, like the first, repaid with affection the tenderness which was lavished upon him. Yet Sheridan's life was blighted and his career was downward after burying his wife and only daughter. The memory of the incomparable woman whom he had wedded in youth was always kept green and was always cherished. When her youngest sister's singing was praised, he cried out : "Oh heavens! if you had heard Mrs. Sheridan sing that song." In 1813, Wilberforce was at the exhibition of pictures at the British Institution Rooms, and then he records that, "Poor Sheridan took me up to his first wife's picture, and stood with me looking at it affectionately for some time."[1] After the death of Sheridan's grandfather, Swift sadly remarked : "Oh! I lost my right hand when I lost him." When Sheridan's first wife died, he lost not only an adorable companion, but also his guardian Angel upon earth.

[1] *Diary* of Wilberforce, vol. iv., p. 114.

VI.

THEATRE AND PARLIAMENT.

COMPETENT surveyors reported in 1791 that Drury Lane theatre was unsafe and must be rebuilt. The proprietors agreed to erect a new edifice on its site and provided the required sum, which was £150,000. They resolved that the new theatre should be much larger than the old one, and they did so without foreseeing the greater difficulty of making the larger house profitable, and the impossibility of rendering it as suitable as the smaller for artistic representation.[1]

While Garrick managed the theatre which was pulled down, the balance at his bankers' steadily increased. Though he may have paid his company small salaries, he kept his word. Sheridan is accused of being lavish in promises and of never keeping them, and it has been represented that the

---

[1] Mr. Fitzgerald takes the enlargement of the theatre so much to heart as to write that, owing to it: " Sheridan may be said to have had the discredit of the destruction of the drama and thus in his reckless fashion was to shipwreck what it had taken Garrick's long and respectable life to construct." My own opinion is that the drama was not wholly destroyed by Sheridan.

members of his company were always on the brink
of starvation. Why, then, did they continue their
services year after year?

New Drury was opened on the 12th of March,
1794, with a concert of sacred music. Many
obstacles had impeded the substitution of this
structure for the old one. The Duke of Bedford,
as landlord, objected to extending the lease on the
ground that the monopoly might soon end. A
patent which was granted to Killigrew by Charles
the Second, had been overlooked ; but it was believed
to be valid, and its holders parted with it for sixteen
thousand pounds. When the proprietors had obtained this Patent and an extension of their Patent
from the Crown for twenty-one years, the Duke
declared himself satisfied and renewed the lease.
For the proprietors, however, the prospect was
gloomy and disheartening. During the four years
that Drury Lane theatre was rebuilding and the
company occupied that in the Haymarket, the
receipts never covered the expenses. Moreover,
six thousand pounds had gone to pay interest on
the capital, and, what was still worse though not
unprecedented, the cost of construction had exceeded
the estimate by £70,000. If Sheridan had been
less sanguine by nature, he would have been dis-
mayed and given way to despair. Yet he felt confident of retrieving what had been lost and warding
off impending ruin. He did not suspect at the time,
what he learned to his mortification in later years,
that he had been as wax in the hands of unscrupulous
and wily men who were enriching themselves at his

expense all the time he thought they were faithfully serving him.

The first theatrical performance in the new theatre took place on the 21st of April, 1794, *Macbeth* and *The Virgin Unmasked* being the pieces chosen for the occasion.   An address was delivered by Miss Farren, whom Horace Walpole had termed, eight years before, " the first of all actresses," and who, three years afterwards, became Countess of Derby. Neither the acting of Mrs. Siddons and John Kemble, nor the delightful intonation of Miss Farren's voice produced as profound an impression, however, as a display of the elaborate precautions which had been taken against danger from fire.   A massive iron curtain was lowered, and " struck with heavy hammers in order to prove that it was something more than stage iron, which by its clang, reverberated through the house, mingling with the uproarious clamour of a delighted audience.   On its being raised, another burst of applause rung from every quarter on the exhibition of a cascade of water rushing down from tanks with which the roof had been supplied, roaring into a huge basin which had been prepared for its reception ; dashing, splashing, tumbling over artificial rocks, but bearing no doubt of its own reality, and clearly showing that in such an awful event as that of fire, they could not only extinguish the flame upon the instant, from whatever quarter it could originate, but actually drown the theatre."[1]

On the 24th of February, 1809, fifteen years after

---

[1] " Sheridan and his Times," vol. ii., p. 230.

this exhibition, the House of Commons was reddened
with the glare of a great conflagration.   A debate
was then in progress on the conduct of the war in
Spain.   Ponsonby, who originated it on the part of
the Opposition, had moved for an inquiry.   Castlereagh, as Foreign Secretary, opposed the motion
on the part of the Government.   Canning, who
was Home Secretary, did so likewise and his speech
was repeatedly interrupted, towards the close, by the
cry of " Fire !"   Sheridan whispered across the table
that Drury Lane theatre was burning.   Windham
had risen to reply to Canning, but resumed his seat
on Lord Temple suggesting the adjournment of the
debate " in consequence of the extent of the calamity,
which the event just communicated to the House
would bring upon a respectable individual, a member
of that House."   Thereupon Sheridan rose and said
that, " whatever might be the extent of the individual
calamity, he did not consider it of a nature to in-
terrupt their proceedings on so great a national
question."   Mr. Ponsonby agreed with Lord
Temple ; Mr. Perceval, the Chancellor of the
Exchequer, took an opposite view, assigning the
reason that, as there was no performance at the
theatre, it was absurd to feel apprehension concerning the fate of the friends or relatives of
members.   General Mathew did not envy the Chancellor of the Exchequer or share his optimism, and,
dreading lest a part of London might be burnt
down while the House was debating, he moved its
adjournment and Mr. Herbert seconded the motion.
Wilberforce said that he would vote with General

Mathew if, by so doing, the fire would be extinguished, urging, however, the absurdity of adjourning an important debate for the reasons which had been stated. The motion was withdrawn by consent and the debate continued till a division took place at half past three in the morning.[1]

Drury Lane theatre rose from its ashes, but the fire which destroyed it in 1809 beggared Sheridan as completely as an organized riot in the Theatre Royal at Dublin had beggared his father in 1754. He was now burdened with a load of liabilities, for which he had accepted the responsibility with a chivalry which never received recognition. What happened, forms part of the history of the theatre. The facts of biographical value will be set forth in another chapter. Suffice it for the present to show how Sheridan continued to render the theatre as attractive during the later as it had been during the earlier period of his management.

He adapted pieces for it which were applauded by playgoers, one being *The Stranger* and another *Pizarro*, and both being taken from the German of Kotzebue. Three English versions of *The Stranger* had appeared, that followed by Sheridan having been made by Benjamin Thompson. The acting version is not a slavish reproduction; the hand of a master being unmistakeable, and Sheridan told Rogers that every word of it was from his pen. His version of *Pizarro* by Kotzebue made a still deeper and more lasting impression. It differed so greatly from the original as to be thought worthy of

---

[1] "Parliamentary Debates," vol. xii., pp. 1105, 1206.

translation into the tongue in which the original was composed.

Pizarro contains more splendid claptrap than any piece which has been very popular on the English stage. It gratified the King and Queen in the royal box as much as the patriotic crossing-sweeper in the upper gallery. It was first represented at Drury Lane Theatre on the 24th of May, 1799. Moore wrote to his mother on the 11th of June in that year: "I have not yet been to this wonderful *Pizarro* of Sheridan's, which is putting all London into fevers."[1] If Sheridan had produced no other pieces than his adaptations of *The Stranger* and *Pizarro* no praise would attach to his name as a dramatist. These were produced, however, in his capacity of responsible manager of the theatre upon which he depended for his daily bread. Measured by pecuniary results his labours were praiseworthy. The performances of *Pizarro* caused £15,000 to flow into the treasury. When the country was threatened with invasion Pitt was urged to have some of the patriotic tirades in the piece reprinted as the best possible incentive to recruiting the army.

A great blunder, however, must be laid to his charge. He was shown the manuscript of an unpublished play by Shakespeare and he shared the

---

[1] "Memoirs" of Moore, vol. i., p. 90. In his "Memoirs" of Sheridan, vol. ii., p. 287, Moore does not overpraise this play, while he makes the mistake of writing: "In the plot, and the arrangement of the scenes, it is well known, there is but little alteration from the German original." If he had read the original he would not have penned these words.

conviction of Dr. Parr, Dr. Wharton, Erskine,[1] and many others that the tragedy of *Vortigern and Rowena* was the work of the greatest among dramatists. James Boswell kissed the pages which he accounted priceless and exclaimed that he could now die happy.

Mr. Harris, the manager of Covent Garden Theatre, competed with Sheridan for the privilege of representing the tragedy. But the terms offered by Sheridan induced Ireland to consent that it should be first acted on the stage of Drury Lane. Three hundred pounds were to be paid down and half the profits given for sixty nights. Before signing the agreement, Sheridan called upon Ireland accompanied by his friend Richardson, to examine the manuscript of the tragedy. After reading several lines, he came upon one which he told W. H. Ireland " was not strictly

[1] Erskine wrote as follows to Dr. Parr on the 31st of December, 1795 : "I went to Ireland's from curiosity, having heard from several quarters that the new Shakespeare was a forgery, and having seen an advertisement from Malone upon the subject. All I can say is, that I am glad I am not the man who has undertaken to prove Malone's proposition; for I think I never saw such a body of evidence in my life to support the authenticity of any matter which rests upon high authority. I am quite sure that a man would be laughed out of an English Court of Justice who attempted to maintain Malone's opinion in the teeth of every rule of probability acknowledged for ages as the standard for investigating truth."—" Works of Samuel Parr," vol. vii., p. 120. Erskine is not the only great advocate, who became Lord High Chancellor, whose opinion on a point of literature excites the ridicule of those who had no title to forensic talent and had a legal training inferior to his. Lord Campbell wrote that Lady Francis's random remarks had convinced him that Sir Philip Francis was the author of the Letters signed Junius.

poetic " and turning to Ireland's father, he remarked :
" This is rather strange ; for though you are acquainted with my opinion as to Shakespeare, yet,
be it as it may, he certainly always wrote poetry."

Having read a few pages, Sheridan laid the
manuscript down and said in substance that some
of the ideas were bold, yet crude and undigested
and must have proceeded from Shakespeare when a
young man, and that, as the papers bore undoubted
marks of age, the contents must be genuine. Porson,
among great scholars, and Malone, among Shake-
spearian students, were conspicuous in denying the
authenticity of the tragedy. John Kemble sided
with them.

The tragedy of *Vortigern and Rowena* was performed for the first and last time on the evening of
Saturday, the 2nd of April, 1796. Drury Lane
Theatre was besieged by a crowd of playgoers eager
to gain admission. Every seat in the boxes had
been taken beforehand. Those who found the
entrance to the pit blocked, paid for a box and
dropped down from the box-seat into the vacant
places below. The epilogue was spoken by Mr.
Whitfield to an anxious public which was called
upon to determine the authenticity as well as the
merit of the piece :

> " No common cause your verdict now demands,
> Before the court immortal Shakespeare stands."

Sir James Bland Burges, a friend and supporter
of Pitt and an admirer of the tragedy, wrote the
prologue which was spoken. The " tuneful Pye,"

as Byron irreverently styled the Poet Laureate, had written one which Sheridan pronounced too depressing. Mr. Robert Merry prepared an epilogue which Mrs. Jordan would have spoken, if she had been afforded the opportunity. Two acts were performed without protest, and Mrs. Jordan congratulated W. H. Ireland, at the beginning of the third, on the success of the tragedy which he was supposed to have rescued from undeserved oblivion.

He told her that he had a presentiment the piece would not be performed a second time. The fifth act was in progress before any demonstration occurred. In the second scene Kemble, who filled the part of Vortigern, spoke the line, "And when this solemn mockery is ended,"[1] and then, to use Ireland's own words, "The most discordant howl echoed from the pit that ever assailed the organs of hearing." He added that he slept soundly during the night after his forgery had been detected. Indeed, he found it easier to figure as a forger than as Shakespeare. His bitterest disappointment was the monetary result. The surplus left by the night's performance was £206, and this was divided between Sheridan and Ireland's father; the amount which Ireland obtained from his father was £30; he had received £60 out of the sum paid for the right to represent

---

[1] This line is taken from the version of the play published in 1799. In W. H. Ireland's "Confessions," the line runs, "An when this solemn mockery is o'er." William Earle. the "Octogenarian," in vol. ii., p. 240, of "Sheridan and his Times," says that he was in the theatre and that the tumult began when Kemble spoke the line, "Death with his icy hand now drags me down."

the tragedy and he was better remunerated than
Chatterton for still more skilful fabrications.[1]

The appearance of young Roscius at Drury Lane
Theatre was more profitable to Sheridan than the
representation of Ireland's tragedy.   This lad represented Norval in *Douglas* on the 10th of December,
1804,[2] and he received fifty guineas nightly during
his engagement, which lasted twenty-eight nights ;
the nett receipts were £200 nightly.

Despite Sheridan's exertions he could not rid
himself of financial obligations in connexion with
the theatre and, in 1802, a bill was filed in the Court
of Chancery by creditors who denied the right of
the performers to the first claim upon the receipts.
Lord Campbell, who was then a student of Lincoln's
Inn, records that never had he seen a greater crowd
at Drury Lane Theatre when Mrs. Siddons appeared
as Lady Macbeth than he did in the Court
of Chancery when Sheridan argued his cause in
person.[3]   Charles Butler, who was in Court, records
that Sheridan spoke for two hours ; the speech was
" perhaps his most splendid exhibition."   He spoke

[1] My narrative is founded on "The Confessions of W. H.
Ireland," published in 1809, and "An authentic account of the
Shakesperian Manuscripts," published in 1796.

[2] The boy's name was William Henry West Betty.   His first
appearance on the stage was at Belfast on the 19th of August,
1803, when he was eleven years old, the part he took being
Osman in *Zara*.   He played with applause in Dublin, Cork,
Waterford, Glasgow, Edinburgh, and Birmingham before facing
and turning the heads of a London audience.—" Dictionary of
National Biography," vol. iv., p. 442.

[3] " Lives of the Chancellors," vol. ii., p. 156, footnote.

"with amazing shrewdness of observation, force of argument and splendour of eloquence, and as he spoke from strong feeling, he introduced little of the wit and prettyness with which his oratorical displays were generally filled. He was heard with great attention and interest : while his speech lasted a pin might be heard to drop."[1]

Mr. Mansfield appeared as counsel for the trustees at whose instance a bill had been filed against Sheridan, and abused his position to import personalities into a legal argument which would not have been tolerated by any other Lord Chancellor than Eldon. But Mr. Mansfield considered himself justified by the affidavits, and held that he was entitled to disregard good taste by repeating what he must have known to be statements which were highly coloured, exaggerated and possibly untrue. Yet the Lord Chancellor acted with still greater partiality and disregard of practice. He decided in Sheridan's favour ; but he forgot the Judge in the partisan and addressed Sheridan in terms such as those which Dr. Johnson had used when moralizing upon the career and death of Savage. Having gained his cause, Sheridan could forgive the Chancellor for his remarks. If the Chancellor had any justification for identifying Sheridan with Charles Surface, posterity has found in Trapbois a perfect representative of the worst side of his own character. Though the feelings of an audience in a Court of Justice have little or no weight when a decision of the Court is criticized,

---

[1] "Reminiscences" of Charles Butler, vol. ii., p. 87.

yet it is worthy of note "that Sheridan was loudly congratulated when he left the Court."[1]

He had vexations far more difficult to endure than any which Eldon could inflict. The deaths of Tickell and Richardson removed two of the trusted friends in whose society he forgot his troubles and by whose advice he often benefited. Both Sheridan and Tickell were delighted, when past middle-age, in performing those practical jokes in which youthful exuberance finds a vent and relief. While on a trip to the West of England in 1786 with their wives, the pair indulged in games which young children might think amusing. They stopped at Broadlands for a few days, when Mrs. Sheridan wrote to Mrs. Stratford Canning, and said they went every morning " in different boats, on the river which runs through Lord P[almerston's] grounds, splashing one another till one confessed himself conquered by running away, after which they used to come puffing to us, like two Tritons in a sea-piece, dripping from all parts."[2]

There is not much fun in this performance, neither is there any more in what occurred, according to Rogers, when they were staying at Crewe Hall : " Mrs. Sheridan and Mrs. Crewe would be riding out in the carriage, Sheridan and Tickell riding on

---

[1] " Reminiscences " of Michael Kelly, vol. ii., p. 190.

[2] In the letter from which the above extract is made, Mrs. Sheridan depicts the Lord Palmerston of the last century as "a good-natured, poetical, stuttering Viscount, and [his wife] as a pleasing, unaffected woman, who though she *did* squeeze through the City Gate into a Viscountess, bears her blushing honours without shaking them at you every moment."

before them : suddenly the ladies would see Sheridan stretched upon the ground in the agonies of death, and Tickell standing over him in a theatrical attitude of despair."[1]   On the 4th of November, 1793, Tickell was the actor in a real tragedy.   His lifeless body was found lying below the windows of the rooms which he inhabited in Hampton Court Palace. He was a clever man and a disappointed politician, being one of the many who considered that the party which he served had not done enough for him. Party ingratitude is always cynically displayed when the services rendered are most conspicuous.   Tickell would have been forgotten now if he had not been Sheridan's brother-in-law and friend.

Richardson died ten years after Tickell, and Sheridan lost in him a true and most serviceable, as well as a highly valued friend.   Joseph Richardson, who was Sheridan's junior by four years, was born at Hexham in Northumberland.   He distinguished himself at Cambridge : he was called to the Bar by the Middle Temple ; he gave more of his time, however, to literature than to law, and was brought into Parliament by the Duke of Northumberland as member for Newport, in Cornwall.   He was a silent member.   He feared, with a modesty which is unknown now, lest his mode of speech would be unwelcome to his hearers.   However, he made his mark and his influence felt by contributing to the *Rolliad* and *The Probationary Odes*.   He composed *The Fugitive*, a comedy which was played at the Haymarket Theatre by the Drury Lane com-

[1] Table-Talk, p. 65.

pany on the 20th of April, 1792, the prologue being
written by General Burgoyne and the epilogue by
Tickell, and the piece was so favourably received
as to be performed thirteen times in succession.
Richardson was first a contributor to *The Morning
Post* and afterwards one of its promoters. The
Duke of Northumberland advanced the money
wherewith he bought a share in Drury Lane
Theatre which yielded him a weekly return of fifteen
guineas.

Between Tickell and Sheridan there was an
undercurrent of rivalry, and Tickell was absurdly
jealous of his more accomplished and successful
brother-in-law. But the relation between Sheridan
and Richardson was unmarred by any other drawback than Richardson's inordinate liking for dispu-
tation. He disliked as greatly as Anthony Trollope
to agree with anybody ; and he was not perfectly at
ease when anybody ostensibly coincided with him.
No other man, however, had more influence over
Sheridan, nor could anyone have used it to greater
advantage. In consequence of this, Richardson's
good offices were frequently invoked. Boaden
records that, "if anything was really pressing,
Richardson would speak to Sheridan about it,"[1] and
the desired result was usually attained.

Not long before his friend's death, Sheridan related
to Michael Kelly that when he and his second wife
were staying at Bognor, and Lord Thurlow was
a visitor, Richardson visited the place also, because
he was acquainted with them all and hoped, more-

---

[1] "Life" of Mr. Jordan by John Boaden, vol. ii., p. 141.

over, to enjoy himself in their company at the seaside.

" Nothing can be more delightful," he said of his contemplated visit. "What with my favourite diversion of sailing, my enjoyment of walking on the sands, the pleasure of arguing with Lord Thurlow and taking my snuff by the sea-side, I shall be in my glory." The first day after arriving, he sprained his ankle while stepping into a boat and he was carried to his lodgings, from which there was no view of the sea. Next morning, the barber cut him severely under the nose, and at breakfast the head of a prawn stuck in his throat and caused so much pain and inflammation that his doctor forbade him to speak for three days. " Thus," added Sheridan, " ended in four and twenty hours his walking, his sailing, his snuff-taking and his arguments."[1]

Richardson was staying at the Wheatsheaf Inn, near Virginia Water, when he died, and his remains were buried in the neighbouring church-yard at Egham on the 13th of June, 1803. Sheridan, John Taylor, Richard Wilson, and Dr. Coombe agreed among themselves to attend the funeral at the hour of one. The carriage which conveyed them from London arrived fifteen minutes late, and they were astonished to learn that the burial-service had been performed. Sheridan was particularly affected, saying that he would be accounted so careless as not even to have attended in time " to pay respect to the remains of his dearest friend." The undertaker

[1] " Reminiscences " of Michael Kelly, vol. ii., pp. 358, 359.

was to blame. Being in a hurry to attend a funeral elsewhere, he would not wait for the arrival of the mourners. When the vicar was made aware of what had occurred, he permitted his son, the curate, to repeat the service, and this, as Mr. Taylor writes, gave "a sort of mournful exultation to Mr. Sheridan," who felt that he could now meet his friends in London without being stung by their reproaches.

The party stopped to dine at Bedfont on the way back and then, Mr. Taylor adds, "Mr. Sheridan entered into a eulogium on his deceased friend, of whom he spoke with sincere emotion and affecting eloquence." When he and Mr. Taylor parted in town, "he manifested great emotion, and in the agony of his feelings struck his head against the door of the nearest house, exclaiming that he had lost his dearest friend, and there was now nobody who could enter into his domestic cares."[1]

The domestic cares to which reference has just been made were the consequence of a second marriage, of which I shall postpone a description till I shall have described Sheridan's last appearance at the trial of Warren Hastings. No chapter in the vicissitudes of existence could be more varied and startling than that which should faithfully record the changes that occurred while Warren Hastings was a victim of the malignity of Francis

---

[1] "Records of my Life," by John Taylor, vol. ii., p. 171. The version given by Moore of what occurred at Richardson's funeral differs from that of Mr. Taylor owing to Moore having incorrectly repeated what Mr. Taylor told him.

and of the eloquence of Burke. In 1788, when Sheridan made his memorable speech in Westminster Hall on the charge concerning the Begums of Oude, the Peers constituting the Court numbered 186. When, in 1793, Mr. Law rose to set forth the defence of Hastings on that charge, the number of peers present ranged from 22 to 28, while the changes in the interval owing to death and new additions to the peerage amounted to 121. The Managers for the House of Commons were at unison in politics at the outset of the Impeachment; long before it closed, the most noteworthy among them were at daggers drawn.[1]

When the Impeachment was opened, the Managers of it were chiefly concerned about the condition of India; at its close the condition of France was the main subject of their thoughts. Fox and Sheridan then rejoiced that the House of Bourbon had ceased to reign over France and trouble the peace of Europe, while Burke and Windham deemed it a patriotic duty both to assist that House to regain its former status and to keep in subjection those of their poorer fellow-countrymen who desired to be entrusted with the Parliamentary suffrage and whom they styled "the swinish multitude." Burke closed his long reply to the evidence with an expression of

---

[1] The Committee of Managers was composed of Burke, Fox, Sheridan, Pelham, Windham, Sir Gilbert Elliot, Grey, Adam, Sir John Anstruther, M. A. Taylor, Viscount Maitland, Dudley Long, General Burgoyne, E. A. North, Andrew St. John, Colonel Fitzpatrick, Wilbraham, Courtney, Sir James Erskine and F. Montagu.

fear lest the august tribunal he addressed, which stood amid the ruins caused " by the greatest moral earthquake that ever shattered this globe of ours, might be swept away in turn by a revolutionary shock," and his apprehensions agitated the minds of many inferior and fallible men. No such dread was entertained by Sheridan and his reply contains no references to matters which were alike extraneous and misrepresented.

Sheridan's speech in reply, though wonderfully able, has received but little notice, and no complete report of it was published till 1861.[1] He procrastinated making preparations for its delivery, and he had to request the Lord Kenyon to grant him further time. He occupied three days and the greater part of three nights at Wanstead in reading over papers, making notes and mastering the points to be discussed.

In this speech he was less rhetorical than in many others ; yet he was quite as clever in presenting his case. He skilfully ridiculed the allegations of counsel for the defence and their complaints about the verbosity of the Managers, saying that some who had promised to set forth the facts in a narrow compass had taken four days to perform the task. He retorted upon Plumer, who had rebuked his poetical

[1] If Moore had seen this report or been aware of its existence, he might have written less absurdly about it. In the verbatim report words which Moore quotes do not occur, while the passages from the evidence which Moore said he did not read, are inserted because he had read them.—" Memoirs " of Sheridan, vol. ii., pp. 248, 249.

flights, that his own phrases were equally high-flown, adding, that their Lordships must have observed the critics of himself and his fellow Managers, " venting the most fanciful spleen against our indulgence in flights of imagination, and dealing in most figurative lamentation at our addiction to metaphor and ornament." He acutely remarked how cleverly the counsel for the defence laboured to establish what was indisputable and took for granted the points in dispute :—" Whenever they want to establish any self-evident proposition, any palpable truism, they proceed with the utmost degree of diffidence ; when anything very silly is going to be produced, it is countenanced by a quotation from Puffendorf! I am certain if the counsel had occasion to risk the assertion that two and two make four, they would quote Cocker's arithmetic. It is not a want of art, for they want to impress upon your Lordships' minds that they will risk nothing, hazard no assertion ; that they will bring their authority with them every step they take ; and when they have established, as they think, that sort of character for diffidence and caution, whenever they come to facts or to real important matter they make no scruple of assuming the whole, not only without any proof or evidence, but in the very teeth of proof, evidence and fact."[1]

Professor Smyth, who repaid Sheridan's kindness to him in early life by printing much about him that

---

[1] "Speeches in the Trial of Warren Hastings," vol. iv., pp. 106, 108, 130, 131.

was discreditable and untrue thirty-four years after
his death, heard this speech and his testimony as to
its character and effect can be accepted as being
entirely free from the taint of partiality.   He records
that when Sheridan stood up in the Managers' box,
"his countenance had assumed an ashen colour that
I had never before observed, that he was evidently
tried to the utmost—every nerve and faculty within
him put into complete requisition."   He had been
apprised of Sheridan's intention to rebuke Mr. Law
[afterwards Lord Ellenborough] for attacking him
on account of a statement which had actually been
made by Lord Camden, and Smyth, knowing the
facts, avows himself to have been the more interested
in the way that Sheridan turned them to account.
He notes that he could never forget the dignity of
tone and manner with which Sheridan turned to
Mr. Law to tell him of his error and to warn him
against ever again wrongfully imputing conduct to
others from which he himself would recoil with
horror.   Smyth continues to say that "Sheridan
proceeded in this strain for several minutes, and
during all this time the audience sat breathless.   I
myself grew hot and cold ; and happening to look
up to Richardson to express my admiration, I saw
his features quivering and his eyes filled.   What
became of Law I could scarcely consider ; but I
remember seeing him start up and tremble over his
papers in a hurried manner ; and though a more
imperturbable and invincible front was never placed
even under a lawyer's wig, I saw him soon change
colour, and, evidently in a state of great confusion

and distress, hide himself as well as he could in the bottom of his box and sit down."

The impression which Sheridan made as an orator upon Smyth was never effaced. When writing in after years, Smyth expressed it in the following terms which possess a value, for the reason already assigned, far greater than the reminiscence of a friend or enthusiastic admirer : " On this day the appearance of Sheridan, as it struck me, was that of a perfect actor. The voice was so fine, the manner so dignified and graceful, the flow of words so unembarrassed, the expressions sometimes so beautiful, the rapidity and fire of the eloquence sometimes so overpowering, the statements so clearly made, the appeals deduced from them so forcible, that the impression on my mind, as I sat under him in the Managers' box, was quite that of listening to some being of a totally different nature from my own, one that could not possibly be measured by any standard within my comparison."[1]

After the Managers of the Impeachment had performed their commission, Pitt moved a vote of thanks to them in the House of Commons. Objections were raised by members who were dissatisfied with Burke, one of the Counsel for Hastings affirming that Burke's conduct " had entailed shame and disgrace upon the House of Commons." Both Fox and Sheridan defended him with warmth and effect, Fox expressing the opinion of his colleagues when he said of Burke that he was a man, " with whom it was their boast and glory to

---

[1] " Memoir of Mr. Sheridan," pp. 31 to 35.

be identified." A large majority assented to Pitt's
motion and, after the Speaker had thanked the
Managers, Burke replied for them in a few dignified
and graceful words which were well received, the
occasion being the last on which he addressed the
House.

With the wanton deliberation which the Peers had
displayed throughout the proceedings, their verdict
was postponed for nearly a year after the Impeachment had ended. On the 23rd of April, 1795, twenty
peers were present when the vote was taken, the
result being the acquittal of Warren Hastings on all
the charges. Burke keenly felt the miscarriage of
his hopes, and he even held that the Peers had condemned themselves by letting Hastings go free.[1]
He purposed writing a history of the whole proceedings ; but, being hindered by illness, he implored
his friend Dr. French Lawrence to make manifest
to the world, "the cruelty of this pretended acquittal."
Fox was as earnest as Burke, though not quite so
much under the influence of Francis, and he had
given up all hope of conviction long before the trial
ended. Sheridan told the tribunal before which he
urged the conviction of Hastings that, while regarding an adverse verdict on the second charge as a
thing "absolutely impossible," yet that the decision

---

[1] Writing to Malone from Beaconsfield he says : " It is very
true that my business with the House of Lords is over for the
present ; for they have, or a *rump* of them, done their own business pretty handsomely. *Fuerunt.* There is an end of that part
of the Constitution ; nor can it be revived but by means that I
tremble to think of."—" Works," vol. ii., p. 297.

would be accepted by him "with respectful submission."[1]

The Prince Regent is said to have tried several years afterwards to make Sheridan and Warren Hastings personally known to each other. Adolphus narrated, on the authority of "private information," what he styled a remarkable incident : "Mr. Hastings appeared by invitation one evening at Carlton House, when the Prince Regent, with his usual gracious politeness, requested leave to introduce a friend. Mr. Sheridan was the individual brought forward; he took Mr. Hastings by the hand, burst into tears, and rushed out of the room."[2]

Two biographers of Hastings have given currency to a different story, Sir Charles Lawson having been the first to do so and Colonel Malleson having followed him, and added, for no obvious reason, that Sheridan had acted as "a hired bravo." Sir Charles has affirmed that the two [Hastings and Sheridan] met, many years after the trial, as the guests of the

[1] A Committee of the House of Commons reported that the trial lasted six years, during which the Court sat for 118 days, and that Warren Hastings continued in legal custody from first to last. Whether the Court sat or adjourned, costs were incurred which he had to pay after having been pronounced not guilty. Three days were occupied in reading the articles of Impeachment and the answer and in debating as to the form of procedure; nineteen in hearing the opening and closing speeches for the Managers; fifty-two in hearing their documentary and oral evidence and twenty in hearing the opening and closing the defendant's counsel and his own defence, and twenty-three in hearing the documentary and oral evidence for Hastings.—"Parliamentary History," vol. xxxi., pp. 287, 290.

[2] "History of England," by John Adolphus, vol. vi., p. 221.

Prince Regent, in the Pavilion, at Brighton ; and Sheridan, at the prompting of the Prince, advanced to Hastings, and said that, " The part which I took in events long gone by must not be regarded as any test of my private opinions, because I was then a private pleader, whose duty it is, under all circumstances, to make good if he can the charges which he is commissioned to bring forward." But Hastings drew back a step ; looked Sheridan in the face ; made a low bow ; and remained silent. " Had he," Hastings subsequently said, "confessed as much twenty years ago, he might have done me some service." Sir Charles Lawson omits to add the name of the person to whom the statement was made. He may have also omitted to read the declaration of Sheridan in the House of Commons, on the day after the delivery of his speech on the Begums of Oude, that " he neither felt nor professed to feel any malignity against Mr. Hastings. Those who knew him most intimately, he believed, indeed, he might say without vanity, knew that he had no malignity in his composition, and that he was not capable of feeling such an unworthy passion against any man."[1]

The two stories clash. A third, given by Moore

[1] "Speeches," vol. i., p. 243. Though these words were heard without a syllable of protest from the friends of Hastings and are accessible to the world, Colonel Malleson deemed it seemly to write that Sheridan's speech in the House of Commons on the Begums of Oude, " was the result of the prostitution of splendid talents to the gratification of personal hatred and the desire of personal vengeance of his friends."—" Life of Warren Hastings," p. 462.

on Creevy's authority, differs from either. Moreover, it is incredible that Sheridan could have spoken to Hastings in the manner attributed to him, seeing that Hastings had heard him repudiate in Westminster Hall on the 14th of May, 1794, that he was acting as Counsel and assert that, as a Manager, his position was entirely different, adding, " I do protest for one, that, entering into this cause with a peremptory conviction of the guilt of the person whom we were bound to arraign, and regretting as I do that that impression has not been diminished but strengthened by the defence which I have heard, if, in the course of it, I had found by reasoning or by evidence that I had embarked in error and that the person was innocent—if that previous conviction in my own mind had been removed—I would have returned to the Commons and said that it was my duty to decline the office, and that some other person ought to be appointed in my place."[1] That Sheridan may have met Hastings at Brighton or Carlton House is possible, that he should have made a friendly overture to him is in accordance with his nature ; but what actually happened at such a meeting cannot be gathered from the contradictory statements on the subject which have been printed. Those who blame Sheridan for any injustice of which Hastings was the victim must have forgotten, or do not care to recall, that the Impeachment was due to the speech and vote of William Pitt and also that his refusal to sanction a grant in payment of Hastings' expenses

[1] " The Trial of Warren Hastings," vol. iv., p. 128.

after acquittal deepened the cruelty of which he was the victim and which his admirers have rightly condemned.

There is no doubt of Sheridan's commanding position in the country when, in May, 1797, there was a mutiny in the fleet at Portsmouth. He attributed it to dry-rot; he was impressed from the first by the danger; yet he knew better how to meet it than to explain its origin. The seamen had grievances which were investigated and admitted; but an unfortunate delay occurred before redress followed. He had urged conciliation, and he was emphatic in denouncing the mutineers, who denounced him in turn. He defended himself in the House of Commons against the unfounded allegations of the ringleaders and said that he laughed at their libels. It was partly due to his remonstrances that official sloth was quickened into action, that the mutiny was quelled and the fleet converted from a danger to the land into a bulwark of it.

Yet when the report from the fleet at Portsmouth ran " All's well," a still fiercer mutiny broke out in the fleet at the Nore, with a ringleader in the person of Parker, who proved to be much more mischievous and daring than anyone in the fleet at Portsmouth. In both cases a man named Duckett, who was in the pay of France, fomented the outbreak. He acted under the instructions of La Croix, the French Minister of War, and with the cognizance of Truguet, the French Minister of Marine, who hoped that the result would be England's downfall. Wolfe Tone was quite as anxious for this consummation ; but he hated Duckett and rejected his co-operation. The Ministry could not be ignorant of what was impending as Turner, a spy, had disclosed Duckett's plans. There was a strange hesitation, however, in acting with promptitude and firmness.

Then it was that Sheridan, from his place in the House of Commons, indicated the path of honour and safety. He declared that party strife must be suspended and that the Ministry must receive un-divided support in carrying into effect the most drastic measures. Before doing so he had called upon Dundas and told him : " My advice is that you cut the buoys on the river, send Sir George Grey down to the coast and set a price on Parker's head. If the Administration take this advice in-stantly they will save the country, if not they will lose it, and on their refusal, I will impeach them in the House of Commons this very evening,"

The advice was taken : the country was saved. A bloody fight took place before Parker was cap-tured. On the 30th of June, 1797, he was hanged.[1] Some of the vessels which he desired to transfer to France formed part of the fleet which check-mated Bonaparte, that fleet which, in the imperishable

---

[1] The nature of Sheridan's service was not made public till twenty-eight years after it had been performed, when Moore authoritatively stated that hesitation prevailed in the Ministry at the moment when he counselled immediate action.—" Memoirs " of Sheridan, vol. ii., p. 271. Mr. Fitzpatrick's admirable work on " Secret Service under Pitt " contains other particulars of great interest about the mutiny in the fleet, pp. 111-115.

words of Captain Mahan, though composed of " far-distant, storm-beaten ships upon which the Grand Army never looked, stood between it and the dominion of the world."[1]

The word in season is the word which works as great miracles as faith. It was spoken by Sheridan when the mutiny at the Nore had imperilled his country and caused general consternation. Dundas expressed the feeling, on the part of the Ministry, that "the country was highly indebted to Sheridan for his fair and manly conduct."[2] A writer who differed with him in politics, but desired to deal justly by him, declared after his death that he had earned " the gratitude of the Empire " for his services in connexion with the Mutiny at the Nore.[3] If the custom had prevailed in his time which was followed in the days of Rome's greatness and power, when patriotism was ranked and revered as supreme among the virtues, his conduct would have been the theme of many a splendid oration, and his statue would have occupied a conspicuous place in the temple of national glory.

[1] " The Influence of the Sea Power on the French Revolution," vol. ii., p. 118.

[2] " Parliamentary History," vol. xxxiii., p. 804.

[3] *Blackwood's Magazine* for March, 1826, p. 352.

VII.

SECOND MARRIAGE AND AFTER YEARS.

MR. EDGEWORTH's chief title to remembrance is to have been the father of Maria, and an expert in matrimony. He was the loving husband of four wives and the proud father of twenty-two children. In his opinion, "nothing is more erroneous than the common belief that a man who has lived in the greatest happiness with one wife will be most averse to take another. On the contrary, the loss of happiness which he feels when he loses her necessarily urges him to endeavour to be again placed in the situation which constituted his former happiness."[1]

Whether a widow or widower should remarry depends on circumstances with which the public has no concern. There are many cases in which a second marriage may jeopardize the comfort or prospects of children by the first, yet a widow or widower must bear the responsibility of this, even in defiance of good and unpalatable advice, if either should endeavour to mitigate the rigour of lamenting the departed by forming a new union in the hope of receiving solace for the present, and of

[1] "Memoirs" of Maria Edgeworth, vol. i., p. 8.

having in the future another family to rear and cherish.

It is indisputable that Sheridan sincerely mourned the death of the wife to whom he owed more than he may ever have realized. Michael Kelly records : " I never beheld more poignant grief than Sheridan felt for the loss of his beloved wife ; and although the world, which knew him only as a public man, will perhaps scarcely credit the fact, I have seen him, night after night, sit and cry like a child, while I sang to him, at his desire, a pathetic song of my composition : ' They bore her to her grassy grave.' "[1]

One day Michael Kelly called upon Sheridan and while waiting for him, he picked up a paper which had been thrown under the table in his room. He took it home, set to music the lines which Sheridan had written upon it, and often sang them to him :

I.

" No more shall the spring my lost pleasure restore ;
   Uncheered, I still wander alone,
And, sunk in dejection, for ever deplore
   The sweets of the days that are gone.
While the sun as it rises, to others shines bright,
   I think how it formerly shone ;
While others cull blossoms, I find but a blight,
   And sigh for the days that are gone.

II.

" I stray, where the dew falls through moon-lighted groves
   And list to the nightingale's song :
Her plaints still remind me of long banished joys,
   And the sweets of the days that are gone,

---

[1] " Reminiscences," vol. ii., p. 129.

> Each dew-drop that steals from the dark eye of night
> Is a tear for the bliss that is flown ;
> While others cull blossoms, I find but a blight,
> And sigh for the days that are gone."[1]

On the 12th of April, 1797, Sheridan wrote from London to his second wife :—"What a heavenly day this has been ! The first sweet spring day [makes] me melancholy always, for a particular reason," and on another occasion he said : " The truth is that the death of time and the recollections of departed hours, if happily spent, can never be cheerful recollections, and if there is added to that the regret that those hours have not been prized enough, in all the happiness attached to them which might have been, the reviewing them and reflecting on them is still more painful."[2]

The foregoing sentences are in perfect unison with the verses which precede them, and both prove how profound and lasting had been the impression on Sheridan's mind of the happy spring days when he and Miss Linley became man and wife.

His second wife was Ester Jane Ogle, the eldest daughter of the Dean of Winchester. He was forty-two and she was twenty at the date of their marriage. Unauthenticated gossip has been printed to the effect that the pair first saw each other at Devon-

---

[1] " Reminiscences," vol. ii., 289, 290.

[2] These extracts and others which will follow, are from a series of ninety-six letters written by Sheridan to his second wife and unpublished. His idea in the verses and in prose had been thus expressed by Dante :

> " nessun maggior dolore,
> Che ricordarsi del tempo felice
> Nella miseria."
> *Inferno*, Canto V., lines 121, 122, 123.

shire House, and that Miss Ogle then called out to Sheridan, " Keep away, you terrible creature." Being piqued, Sheridan exercised his power of fascination, with the result that Miss Ogle most gladly consented to marry him.   The story resembles that in which the Duchess of Cleveland is represented as addressing Wycherley before avowing her passion for him, and it may be quite as true.[1] *The Gentleman's Magazine* for 1795 contains this announcement—" 27th of April, at Winchester Collegiate Church, Richard Brinsley Sheridan Esqre. M.P. for Stafford to Miss Ogle, only daughter of the Dean of Winchester Cathedral." According to Madame D'Arblay Miss Ogle had sisters, as she refers to " Mrs. Ogle and her sprightly daughters." She depicts the Dean himself as " a man of facetious pleasantry, yet of real sagacity ; though mingled with eccentricities, perversities and dreadful republican principles."[2]   His wife was the daughter of the Bishop of Winchester who had been tutor to George the Third.

Dr. Ogle was careful of his daughter's monetary

---

[1] It is supposed that Sheridan's rubicund face, which may have repelled Miss Ogle, was the consequence of his intemperance. Those who drink nothing stronger than claret or water may have very red faces.   Mr. Malcolm Morris, the eminent dermatologist, who has carefully considered all the facts which are extant about Sheridan's constitution, has arrived at the conclusion, which he has kindly permitted me to make public, that Sheridan may have suffered, as even water-drinkers often do, from a disease of the skin called *acne rosacea.*

[2] " Memoirs of Dr. Burney," by his daughter, Madame D'Arblay, vol. i., pp. 338, 339.

interests.   She had a dowry of £5,000.   Sheridan undertook to settle that amount upon her and to add £15,000 to it.   The estate of Polesden in Surrey was bought by the trustees of the marriage settlement, who were Mr. (afterwards Earl) Grey and Mr. Whitbread, and this property passed after the death of Sheridan and his second wife to their only child Charles Brinsley, who was born on the 14th of January, 1796, and who died unmarried on the 29th of November, 1843.[1]

The property became a drain upon his purse, when, as he wrote to his wife, he had resolved upon building a good house on the site of "the shameful ruin" at Polesden.   Moreover, having yielded to the temptation to add acre to acre, as Sir Walter Scott unfortunately did after buying a small farm at Abbotsford, he became the owner of several farms near Polesden, and his delight at the acquisition is shown in a letter sent to his wife shortly after marriage :—"I have every hour some new reason to be satisfied with our purchase.   Hammersley [his banker] has had repeated offers of great advantage for the bargain.   My negociation for the lovely farm adjoining goes on well and then we shall

[1] Charles Butler, in his "Reminiscences," refers to the neglect of Sheridan paying for an estate in Surrey which he had bought of Sir William Geary (vol. ii., p. 82).   Mr. Percy Fitzgerald, at p. 410, vol. i., of "Lives of the Sheridans," comments upon Sir William Geary and the trustees of the wedding settlement being victimized by Sheridan.   Even if as unscrupulous as Mr. Fitzgerald seems to think, he could not deal with funds which were in the hands of trustees.

have the nicest place, within a prudent distance of town, in England."

Sheridan took to farming with all the ignorant enthusiasm, and all the determination to succeed, of one who had frequently led fortune captive. At one time he writes to his wife that his zeal for politics has cooled, adding, " I think a great deal more of two great china jars I have bought for our dairy— and such a bargain." On the 5th of September, 1800, he writes that Tom and he had " got to town, but in rain at last, which made my bones ache for my harvest. O! ye Gods, that my ricks had been thatched even with ' fern and green boughs.'" He took a personal interest in the enclosure of Commons which, in his day, was conducted with a disregard to justice, that, thanks to the Society for the Preservation of Commons,[1] is now impossible. It was the exception for anyone in his position to be the advocate of fair play for men whose poverty was too great to enable them to appeal to a Court of Justice in defence of their legal position, their ignorance of their rights being equal to their poverty. On Thursday, the 15th of November, 1804, he wrote :—" I go to Polesden at six o'clock to-morrow morning. There is a meeting on the business of enclosing all the Commons, Ransmore, Bookham, etc., etc., and, if I am not on the spot, they will cheat me egregiously, and perhaps ruin the

---

[1] A most interesting account of the warfare for the preservation of Commons in recent years is contained in " English Commons and Forests " by the Rt. Hon. G. Shaw Lefevre, who was foremost among the heroes of the good fight.

beauty of Polesden ; but they cannot and shall not move an inch without me and so I have given Sumner and Launell to understand. . . . Nothing can be more for our interest than the enclosure if I have my due ; but I will see real justice done to the cottagers and the poorest claimants. Timber-Toe Wood is the village Hampden." Subsequently, he said that he had attended a meeting concerning the Bookham enclosure, adding, " I was called to the chair to resist Sumner's unpopularity, the poorer claimants putting their cases entirely into my hands." Popularity is more to be desired and honoured under these conditions than when shown by the applause of a theatre or a senate.

A letter supplied by his nephew, Nathaniel Ogle, furnishes conclusive proof why the poorer persons at and near Polesden should have regarded Sheridan with entire confidence and considered, with perfect justice, that their true interests were safe in his hands.[1] His letter, which is dated the 17th of February, 1819, states that, early in the summer of 1815, the writer accompanied his uncle to Polesden and stayed a few days with him. Every morning Sheridan rose early and went round his property after breakfast, " making minute inquiries relative to his affairs, about which he seemed very

---

[1] Moore wrote in his *Diary* for the 22nd of February, 1819 : " Received a letter from Mr. Ogle, Charles Sheridan's cousin, containing an anecdote very creditable to Sheridan," vol. ii., p. 271. Moore received other letters containing statements which were " very creditable," but he forgot to insert them in his " Memoirs " of Sheridan.

anxious. After having completed his inquiries for the day he dismissed his attendants and reclined beneath the shade of some favourite tree to partake of refreshments. In one of these walks, when approaching a neat farmhouse, he said to me. ' The inhabitant of that house is a man whose bread has been dipped in tears, but I trust the assistance I have given him, united with his own industry, will extricate him from his difficulties and enable him to provide for his family.'

" On entering the wicket near which several children were at play, he was recognized by them. and they shouted with one voice as they ran towards their home, ' Here's Mr. Sheridan.' Immediately a venerable-looking old man, his son, a man of about fifty (the father of the numerous offspring before mentioned), and his wife came to the door and, with looks of joy, saluted him. We entered the dwelling. Mr. Sheridan, being seated, kindly inquired after the health of the family, the state of the crops on the farm and the probability he had of success. From the answers of the man I easily discovered that Mr. Sheridan was well acquainted with his affairs and had interested himself on his behalf." Mr. Ogle learnt from the wife, after her husband had left the room with Sheridan, that the family had been evicted from a farm in the neighbourhood, that Sheridan, hearing of their case and thinking it hard, accepted them as tenants of a farm, charging no rent for a year, and advancing money for their needs. To him, then, they owed their fresh start in life and the prospect of being more fortunate than before. Mr.

Ogle notes that the gratitude displayed by the family moved Sheridan to tears and made him hurry away, and that he was desired by him " not to mention the circumstance." He winds up his letter by saying " that a sense of duty and sincere affection for Mr. Sheridan alone induce me to offer this communication to you."

The disparity in years between Sheridan and his second wife, was not more marked than the disparity in their tastes, characters and inclinations. He was absorbed in politics : she detested them. He was the first dramatist of his day and she regarded the theatre as merely a place from which she obtained sums of money at irregular intervals. They had nothing in common, except natural fondness for their son, Charles Brinsley. Yet her admiration for him was unbounded, as is shown by the words which Thomas Grenville has put on record : " As to my husband's talents, I will not say anything about them, but I *will* say that he is the handsomest and honestest man in all England."[1]

It is true, moreover, and worthy of commendation, that she shared with her husband an intense affection for his son Tom, and the letters which passed between Tom and his step-mother betoken a community of sympathy which is as admirable as it is uncommon. Her shortcoming, as Mr. Mulock stated from personal knowledge, was to have " contributed to swell her husband's embarrassments " and to be " careless and self-indulgent."[2]

[1] Moore's *Diary*, vol. iv., p. 134.
[2] I quote from a letter written by Mr. Mulock in 1861, to the

Sheridan had to remonstrate with her repeatedly for demands for another house or another horse, at a time when the claims upon his purse were legion and the purse itself nearly empty. His patience with her was exemplary and almost inexhaustible, and his tone was always kindly when answering her inconsiderate requests : "You may be assured that if I cannot always immediately meet your wishes in money matters, it is because it is absolutely out of my power, and never from the slightest consideration of myself, or from my ever being disposed to pay anything in preference to any one claim in which you are concerned. The delight of my life is to see you cheerful and without care, and in future we shall have no money anxieties let what will give way ; but to follow up my present plan effectually we must be as careful as ants. . . . I employed Tom's man to collect for me the bills at Richmond ; the amount is frightful, more than four times what I expected, for since the short time we had it, I had twice cleared them off."

Miss Berry professed her inability to understand Mrs. Sheridan. Calling upon her on the 1st of August, 1811, she had "a curious conversation on the subject of her husband and their pecuniary necessities." On the following day, she saw her at Mrs. Villiers' ; "To my utter amazement," Miss

Honourable Caroline Norton, when she contemplated writing a biography of her grandfather. Mr. Mulock is less known than his daughter, whose writings, in her maiden name and that of Mrs. Craik, are among the pleasantest and most popular in the lighter literature of this century.

Berry adds, "after the conversation we had had the day before, Mrs. Sheridan was waltzing away there, the gayest among the gay."[1]

Sheridan's devotion to his second wife was as impassioned as that of his first wife to him. He gazed upon her with the eyes of a moon-struck lover, and he wrote to her in terms befitting an Oriental rhapsodist. His expressions of tenderness are as novel and varied as the illustrations given by Bob Acres of the " oath referential, or sentimental swearing." His pet name for his second wife was Hecca, and he began letters to her in terms such as these : " My sweet Hecca "; " My dear, dear Hecca "; " My sweet beloved "; " My only delight in life "; " My own Gypsey "; " My soul's beloved "; " My darling Wench "; " My life's delight "; " My life, my soul "; " My pretty Wench "; " My own dear bit of brown Holland " and, by way of climax, " Prettiest of all that my eyes ever thought pretty, dearest of all that ever was dear to my heart." The endings of his letters are as high-flown and original :—" Bless your bones "; " Bless your low forehead and your round plump elbows, and your flowing tresses ";

---

[1] " Journals and Correspondence," vol. ii., pp. 483, 484. I have found in a scrap-book at Stowe which belonged to Thomas Grenville, the following lines from the pen of his friend, Sheridan. They must have been written before those by Byron styled : " The Waltz : An Apostrophic Hymn."

> ' While arts improve in this aspiring age
> Peers mount the coach box, horses mount the stage,
> And waltzing females with unblushing face
> Disdain to dance but in a man's embrace.
> While arts improve and modesty is dead,
> Sound sense and taste are, *like our bullion*, fled."

"Bless you, my own Wench, my Hecca, that I never see without loving better, nor leave but with increased regret"; "Bless your eyes"; "Bless your knees and elbows"; "Bless you ever and ever and all over"; "Bless thy heart, my only real pleasure on earth"; "Bless your eyelids, my beloved"; "Bless your days and nights."

His extravagant apostrophes to her and his comprehensive blessings, are not more curious than his admiration for her eyes, which he called green, a colour that is not commonly associated with other eyes than those of a cat or a tiger. When she had been complaining about her sight, he wrote to reassure her and said, "as for your emeralds, I will guarantee them." He wrote on other occasions, "By Jove, I will see my emeralds on Friday"; "now you are fast asleep, your green eyes closed and your arm round one of your rosy cheeks"; "I will kiss your green beads on Saturday."

He expected her to be a regular and faithful correspondent, and there is something ludicrous in the vehemence of his complaints when a day had passed without a letter arriving. For example :— "Gracious God! not a single line. If a voice from Heaven had told me that any human being should have treated me thus, I should not have believed it. No matter." Her difficulty in writing is candidly set forth in one of the few letters which have been preserved. She tells him that her letter is sent to prevent him feeling annoyed, though she has literally nothing to say now that her cold is better, adding, "Pray dear S. write, for I like of all things to hear from you and when you write I feel as if I had something to say." He complained of her mode of addressing him, yet he could scarcely have expected her to rival him in variety of superlatives and fanciful epithets. He wrote: "When your letter this morning began 'My dear S.,' as formerly, I felt my gloom-sprite more chased away than by any other circumstance." The warmest and most endearing terms which she used: "What a sweet morning. O! Sheridan, if you were but here Hecca would be quite happy. . . . Sheridan! how much better you are than anything on earth, and how well I love you. I will hate everything you hate and love everything you love, so God bless you."

Many passages in his letters refer to sufferings in body and mind; both of which were often extreme; but he found the mental harder to bear than the physical. On one occasion he said:—"I have been sitting by myself most melancholy and gloomy ever since, but much better of my complaint. Great pain is a very bad thing; but I think a fit of my low spirits in solitude as bad." Not long after marriage he wrote: "My cold is going, but I am not well! 'I see a hand you cannot see,'" and this passage is in the same strain:—"How unceasingly do I meditate on death, and how continually do I act as if the thought of it had never crossed my mind."[1]

Yet, when his wife complained of her health, he was so filled with anxiety as to forget his own pains or premonitions: "I should have felt glad and

---

[1] Thiers, when over eighty, put the case in this pointed fashion: "Of course we shall all die; only we don't believe it."

grateful at finding myself better after having, according to my usual and nervous superstitions, put myself down for dying yesterday morning; but your applying that word to yourself undoes all care about myself. Think as you will, my Hecca, but I would with the hand I am now writing with, I would cut off the other to ensure your health and life." The complaints about himself were not wholly due to hypochondria ; neither were they always induced by over-indulgence in stimulants. His favourite wine was claret; Dundas and William Pitt preferred port ; Boswell, who was given to drink and repent during a life that ended when he was fifty-five, preferred old hock; while Fox had an eclectic taste, though punch pleased him the most ; yet Pitt, Boswell, and Fox, whose lives were shortened by drinking to excess, were all much younger than Sheridan when they died. His face at the age of forty resembled, as I have said, that of a man who was a constant wine-bibber ; but he constantly affirmed in his letters that a pint of wine was all that he took. Towards the end of his days, he gave way to the seduction of brandy, as the pious Dr. Johnson had done before him, pronouncing brandy to be suited for heroes ; still, when he was far more abstemious than many a contemporary, the stranger who looked at his face, or saw it in the caricatures of Gilray, was led to conclude that no man could have such a purple skin without being a habitual drunkard. He was unjustly judged by appearances, the truth being, as I have already explained, that he suffered from an affection of the skin which is just as common among those who drink nothing but water, as among those who drink little except alcohol in various forms.

He was of a nervous temperament and his health had never been robust. The veins of his legs were swollen and inflamed and they caused him intense and unintermitted suffering during many years. His letters contain frequent and touching references to his "poor veins," and Cline, the most eminent surgeon of his day, could not give him relief. He had long been a martyr to insomnia, an equally grievous malady. How greatly he suffered may be inferred from the following sentences :—" I am better, though I literally have not slept four hours in the last four nights. I have left off opiates, but touch not one drop of wine, only sleep will not come near me, and yet I am sure I have had no fever; so much for an interesting subject—myself." Again, he says that he has not slept for two nights and has got up to write to his wife so as to chase away horrid thoughts. In January, 1809, he tells his wife, "I am very unwell myself, and have lost all power of sleeping and yet, upon my soul, I drink little wine." He appeals to her more than once in this strain. "Sweet Hecca, be kind to me," or "think kindly of poor Dan." By his first wife, he was commonly styled "Dick" which was appropriate as the contraction of Richard ; his second one appears to have preferred an abbreviation of his surname. Sometimes he uses a mocking fashion in which to set forth his complaints ; as when he tells her : "For my part I mean to die in a Hermit's cell," "I am fast turning into a Hermit and like nothing but shade and solitude," again, "It is clear to me that I shall become a Zimmermanian,[1] a Hermit, only that I shan't have beard enough. I know a nice spot for my cell."

There was nothing jocular, however, in a letter written on the evening of the 25th of December :— " It ought to melt a heart of Scotch pebble to have seen how I have passed this, my Christmas day. There is no peer, no gentleman, no Christian sweep that does not make something social out of it, and I suppose I am the single person not manacled who has spent it in my cell without communion with any fellow-creature."

While Sheridan characterized some of Hecca's letters as being his " heart's food and rayment," he would have been happier if she had not addressed others to him. He writes in 1805,[2] that " she supposes he had been affronted by her manner of addressing him," and adds " I assure you it had not ; but I should be false if I did not own that I had been extremely hurt at it." A letter written from Savile Row, probably in 1810, is couched in terms of reproof :—" I grieve about many things ; but one thing chiefly hurts and depresses me more and oftener, I am sure, than you think. You allow yourself to get into a habit of frequently being very unkind and even contemptuous in your words and manner towards me. I don't fancy that an ironical shuffling tone or tones can well become any living

---

[1] Sheridan had probably been reading the translation of Zimmerman's " Meditations on Solitude," which appeared in 1806.

[2] Few of these letters have dates, and their arrangement in chronological order is conjectural.

person in speaking to *me* and surely not *you*. I never so express myself to the meanest intellect."

Husband and wife are not always in perfect accord, yet the pendulum of affection seldom oscillates so greatly between married couples as it did between Sheridan and his second wife. It had swung violently to the one side when she gave Sheridan occasion for writing, as he did on the 30th of June, 1803 : " By my life and soul if you will talk of leaving me now you will destroy me. I am wholly unwell and neither sleep nor eat."

He covered four quarto pages with explanations in reply to several charges, doing so when sleep had deserted his eyelids and when he preferred writing to her to remaining haunted with phantoms of misery. He began : " You have never known me, though I am aware you are confident that you do. We shall see." She appears to have accused him of misrepresentations as to his affairs before marriage, and his explanation is that, after money had been provided for rebuilding Drury Lane Theatre, " the detected villainy of two lawyers and one banker stole £30,000 from the fund ; the architect's excess of expenditure beyond the estimate, about the same sum, no vigilance or exertion on my part could have guarded against much of this." Sir Arthur Pigott had investigated his affairs before marriage at her father's request and reported he could reckon on a permanent income of £10,000 ; " the theatre then being all my own."

She repeated her complaints and accusations in the year 1810, and he dealt with them in detail.

His statement, covering twenty-four closely-written pages of quarto paper, is written in excellent tone and temper, and it is a most able and minute exposition and defence of his life and conduct during his later years. It is too long for quotation. I reserve this document and many others for publication in full hereafter. I shall quote enough, however, to exhibit its tenor. The date is " Richmond, 20 April, 1810," and he tells her that he had burnt a letter in reply to hers which, on reflection, he considered to be too strongly worded, and he was determined not "to utter an unkind or even an expostulatory expression" concerning her.

He continues : " No one can be in smaller affairs of the world of a more negligent, forgetful and procrastinating habit of mind than I am, united at the same time with a most unfortunately sanguine temper, and a rash confidence that I am capable of exertions equal to any difficulty whenever extremity may call for them. To this frame and temper of mind you may trace the ground of everything you complain of, and not one atom of it to intentional neglect or indifference to your comfort and happiness.

" Stating this I cannot avoid making one observation in passing. I cannot conceive on earth anything more odious than a man's enjoying comforts and ease himself yet perceiving those he professes to love, or who are dependent on him, not sharing them. On this I have only in one word to say that however strongly you paint the distresses and mortifications you have experienced, I am sure you will allow that even, allowing for the great difference between man and woman, they cannot be compared with the privations and vexations which I have been obliged to submit to, and have submitted to with more pleasure when, as has happened, the result produced some accommodation to you and upon perhaps no very important exigency. I have said before you do not know me ; in truth you do not in the least. You should judge of my conduct, character and principles upon a larger scale of observation, and not from the defects of daily life which arise from the failings I acknowledge."

He proceeds to attribute the monetary trials of the moment to his rashness in undertaking the discharge of the liabilities, in excess of the estimate, for rebuilding Drury Lane Theatre. He avows an " inveterate indifference about what the world calls comforts, and much more its luxuries," and regrets that he neglected the smaller domestic affairs, yet "after all," he says, " the bills do get paid and most of the embarrassments turn out to have been unnecessary."

He continues :—" I have all my life kept free from personal obligation on my own account beyond perhaps any case that has existed under the circumstances in which I have struggled through the world. Yet for the sake of Tom and to gratify his ambition and in the hope of finding him serviceable and creditable occupation I have incurred the obligation of the expenditure of not less than £8,000 on the part of the Prince [of Wales], in his three attempts to bring Tom into Parliament, I, who for myself more than once peremptorily refused the offer of a moderate loan from him when I have been in the greatest distress."

Sheridan tells his wife that he had to advance money to keep Tom from appearing in Court, though Tom had been the victim of a swindler ; but that he did so rather than suffer the name of his son or of Lord Moira to come before the public. He estimated his losses in connection with the theatre, in consequence of a decision of the Chancellor, at £7.000, while an even larger sum was lost at Polesden. He undertakes, however, to arrange for paying all his wife's debts and for securing to her in the future a fair and fixed income. To her probable question how this can be accomplished, he replies that, to meet her wishes, " I have broken through the rule of my life which has formed its pride also and have with a broken spirit stooped for the first time to solicit and accept the pecuniary assistance of private friendship." He anticipates with this help bringing his affairs into order, paying his debts and being able to count upon an income of £4,000.

After avowing his readiness to do anything for her family that may be necessary, and stating that he may yet have to help his son and daughter-in-law, he says that he labours the more strenuously to put his affairs in order because of the uncertainty of his own life, adding, " That disorder which I have lately had a return of, from which I have been more than once in greater danger than you have imagined, may at any time return and quickly end me. The same may occur from the condition of my veins, for no operation for life's sake will I ever undergo."

He restates, towards the close, that she did not know him, and repeats that she could do so only if acquainted with all the tests and trials of his former life and his conduct under them. Despite everything, he adds, " I yet preserve my own self-esteem and hold it beyond all price or purchase, nor would I exchange the recollection of acts of kindness, gentleness and benevolence which without ostentation I have in my life done, though accompanied with all my carelessnesses, for the more imposing character which others may have acquired by more prudent and punctual habits than I have had the good fortune to cultivate. And sure I am that there is no person who has been near to me and confidentially acquainted with my private affairs and personal difficulties and who has witnessed my conduct under them, that has not been confirmed or improved in principle and integrity in his views and transactions in this life. You will forgive my having said thus much of myself. It may be egotism ; but it is fact." He informs her that he has carefully avoided contracting new debts ; knowing, as he well does, that were he to involve himself again and fail to obtain a seat in Parliament, which, he considers "a thing infinitely probable," what would become of him ? "You would be sorry to see me dying in a jail." He concludes by mentioning the vouchers which he encloses in support of all his statements, and by hoping that they will be used in a careful investigation of the facts, adding, "And now God bless you and, as I trust you will have pardoned whatever you will have thought amiss in my conduct, so do I from my soul forgive yours."

I infer that Mrs. Sheridan was duly impressed by this letter. After it had been sent, her husband resumed his old style when corresponding with her.

Many things in the foregoing letter were not new to his second wife. In a previous one, he promised to show her instances in which his loss of receipts upon which he was justified in counting, "has not been less than £60,000 without fault on my part, but the rashness of misplaced confidence," and he likewise affirms : " I never have done a dishonest or a base act. I have never omitted to do a kind, a generous, or a benevolent one, when I had the power. But sins of omission, ah! me ;—senseless credulity, destructive procrastination, unworthy indolence, all abetted by one vile habit, somewhat perhaps to be palliated by an original infirmity of constitution (an occasional and unaccountable dejection of spirits without a cause and a constant inability to sleep), but never to be excused." On the 5th of September, 1800, he informs her of the death of Wallis, one of his partners in the proprietorship of Drury Lane Theatre, saying in addition : " I am anxious to know how he has bestowed his illgotten hoards. If he had a living conscience in his bosom when he made his Will, he will have restored me some thousands."

The losses of Fox at play were as attributable to roguery as the debts of Sheridan were to sharp practice of which he had been the victim. His first wife clearly saw that he was a puppet in the hands of men far more astute, and, unlike him, utterly un-scrupulous. Had she lived longer he might have been saved from much ·mortification. She never worried him with anything save good advice which, though generally unwelcome, is easier to bear than re-proaches. She often urged him to put off his "false delicacy" and be as ready to ask favours from others as they were to apply for his aid, and told him that he was "no match" for the men of the world who preyed upon him. When he most required help and sympathy, the clear head and loving heart from which he would have received them had returned to kindred dust, and he had to pen the woeful letters to his second wife from which I have given extracts.

Yet many of his letters are filled with details far more interesting than failures to become rich. They contain information of what passed behind the scenes in the days when Sheridan was a favourite on the stage of public life. An account of his experience at the Levée supplies the seeker after unrevealed facts in history with the valuable information that Queen Charlotte was hindered by corns on her toes from becoming proficient in dancing. Sheridan told his wife that: "The King very gracious, but it is strange to think how he picks up everything that is going on. The first thing he asked me was whether you had recovered [from] the ill effects of your steps? 'tis fact I tell you. He spoke a great deal on the subject and seems a decided enemy to the new capers [waltzes?]. He said your grandfather [the Bishop of Winchester] advised him from a boy never to attempt to excel in dancing, and that the Queen's

corns had providentially interfered with her early
propensity to become a proficient in that frivolous
and often mischievous accomplishment."

When on a visit to Woburn, he wrote : " Fox was
very glad at my coming and we have had a great
deal of talk.   Dinner is at 4, and we walk always
after dinner.   In wine all moderation.   I have
made a rare levy on all for my library.   The
Duke of Devonshire gives me the finest edition of
all Rousseau. . . .

" Nothing can be more complete than the library
here."   In describing another visit, he tells her that
he had played tennis every day, avowing that " he
couldn't play the least "; and adding that, " all strong
exercise " agreed with him.   He further says : " I
must tell you whom we consist of.   1. C. Fox ;
2. Fitzpatrick ; 3. Hare ; 4. Lord John Townshend
(all pleasant as possible) ; 5. Sheridan (stupid) ;
6. Erskine (in great spirits) ; 7. Francis (laughed
at) ; 8. Lord Thurlow (his first question [was] after
Robin [a pet name for their boy], which I told
him I should write you word of) ; 9. Richardson ;
10. Adair ; 11. Lord John Russell (my particular
favourite) ; 12. E. Faulkener ; 13. Dudley North
(very pleasant) ; 14. Lord R. Spencer ; 15. Lord
Holland ; 16. Duke of Bedford."

In the characterization of the guests at Woburn,
nothing is said of Lord Holland ; but I shall repair
that omission by quoting from a letter of a later
date :—" The Hollands are arrived [in town].   The
joyous dear manner in which *he*, seeing me coming
up Berkeley Square yesterday, *ran* like a school

boy, lame as he is, to catch me by the hand quite affected me. He is an excellent creature and the only public man I have any attachment to."[1]

Sheridan was greatly flattered with his reception at Guildhall on the 11th of November, 1803, when his health was drunk, and the toast had such a reception, "as would have gratified Hecca's heart." His shortcomings were not denied by him, neither did he refrain from making confessions which display alike a knowledge of himself and a rare capacity for profiting by it : "A talent for ridicule even to bitterness has not been wanting among such as I possess, but a certain portion of good sense and more of good nature very early decided me to forego the use of it, and I may say, without feeling it much of a boast, that a more inoffensive companion among the various classes it has been my lot to mix with has scarcely been found."

A sentence in another letter is a contribution to his self-portraiture. He had dined at Lord Lynedoch's. The company was composed of military men, all of whom were, as he adds, "new to me, which I hate. However, I think I have lately taken a new turn among strangers and try to be agreeable."

While laudably ready to confess and amend faults in himself, he was also clear-sighted and sensible in dealing with those in his son Charles, from whom he tells his wife he had received a letter in which there

---

[1] Moore would have gratified Lord Holland by publishing the letter from which the extract is taken. It is one of many which I cannot think he read.

is "a *horror* of returning to study which frightens me. If there is not a *sincere* desire to learn and an *ambition* to improve in a boy's mind at a certain age, he will be nothing. *Application, application* without which, says Montesquieu, "there never was or can be a great man. . . . I dislike his using the word *cursed* in his letter to Williams which he wouldn't do in a letter to you or me.'

The references to his son Tom are many and most pathetic. One, which is less painful than the others, relates to visiting Lady Melbourne to please Tom and Caroline, his wife, when *The Rivals* was performed by an amateur company: "They played *The Rivals* really extremely well indeed. Lady Cahir very good and a Mrs. Haseltine, a great Priory personage and a very pretty woman, admirable. . . . I don't know when I have sat out a play before; it made me very nervous. I don't mean the writing or sentiments of the play, but the recollection of the days when, just twenty-one, I wrote it, many years before I knew some *dear friends !* who sat on the bench with me, or their world or their system."

At the time of the letters being written from which I have made extracts, Sheridan was broken in health as well as in fortune, and he had to bear, with all the fortitude at his command, much physical suffering and even more mental sorrow. He had long tried, but in vain, to steel his mind against anxiety for those dear to him; the delicate health of his first wife had kept him in nervous apprehension for years; his second wife fell a victim to an internal malady as hopeless and more painful than that which prematurely ended the days of the first, while his heart was wrung at the spectacle of his son Tom passing rapidly to an untimely grave. His pride in this son is evinced by passage after passage in his letters; a few sentences will suffice to elicit from every compassionate reader true sympathy for the sorely-tried father.

Shortly before Tom left England in the hope of finding at the Cape of Good Hope, where he had been appointed Colonial Treasurer, a relief from his serious ailments, Sheridan wrote to his second wife: "It would half break your heart to see how he is changed. I spend all the time with him I can as he seems to wish it, but he so reminds me of his mother, and his feeble, gasping way of speaking affects and deprives me of all hope. He tries to suppress the irritability of his temper in a very amiable way which makes me fear he thinks ill of himself." Having said that they had arranged to pay a visit together and that Tom had insisted on his father going in the chaise, Sheridan adds :—
" This, poor fellow, was so unlike what in his stouter days would have occurred to him that the very kindness of it grieved me." The expectation that Tom would renew his youth in the balmy climate at the Cape had to be abandoned by his father, who wrote in the depths of his sorrow in terms which can hardly be perused without emotion, and a feeling of sincere commiseration.

" I have endeavoured to escape from despairing about Tom as long as my sanguine heart could hold a hope.   But now, and you must think so too, all hope is over.   It is a heavy stroke and the long postponing of it led to a habit of irrational confidence on the subject, for his malady seemed to have become a part of his constitution and unable to conquer life. . . .   If you were well I would go to him though the scene would crack what nerves I have left. . . .   I try to reserve a ray of hope for thee, my son! for observe what Caroline says of 'his spirits being still excellent' and that, in all events, is a blessed circumstance."   A postscript is added: "A long interview with General Gordon [who had returned from the Cape].   O sad! sad! What shall I do!"

Neither Sheridan's manifold joys and sorrows, nor any of his theatrical entanglements ever made him disregard his duties as a member of Parliament: he was seldom absent from his place in the House of Commons and, during the thirty-one years that he was a member, he filled a prominent part in every important debate and recorded his vote in every important division.   The House always honoured him with an attentive hearing.

It was chiefly in Parliament that Sheridan sought in later years the popularity for which he candidly avowed an excessive liking, though he as candidly admitted, in a letter to his wife, that he had often acted with unwisdom in its pursuit: "I have been always fond of popularity too indiscriminately, and jealous of the world's good opinion, yet have for ever risked the former, in society I mean, by negligence, nor ever possessed the latter with common prudence, but have even felt gratified with setting it at defiance." Though a frequent speaker, he was not a careless one. It was the exception for him to join in debate without having carefully considered the subject beforehand, as the following letter clearly shows :—" I did not speak till 12 o'clock . . . for as I did not look at any of the materials which belonged to the question, I was obliged to wait till others furnished something to remark on. . . . The Ministerial *Times* does me the honour to put my speech in the first person."

With unconcealed and pardonable exultation he wrote to her in June, 1800, that Sir Francis Burdett had moved for an inquiry into "The state and management of the Prison in Cold-Bath-fields," after having postponed his motion in order that Sheridan might be present. The debate took place on the 22nd of July, and Sheridan wrote :—"Yesterday's debate turned out more to my satisfaction than almost anything I ever took part in since I have been in the House of Commons. I made the Speaker blubber, and I really think smote Pitt's conscience : in short, we carried our point and have resolved *nem. con.* on an address to the King to institute an immediate inquiry. . . . I own I am extremely pleased at this event, though it does not seem of the importance of great political questions. The gallery was immensely full, and the result gives universal satisfaction. I don't send you the papers, for there is not one of them that gives an idea of the debate which the listeners who have been with me this morning are outrageous at. However, the good is done."[1]

On the 22nd of November in the same year, he says that his speech on Thursday night, "is horridly given, as no debate was expected," and that he trimmed Pitt, who had attacked him.[2] In 1802, he was seized with giddiness and incapacitated from speaking in the House, and then he writes, "as the question was very particular I got Grey to put off the debate." He had an extreme admiration for Grey, the great Premier of the Ministry which carried the first Reform Act. Writing about him in 1806, he tells his wife : " Only one thing on the subject of Grey. Believe me that there never can be misapprehension or coldness on my part, nor I think on his."

Sheridan expressed his admiration for the manner in which Grey bore his honours and responsibilities after the 8th of October, 1806, when, as Lord Howick, he had succeeded Fox as Secretary for Foreign Affairs and Leader of the House :—" The

[1] Sheridan's statement about the meagreness of the reports in the newspapers can be verified by those who turn to *The Parliamentary History*, vol. xxxv., pp. 463-470.

[2] The report in *The Parliamentary History* gives no clue to the attack, or the retort. A debate took place on the 18th of November, but this was a Tuesday and not a Thursday, the day which he mentions, possibly, by mistake. Mr. T. Tyrwhitt Jones originated the debate, saying in the course of his speech : " I repeat, while there is a single Frenchman in Egypt, England is in danger. . . . I believe, from my soul, her salvation and existence are involved in the evacuation of Egypt " [by the French].—*The Parliamentary History*, vol. xxxv., pp. 587-597.

House of Commons began yesterday. W. Lamb [afterwards Lord Melbourne] acquitted himself admirably, but I really cannot describe how incomparably Grey spoke, or the decided credit he has acquired and confirmed to himself in every respect. It was a very trying moment and occasion, appearing for the first time as Minister and Leader of the House of Commons. Beside excellent argument and statesmanlike, he showed the greatest readiness in replying to every part of Canning's prepared speech, and that is the faculty that takes most with the House. There is but one opinion on the subject and that is, if possible, more favourable than even what I am stating. I assure you from my heart that this has given me the greatest pleasure, as I am sure it will you."

He confided to his wife his personal view of a momentous political question concerning which he had to take a side and ran some risk in so doing : " The country is going to the Devil. I have resisted every effort to induce me not to vote for the Catholic question to-day, under the shabby pretence that it was premature and ill-timed, a ground which some real friends to the Catholic cause mean to take to make court to the Regent, and it is the worst court for him that can be taken. It has been a toss-up whether I should not have taken the Chiltern Hundreds and been out of Parliament this day, but I shall continue to consult nothing as a public man but my own self-esteem." These words ring true. They were justified by conduct. He preserved his political independence as completely as Fox during a long parliamentary career. If he had descended to play the part of Pliable, all the honours and emoluments which he might covet would have been within his grasp.

The path which he trod was hard though most creditable. His noble independence led to the greatest disappointment in his career, his rejection for Stafford in 1812. He had written to his wife, in 1810, that his exclusion from Parliament was "a thing infinitely probable," yet, when the day came that he ceased to be a member and to enjoy the privileges which were then attached to the position, he felt grievously annoyed and was made to feel how much he had lost. The lack of funds wherewith to pay what was indispensable had chiefly caused his defeat, which was rendered more bitter by the fact that a much larger amount than he required was owing to him by the committee which then managed Drury Lane Theatre.

It has been said that the Prince Regent offered to find a seat for him in Parliament, and that he declined the offer.[1] Another writer has affirmed that the Prince advanced the money required for the purchase of a seat and that Sheridan's agent misappropriated it ; but no trustworthy authority has been given in support of the statement. Sheridan says in a letter to his wife : "I am very much pressed to come into Parliament : but of that hereafter ;" again he writes : " My friend the Duke of Norfolk is I fear in a very bad way, indeed, likely

[1] Moore's " Memoirs " of Sheridan, vol. ii., p. 437.

to die. [He died, 16 December, 1815.] He had just settled a plan to give me a seat without expense before the next meeting of Parliament, and he is the only one I would accept one from because he knows my condition of being my own absolute master, and in politics no difference existed between us."[1] This avowal tallies with what he wrote to the High Bailiff of Westminster for publication in 1814, when declining to be a candidate in opposition to Lord Cochrane :—" Never will I accept a seat in the House of Commons but on the sole condition of being master of my own vote and voice, the servant only of my conscience."

I reserve many passages in Sheridan's letters to his second wife for use in connexion with his career in later years, and I shall now give but two which are of general interest. Writing in the year 1809, he asks her to tell Tom that he is bringing a book which he is sure Tom will read " with pleasure and attention, though all morality and religion, and yet I

---

[1] The story which George IV. told to Mr. Croker, with which I shall afterwards deal, is in direct variance with the statement in the letter from Sheridan to his wife, that the Duke of Norfolk had settled a plan " to give me a seat in Parliament without expense " and with perfect freedom of action. Croker reports the King to have said, "The Duke of Norfolk had a seat to dispose of for which he expected £4,000, but he consented, as he called it, to subscribe £1,000 towards bringing Sheridan into Parliament ; or, in other words, to accept from Sheridan £3,000 for the seat. As even the payment of this sum was not to leave Sheridan personally independent, the Duke expecting that he should vote with him, I did not consider the offer quite so noble as the offer of sub-scribing £1,000 towards bringing Sheridan in, seemed to affect to be."—" The Croker Papers," vol. i., p. 306.

think it the most argumentative, logical, ingenious and by far the wittiest performance I ever met with."

Though the title is not mentioned, the book was probably the " Letters to the Catholics from Peter Plumley to his brother Abraham." And if so, Sydney Smith had in Sheridan a reader whose praise was golden. At the time the authorship of the " Letters " was attributed to Sheridan himself. The last letter to his second wife which has been preserved, was written on a " Sunday Evening " in April, 1815. The whole has not been preserved ; but four quarto pages remain and from them I make the following extract : " I dine again by myself, as indeed I do every day, so I will scribble a little now for fear business should prevent me to-morrow. I was infinitely delighted to get your letter by Henry and in *your own* pencil hand too ma'am ! and the direction by *pen and ink* and in your best copper-plate ! You may imagine I hastened to find out Henry and to ask no few questions about you. I was tolerably satisfied with his answers, but I don't like your living lower than ever, and avoiding any attempt to walk, for you could walk a little without hurting yourself when I left. Then I grieved at your not letting your maid come to you, though I enter into your reasons ; but do let us leave the *Puffin's nest* and get into a *house*.

" I think settled fine weather will come now, though *yesterday*, and I dare say you did not notice the difference, was as detestable a day as ever nipt the nose of April ; but still *ad interim* (you know you are a perfect Latin scholar) let Bloxham send you a substitute, my Mary dear can't do everything. Henry diverted and pleased me extremely by his account of your joint cheerfulness. No two little swallows in their mud tenement under a friendly pent-house, I fancy, ever twittered more gaily.

"Henry says you want the new novel by the *Author of Waverley*. I shall send it to you and when you [are] done with it make it a present to Mary. I spent near three hours this blessed morning, for mind I don't hop, step and jump through a book as some certain people do, in reading the third volume of *Waverley*, having read the first at Leatherhead and the second at intervals since I came to town. I am enchanted with the work. I class it above any book of its character and description that I ever met with in my life. To a Highland Scotsman it must have a tenfold recommendation. Henry tells me you have read it. I wonder at your not having mentioned it [to] me. What relates to the subject of education in the early part of the first volume and the account of Edward's half-idle and desultory reading must have brought Charles to your mind. Charles confessed it did most strongly remind him of himself. He read the book at Leatherhead. We had it Ma'am from our *Leatherhead circulating Library*. I will positively find out the author.[1] I

---

[1] Sheridan correctly guessed the authorship; but the author refused to disclose his name. Rogers states that he and Scott met Sheridan at Lady Jersey's, where Sheridan said, " Pray, Mr. Scott, did you, or did you not, write Waverley?" Scott replied, "On my honour, I did not." This is the only downright denial

... Henry says you want the
... Novels by the author of Waverley
I shall send it to you & when you done
with it make it a present to Mary ...
I spent near three hours this blessed morning,
for mind I don't lay ... I ... ...
a book as some certain people do, in reading
the third volume of Waverley — having
read the first at Leatherhead & the second
at intervals since I came to town —
I am enchanted with the work — I class it ...
... ... book of ... ...
... ...
... ...
... ...
Henry tells me you are in ... ...
... of your ... ...
... me ... ...
... in the early ... the third volume ...
... ... and the ... of ...
half odd I ... time reading ... ...
... ... to you, mind — Charles
... it ... most strongly ...
... ... read the book
at Leatherhead ... had it Ma'am
from our Leatherhead circulating library —
... ... find out the author
... from beginning his new work,
for the present — it would keep me ...
... because — but I will send it ...
& Mary will read it to you — & ...
if you have not read Waverley ...
Now a word of Tom & ... ...
Col. Graham a cousin I think of Lyon
goes to the lake in a week or where ... also

LETTER FROM SHERIDAN ALLUDING TO "WAVERLEY."

abstain from beginning his new work, for the present it would keep me from business. But I will send it you and Mary will read it to you, and, dear Mary, if you have not read *Waverley*, do."

If the sentences which I have quoted from Sheridan's last letter to his wife had been published in 1825, they would have given great pleasure to Sir Walter Scott, who had a greater and juster admiration for Sheridan than his son-in-law Lockhart. The year before this letter was written, Sir Walter had penned these words : " Thomas Sheridan was still more remarkable as the father of the celebrated and highly-gifted Richard Brinsley Sheridan, M.P., one of the most gifted men of a period when talents were the profuse attribute of those who dedicated themselves to the public service."[1]

of the fact which Scott is reported to have made; I think, however, that the form in which he couched it may have been more evasive than the words which Rogers ascribes to him.—" Table-Talk," p. 195.

[1] " Swift's Works," edited by Walter Scott, vol. ix., p. 304.

VIII.

CALAMITOUS YEARS.

SHERIDAN's parliamentary career has been misunder-
stood and undervalued. His oratorical achievements
have had a full measure of praise, yet his regular
work in the House of Commons during thirty years
has not been accounted worthy of panegyric. "A
Constitutional Friend" collected four hundred and
sixty of his speeches and published them in three
octavo volumes.[1] The general public has a very
lukewarm taste for useful works of any class ; still,
those who have written about him might have read
his speeches. They possess a biographical value
which is second only to his letters.

A parliamentary opponent of Sheridan was struck
with the fact that, after being three years a member
of the House of Commons, he began to eclipse
Burke because he exhibited, "almost all the talents
which can meet in man under the control of unalter-
able equality of temper."[2] He was acquainted, however, with his own limitations, and though conscious

---

[1] This work is not complete, the last speech reproduced in it
having been delivered on the 17th of June, 1808. He spoke
frequently between that year and the 21st of July, 1812, when he
addressed the House of Commons for the last time.

[2] Wraxall's " Memoirs," vol. iii., p. 116.

of his oratorical gifts, he was not blind to Burke's greatness and there was critical acumen as well as generosity in his remark to Rogers: "When posterity read the speeches of Burke, they will hardly be able to believe that, during his lifetime, he was not considered as a first-rate speaker, not even as a second-rate one."[1]

The most effective orators in Parliament are also the best debaters. Now, Sheridan could distinguish himself in debate, as well as deliver a set speech, elucidating and adorning all the topics with which he dealt. He did not disdain drudgery. Wherever there was a wrong to be righted or an abuse removed, he willingly lent his aid. His popularity had been honestly earned and was the fitting recognition of untiring and fruitful service to the country which he loved and to the people who loved him.

An appeal made to Sheridan in 1787 to help the Scottish Burgesses to obtain redress promptly received a favourable answer, and he repeatedly brought their grievances before the House of Commons and eloquently urged that they should be modified or removed. He did not seek the office; but there was nothing singular in his accepting it when others, including his own leader, had been invited to undertake it and declined.[2] The origin of the movement for reform was the prevalence

---

[1] " Recollections of Rogers's Table-talk," p. 67.

[2] Moore writes in his " Memoirs " of Sheridan (vol. ii., p. 135), " He had been, singularly enough, selected, in the year 1787, by the Burgesses of Scotland, in preference to so many others professing more personal knowledge of that country, to present to the House the petition of the Convention of Delegates, for a reform of the internal government of the Royal Boroughs."

of the feeling that the tyrannical conduct of the
Councils in the several Boroughs ought to cease.
These Councils were self-elected and they elected
members of Parliament.   There was not even the
semblance of popular representation in Scotland at
the time Sheridan spoke, nor when Moore wrote his
" Memoirs," neither was the voice of the people heard
there at Parliamentary elections till after 1832.

In 1784 a Convention of Delegates from 54 out of
the 64 Royal Boroughs which were represented in
Parliament, met to consider what measure of reform
was necessary, and after long consultation at several
meetings a scheme was drawn up for improving, in
the first instance, the internal government of the
Boroughs.   Mr. George Dempster was requested
to act as spokesman in Parliament for the Delegates ;
he refused, however, on the ground, " that it would
ill become him to attempt the subversion of
magistrates and Town Councils from whom he
derived his seat."   An application was made to Pitt,
which he left unnoticed, and to Dundas, who announced in reply that he was determined to oppose
the wishes of the Delegates.   Mr. Wilberforce, Mr.
Grey, Mr. Lambton and other members of Parliament refused to lend their aid.   A deputation then
waited upon Fox, who urged his " ignorance of the
constitutional law of Scotland " as the reason for not
assenting to the request made to him, while if he had
added that his indolence was equal to his ignorance,
his reply would have been complete.   However, he
recommended the deputation to apply to Sheridan,
who was not better acquainted with Scots law and
who had more business in hand than he could

execute. The advice was taken ; Sheridan was
approached on the subject, and it is recorded that,
" upon his being made acquainted with the case, he
embraced the cause with ardour."[1]

Between 1787 and 1792, Sheridan brought the
subject of the Royal Scottish Boroughs twelve times
before the House. Speaking on the 27th of May,
1791, he classed the grievances of the Burgesses, who
through him had petitioned the House to the number
of ten thousand, under four heads ; first, the exaction
of the land tax by the magistrates without legal authority ; second, disposing of public money at their own
discretion ; third, being self-elected in contravention
of the law, and fourth, the absence of any tribunal in
Scotland to adjudicate on the points at issue. Dundas
admitted the truth of much which Sheridan urged,
but he considered that it was a sufficient reply to
state that the Royal Boroughs had existed since the
year 1469, that the state of English Boroughs and
Stafford in particular was quite as bad. Moreover,
Dundas twitted Sheridan with seeking after popularity and predicted that no statue in his honour
would be erected in Scotland, and received the
retort that he did not desire either popularity or
a statue by the Bill he had introduced and that
Dundas would better deserve a statue by obtaining
free elections for his countrymen instead of manag-
ing election jobs.

Dundas had an incontestable superiority over
Sheridan. Nearly every Scottish member of Parlia-

---

[1] " An Historical Sketch of the Municipal Constitution of the
City of Edinburgh," by Alexander Pennecuik. Published in 1826,
pp. xlix. to liii.

ment had merely to say " ditto " to him, while he dis-
pensed patronage with single eye to ensuring a full
chorus of " dittos," as Mr. Cruger is incorrctly supposed to have done to Burke on the hustings at Bristol.
His statue is as conspicuous an object in Edinburgh
as that of Nelson in London and Dublin. A royal
commission reported that all Sheridan's allegations
concerning the Scottish Boroughs were well-founded,
and an Act accomplished in 1833 what he had
striven to effect between 1787 and 1792. Dundas
was a true prophet, as well as wise in his generation.
Unbought and useful services such as those which
Sheridan rendered to Scotland are seldom commemo-
rated by statues. The Delegates whose cause he "had
embraced with ardour," were truly grateful for his
zeal, energy and consistency, and many communications from them are preserved among his papers
couched in glowing terms of admiration, while the
hope expressed that he will persevere in exerting
" his distinguished abilities with that inflexible firmness and constitutional moderation which have
appeared so conspicuous and exemplary throughout
the whole of his conduct, as to be highly deserving
of the imitation of all good citizens."

Sheridan was as chivalrous in espousing the cause
of an impecunious Prince of Wales as in labouring
to give relief to the deserving and ill-treated Scottish
Burgesses. On the 27th of November, 1788,
Elizabeth Sheridan wrote to her sister in Dublin :
" I should tell you that the latter gentleman [the
Prince of Wales] has more esteem and friendship
for him [their brother] than for any man in England."
There was no trace of the self-seeking ends pursued

by Bubb Doddington, while professing to serve
Frederick Prince of Wales, in Sheridan's conduct
towards his grandson.   Indeed, he suffered in public
estimation by championing the Prince in the House
of Commons, yet his most censorious critics would
gladly have taken his place.   He made a public
defence on the 5th of June, 1795, and said that,
though not occupying an official position, yet "the
Prince sometimes honoured him with his confidence,
and often asked his advice, chiefly from the knowledge of his fixed determination to accept of no
obligation of any kind whatever.   It was not his
custom to answer calumnies, many of which he had
suffered to pass unnoticed ; but he now declared in
the face of the House of the country, that he never
[had] received from the Prince of Wales so much as
the present of a horse or a picture."[1]

The Prince had recourse to Sheridan's pen when
he desired to give telling expression to his thoughts
on questions which were in dispute between himself
and the Government, or his father, the King.   No
mischief can now be caused by publishing extracts
from the confidential letters which the Prince wrote
to Sheridan.   Much of their interest was fleeting ;
but much of their value has become historical.   They
conclusively prove the confidence which the writer
placed in him to whom they were addressed.

In August, 1791, the Prince wrote to Sheridan
and said that Lord Southampton had sent him "a
new publication [probably *An Appeal from the Old
to the New Whigs*] accompanied by a very curious

---

[1] *The Parliamentary History*, vol. xxxiii., p. 107.

epistle which I keep on purpose to show you one of these days." On another occasion, he asks Sheridan to return the letter addressed to the Duke of York, adding: "In the first place I wish much to get it back into my own possession, and in the next place I fear very much that you will either mislay it or lose it." He is anxious, moreover, to receive through Sheridan the opinion of Fox concerning the letter.

A few blotted lines written on the 27th of July, 1803, in "the greatest hurry," according to the Prince,[1] inform Sheridan: "I have received a most impertinent letter and most insincere from Addington and the answer must be with him before one o'Clock to-morrow. You positively must be with me at twelve."

Before quoting a short letter wherein the Prince bestowed on Sheridan an office in his gift, I may state that Sheridan displayed abnegation to a degree which some contemporaries accounted puritanical, and others laughed at as foolishness. In his day the men who could get anything never thought that they had received enough. The chase after sinecures was considered to be the duty of every loyal citizen, and none who had the remotest prospect of success, hesitated in striving, without scruple, to command it. When Lord St. Vincent desired to show his high appreciation of Sheridan's patriotic service by appointing his son Tom to the office of Registrar of the Admiralty Court at Malta, an office

---

[1] Moore records in his *Diary:* "Found some letters of the Regent's, one of which seemed to be written when he was drunk," vol. i'., p. 235.

Dear Sheridan,

You well know that I never forget my old friends, the death of Lord Elliott affords me the opportunity of offering you a trifling proof of that sincere friendship I have always professed & felt for you through a long series of years. I wish to God it was better worth your acceptance.

ever affectionately yours

Carlton House.
Monday night.
Feb.y 20. 1804.

LETTER FROM THE PRINCE REGENT TO SHERIDAN.

which, in time of war, was extremely lucrative,
Sheridan's unbending consistency was vindicated by
his declining the offer, and his wife thought he had
acted rightly.   She was most anxious, however, to
smooth her stepson's path through life, and told her
husband that she was willing [for the sake of his son
Tom] "to make any sacrifice in the world and to
live in any way whatever."

On the 20th of February, 1804, the Prince wrote
from Carlton House : " Dear Sheridan, You well
know that I never forget old friends.   The death of
Lord Elliott affords me the opportunity of offering
you a trifling proof of that sincere friendship I have
always professed and felt for you through a long
series of years.   I wish to God it was better
worth your acceptance.   Ever affectionately yours.
George P."

This office was the Receivership of the Duchy of
Cornwall, of which the salary, though fluctuating,
seldom fell below £800.   Sheridan considered it his
duty to inform Addington, who was then Prime
Minister, of the offer and of his acceptance, telling
him also that, while he had plumed himself on acting
for the Prince with perfect independence, he thought
"it would have been false pride and apparently
mischievous affectation " to have declined this mark
of the Prince's confidence and regard.   Moreover,
the advice given by him when the Prince and
Addington were in disagreement, had been alike
uncourtierlike and unwelcome.   Sheridan desired
that Addington and the Prince should come to an
understanding and act together, and he exerted

himself to promote harmony between them. His
conduct on this occasion was due to aversion for
William Pitt, rather than to admiration for Addington.   Jealousy, rivalry and unconcealed dislike had
existed between Pitt and Sheridan since the days
when they exerted themselves in concert to overturn
Lord North.   Their minds were cast in different
moulds; yet, if Sheridan had occupied the position
which Dundas did, the influence of Pitt for good
would have been doubled, while some of his mistakes
might have been avoided.   During Addington's
tenure of high office under sufferance, Sheridan frequently visited him.   One evening after dinner at
his house in Richmond Park, Sheridan candidly and
truthfully remarked, as Addington records: "My
visits to you may possibly be misconstrued by my
friends; but I hope you know, Mr. Addington, that
I have an unpurchaseable mind."[1]

If Sheridan had been less scrupulous he would
have received higher praise.   His contemporaries
and their successors have accused him of failings
from which he was free, because he practised virtues
which they regarded as utterly Quixotic.   It seemed,
however, as if the fates were adverse to Sheridan's
enjoying the Receivership of the Duchy of Cornwall.

General Lord Lake put forward a claim to the
reversion of it.   Some correspondence passed between Sheridan and the representatives of General
Lake, and these letters have been printed.   The
facts were set forth by Sheridan himself in the
House of Commons on the 17th of June, 1812, a

[1] "Life of Lord Sidmouth," vol. ii., p. 105.

version which is alike clear and consistent and one which has never been disputed. He said : " The income which I derive from the bounty of the Prince is the only thing I have, [here Mr. Sheridan appeared somewhat agitated] and I shall explain to the House how I came to receive it. On the death of Lord Elliott, when the office of Receiver of the Duchy became vacant, the Attorney-General, Mr. Adam, and a number of other learned gentlemen, some of whom are now in the House, who were then consulted, agreed in thinking that Lord Lake could not accept the situation when he was absent from this country, and it was then proposed that I should take it. I apprized his brother, in the presence of the Duke of York, that if I took it, I should immediately resign it on Lord Lake's return ; and accordingly I did resign it when he returned. When he died, the Prince was pleased to give it me by Letters Patent for my life, in the same manner as it had been given to Lord Lake."[1]

At half-past 11 a.m. on the 5th of March, 1804, the Prince wrote to Sheridan from Carlton House : " Pray come here as soon as you can, for I have got hold of almost all the circumstances that have happened respecting the interview of yesterday, and which is most essential should be communicated previous to the debate of to-day. The sooner you come the better." On the 31st of December, in the same year, the Prince reproaches him with neglecting to keep an appointment ; in this matter, Sheridan was no respecter of persons.

[1] *Parliamentary Debates*, vol. xxiii., pp. 554, 555.

He wrote again : " I have received this moment a letter from the Chancellor that demands a very smart reply from me, and I therefore write to you in the hope that you will *instantly* come to town on the receipt of this letter, as I should be sorry to send an answer of the important nature which the answer to the Chancellor must be, without availing myself of your advice."

A letter in the same familiar strain, is dated the 29th of April, 1805 :—" According to your desire I have put off Lord Grenville till four o'Clock to-morrow, in the hopes of seeing you first at an *early* hour. I hope you have not forgot to appoint Wilson according to your promise at 1 o'clock to-morrow at MacMahon's [the Prince's Private Secretary], and that you would call upon me at that hour in order to go with me there. Pray write me a line to-night before you go to bed to say whether it is possible for you to do so after all your fatigues in the House of Commons, or if you have any doubts as to your being able to be in time, if so will appoint him to be at MacMahon's between eight and nine to-morrow evening, it will be quite as convenient to me, and in that case possibly you would dine with me at Mrs. Fitzherbert's at six o'clock to-morrow, and then we could go together to MacMahon's in our way to the Opera." The Prince adds in a postscript : " Do not forget to write me a line before you go to bed."

The following imperative summons was despatched from " Carlton House, Saturday, ¾ past 6, January 25th, 1806 ": " You must positively be with me at *eight o'Clock* to a minute, as I have something of the *utmost importance* to communicate to you ; I have just written to Charles [Fox] to be with me at the same time as I shall see *no one* till I have first communicated with both of you.   Not a moment of time is to be lost, therefore *you must* be punctual. Not a word to any soul living of the contents of this."

· Though the Prince was usually as precise as his father in noting the hour, as well as the day and date when a letter was written, yet he sometimes left too much to the imagination by omitting the date, and writing " Saturday night, 10 o'clock." The few lines thus headed are as confidential as any which I have quoted : " I wish much to have a conversation with you this evening on *particular business*, and a paper to show you.   This is a circumstance that does not admit of delay, or I should not press so urgently the seeing you to-night."

The last letter from which I shall make extracts at present is dated " Carlton House, Sunday, ½ past 7 p.m.," and begins with the remark that he had waited from a quarter past six for Sheridan to call. He begs him to be very firm in treating with the Chancellor, " at the same time expressing the readiness with which I should listen to anything from the K— were it not from the strong founded impression there exists in my mind, of his *rooted antipathy to me*, and which nothing but what you know I have so much *at heart*, and feel myself *so pledged to*, being *undone* can possibly give me the smallest hope of being otherwise, and indeed without such a public testimony on the part of H⁵ M⁷, it would really render all assistance on my part to the K— of no avail, as it would make me appear in the eyes of the public, jumping at the very first overture, and lower me in the eyes of the person, in whose eyes of all others, it is both my intention as well as my wish to stand the highest, namely *my own.*"   I hope that Sheridan understood all that the Prince intended to convey by the foregoing passage.

Though the Prince of Wales had treated Sheridan as his confidential adviser for many years, the circumstance was long kept a secret.   Many persons who were indignant when the truth was revealed would have been delighted had they occupied Sheridan's position.

His situation appears to me alike intolerable and unenviable ; yet in his day it was coveted by thousands.   To play the part well, requires talents which are rare and mental qualities which are rarer ; the mere courtier finds no difficulty in pandering to the vanity of any Prince ; but Sheridan made himself indispensable because he never withheld the truth. He frequently gave advice which was unpalatable, and the Prince deserves credit for sometimes taking it.   He probably discerned that no other man among those who called themselves his friends would have had the courage to be as outspoken and honest. Leigh Hunt harshly blamed Sheridan in *The Examiner* for not giving the Prince such advice[1] as should have had the effect of making him "conquer his bad habits," and "become a reformed character." Even Sheridan could not perform impossibilities.   A

[1] *The Examiner*, 21st June, 1812.

letter to his second wife, which is dated Monday, the
27th February, 1804, contains this passage:—"There
never was known before anything equal to the
agitation of people's minds at this moment, and the
Prince, just recovered from an illness in which his
life was despaired of for two days, is so nervous and
anxious that it is not easy to thwart him, though he
runs a great risk of making himself ill again.   I now
see him openly, but till lately I never saw him till
twelve at night, and he has often kept me till 4 in
the morning, not supping or with a drop of wine,
but in his bedroom."   Several years later he wrote
to her : " Pray, pray never suspect or decry the
Prince.   He is acting as honourably as man can
do, and gives me his entire and unqualified confidence."

The private letters of Sheridan do not confirm the
allegation that lust for office was one of his besetting
sins.   Unfortunately, his great capacity for the
business of statesmanship never had free scope, and
Fox, his friend and leader, laboured under the like
disadvantage.   What Plunkett said to Lockhart
when he and his great father-in-law visited Ireland
in July, 1825, applies as forcibly to Sheridan as to
Fox : " Plunkett said how much better men and
greater statesmen would Fox and Pitt have been,
had the one spent half his time in power, the other,
half of his in opposition."[1]

On the 20th of September, 1799, Sheridan wrote
to his wife : " Lord Malmesbury is now in London,
and all hopes of peace gone.   It will end in our

[1] "Familiar Letters of Sir Walter Scott," vol. ii.; p. 304.

coming into office which I solemnly protest I hate
the thoughts of." Earlier in the same year, he had
taken an active part in the debates concerning the
projected Union between Great Britain and Ireland,
fighting, as Mr. Lecky puts it, " a hopeless battle
it opposition, with conspicuous earnestness and
courage."[1] When the subject was formally introduced on the 23rd of January, 1799, he said : " My
country has claims upon me which I am not more
proud to acknowledge than ready to liquidate to the
full measure of my ability."[2] In his opinion, as in
that of other leading Whigs, the final bargain
between Great Britain and Ireland had been concluded in 1782, when Grattan's Parliament was
established and its legislative independence formally
acknowledged. Neither Sheridan, nor the twenty-
five members of the House of Commons who
followed him, were aware how greatly the influence
of the French Revolution had operated in Ireland,
or that the powerful party called United Irishmen
was opposed to the Irish Parliament and working for

---

[1] " History of England in the 18th Century," by W. E. H.
Lecky, vol. viii., p. 356. Mr. Lecky further points out that
Sheridan and his small band of followers did not direct their chief
arguments against a legislative union, their main position being,
" that no such Union could strengthen the connexion, if it was
carried by corruption and intimidation, without the free consent
and real approbation of the two Parliaments and nations."

[2] These words were sincere. His sister Elizabeth wrote on the
15th of June, 1785, to Mrs. Lefanu in Dublin : " Let us know
what Grattan does. Dick is a very warm friend to the Irish.
Mrs. Sheridan cannot conceive the violent attachment he has to
that country."

the declaration of a Republic or the annexation of Ireland to France. Yet, though the reasons for a Union, on the ground of expediency, were more cogent than Sheridan supposed, the manner in which the Union was achieved deserved all his criticism.

He argued with warmth and in the most logical fashion yet he failed to move his hearers, many of whom were better acquainted with certain facts than he was, or than he acknowledged himself to be. Still, it is difficult now to understand why his impassioned speeches produced so little effect and why all his resolutions were contemptuously rejected. At the end of January, 1799, and in the first week of February he vainly implored that no Union should take place unless it were based on "the manifest, fair and free consent and approbation of the Parliaments of the two countries." Neither is it easy to understand why the further motion should have received as little favour which declared the man to be an enemy to the King and Government who tried to bring about a Union "by employing the influence of Government for the purposes of corruption and intimidation." He fought a losing game and he did so chiefly because, as I have hinted, he fought in the dark. The most deplorable circumstance is that the removal of religious disabilities, and the endowment of Roman Catholic priests in Ireland, which Pitt contemplated, each being the natural and inevitable sequence of his scheme of Union, should not have received the support of Parliament because George the Third had declared that he would never give his consent. Pitt took a manly part and resigned.

If he had refused to accept office again unless his Irish policy received the King's sanction, he would probably have had his own way, and in that case many bitter thoughts would never have filled men's minds subsequently, while the annals of Ireland might have been far less painful and depressing reading.

None of the Administrations of George the Third was more ludicrous and more congenial to him than that of Addington. Farmer George delighted in exercising patronage, and if the Whigs had been ready to indulge him in this respect, he would have given them his confidence. William Pitt was shrewd enough to ascertain the King's weak side, yet he had failed to learn the depth and strength of his bigotry on subjects which Pitt held as strongly as Fox to be matters of expediency. Both of these statesmen agreed in regarding the interests of the State as paramount, and both were ready to face the wrath of Prelates when acceding to what these Prelates deemed to be the inadmissible demands of Protestant Nonconformists and members of the Church of Rome to exercise freely and fully all the rights of citizens.

Addington was one of the happy men who have no original ideas to distract their minds, nor any doubts as to the divinity of their rulers. The most gladsome event in his life took place on the 29th of December, 1804, about which he wrote to his brother : " I am just returned from Kew, where I passed an hour and a half with his Majesty, and partook of his dinner, which consisted of mutton chops and pudding."[1]

[1] " Life of Lord Sidmouth," vol. ii., pp. 342, 343.

He was not the pilot in extremity, and, when Bonaparte resumed his career of conquest and rapine and the nations of the Continent trembled at his nod, Addington had to give place to William Pitt who, if he ever felt fear, did not show it, whose presence at the head of the Government inspired the timorous with confidence, and whose death in 1806 would have caused a panic, if there had been any chance of Addington, then Lord Sidmouth, succeeding him. Confidence was unimpaired when it became known that the King had consented to the formation of a Ministry in which Charles James Fox was to be the Secretary of State for Foreign Affairs. The King's insane hatred of Fox lasted till Fox was in his grave, and then the King regretted the loss of the truest statesman of his reign.

Sheridan was made a Privy Councillor and appointed Treasurer of the Navy, the office that had been reserved for him in the Whig Ministry that was to have been formed in 1789 had the faculties of George the Third continued in eclipse. It was not considered expedient that he should enter the Cabinet; yet, with the exception of Fox, his qualifications and his claims for Cabinet rank were superior to those of all who obtained it.

The Ministry over which Lord Grenville presided is known as that of All the Talents. In reality it was an agglomeration of discordant elements. Ellenborough, the Lord Chief Justice, was included in it to please Sidmouth, who had had no claim to be accounted a man of talent or a Whig.

Sheridan did not assent to his exclusion from the

Cabinet without murmuring against his Whig friends, who were then as ready, as they had previously been, to reserve office and emolument for those who had been cradled in historical Whig nurseries. He rightly held that he had been unfairly treated, and wrote to Fox :—" I tell you frankly that I take that office without the slightest feeling of obligation to anyone living ; perhaps I might say more. It is seventeen years since, when you professed to me that I should not be content to accept that alone." He contended, moreover, that a seat in Parliament should be found for him, or that the expense of his re-election for Stafford should be defrayed out of the party funds, and also that, in accordance with promises frequently renewed, some provision should be made for his elder son.[1]

Nine months was the brief life of the Administration over which Lord Grenville presided, and of which Charles James Fox was the soul. Sheridan had seldom occasion to address the House while in office; his most important speech as Treasurer of the Navy was made on the third reading of the Bill for the repeal of the Additional Force Act,

---

[1] I have before me the letters which passed between him and Fox in which these points are set forth and discussed.

He thought himself entitled to dispense more patronage than he was permitted to do. If the following passage in the " Biographical Index to the House of Commons " published in 1808 be correct, then there was nothing mercenary in Sheridan's expectations : " Nor ought it to be forgotten, that it was proposed by Mr. Fox to render him independent for life, by the offer of a patent place of £2,000 per annum, which he had the magnanimity enough, notwithstanding his obvious necessities, to refuse."

and the most memorable passage in that speech referred to William Pitt, of whom he nobly and finely said :—"There were many who flattered him more than I, and some who feared him more ; but there was no man who had a higher respect for his transcendent talents, his matchless eloquence and the greatness of his soul ; and yet it has been often my fate to have opposed his measures. I may have considered that there was somewhat too much of loftiness in his mind which could not bend to advice, or scarcely bear co-operation. I might have considered that, as a statesman, his measures were not adequate to the situation of the country in the present times ; but I always thought his purpose and his hope was for the greatness and security of the Empire."[1]

In letters to his second wife, Sheridan describes what passed behind the scenes while the Ministry of All the Talents was in office. He was personally active in the advancement of Lord Grey, who had been created Baron Grey de Howick on the 27th of June, 1801, to the rank of Viscount Howick and Earl Grey, and who would not apply to Fox for the promotion which he desired. Moreover, as Sheridan notes, Fox was debarred from making further recommendation concerning peerages. Sheridan writes :—
"I saw that the only way to effect it was through the Prince, and I went immediately to him. You know that there has been always a distance not to say dislike between him and Grey. I never omitted an opportunity to remove this. I urged to him the good

[1] "Speeches," vol. iii., p. 504.

on every account of convincing Grey of his good-will towards him and gaining his personal attachment. Whitbread had stated that the thing would be most grateful. I represented to him that if anything were to happen to Fox and me, both as his Minister and private friend, he would look nowhere for anyone to be put in competition with Grey. The P. adopted the whole idea most cheerfully, and assured me he would propose it to Grey at D[evonshire] House in the evening and afterwards make a point of it. Observe he was not asked for one tittle for anyone himself. This he has accordingly done, and I have no doubt it will succeed. He must have the exclusive merit of it with Grey, who of course must know nothing about me in the matter."

This instance is one out of many in which Sheridan helped his friends without parade and even without their knowledge. Not a single one is on record of his political friends helping him. Twice only did he ask a personal favour. He applied to Thurlow, at the request of his first wife when on her death-bed, to give a living in his gift to her brother, Ozyas Linley. He applied to the Prince Regent, at the request of his second wife, to pardon a man who had been sentenced to death for horse-stealing. His first wife taunted him with a reluctance to be as forward in asking for himself as he was in doing so for others. She was quite right. None knew better, how much he suffered and lost by false modesty. Like his paternal grandfather, he was the useful friend of everybody whom he knew and esteemed, and his own worst enemy.

After the death of Fox in 1806, Sheridan naturally desired to succeed him as member for Westminster. Lord Grenville had resolved, however, that Lord Percy, whose only claim on the Whig party was to be the son of the Duke of Northumberland, should represent Westminster in Parliament. It was admitted, when too late, that a mistake had been made, and alleged that the cause of it was a misunderstanding; yet the unpublished letters which I have read justify me in affirming that Sheridan's wishes had not received the slightest consideration. He was doomed as a politician to hew wood and draw water, while the aristocratic Whigs were clad in purple and fine linen and fared sumptuously in high office. George Canning informed Sheridan that he could not join the Whig party because it was too aristocratical. He lived to be stigmatized as an adventurer by the Tories, who, in his case as in that of Disraeli, deemed his brilliancy unconstitutional and his rare eloquence revolutionary. Sheridan, who had joined the Whigs owing to his admiration for Fox, was too independent to be their patient tool or their uncomplaining victim. At the general election in 1806 he was returned for Westminster along with Sir Samuel Hood; but he was defeated at the general election in 1807.[1]

This rejection depressed and grieved him. He knew that Fox had spoken with greater authority in the House because he was the representative of

[1] The third Parliament of the United Kingdom of Great Britain and Ireland sat for one session only.

the city in which the House was situated.   Sheridan
thought that his own services to the country would
receive from the electors of Westminster a well-
merited as well as marked recognition and reward.
The ingratitude of the people often matches that of
Princes.   However, he re-entered the House in
1807 as a member for Ilchester, his colleague being
Michael Angelo Taylor.   His hope was to have had
a seat for Westminster, while his son, Tom, had one
for Ilchester, and that they should sit together in
Parliament.

In 1812, Sheridan wrote to his son Tom :—
"Another thing that threw cold water on my wishes
as to Stafford, was the Prince's confessed dislike to
my declining to continue to be brought in by him.
This, observe, months before his decision to continue
his present Ministers ; but while he continues them
arrayed against the Catholic claims, they cannot
have a vote in their support from me, and therefore
I ought not to continue to owe my seat to their
master."   This seat, be it noted, was that for
Ilchester which Sheridan had held from 1807 till
1812 and if the words quoted about it be taken in
their natural sense, it follows that the Prince paid for
Sheridan's seat at Ilchester.

At the general election in 1812 he made an
endeavour to be returned again for Stafford ; but he
could not pay the price exacted by the free and
independent burgesses, owing to Whitbread refusing
to advance the money, though a sum equal to three
times the amount was due to Sheridan and in Whitbread's hands, the result being the final severance of

a connexion with the House of Commons which had lasted unbroken through thirty-one years. Before ceasing to be a member of the House, he had withdrawn his confidence from the new leaders of the Whig party.

The bitterness of his disappointment was deepened by previous over-confidence. He knew that a new generation had grown up since he first represented the Borough, while he did not realize that many supporters had felt aggrieved at his leaving Stafford to represent Westminster. He made the further mistake of thinking that, while he sat for Westminster, the Stafford burgesses would gladly be represented in Parliament by his son. Two letters have been preserved which he wrote to Mr. Perkins, one of his chief supporters, and they contain a picture of the feelings which animated him. The one was written before, the other after the election ; the first is dated Cavendish Square, the 29th of November, 1811 : "I have really been so incessantly engaged that it has not been in my power to keep my promise of writing to you by last Monday's post. I have now to say that upon mature consideration and reviewing those accounts I have received of the disposition of your borough, I have decided in my own mind to embrace the present opportunity of declaring again for Stafford.

" I am not only secure of Ilchester for myself, but also of the second seat for my son, yet I pant for my old independent seat, and my own means as well as the assistance I can receive if necessary from another quarter, enable me to meet any opposition. You are a sportsman, and as all lovers of field sports must be more or less friendly to poetry, I may refer you to Goldsmith for my feelings on the present occasion :

> " ' And as a hare whom hounds and horns pursue,
>   Pants to the goal from whence at first she flew,
>   I still have hopes, my long vexations past,
>   There to return and die at home at last.'

Political death, mind, I mean. But even before that I trust that we and the few surviving old friends may yet spend some pleasant days together."   .

Though the second letter has no other date than "Tuesday, June 6," yet it must have been written after that from which I have made a quotation. Sheridan had never forgotten, he writes, the uniform and generous attachment to him of Mr. Perkins, "a remembrance," he adds, "much enhanced by your continuance of it to my son ; your kindness to him has been such, that I know you will feel, almost as some return for it, my informing you that the accounts of him are most favourable and particularly from the personal observation [of] a friend lately arrived from Cadiz. I trust you will receive him and his excellent and lovely wife again at Rickerscote. I hear you are becoming at Stafford all purity and patriotism ; never fancy this attainable or men just. Among the latter class of our friends, I have experienced ' the utmost honour and disinterestedness'; but while poor and working men have votes they will ' keep the borough free.' "[1]

[1] I am indebted to Major Knight, of Camden Place, Stafford, for having procured copies of these letters, and other interesting details for my use, all of them showing how popular a member

He had been proposed for the County of Wexford, at the general election in 1807, by some Irish admirers without solicitation on his part or even communication with him. This incident in his career has been strangely overlooked or suppressed by his biographers.[1]

Mr. John Colclough, who had represented the County of Wexford before, was a candidate again and he joined Sheridan's name to his own as the candidate for the second seat. Colonel Ram and Mr. Alcock were the rival candidates. The tenants of one of Mr. Alcock's supporters declared that they would vote for Mr. Colclough and "the great Sheridan." As Mr. Colclough and Sheridan were the popular candidates, their return appeared to be certain. The partisans of Mr. Alcock were enraged

---

Sheridan had been, and some proving how much he contributed to find, for the staple industry of Stafford, markets abroad which are still retained.

[1] Sir Jonah Barrington, who gives a full account of the Election for Wexford in " Personal Sketches of His Own Times," introduces it with the following comments, at p. 298 of the second volume, on Sheridan's biographers : " These writers have raked up from his ashes, and exposed to public indignation, every failing of that great and gifted man ; so that, if their own productions were by any chance to become permanent, they would send him down to posterity as a witty, but low and dissipated *sharper ;* or, in their very best colouring, as the most talented of mean and worthless mendicants. But Sheridan's reputation will outlive all such attempts to obliterate it ; while the ignorance of his libellers is conspicuous from their entire omission of some of the most interesting events of his career, at the same time that others are vouched for which to my individual knowledge are gross misrepresentations."

at the defection of electors upon whose support they had counted, and they attributed this to undue influence. When told that, if he received the votes which ought to have gone to Mr. Alcock, he would have to fight with him, Mr. Colclough disregarded the warning and was challenged to a duel in which he was shot through the heart. After the lapse of an hour, during which no votes were recorded save for Colonel Ram and Mr. Alcock, the poll was closed, and they were declared to have been duly elected. Mr. Alcock subsequently lost his reason, and died in an asylum for lunatics: his sister had the same miserable fate.

IX.

EYES CLOSED "IN ENDLESS NIGHT."

I ENDED the last chapter with a reference to the attempt, which had a tragic ending, to seat Sheridan in Parliament as the representative of an Irish constituency, a position he would have filled more appropriately than Fox did when representing a Scottish one. While Sheridan's biographers never mention the contest in the County of Wexford where he had been nominated and received many votes, neither have any of them, except Dr. Watkins, devoted a single word to a visit which he paid to Scotland in 1805. It is true that little more can be done than to mention the fact; yet the fact itself deserves record.

His habits changed after his second marriage. Before then he yearly paid a round of visits in his wife's company to the country seats of persons of note and rank when Parliament was not sitting. Afterwards, his favourite relaxation was visiting the abodes of his second wife's relatives near Southampton and in the Isle of Wight, and yachting with them. In one of the notes to his sister-in-law, Mrs. Ogle, addressed by him from West Cowes to her house in Orchard Place, Southampton, he requests her to forward some fruit and also some red mullet, as fish was scarce at Cowes. He complains in many letters written during the later years of his life about difficulty in sleeping. In a note to Mrs. Ogle he says : " You save my life by offering me a quiet bed to-night, for an Inn kills me and I have lately been sleeping in none but quiet rooms." The Marine Hotel at West Cowes did not suit him, and he writes : " I have scarcely closed my eyes since I have been in this infernal noisy hotel."

At the middle of August, 1805, his wife and he were present at an entertainment on a grand scale at Stowe. Though the newspapers were not so well informed then as to the doings and intentions of notable persons as they now are, yet the invention of news was not unknown and a paragraph in *The Caledonian Mercury* announced the arrival of Sheridan at Edinburgh when he was the guest at Stowe of the Marquess of Buckingham. On the 19th of September the same paper correctly stated that " R. B. Sheridan, Esq., M.P., and lady " had arrived at *Oman's Hotel*, in West Register Street, on the 17th of September, being Tuesday, and that " R. B. Sheridan, Esq., M.P. and party," had started for " a tour to the North " on the following Sunday. Another journal, of the same date, *The Edinburgh Evening Courant*, contained the same announcement, slightly varied : " Arrived at *Oman's Hotel* on Monday, Mr. and Mrs. Sheridan, Mr. and Mrs. Ogle, Mr. and Mrs. Scott, etc., etc., from London." In the impression of the *Courant* for the 12th of October, 1805, this paragraph appeared : " Set out yesterday from *Oman's Hotel*, Mr. and Mrs. Sheridan, Mr. and Mrs. Ogle and Mr. and Mrs Scott, etc., for London."

While detailed information is lacking concerning most of the interludes in Sheridan's political career, there is a full supply of particulars connected with his visit to Oxford in 1810 at the request of Lord Grenville, who had been elected Chancellor of the University in succession to the Duke of Portland. The election had been hotly contested. Lord Grenville, Lord Eldon and the Duke of Beaufort were the candidates, the first receiving 406, the second 393 and the third 288 votes.

The new Chancellor put Sheridan's name on the list of those to whom he thought the University ought to grant the honorary and honourable title of D.C.L. He may not have known that, when Burke was nominated for the like degree in 1790, the University had pronounced him unworthy to receive it. Some members, whose names would have been pilloried for all time if they had been disclosed, objected to Sheridan receiving any degree. They were doubtless unaware that by accepting one, he would have conferred, as Burke would have done also, an honour in return. Public feeling in Oxford was aroused; sides were taken and a hand-bill containing the following appeal was circulated: "It is humbly asked of the justice and generosity of members of Convocation whether the public merits of the Right Honourable Richard Brinsley Sheridan do not claim, upon the present occasion, the usual honorary rank and their respect? and whether it be

consistent with the spirit of their honours to withhold them from a man whose talents have through
a long and arduous career eminently adorned, and
whose patriotism has, upon every trying occasion,
stood forward to support the general interests of his
country."

It was not pleasant for Sheridan to visit Oxford
by invitation and, instead of being rewarded for
his services, to be treated with churlishness. He
acted on the trying occasion with a tact and good
feeling which heightened his reputation. His name
was withdrawn at his own request, and the University lost more than he did.

Yet he had a triumph which was alike consolatory
and unexpected. Being invited to attend the ceremony in the Sheldonian theatre, he entered it
before the procession. An eye-witness records that,
"he was at once tumultuously recognized by the
whole assembly. . . . As all other proceedings
would evidently be suspended (the procession not
yet entered, nor Convocation been formally opened)
he was *by acclamation* voted to the Doctor's *seat*,
and conducted thither by the Curators of the theatre,
though without a *Degree*."[1]

No other man than Sheridan has been the re-
cipient of a unique honour both in the House of
Commons and at Oxford. The House adjourned
because deliberation was impossible while the words
from his eloquent tongue were still sounding in the
ears of the members. He was treated at Oxford as
a Doctor of Civil Law after it had been decided that

[1] " Recollections of Oxford," by G. V. Cox, p. 70.

the degree should be withheld from him. Though his enemies in Oxford perceived they had blundered, they were so despicable as to spread the report that he had organized the proceedings in the Sheldonian theatre. It is unfortunate that the letter which Sheridan forwarded to the Vice-Chancellor from New College, before leaving Oxford, was not made public at the time ; it will be read with great interest now :

" Sir, Having been informed by a friend that an attempt has been made to circulate a report that upon my name being withdrawn from the list of those to be proposed for a degree at the Installation, I had expressed myself in terms of most unbecoming disrespect both with regard to the honour in question and those who alone were entitled to confer it, I cannot leave Oxford without so far intruding on your attention as to deposit in your hands my solemn assertion that from me there never proceeded the slightest expression or pretence to give rise to so unjust and false a rumour.

" I came here late on Monday night or rather early on the Tuesday morning entirely unprovided and in my opinion unentitled to partake of the honorary compliment attached to the occasion. Accordingly when I learnt that my name was in the list, but that it was likely to be productive of some degree of contention, I deemed it incumbent on me, without feeling myself entitled in the slightest degree either to be hurt, or to complain of those with whom the objection originated, to write to Lord Grenville before I went to rest in terms I trust far different from those which the report I have alluded to has attributed to me, respectfully to suggest that my name might be withdrawn.

"Your polite attention, Sir, to me on that day followed by a similar conduct from other Colleges entertaining Lord Grenville convinced me that I had judged rightly in avoiding as far as lay in my power any occasion of my name becoming a topic of dispute, or the cause of interruption to the harmony and dignity of a proceeding so essential to the high character of the Convocation.

"With regard to what occurred on the Friday I can only in one word declare to you upon my honour that I was utterly uninformed of any disposition towards the irregularity which took place and that, had it been referred to me, no effort on my part would have been wanting to have prevented it.

"Again apologizing for the liberty I have taken in making this address to you, I have only to add that, with a due regard to your situation and a just esteem for your character and with the most sincere respect for the University, I have the honour to be, your obliged and obedient servant, R. B. Sheridan."

The undergraduates of Oxford were doubtless aware that Sheridan's speeches in Parliament were then as remarkable and fine as those which they may have heard their fathers praise. A speech delivered on the 13th of August, 1807, would have been classed among his best, if an accurate report had appeared in the newspapers. It concerned a motion on the state and condition of Ireland. Grattan did not support him; yet he declared that Sheridan had that night: "reasserted his claim to the due applause of past times and the disinterested admiration of impartial posterity." A report filling five columns appeared in *The British Press* and a copy with the reporter's corrections has been preserved. I shall extract from it some of the more notable passages. After stating that Irishmen were the most useful and hard-working dwellers in London, he asked : " Am I to be told that these are the people whom, on their native soil, you have described as a barbarous, savage and indocile race ? No! this cannot be the case. Shall I then be told that they possess all ill qualities upon their native soil, and that when separated from it they possess every attribute which gains respect ? That cannot be without a miracle."

Having remarked that it was a commonplace to call the occasion the most perilous ever experienced, he said that he was tired of hearing of " the magnanimous Emperor of Russia who appears at this moment to be more proud of being enrolled in Bonaparte's Legion of Honour than of co-operating with this country in rescuing from oppression the fallen nations of Europe. The Emperor Alexander returns back to his country, exulting in his acquired territory; but how acquired? It was by the spoliations of Bonaparte and himself from his sunk and degraded ally the King of Prussia. . . . When I look, Sir, at the map of Europe, I may say, that I now see nothing but France. How different this from the anticipation of the celebrated Mr. Burke, who, at the commencement of the French Revolution, had predicted that France would be but a blank upon the map of Europe ! . . . Look at the conduct of Bonaparte.

See what he has made of France herself : see how he has surrounded her! He has even exceeded the vain boast of Lewis the XIV. He has bounded his territories, not by an iron frontier, but by kingdoms of his own creating. He has fixed the bonds of affection in the breasts of his own heroes, and finds in the gratitude of great minds, a hostage for their fidelity : while he has the fears of others as the pledge of his own security. Sceptres are the palisadoes of his entrenchments, his Martello Towers are thrones : his sentinels are sovereigns. . . .[1]

" Can any man doubt, there remains but one object only to complete the ambition of his heart, and that is the annihilation of the glory and the honour and the independence of our country. . . . Therefore I would press upon gentlemen the necessity and importance of a close union and affection between this country and Ireland. . . . I call upon you, instead of subsidizing the foreign Powers of the Continent, to subsidize Ireland : and what is to be that subsidy ? Nothing but your justice, your confidence and your conciliation, and not to disappoint

[1] The uncorrected version of this passage in Sheridan's published speeches has been rendered nonsensical by the reporter trusting to his imagination instead of his note-book :—" Petty squabbles should not be thought of while Bonaparte is grasping the nations ; while he is surrounding France, not with that iron frontier for which the wish and childish ambition of Lewis XIV. was so eager, but with kingdoms of his own creation, securing the gratitude of higher minds as the hostage, and the fears of others as pledges of his safety. His are no ordinary fortifications. His Martello Towers are thrones ; sceptres tipped with crowns are the palisadoes of his entrenchments, and kings are his sentinels."— " Speeches," vol. iii., p. 535.

those hopes of kind concessions which you have suffered them to indulge; not to break those promises which you made at the Union. . . . I think we shall still have success under Providence, and if not, we shall at least give the historian—if the tyranny of the present or any succeeding ruler of empires should allow the historian to do our memory justice—an opportunity to record of this nation, that we were not merely fighting for our own honour and fame but were animated with this conviction, that to these two little Islands, as to an altar, the freedom of the world had flown for protection; acting with the valorous fury of those defending a violated sanctuary, the liberty of man fell, and we fell with it bravely."

Towards the end of the year 1810, the question of appointing a Regent during the King's incapacity occupied the mind of Parliament. Sheridan was the notable survivor of the statesmen who had dealt with the problem in 1788 and he could speak and act with an authority derived from experience, and with an ability all his own. Precedents were followed and the Prince of Wales was appointed Prince Regent subject to certain restrictions for a year. As his father did not recover, he continued to act as Regent till his father's death. It was thought that the Prince Regent would call the Whigs to his councils and Sheridan was blamed because Spencer Perceval and his Tory colleagues remained in office at the Prince's request. If a change had been made, Sheridan would have been a member of the Ministry. The truth is that the influence of Sheridan was as much exaggerated as the Prince's good faith. The Prince had cajoled the Whig leaders into thinking him their friend; but he did not help them to form an Administration because he thought himself better served by their opponents, with whom he was, moreover, in entire sympathy. Mr. Tierney, who had become conspicuous among the Whigs and was regarded by many as the successor of Fox, had no illusion concerning the action of the Prince Regent and had predicted what did happen, as any man could have done in the circumstances. It is true that the Prince suggested a coalition between Lord Grey and Grenville and Perceval and his followers, feeling confident that nothing would come of it. The official Whigs, who were hungry for office, blamed Sheridan for their having been ostracised. He could not have served them. Why should he have done so? They had seldom treated him with ordinary courtesy and he rightly objected to acting the part of "Whipping boy," which Buchanan thought it no shame to fill for King James the Sixth of Scotland and First of England.[1]

Writing to his second wife, Sheridan laid bare his

[1] The facts are most clearly set forth in the "Memoirs" of Plumer Ward, vol. i., p. 418. The statements in Moore's "Memoirs" of Sheridan are quite untrustworthy. He admits in his *Diary* that he dared not say anything unpleasant to his Whig friends, and the Whigs preserved the tradition for many years that, if it had not been for Sheridan, they would have been called to office in 1812. Moore wrote that, "in helping to disband his party, Sheridan had cashiered himself." Charles Brinsley, the son of Sheridan by his second marriage, makes this marginal note on his copy of Moore's "Memoirs" of his father: "The coalition of Grenville and Grey was no longer 'his party,' but Whiggism corrupted."

inmost thoughts on a political episode of which he has been made the scape-goat : "As to politics nothing can be worse. I am doing and shall do nothing but what is honest and disinterested. At the same time it is a mortifying situation to endeavour to promote the views of persons who have treated me as they have done, and are entitled to no service from me [and] to find them returning from their confidential meeting with Tierney, Whitbread, etc., and confidently expecting every co-operation and common cause from me. But no matter. I act as in my conscience I think is best both for the Prince and the country." In a letter to his son Tom, written in 1812, he says that his object for several years had been that which his son had told him was the one at which he should aim ; and he quoted his son's words :—"What a situation would yours be could you now stand between the Prince and the people, possessing the confidence of both." This represented Sheridan's ideal, one which was creditable to him and utterly impracticable.

One of these letters ends with the words : "since writing the above Perceval is confirmed" [as Premier]. Again, he says : "Pray, pray never suspect or decry the Prince. He is acting as honourably as man can do and gives me his entire and unqualified confidence. . . . I wrote his answer to Perceval's communication. I must feel a little proud to see the turn my *friends'* opinions have taken on my conduct." In another letter he tells her :—"I must dine at Carlton House to settle a paper for the Prince, not a political one you may be sure for never will I have anything to do with double advice. Pray copy the Prince's reply to Perceval and Perceval's answer," he added, " Perceval's reply is mean and miserable." Again : " The rascally Minister [Perceval] tried to put an infamous speech in the Prince's mouth to the City Address. He should turn them out rather than speak it." Readers of the foregoing extracts will not think that Sheridan entertained any personal desire for Perceval continuing Prime Minister ; and they will probably consider it obvious that Perceval was continued in office by the Prince Regent, not on account of Sheridan's machinations, but because the Prince preferred a Tory to a Whig Cabinet. In a debate on the 11th of June, 1812, in which the subject was dealt with, Mr. Matthew Montague thus pointed the moral of the whole matter : " Confidential friends of hereditary princes who encouraged and supported them in opposition to their sovereign, were uniformly discarded when these princes came into power."[1]

Once in his career, Sheridan had to defend in the House of Commons the theatrical property for which he had paid dearly. This was in the spring of 1811, when a Bill was introduced for establishing another theatre, and he based his opposition to it on the ground that the proprietors of Drury Lane ought to be authorized to build one, if another were required. He carried the House with him and he received many flattering compliments during the debate. Mr. Peter Moore, the Chairman of a Committee to examine into the affairs of Drury Lane Theatre,

[1] Parliamentary Debates, vol. xxiii., p. 406.

which had been the subject of a special Act, avowed that the several claimants had acted with great consideration, and he added : " Nor had his Rt. Hon. friend [Mr. Sheridan] been behind them in liberality and an anxious expression to devote his private to the general interests. As in his whole political and private life, so he had on this occasion evinced the utmost disinterestedness, and in giving up his own rights, had proceeded till the Committee thought it necessary to put a stop to it : all that he had ever said was, ' Do all you can for the sufferers.' " General Tarleton, who seconded an amendment for postponing the Bill, " appealed to the feelings of the House, and called on them to consider the immortal works of Mr. Sheridan and the stoical philosophy with which in that House he had witnessed the destruction of his property. Surely some indulgence was due to such merit." Mr. Morris said " they should recollect how much the Drama was indebted to him whose interest was concerned in the present motion." Sheridan informed the House how the question at issue had been argued by him before the Privy Council, and that he had obtained a decision in his favour, while he deprecated upsetting that decision by legislation. A majority of 57 gave him a complete victory.[1]

The only account which I have met with of his appearance before the Privy Council is that in a letter to his second wife :—" I have but one moment to tell you in one word the good news that the Council have unanimously decided in our favour on

[1] Parliamentary Debates, vol. xix., pp. 1142-1145.

the patent right question, and now I shall get my affairs right, and you shall never know a plague again; otherwise irretrievable ruin must have been the consequence to me and poor Tom and his family. It was going against us till I spoke on Monday, and is decided entirely on the ground I put the question on. I spoke for nearly two hours."

He thus wrote to her relating to the theatre when no longer a member of Parliament :—" I have been arranging and winding up all my affairs and accounts as if it were certain I could not outlive the next three months. . . . My settlement with the theatre is an *arduous* and *complicated* business; it requires reference to many written documents exchanged through the course of three years, my share of which, though I have not lost or destroyed them, gives me no small labour to search for and produce. Then come discussions and communications with individuals of the Committee, who mean me well, and who are no longer disposed to bow implicitly to the nod of Kehama."[1]

By Kehama, in the foregoing extract, Sheridan meant Whitbread. It was at Sheridan's request that Whitbread undertook to preside over the Committee appointed by Act of Parliament to regulate the affairs and provide for the re-building of Drury Lane Theatre. It has been alleged that Sheridan considered his exclusion from that Committee a slur and a disgrace. The following letter proves the

[1] Southey's "Curse of Kehama" appeared in 1810. The above reference implies that Sheridan was acquainted with the book.

statement to be one of the many fictions current about him :—" The first general meeting of our theatre grand corporation is on the 4th of October, and every exertion of my mind and every hour of my time must be employed to meet that occasion. Oh! how I long to be fairly and honourably freed from all connexion with this to me disagreeable property! Yet in the new hands in which it will be placed it will be their own fault if it does not prosper."

The settlement which Sheridan desired was postponed longer than he had expected. A sum of £28,000 was admitted to be due to him, but he sought in vain for payment. He had undertaken to discharge debts which he had not incurred, yet for which he rashly made himself responsible, and rather than contest the claim of anyone styling himself a creditor he undertook to pay the sum demanded. He wrote: "A final theatrical settlement by arbitration with Whitbread is one of the important things that ties me by the leg. . . . If I am fairly dealt with the difference will be very many thousand pounds to me, and looking to my grandchicks I am bound not to allow myself to be fooled if I can help it." Again, he assured his wife, "that in most of the great cases in which I have suffered by eagerness of anticipation the cause has been more infinitely in the roguery and insincerity of others than in my own credulity and indolence."

The natural result of pressure from his creditors on the one hand, and the withholding of the sum due to him on the other, was his arrest for debt in August, 1813. He was conducted to a sponging-house in Tooke's Court, Cursitor Street, where, since the abolition of imprisonment for debt, printing offices have taken the places of sponging-houses, wherein compositors convert manuscripts which cannot be read with ease into printed pages which may be read with pleasure. In bygone and less civilized days, a sponging-house was the Purgatory from which debtors either returned to the Heaven of their homes or were transported to the Hell of the Fleet prison. The inmate of a sponging-house had to pay heavily for the privilege of being detained in it. Wraxall records that a young friend of his was one of Sheridan's companions in adversity, and that another was Sir Watkin Lewis, who had been a man of substance and Lord Mayor of London. Sheridan's detention was soon cut short by Whitbread paying, out of funds belonging to Sheridan, the amount for which he had been arrested.

Though Whitbread was highly respected, he was a very hard man in business matters. His philanthropy was directed to bettering the condition of the agricultural poor. His theories excited greater surprise in 1796 than they would do in 1896, one of them being that a *minimum*, or living wage, should be fixed by Act of Parliament. His speeches were listened to because he had the reputation of being a thoroughly practical man. Country gentlemen have as much respect for a man conversant with the details of business as they have for their family solicitors. Moore thought that Whitbread's reputation was fully merited ; but Charles Brinsley, the second son of Sheridan, differed from this opinion and wrote as follows to Moore on the 6th of October, 1826 : " Whitbread's disposition to details and my father's to generalities, I think just the difference between the mind of a store-keeper and of a statesman ; but then I think my father *had* great talents for business and that his *pre-eminent* quality was his sagacity; what he wanted was self-denial; the power of overcoming the inclination of the moment."

As Chairman of the Committee for settling the affairs of Drury Lane Theatre, Whitbread retained large sums which were due to Sheridan and did so on the ground that William Taylor of the Opera House had made a claim for a still larger amount ; the truth being that the claim was baseless. A physical reason for Whitbread's eccentric conduct was discovered after his untimely death by his own hand, on the 6th of July, 1815, when he was in his fifty-fifth year. Sheridan sent the following particulars to his son Charles about " the deplorable death of our poor friend " :—" I only add a line to mention a circumstance in which the family and friends find a melancholy consolation. On the head being opened by Cline, part of the skull and brain were found in such a state that it is impossible he could have kept his senses, or indeed have retained a painful existence but for a very short time. I know, my dear boy, you will regret him feelingly."

The last years of Sheridan's life were filled with bitterness. His wife suffered anguish from an internal cancer for which there was no cure. His elder son was dying of consumption. He himself was afflicted with a painful and weakening malady of which his friends knew nothing, and about which he had written to his son Tom shortly before his departure for the Cape in the autumn of 1813 :—" I continue very unwell and the progressive bad state of my varicose veins, my secret alarming complaint, preys on my hopes and spirits, for I never will have to do with any operation."   In these later years he kept apart from his friends and nursed his grief alone in London, his wife preferring to live in the country.   He was in daily expectation of effecting an arrangement whereby his creditors would be satisfied, and the load on his mind might be lightened. Yet he was wasting his strength in trying to accomplish impossibilities.   His creditors demanded cash, while the sums due to him were paid in shares.

His health finally broke down under the struggle to free himself from liabilities.   He had long been a victim to insomnia, yet his appetite had continued good ; now, however, he could neither eat nor sleep ; an abscess formed in his throat, and his life slowly ebbed away.   The last notice of his appearing out of doors is from the pen of John Taylor, who saw him walking along Oxford Street, "leaning on his servant's arm."   Mr. Taylor took the servant's place and supported him, as they walked together, to the top of Bond Street.[1]

There is neither peace nor mercy for the dying lion after the wolves and vultures have marked him for their prey.   As soon as Sheridan's illness became known, his creditors redoubled their efforts

[1] "Records of my Life," vol. ii., p. 177.

Drawn & Engraved by Geo. Clint 1816

THE LAST PORTRAIT EXTANT OF SHERIDAN.

Vol. ii. To face p. 280.

to compel him to satisfy them at once.   A sheriff's officer, named Thomas Hurst, succeeded in entering 17, Savile Row, where he lived, and serving a writ upon him.   In accordance with the barbarous laws which were in force in his day, and are now but records of an unenlightened past, he might have been carried from his death-bed to a prison.   However, Hurst proved amenable to the remonstrances of Dr. Bain and, by electing to remain in the house, he hindered others of his fraternity obtaining admission on a like errand.

If time had been accorded, Sheridan could have discharged all his liabilities; it was wrongly inferred that, because he could not do so at a moment's notice, he was in destitution.   An appeal to help him was made by Denis O'Brien in the columns of *The Morning Post*, and many offers of money were made in consequence.

Michael Kelly, whose acquaintance with him was of many years' standing and whose admiration for him was great, read with astonishment and vexation what he styles the groundless reports about Sheridan which had been fabricated to produce a sensation. He learned from Sheridan's man-servant that his master was in want of nothing that his condition required, yet this knowledge does not detract from the kindness of the offer to supply anything that was necessary on the condition that his name was not mentioned.[1]

Professor Smyth journeyed from the country to

---

[1] " Reminiscences " of Michael Kelly, vol. ii., p. 343.

visit the sick man, to whom he was under more obligations than he cared to acknowledge. Smyth did admit, however, the great consideration with which he had been treated.[1] He learned from one of the old servants that Sheridan was believed to be on his death-bed. He saw "strange-looking people in the hall." He took up a piece of paper which, as he thought, had been "thrown [on the table] carelessly and neglected," and he found that it was a prescription from Sir Henry Halford for a strong cordial. Mrs. Sheridan admitted him into her room and she took a message from him to her husband, and he replied that he would get ready to see him, but afterwards sent another to say that he " was not equal to the interview." Smyth declined the refreshments which were offered, and when he called again Sheridan was worse.

Among the callers at 17, Savile Row, who were admitted to Sheridan's bedside were Lord Holland, Moore, Rogers, and Howley, the Bishop of London. None of them saw anything more worthy of note than what Smyth has recorded. In the number of *The Quarterly* for March, 1826, a review of Moore's " Memoirs " of Sheridan contained particulars about Sheridan's last days which were put forward as authentic and in correction of the story which Moore had told. These particulars had been obtained by

---

[1] " Through the remainder of his life, Sheridan was never wanting to me in expressions of kindness whenever he met me. In 1806 when the Whigs came in, he desired me to let him know if he could be of any assistance to me or my family."—" Memoir of Mr. Sheridan," p. 66.

Croker from George the Fourth. They were re-printed in full ten years ago.[1] If proceeding from any other authority, they might have commanded attention and wrought still more mischief. Croker was accustomed to talk about his "royal friend, George the Fourth."[2] He was professedly ignorant of things which were familiar to schoolboys, such as that Rigby in Coningsby was the counterpart of himself. Yet he was probably the only living man who did not know that the worst enemies of George the Fourth had never charged him with speaking the truth.[3]

I hesitate to affirm that Croker communicated for publication during his lifetime, and left for publication after his death, statements about Sheridan which he knew to be lampoons. He may not have been so bad and ignorant as Macaulay supposed, neither was he, perhaps, a universal genius. His opinion of himself may have been as inaccurate as that of his critics. Yet he can be acquitted of acting vilely and

---

[1] "The Croker Papers," edited by Louis J. Jennings, vol. i., pp. 288-312.

[2] "Mr. Croker singularly entertaining and disagreeable; a handsome, disingenuous face, eyes catering all round for hearers to his tongue . . . Mr. Croker began to talk about 'his royal friend George IV.' Mr. Lockhart growled emphatically, 'Ah! the old story.'" June 5th, 1846.—"Memoirs" of Lady Eastlake, vol. i., p. 165.

[3] In an interview with Lady Spencer, the Prince Regent observed: "You know I don't speak the truth, and my brothers don't, and I find it a great defect, from which I would have my daughter free. We have always been brought up badly; the Queen having taught us to equivocate."—"Memoirs" of Lord Melbourne, vol. i., p. 157.

cowardly towards Sheridan on the sole ground that he acted in impervious, if not wilful ignorance. His credulity cannot be matched, if he honestly believed the King's story to be trustworthy.

The substance of what Croker narrated on the King's authority and of which he could easily have ascertained the falsity was that, when he heard of Sheridan's illness, he commissioned Mr. Taylor Vaughan to call and present him with £200 as an instalment out of £500 for the relief of his necessities, that Vaughan did call, that he found Sheridan lying on a truckle bed in an attic, neglected by everybody, his wife included, and that he expended £140 in procuring ordinary comforts for him.

The tale is replete with loathsome particulars and it is wholly untrue. Vaughan did see Dr. Bain at his own house, told him that he was commissioned to hand over a sum for the relief of his patient, and, on being informed that money was neither required nor would be accepted, he carried back the sum with which he was entrusted, never having set his foot in Sheridan's house.

The malicious and false narrative concerning Sheridan was dictated to Croker by the King on the 26th of November, 1825, nearly ten years after Sheridan's death. Immediately after the funeral, he had received Peter Moore, member for Coventry, in audience for the purpose of learning the circumstances of Sheridan's last days on earth. He listened to the account with a feeling for which Peter Moore had not given him credit, and remarked at its close : " Sheridan was a great man, but in the simplicity of his nature he never knew his own greatness. His heart was too much enlarged to be governed by his head. He had an abounding confidence in every man ; and although his pen indicated a knowledge of human nature, yet that knowledge was confined to his pen alone, for in all his acts he rendered himself the dupe of the fool and designing knave. . . . He was a proud man, sir, a very proud man, with certain conscientious scruples always operating against his own interests. He was a firm and sound adviser ; but he was so systematically jealous of his own honour, that he was always willing to grant what he was not willing to accept in return—favours, which might be interpreted as affecting his own independence."[1]

If the Prince Regent had been as other men he would have mourned bitterly when informed on the afternoon of Sunday, the 7th of July, 1816, that the truest of his friends, and the most illustrious member of his Household had joined the great society of the noble dead.[2] I should have refrained from saying or quoting anything about the passing away of the greatest orator and dramatist of his age, if the actual facts had been generally known. An accident, which really deserves to be styled happy, has enabled me to set forth the truth for the first time, and those who peruse the documents which I am about to print

---

[1] "Sheridan and his Times," vol. ii., pp. 316, 317.

[2]   "There is
One great society alone on earth,
The noble living, and the noble dead."
                              The Prelude.

will be the harshest critics of that which Croker caused to be circulated and scandal-mongers have retailed with gusto.

I have already said that, not many years before Sheridan's death his son Tom was appointed to the lucrative office of Colonial Treasurer at the Cape of Good Hope, and that he went thither with his wife and children in the expectation of finding a cure for his diseased lungs and of being able to educate his family. His half-brother wrote to him shortly after their father's death and this letter, which was brought back to England and has been preserved among the Sheridan papers as a precious relic, is now made public for the first time. It is as well, perhaps, for Croker's peace of mind, that he has not lived to read it. The letter was written from Fulham Palace on the 16th of July, 1816; Mrs. Sheridan and her son having taken up their abode there at the invitation of the Bishop of London : " Before you open this you will have learned the melancholy tidings, which it was to have conveyed, from others. The particulars which I must add, though melancholy, must be consolatory. You will be soothed by learning that our father's death was unaccompanied by suffering, that he almost slumbered into death, and that the reports which you may have seen in the newspapers of the privations and the want of comforts which he endured are unfounded ; that he had every attention and comfort which could make a death-bed easy.

" From the first moment when my father grew worse, his recovery was hopeless. The physicians, however (Bailie and Bain), said that letting him know the full extent of his danger might by the shock and depression of spirits it would occasion preclude the *possibility* of his recovery. It was therefore delayed as long as possible ; apparently the first certainty he received that he could not live was the Bishop of London reading prayers to him. This was when he was no longer able to speak, but he joined in them with the most animated expression of his countenance and clasping of his hands ; and the Bishop said he never saw a more fervent and unaffected expression of piety.[1]

" There was not the least struggle or suffering, at the moment of decease ; it was even impossible to perceive from the countenance when it took place ; the eyes had to the last a most beautiful and touching expression, a sort of subdued and softened

---

[1] It was not customary in Sheridan's day for statesmen to parade their religious opinions. The following passage from a letter which he wrote in 1786 to Mrs. Stratford Canning when on a tour in the West of England with his wife, his sister-in-law and Tickell, discloses his feelings concerning the Church : " The others have led a most ungodly life—never once have they been in the inside of a church, nor permitted me, though I often got up early in the morning on purpose. However I took my opportunities, when I could steal a few minutes to myself, to express my gratitude to the Maker of all the woods, hills and lakes which they admired as heathens would. The church at Axminster is a very good building, as is that of Bridport, but I found the greatest comfort in the new chapel at Totness, where I heard a very fine discourse from a young man who is curate with a large family and only £40 per annum, so unequal are the distributions of church emolument in this country, which is a reproach to Christianity, and has often led me to reflect how—— I beg pardon, I must break off as I hear the last bell tolling for the Garrison prayers [at Plymouth] which I mean to partake of before we set off."

brightness. You will be gratified by seeing the public feeling of respect and admiration which has been called forth ; I will not enter into any details, for the papers of the day will give you a much more lively idea of it.

" My mother has of course been thrown back[1] dreadfully by the affliction and fatigue which she has gone through. She attended my father to the last,[2] though ordered not to move from a sofa ; while the painful scene lasted, the anxiety of her mind gave her, in spite of the pain she was in, a degree of strength which, in her state, astonished me ; but as soon as it was over she completely sunk under it. She is at present here at the Bishop of London's, Fulham, and recovering a little.

" I hardly know whether you have reason to regret not having been in England, except on account of the pleasure which your presence might have given your father, though latterly he seemed to take very little notice of those around him. You have been spared a most agonizing scene, that of seeing death gradually and inevitably creeping on a person you love, knowing the certainty of it, and compelled to avoid betraying it to that person, to assume cheerfulness, and all this lasting for weeks. I wish I could put time forward ; our anguish is past and has

---

[1] She did not long survive her husband, dying on the 27th of October, 1817, at the age of 41.

[2] George the Fourth audaciously said, as chronicled by Croker : "It is stated in Mr. Moore's book that Mrs. Sheridan attended her husband in his last illness. It is not true; she was too ill to leave her own bed."—"Croker Papers," vol. i., p. 311.

left only a feeling of melancholy and regret and I feel while writing that a month or two hence you will suffer all the sorrow we have gone through ; that you have it all to come. I have only one consolation to offer you, that the event could not in the nature of things have been protracted much longer, and that it could not have happened in a manner less painful or more honourable. This, however, did not comfort me in the first moments, and I am afraid it will not you ; but you will find it a consolation after-wards.

" In looking over my father's papers which lay in his bedroom, I found a letter from me to you which I thought had been sent, but it seems never was ; I will now send it with this ; not from thinking it worth reading at this distance of time, but to show you that I never neglected writing ; I cannot help thinking some other of my letters have missed you, which I am very sorry for as it has deprived me of your answers. My mother sends her kindest love to you and Caroline, to which I beg you will add mine and believe me, your affectionate brother C. B. Sheridan."

Another letter adds to our knowledge of the facts and must increase the contempt, if that be possible, for the purveyors of foul fiction about Sheridan's last days upon earth. The writer, Mrs. Parkhurst, was acquainted with Sheridan and his elder sister, Mrs. Lefanu, to whom the letter was addressed, and it has been preserved among the Lefanu papers which I have been allowed to examine and from which I have already given extracts. It is dated the 22nd of July: "I know all letters of consolation in the first hours of sorrow are ill-judged. The time is too sacred for even the intrusion of friendship. Your loss is great, and England has lost the last of that brilliant constellation of men that adorned her Senate in my youth. Mr. Sheridan wanted neither medical aid, the attention of true affection, the consolations of piety or the exertions of friendship. He had three of the first physicians of London [Sir Henry Halford, Dr. Bailie and Dr. Bain ?]; every day, his wife, his son and his brother-in-law were constantly with him, the Bishop of London saw him many times, and [Lord] Lauderdale did all he could for the regulation of his affairs.

"May I say to you, that he was fixed in a country you never intended to visit, that he is gone where you and all of us must follow him, that he is no longer before hard mortal judges who could only know his actions; he is before the God who created him, who knows the strong temptation of his nature, who will make account of when he resisted as well as when he yielded; he has taken with him a thousand charitable actions, a heart in which there was *no hard part*, a spirit free from envy or malice, and he is gone in the undiminished brightness of his talent, gone before pity had withered admiration. These thoughts have presented themselves to me when I intended simply to have stated such facts of his illness as distance might prevent your knowing. Excuse them from a person who sincerely admired your brother and who is in truth sorry for your sorrow."

LETTER FROM THE DUKE OF WELLINGTON REGARDING
SHERIDAN'S FUNERAL.

Vol. ii.   To face p. 291.

A letter of condolence to Tom Sheridan at the Cape of Good Hope was sent by the Duke of York and Albany from Brighthelmstone, on August 20th: "You will long ere this reaches you have received the account of your poor father's death. His sufferings were long and so severe at the same time that for two months there was no possible chance of his recovery; it was therefore a mercy that he was released. It is impossible, however, for those who, like myself, have the advantage of knowing him and were fully acquainted with his many amiable and pleasant qualities but to regret sincerely his loss. . . . Adieu and believe me ever with the greatest regard, dear Tom, yours most sincerely, Frederick."

No message of sympathy was sent by the Prince Regent to the widow or sons of the most faithful of his servants, to whom he wrote in 1804 of the "sincere friendship I had always professed and felt for you through a long series of years." Moreover, a few years before his death, Sheridan stated in the House of Commons, and it is possible that Croker was among the members present: "the protecting friendship with which his Royal Highness had condescended to honour him for so many years, formed the just pride of his life."[1]

"That man of men, the Prince of Waterloo," neither made empty professions of friendship, nor bore false witness against any one to whom he had been indebted for honest service. Having received an invitation through Lord Lauderdale to attend

[1] *Parliamentary Debates*, vol. xviii., p. 825.

Sheridan's funeral, the Duke of Wellington replied from Cheltenham on the 11th of July: "I received your letter of the 9th and although I go to Town to-morrow I am afraid I cannot attend poor Sheridan's funeral, as I leave Town early on Saturday morning.

"Instruct me as soon as possible respecting the state of Sheridan's affairs in order that I may apply without loss of time for his family, and I only beg that nothing may be done from any other quarter till I shall have tried what I can do. Ever yours most faithfully, Wellington."

The Marquess Wellesley had also been invited to the funeral of him with whom he had battled in Parliament and by whom his conduct in India had been severely criticized. Yet the terms in which he wrote from Ramsgate, on the 16th of July, to Sheridan's son, do as much honour to himself as to the object of his praise: "I have the honour to acknowledge the receipt of your invitation to your father's funeral; and to return you my thanks for that mark of kindness and distinction. Lord Lauderdale has apprised Mrs. Sheridan of the circumstances which have prevented my attendance: I will only add my sincere regret, that my unavoidable absence from London has deprived me of the opportunity of assisting you in discharging the last duties of affection and honour towards a character which I shall always remember with grateful admiration. Believe me to be, Sir, your faithful servant, Wellesley."

The great Duke laboured under a misappre-

**LETTER FROM THE MARQUESS OF WELLESLEY REGARDING
SHERIDAN'S FUNERAL.**

hension which was general at the time and has been fostered by those who, if they had chosen, could have ascertained the truth. Sheridan's affairs were involved at his death; yet his debts were a little over five thousand pounds and they were all liquidated by his family. William Pitt had received £8,000 annually from the public purse during twenty years; he never married, neither had he a large family to support, like that zealous churchman, Lord Chancellor Thurlow, who was a bachelor also; his purse was not emptied, as Fox's was, at the gaming-table and on the turf; he had none of the liking of his friend the Duke of Rutland for buying expensive works of art, neither did he collect rare books, like Thomas Grenville; his charities were not on the scale of Burke's, neither did he take Sheridan's delight in paying the debts of others and entertaining his friends at costly banquets, yet, when he died, his debts amounted to £40,000, and the nation paid them. Sheridan's widow did not require pecuniary help[1]; both she and her son were amply provided for, and her son lived in comfort till his death in 1843, upon the provision which his father had made for him. Sheridan's son by his first marriage was in the annual receipt of £1,200 as Treasurer at the Cape, a salary sufficient for the

[1] Mrs. Sheridan requested the Duke to apply for some office for a connexion of her own, and she received this reply in a letter from Paris on the 27th of February, 1817: "Lord Castlereagh desired me in consequence of my application to him to offer Mr. H. Scott the Consulship of Bahia; and I am certain that he was induced to make the offer not less by respect for Sheridan's memory than by my application."

support of himself and his family. It is true that Sheridan was baulked in leaving to his "grand-chicks," as he fondly termed them, the sum which he desired; but for this he is not blameworthy.

Sir Thomas Browne remarks in his *Hydriotaphia* that " Ulysses in *Hecuba* cared not how meanly he lived so he might find a noble tomb after death." Sheridan's ambition was to be laid in Westminster Abbey; but it was not wholly gratified, as he desired to sleep in death near Fox and Pitt, instead of the poets among whom he reposes.[1] His funeral was on a grand scale. His wife, and his friends, Peter Moore and the Earl of Lauderdale, had issued invitations to which the response was general. Sir Samuel Romilly has recorded his astonishment at seeing Royal Dukes and the flower of the peerage at a funeral which he expected to be " very private."[2] If Sheridan's own wishes had prevailed there would not have been a pompous funeral array. He wrote to his second wife, after returning with his son Tom from the funeral of Mrs. Ward, whose maiden name was Jane Linley, that the simplicity and quietude of the ceremony had pleasingly impressed him by comparison with what occurred at the burial of her sister in Wells

[1] Lord Thanet informed Moore " that Sheridan, at no part of his life, liked any allusion to his being a dramatic writer, and that if he could have spoken out when they were burying him, he would have protested loudly against the place where they laid him, as Poets' Corner was his aversion; he would have liked to be placed near Fox."—*Diary* of Moore, vol. iii., p. 233.

[2] " Memoirs " of Sir Samuel Romilly, vol. iii., pp. 261, 262.

Cathedral, adding, "and so shall be my own passage to the grave."

The procession started from Peter Moore's house in Great George Street, Westminster, and its length was so great that the bier had been carried into the Abbey before all the mourners had moved from the starting point.[1]   An eye-witness records that "the whole line of the procession was densely crowded with spectators, preserving the greatest order and decorum, and to all appearance deeply impressed with the solemnity of the ceremony.   Blessings were poured out on the coffin as it passed and half-

---

[1] It is difficult to determine which statement in "Sheridania" is the falsest and most ridiculous, yet the one on page 245, to the effect that the funeral procession was stopped while a bailiff had the coffin lid removed, arrested the deceased for debt and ha to be paid £500 before the mourners could move on is, perhaps, the one deserving pre-eminence in folly.   Lord Chief Justic Ellenborough affirmed in 1804 that the arrest of a dead body for debt was not only shocking to the feelings, "but absolutely illegal." Yet the concocter of this absurd fiction was of opinion that the remains of Sheridan were intact when he was carried to the grave. As in other cases, so in this : one story of Sheridan is contradicted by another, equally absurd.   Mr. Stratford Canning is said to have been struck with a skull "in Delville's shop in the Strand . . . and he exclaimed, 'Surely that is Sheridan's!' and it was." ("The Life" of Stratford Canning by Stanley Lane-Poole, vol. i., p. 14.)   Dr. Watkins deserves credit for having written sensibly and truthfully on this subject: "Some stupid accounts have strangely ascribed the removal [of the body from Savile Row to Great George Street] to the fear of Mr. Sheridan's friends that the corpse would be arrested in its progress to the grave ; an idea that never occurred to any imagination except that of the ignorant fabricator of the report."—"Memoirs" of Sheridan, vol. ii., p. 530.

suppressed tears and lamentations of the many testified to his worth. The good-natured man had passed away from among the living; but his charities, which had been administered with unsparing hand until he himself had been reduced to need, stood now confessed, attested to by tears."[1]

His death was sincerely mourned by all who were conversant with his career and aspirations, and were conscious of his extraordinary merits. Ribald party hacks acted after their kind. Michael Kelly confesses that the newspaper reports concerning Sheridan were malicious and groundless, "and fabricated for the most atrocious purposes of party scandal."[2] The outrages which are committed in the name of a political party often equal, and sometimes surpass in malignity, in hypocrisy, and unimpeachable vileness, the most ignoble and unpardonable crimes for which the holy name of Liberty has been invoked and profaned. Lies attract and gratify the multitude, as carrion does flies and vultures. Like noxious weeds which flourish in any soil and defy the efforts of the most vigorous exterminator, the cruel and baseless calumnies of which Sheridan was the victim have survived and been cherished by the enemies of whatever in his character is noble and true. The trail of the dull and rancorous bookmaker is over his memory.

I have narrated the facts of his life. I join in spirit with those who, when he was carried to his

[1] "Sheridan and his Times," vol. ii., p. 314.
[2] "Reminiscences," vol. ii., p. 342.

last home, bowed their heads under the weight of a great sorrow, and sincerely mourned the loss of the finest and most refined spirit of his age. Before summing up his character as a whole, I must criticize him as a dramatist and an orator. Meanwhile, I shall represent the general impression which prevailed among those who were neither fraught with unextinguishable prejudice against him, nor misled by unreasoning friendship, by quoting the following passage from an article in *The Times* which appeared on the morning after Sheridan's death :—" It extends our charity, and abates our pride, to reflect with calmness on the fate of one who was equally the delight of society, and the grace of literature—whom it has been the fashion for many years to quote as a bold reprover of the selfish spirit of party ; and throughout a period fruitful of able men and trying circumstances, as the most popular specimen in the British Senate of political consistency, intrepidity and honour."

X.

CHARACTERISTICS AS A DRAMATIST.

No plays which delighted the public when represented for the first time in 1775, 1777, and 1779 are now better worth seeing on the stage or reading at home than *The Rivals*, *The School for Scandal* and *The Critic*. Since he who wrote for all time went to his last home two centuries before Sheridan, no comedies have equalled Sheridan's in freshness, point and inimitable finish, in qualities which defy successful imitation, and in being permeated with the divine and impalpable essence which defies decay.

The distinguishing marks of Sheridan as a playwright are many, rare and wonderful, yet his powers are most conspicuous and telling within a narrow circle, and his limitations are as indisputable as his talent. If genius be unconscious and imponderable force manifesting itself in unusual forms and at unlooked-for times, and if talent be conscious capacity developing and disciplining itself in regular order in accordance with set rules, carefully adapting means to ends and never producing a result wholly novel and unforeseen, then Sheridan must be classed among the men of supreme talent who are often and may easily be mistaken for men of genius. Among

Sheridan's contemporaries, the only one who could be matched with him was Oliver Goldsmith, and in the case of Goldsmith, as of his own, the partition between talent and genius was very thin and not discernible at a glance.

Critics of Sheridan who unsparingly denounced his political views and action, have displayed an admiration for him as a dramatist which is almost sublime. At the time of the publication of Moore's " Memoirs " of him, *Blackwood's Magazine* was, as it continues to be, the friendly rival of *The Quarterly* in literature and politics. Since then, both the lively *Magazine* and the staid *Review* have renounced, in common with the organs of their political opponents, the mistaken policy of importing party considerations into the literary domain.

When *Blackwood* dealt with Sheridan's career and character in February, 1826, the judgment passed upon both was unfavourable in the extreme, yet his success as a playwright received hearty and judicious praise. The reviewer said there can be but one opinion of Sheridan as a dramatist : " He stands at the head of all Comedy since Shakespeare. . . . *The Rivals* will live as long as the language. . . . *The School for Scandal* stands at the head of our ' Comedies of Manners.' Its wit, the more admirable, not from its remoteness, but from its obviousness, its strong distinctness of character, and its plain' progress of story, leave it without a rival."[1] Lockhart wrote as sensibly and

[1] *Blackwood's Magazine* for February, 1826, pp. 121, 123, 128. Professor Wilson, better known as Christopher North, whose

fairly in *The Quarterly* and said that the dramas of
Sheridan "have placed him at the head of the
genteel comedy of England ; and while truth of
character and manners, chastised brilliancy of wit,
humour devoid of the least stain of coarseness,
exquisite knowledge of stage-effect and consummate
ease and elegance of idiomatic language are appre-
ciated, there can be no doubt that his name will
maintain its place."[1]

It is gratifying to record sayings like these, which
are as intelligent as they are emphatic and flattering.
Yet certain qualifications must be made by the critic
who passes an unbiased judgment on Sheridan's
comedies.   What Byron happily termed "the death-
less wit which knew not what it was to intermit,"
forms their drawback, when considered as works of art.

---

papers styled *Noctes Ambrosianæ* were greatly relished by the readers
of *Blackwood* when they appeared, expressed in January, 1828, a
different opinion of Sheridan from that written in 1826 :—

"SHEPHERD : I canna thole to hear sic a sot as Sherry aye
classed wi' Pitt and Burke."

"TICKLER. Nor I.   A couple of clever comedies, a few elegant
epilogues, a so-so opera, some spirited speechifyings, a few fitful
flashes—some composed coruscations of occasional wit—will not
make a great man."

"NORTH. . . He was but a town-wit after all, and of a very
superficial fancy.   He had no imagination."

Christopher is severe ; but he does not treat Sheridan with
greater contempt than he did Wordsworth when saying that
Wordsworth wrote "like an idiot," when he penned the line concerning Milton that "His soul was like a star and dwelt apart,"
and again : "I confess *The Excursion* is the worst poem, of any
character, in the English language."

[1] *The Quarterly*, vol. xxxiii., p. 592.

Sheridan was able, almost by intuition, to group the personages and arrange the incidents in his comedies in such a manner as to render them acting plays of highest class.   Many of the characters seem artificial when judged alone.   What coachman and valet ever talked in the flesh as Thomas and Fag are made to do in *The Rivals?*   Fag says in reply to Thomas: "Why, then, the cause of all this is love—love, Thomas, who (as you may have got read to you) has been a masquerader since the days of Jupiter." Again, Fag thus describes the fortune of Miss Lydia Languish : "Rich!—why, I believe she owns half the stocks!   Zounds! Thomas, she could pay the National Debt as easily as I could my washer-woman!   She has a lap-dog that eats out of gold ; she feeds her parrot with small pearls ; and all her thread-papers are made out of bank-notes."

Fag uses the same artificial style when addressing his master, Captain Absolute, saying in reply to his master's remark, "You blockhead, never say more than is necessary," "I beg pardon, Sir,—I beg pardon—but, with submission, a lie is nothing unless one supports it.   Sir, whenever I draw on my invention for a good current lie, I always forge endorsements as well as the bill."   Captain Absolute returns the ball ;—"Well, take care you don't hurt your credit by offering too much security."   Again, Fag indulges in what his master calls impertinence, but the author may have deemed smartness.   Sir Anthony Absolute having quarrelled with his son, Fag remarks : "Upon my credit, Sir, were I in your place and found my father such very bad company, I should drop his acquaintance."

Sir Anthony Absolute is a country Squire after the model of Squire Western, yet he talks in a strain that would have made Squire Western stare and which excited the envy of George Selwyn and Horace Walpole. Replying to Mrs. Malaprop's remark that circulating Libraries are vile places; "Indeed!" he smartly says, "Madam, a circulating Library in a town is as an ever-green tree of diabolical knowledge! It blossoms through the year! And depend on it, Mrs. Malaprop, that they who are so fond of handling the leaves, will long for the fruit at last." When his son tells Sir Anthony that he is in love and has pledged himself to marry the lady of his heart, he retorts in a strain not commonly used by Somerset squires in Sheridan's boyhood;—"Let her foreclose, Jack; let her foreclose; they are not worth redeeming; besides, you have the angels' vows in exchange, I suppose; so there will be no loss there." Sir Lucius O'Trigger, fortune hunter and fire-eater, is even more elaborately witty than the jovial and epigrammatic Irish patriots of his own generation. A silly letter from Mrs. Malaprop causes him to exclaim: "Faith, she must be very deep-read to write this way—though she is rather an arbitrary writer, too—for here are a great many poor words pressed into the service of this note that would not get their *Habeas Corpus* from any court in Christendom."

Bob Acres is depicted as a country bumpkin, and he talks like a court gallant. Upon entering, he says to Captain Absolute: "Ha! my dear friend, noble captain, and honest Jack, how dost thou? Just arrived, faith, as you see.—Sir, your humble servant

[to Faulkland, who is present].   Warm work on the
roads, Jack !   Odds whips and wheels !   I've travelled
like a comet, with a tail of dust all the way as long
as the Mall."   Other sayings of his are far-fetched
rather than characteristic ; such as, " Your words are
a granadier's march to my heart," and " the thunder
of your words has soured the milk of human kindness
in my breast."   David, his servant, is introduced as
a clown and he talks like a fop.   Acres having remarked,—" But my honour, David, my honour !   I
must be very careful of my honour ;"   David adds
these comments : " Ah ! by the mass !   And I would
be very careful of it ; and I think, in return, my
honour couldn't do less than to be very careful of
me."   *Acres :* " Think what it would be to disgrace
my ancestors !"   *David :* " Under favour, the surest
way of not disgracing them is to keep as long as you
can out of their company.   Look'ee now, master, to
go to them in such haste,—with an ounce of lead in
your brains, I should think might as well be let alone.
Our ancestors are very good kind of folks, but they
are the last people I should choose to have a visiting
acquaintance with."

This is brilliant ; it is a lost art among British playwrights.   An actor has no objection to fill a minor
part when he has to utter such pointed phrases.
Devon is a beautiful county and the inhabitants are
as envied for their cleverness as the county is praised
for its beauty, yet I fear that it did not deserve in the
eighteenth century the credit of producing servants
who conversed like David—which is not a name racy
of the soil—nor that it does so even in these days of

general polish and education. Sheridan did not venture to make Acres and his servant speak the dialect which was more natural to them than epigrams.

The female personages countenance the male in ability to utter unexpected and pithy phrases. Yet, however absurd their speech, they do not render their parts ridiculous. Sheridan's mother gave him a hint for Mrs. Malaprop, yet he moulded her in his own image and has a right to the title of her creator. Miss Lydia Languish is a child of his brain and, though a departed type of those whom he had met in the flesh, she has a truth and an individuality which have kept her alive during the changing years that have elapsed since she fell in love with Beverley, and will serve to make her the subject of interest and amusement to generations yet unborn.

Julia and Faulkland were adapted to the age in which *The Rivals* appeared and they are quite as artificial. Both converse in metaphor run to seed. Julia, offering to accompany Faulkland in the flight from Justice which he affirms must be taken, and professing unabated constancy, adds that she is still ready to marry him and "then on the bosom of your wedded Julia you may lull your keen regret to slumber ; while virtuous love, with a cherub's hand, shall smooth the brow of upbraiding thought, and pluck the thorn from compunction." Faulkland exclaims that he is bankrupt in gratitude. In reality, he was not able to cope with Julia in metaphor. At the end of the scene he shows that his capacity for talking foolishly had been temporarily interrupted only, and he exclaims in superfine language : "O

love! tormentor! fiend! whose influence, like the
moon's, acting on men of dull souls, makes idiots
of them, but meeting subtler spirits, betrays their
course, and urges them to madness." He tries to
excite Julia's pity, after tormenting her beyond
endurance, by appealing to her in metaphor :—
"How can I sue for what I so little deserve? I
dare not presume, yet Hope is the child of Penitence."
To use the well-known phrase of Charles the Second,
"his nonsense, suited her nonsense." Lydia Languish's parting speech is "Our happiness is now as
unalloyed as general," and then Julia pleases Faulkland and solemnly ends the play by saying :—

"Then let us study to preserve it so ; and while
Hope pictures to us a flattering scene of future bliss,
let us deny its pencil those colours which are too
bright to be lasting. When hearts deserving happiness would unite their fortunes, Virtue would
crown them with an unfading garland of modest
hurtless flowers ; but ill-judging Passion will force
the gaudier rose into the wreath, whose thorn offends
them which its leaves are dropped."[1]

Though many other passages are devoid of
simplicity and unadorned beauty, yet the literary
defects of the play do not mar its effectiveness on the
stage. Some of the personages are inartistic ; some
of their sayings appear to be out of place. That so
young and inexperienced a writer as Sheridan should

---

[1] In the list of personages, Faulkland appears without a Christian
name, and Captain Absolute addresses him by his surname till
near the end of the play, when he calls him "Jack." This is a
slip which no commentator has noted.

have displayed in it the trained hand of a master, surprised his contemporaries and remains a riddle. It abounds in telling parts which performers love ; it contains many scenes which always delight an audience, and neither forced wit nor false sentiment detracts from the pleasure which is afforded in abundant measure by the clever buffoonery of Bob Acres, by the farcical exaggeration of Sir Lucius O'Trigger, the boisterous yet genuine humour of Sir Anthony Absolute, the incomparable blunders of Mrs. Malaprop, and the ingenuous maiden fancies of Miss Lydia Languish.

Though *The Duenna* has fewer faults of the kind which I have just noted, yet Don Jerome, the irascible father, is guilty of one which is quite as noteworthy as any of them.   He tells his son, in his daughter's presence, after interrupting a serenade : " What! I suppose you have been serenading too ! Eh, disturbing some peaceable neighbourhood with villainous catgut and lascivious piping ! Out on't ! you set your sister here a vile example.   But I come to tell you, Madam, that I'll suffer no more of these midnight incantations—these amorous orgies, that steal the senses in the hearing ; as, they say, Egyptian embalmers serve mummies, extracting the brain through the ears."[1]

[1] This simile had been used by Goldsmith ten years before in the 84th letter of his *Citizen of the World.*   " You love harmony," says Mê, the philosopher, " and are charmed with music.   I do not blame you for hearing a fine voice, when you are in your closet with a lovely parterre under your eye, or in the night-time, while perhaps the moon diffuses her silvery rays.   But is a man to carry this passion so far as to let a company of comedians,

Though Donna Louisa is far too sparkling to be natural, yet it would be affectation or blindness to deny the charm of her humour. If her looks were equal to it, she must have been bewitching. Her father says that the man she is to marry had renounced Judaism six weeks before, and her brother observes, "Ay, he left his old religion for an estate, and has not had time to get a new one," whereupon she caps his comment with the happy speech,—"But stands like a dead wall between church and synagogue, or like the blank leaves between the Old and New Testament."

For wit of the first water and in over-flowing measure, wit polished, too, till perfection had been attained, and scattered as profusely as Monte Christo did his riches, *The School for Scandal* has no superior among modern English comedies. The reader is dazzled with the excess of brilliancy. Piron was termed by Byron a machine for the production of epigrams, yet his verbal felicities were not produced in greater number and with greater ease than Sheridan's witticisms. At first sight they are less effective than after being carefully scanned. Then it is that their genuineness and appropriateness become clear and the reader is no longer tempted to apply the words of Cowley :

> "Several lights will not be seen,
>   If there be nothing else between.
>   Men doubt, because they stand so thick i' the sky,
>   If those be stars which paint the Galaxy."

musicians and singers grow rich upon his exhausted fortune ? If so, he resembles one of those dead bodies, whose brains the embalmers have picked out through its ears."

Yet it is difficult to repress astonishment at the fluency and fertility of Maria, the blushing young girl who shuns notoriety, of Rowley, the faithful and unimaginative servant of the family and of Trip, the valet to Charles Surface. Their parts are secondary, but their talk is superlative. When asked why she avoids Sir Benjamin Backbite, Maria replies :— " Oh, he has done nothing, but 'tis for what he has said : his conversation is a perpetual libel on all his acquaintance." She piquantly comments on scandal :—

" Well, I'll not debate how far scandal may be allowable ; but in a man I am sure it is always contemptible. We have pride, envy, rivalship, and a thousand motives to depreciate each other ; but the male slanderer must have the cowardice of a woman before he can traduce one." Mrs. Candour's remarks are in the style of the ladies at the Hôtel Rambouillet :—" Why, to be sure, a tale of scandal is as fatal to the credit of a prudent lady of her stamp as a fever is generally to those of the strongest constitutions. But there is a sort of puny, sickly reputation that is always ailing, yet will outlive the robuster characters of an hundred prudes." Sir Benjamin Backbite outvies Maria and Mrs. Candour when defining scandal :—" True, Madam, there are valetudinarians in reputation as well as constitution, who, being conscious of their weak part, avoid the least breath of air, and supply the want of stamina by care and circumspection."

Within the Arctic circle, a few hours intervene between the gloom of winter and the effulgence of

summer.   Lady Teazle undergoes as rapid and
startling a transformation.   She is represented as
having been taken from a dull house in the country,
where she passed the day in doing worsted work,
looking after the dairy and the poultry-yard, making
extracts from the family receipt-book, combing the
lap-dog of her aunt Deborah, and amusing herself
in the evening with drawing patterns for ruffles
which she had not materials to make up, playing
Pope Joan with the curate, reading a sermon to her
aunt, or seated before an old spinet to strum her
father to sleep after a fox-chase.   This young lady,
with such a training and an experience of life,
marries the mature Sir Peter Teazle.   Accompanying him to London, she enters fashionable society,
becomes a member of the Scandalous College, and
flashes out as follows :—" Nay, I vow Lady Stucco
is very well with the dessert after dinner ; for she's
just like the French fruit one cracks for mottoes—
made up of paint and proverb."

When told by her husband that true wit is
very closely allied to good-nature, she replies :—
"True, Sir Peter ; I believe they are so near
akin that they can never be united."   It was not
so strange that Lady Teazle should allow Joseph
Surface to make love to her as that, when he said
her duty was to punish her husband for unjustly
suspecting her, she should exclaim :—" Indeed ! So
that if he suspects me without cause, it follows that
the best way of curing his jealousy is to give him
reason for 't."   When the wily, unscrupulous and
experienced Joseph adds that her character is abso-

lutely dying from too much health, she displays a
cleverness in her reply which Sophia Western, with
a like home-training, would have envied :—" So, so ;
then I perceive your prescription is, that I must sin
in my own defence, and part with my virtue to preserve my reputation."

Sir Peter Teazle is commonly supposed to have
been a superannuated husband, yet, judging by his
talk, he was as young and light-hearted as Charles,
and far livelier than Joseph Surface. He could hold
his own in a tournament of wit with any member of
the Scandalous College. Few who had married in
the same circumstances could equal him in confessing
his mistake :—" Ah ! Master Rowley, when an old
bachelor marries a young wife, he deserves—no—
the crime carries its own punishment along with it."

Sir Oliver Surface, the uncle of Charles and
Joseph, is a merchant who returns from India with a
large fortune and a mine of wit. Most of the nabobs
of Sheridan's day were as rich and dull as the millionaires who are now honoured and envied by the
unthinking, and pitied by all who reflect upon the
inequalities of life. Neither nabob of the past nor
millionaire of the present could match Sir Oliver's
comment in reply to Sir Peter Teazle's remark that
his nephew Joseph was, " what a youth should be,—
everybody in the world spoke well of him." " I am
sorry to hear it ; he has too good a character to be
an honest fellow. Everybody speaks well of him !
Psha ! then he has bowed as low to knaves and
fools as to the honest dignity of genius and virtue."

This untutored merchant sees his nephew Charles

employ the family pedigree as an auctioneer's hammer, and says, as the most cultured of *Punch's* contributors might now do in joke :—"What an unnatural rogue !—an *ex post facto* parricide." Talking with Master Rowley, he thus bemoans the altered habits of servants :—"Ah ! Master Rowley, in my days servants were content with the follies of their masters ; but now they have their vices, like their birthday clothes, with the gloss on." Replying to Rowley's statement that Joseph firmly believes that charity begins at home, he says :—"And his, I presume, is of that domestic sort that never stirs abroad at all."

Not much wit might be expected from old Rowley in real life, yet he shines in *The School for Scandal.* At the end of a speech in the first scene of the third Act he appositely quotes two lines from "our immortal bard," and, when instructing Sir Oliver how to represent the part of Mr. Premium, he advises him to "lament that a young man must be at years of discretion before he is suffered to ruin himself." Again, he speaks as follows of Joseph Surface, concerning whom Sir Oliver had said that he was extolled as a man of the most benevolent way of thinking, "As to his way of thinking, I cannot pretend to decide ; for, to do him justice, he appears to have as much speculative benevolence as any private gentleman in the Kingdom, though he is seldom so sensual as to indulge himself in the exercise of it." Trip, the valet of Charles Surface, does not fall behind his master in cleverness and elaboration of speech. Being asked by Moses whether he can give security for a bill, he replies :—"Why nothing capital of my master's wardrobe has dropped lately ; but I could give you a mortgage on some of his winter clothes, with equity of redemption [what valet knows the meaning of this?] before November, or you shall have the reversion of the French velvet, or a post-obit ; these, I should think, Moses, with a few pair of point-ruffles, as a collateral security—hey, my little fellow ?"

Joseph Surface is a master of fine language as well as of fine sentiments. When Sir Benjamin Backbite repeats his rhymed epigram and his Uncle Crabtree exclaims : " There, ladies, done in the smack of a whip and on horseback too," Joseph neatly adds, " A very Phœbus mounted—indeed, Sir Benjamin." He makes love to Lady Teazle in antitheses. After assuring her that she suffered from the consciousness of innocence, having grown impatient of her husband's temper and intolerant of his suspicions, he adds, " Now, my dear Lady Teazle, if you would but once make a trifling *faux pas*, you can't conceive how cautious you would grow, and how ready to humour and agree with your husband." " Do you think so ?" she asks, and he replies,—" Oh ! I'm sure on't ; and then you would find that all scandal would cease at once ; for—in short, your character at present is like a person in a plethora, absolutely dying of too much health." Joseph's wit is not always unalloyed ; it degenerates into something nearly as bad as the euphuism of Sir Piercie Shafton, when he soliloquises, after getting rid of his uncle Sir Oliver, who had come in the disguise of a poor relation :—" This is one effect of a good character ; it invites application from the unfortunate, and there needs no small degree of address to gain the reputation of benevolence without incurring the expense. The silver ore of pure charity is an expensive article in the catalogue of a man's good qualities, whereas the sentimental French plate I use instead of it makes quite as good a show and pays no tax."

Joseph Surface is more artificial as a villain than Charles is as a spendthrift. Characters such as Tartuffe or Joseph are presented with their worst sides to the spectator, and it is difficult to believe that they may not have possessed some redeeming qualities. The worst hypocrite is a human being after all, and the worst human being is as complex and inscrutable a personage as the best. It is doubtful whether the vilest man is conscious of his evil traits and it is certain that, unless he be a braggart or an impostor, he will not make a senseless parade of his villainies.

Dryden's acuteness as a critic was equal to his poetic gift, and he justly remarks in the preface to *Troilus and Cressida* :—" To produce a villain without other reason than a natural inclination to villainy is, in poetry, to produce an effect which is much stronger than the cause." Now, Joseph Surface's profession of scoundrelism is too extreme and artificial for a genuine hypocrite ; he is never the dupe of his own deceit. Blifil is more natural. He does not parade his wickedness. Joseph ostentatiously admits that he is but acting a part and not living a life when, after saying before Lady Sneerwell, "The man who does not share in the distresses of a brother, even though merited by his own misconduct, deserves—" pauses, upon being told by her that he need not moralize among friends, and adds, "Egad, that's true! I'll keep that sentiment till I see Sir Peter." Now, however clever and plausible, untruthful and self-confident Joseph may have been in fact, he should not have betrayed his weaknesses and wickedness even to intimate friends. A true hypocrite keeps up the part even in his dreams, when the part has become a second nature to him. He has no mask to throw off. His turpitude is not assumed. The artificiality in Joseph's character is rendered the clearer when he remarks to Lady Sneerwell, after exposure has occurred and final discomfiture is impending :— "Well, I admit I have been to blame. I confess I deviated from the direct road of wrong." As a personage, Joseph Surface is deficient in flesh and blood ; but he serves as a foil to his brother Charles and he points the moral which playgoers are never weary of hearing and applauding.

Charles, a professed rake, is as witty as the cleverest and most finished man of his class. He is perfectly satisfied with himself, and he never gives a thought to his shortcomings ; perhaps, he was unconscious of them, his object being to enjoy life in the way which he thought best. So long as he lavishes money he is happy and, when his purse is empty, his epigrams are scattered as profusely as his guineas. He is far more natural than his brother

without being any better at bottom. His liveliness
is contagious and, by making no pretence of goodness, he gets credit for being an excellent fellow whose
only fault was to be rather wild. The ripe and
experienced widow, Lady Sneerwell, falls in love
with him. The young and ingenuous Maria adores
him. His levity proves to be the best policy, and
his jesting the truest wisdom. His uncle Oliver
raises him from beggary to affluence, and the
audience before which he figures thinks that his
rich reward has been rightly earned.

Though *The School for Scandal* scintillates with
wit, it is none the less an acting comedy of the
highest class. Never, since being first put on the
stage, has it failed to attract and charm. Some of
the finest gems have flaws, yet they are valued and
admired despite their imperfections. The choicest
work of Nature or the most finished work of Art
which receives unalloyed and general praise is an
unquestionable treasure and *The School for Scandal*
has been praised in such a manner and deserves it.[1]

[1] Cumberland, who was jealous of Sheridan, says in his
" Memoirs," with reference to criticisms on the use to which he
had turned a screen in his comedy, *The West Indian:* " I could
name one now living who has made such happy use of his screen
in a comedy of the very first merit that if Aristotle himself had
written a whole chapter professedly against *screens* and Jerry
Collier had edited it with notes and illustrations, I would not have
placed Lady Teazle out of ear-shot to have saved their ears from
the pillory ; but if either of these worthies could have pointed
out an expedient to have got Joseph Surface off the stage, pending that scene, with any reasonable conformity to Nature, they
would have done more good to the drama than either of them
have done harm, and that is saying a great deal."—Vol. i., p. 303.

Though *The Critic* is not one of Sheridan's great works, it is so brilliant a farce that his name would have been remembered if he had written nothing else. Mr. Puff is an original creation; he is as natural and impersonal as Falstaff. Sir Fretful Plagiary, though a caricature of Cumberland, is life-like. Sheridan had a keen eye for the faults or whims of others, yet he was not blind to his own failings. Hence he makes Mr. Sneer say:—" But Mr. Puff, I think not only the Justice, but the clown seems to talk in as high a style as the first hero among them." Mr. Puff's reply is:—"Heaven forbid that they should not in a free country! Sir, I am not for making slavish distinctions, and giving all the fine language to the upper sort of people."

Sheridan and Congreve are often coupled together as masters in wit. The personages in Congreve's comedies utter fine things; the sparkle of champagne brightened their talk; but the effervescence soon passed off. Hundreds of jokes give pleasure to one generation and are problems to another. The audience which Congreve amused did not long outlast him; while the attractions of his plays faded with the generation which had welcomed them and passed away. Of no dramatist, however, with the exception of Shakespeare, can it be said that the author of *The Rivals, The School for Scandal,* and *The Critic,* has added more allusions and quotable phrases to our daily speech and writing than can be found in any three of his plays. A few examples will suffice, if, indeed, it be necessary to advance proof of what is self-evident. Bob Acres is an accepted type of poltroonery and his courage oozing out, as it were, at his palms is a happy illustration of it. Sir Lucius O'Trigger shares the immortality of Ancient Pistol and his remark will never be forgotten if the writers of leading articles can help it :—" Pray, Sir, be easy ; the quarrel is a very pretty quarrel as it stands." The very name of Mrs. Malaprop is as happy a thought as any of her incomparable sayings, many of which, such as " She's as headstrong as an allegory on the banks of Nile," and " I own the soft impeachment," will be quoted as long as the language endures.

Sir Benjamin Backbite uttered a phrase which is often repeated, but for which he does not always get the credit ; he tells Maria that she will like his love elegies when she shall see them " on a beautiful quarto page, where a neat rivulet of text shall meander through a meadow of margin." " Too civil by half," is an "aside" by Sir Oliver Surface. Mr. Sneer is the father of, " a most happy thought, certainly," as well as, " no scandal about Queen Elizabeth, I hope." Mr. Puff said, "when they do agree on the stage, their unanimity is wonderful." Two lines from his tragedy will be remembered as long as the one which he reproduced from *Othello* :

> " The Spanish fleet thou canst not see—because
> It is not yet in sight !"

Shakespeare and Sheridan wrote for the stage and their plays lose much in the reading. Byron wrote plays for the study, therefore they are ineffective on the stage. Everybody is aware that Gervinus and other learned German commentators have discovered that Shakespeare had certain reasons for writing as he did, of which he may have been wholly unconscious. Philarète Chasles, a very able French critic, has favoured Sheridan in a like way, and pointed out that he drew Joseph Surface to represent and satirize the social hypocrisy of his day, when everything was done for the sake of form and of respectability, all true virtue and heroism being treated with contempt.[1]

It is very easy and utter waste of time to discuss and determine what any writer intended; all that can be known about his purpose is what he has disclosed, and all that repays attention is the actual product. From the time of their first representation till now, the plays of Sheridan have been admired by playgoers, and it is improbable that they will ever cease to give pleasure when faithfully represented.

The popularity of Sheridan as a dramatist has never waned in the United States of America since his great comedy was first represented in New York on the 16th of December, 1785. Washington was a frequenter of the theatre and *The School for Scandal* was his favourite piece. At the present day this comedy, when adequately performed, never fails to attract American playgoers.[2]

Translations of it have appeared in all civilized

---

[1] *Le Dix-Huitième Siècle en Angleterre*, p. 235.

[2] Mr. Augustin Daly, the proprietor and popular manager of theatres in New York and London, is my authority for this statement.

countries ; several exist in French, and it has frequently been represented with applause on the
French stage.   Its humour is so genuine that, as
was remarked by Villemain, it stands the supreme
strain of reproduction in another tongue without
loss.   The original is used as a text-book throughout France to teach boys English.   It has been
often performed on the stages of Italy, Holland,
Germany and Austria.   That it can be read in the
languages of Europe and India proves its attractive-
ness to be as wide as the world.[1]

Popularity is not a sure test of vitality.   Mr.
Caxton's projected " History of Human Error,"
would require a supplement nearly as voluminous,
if the story of dead reputations were narrated at
length.   Garrick was enthusiastic about *The School
for Scandal* before and after its representation, yet
he would not have ventured upon the hazardous
prediction that the bloom of youth would be upon
it at the end of a century.

The Rivals fills a London theatre now as it
did in 1775, when first performed.   The difficulty
is to find performers capable of filling the parts.
The actors and actresses of the last century were
carefully trained and their highest ambition was to
do justice to their parts.   No managers of London
theatres have had wider experience or greater

[1] Nothing is better worth reading about Sheridan and his plays
than what is contained in the edition of *The Rivals* and *The
School for Scandal* by Mr. Brander Matthews published in 1888.
Some of the above remarks about translations are condensed
from what he has written.

success in representing Sheridan's plays than Mr. and Mrs. Bancroft, and I invite the reader's attention to the following remarks concerning these plays with which Mr. Bancroft has favoured me: " The original cast of the *School for Scandal* must, I often think, have been perfect. King, who—alas, like many a great comedian's fame—is almost unknown now but to those who are a little learned in stage lore—beyond doubt excelled as Sir Peter. Smith—the first actor, I think, to whose name the detestable prefix "Gentleman " was attached—and then, if I remember rightly, about 47, has left a great reputation as Charles Surface ; he continued to play the part until his old age : aided no doubt by the non-discovery of electric light and the dim illuminating powers of oil lamps and tallow. Palmer was, of course, famous in the hypocrisy of Joseph ; while the lovely Mrs. Abington, beautiful still, although the charm of youth had left her, bewitched her world as Lady Teazle.

" Let me now recall, briefly, some recollections concerning the revival of the immortal comedy, and of its companion *The Rivals*, during the days of management by Mrs. Bancroft and myself at the old Prince of Wales's and the Haymarket theatres. It was a high ambition to try and worthily place Sheridan's masterpiece on the stage of the little house in Tottenham Street, and the result of more than a year's hard work and anxious thought, begun by exploring the mines of wealth stored in the print-room of the British Museum, and by delightful pilgrimages to Knole. It was then that a stately minuet —Mrs. Bancroft's happy thought—was danced by

Lady Sneerwell's guests for the first time: and several transpositions in the text and sequence of the scenes, made with all reverence and respect to heighten their stage effect, as, for instance, by combining the banquet scene with the sale of the Surface ancestors, were the signal for their subsequent general adoption. The performance enjoyed a great and long success, the acting being as highly praised as was the production of the play. A delightful remembrance of one of many pictures is painted on the curtain of the Haymarket Theatre, and I always regard it as a masterpiece in distemper.

"*The Rivals*, from the date of its first night's failure, has neither merited nor enjoyed a like measure of success as, throughout the world, has followed the *School for Scandal;* while I venture to think the incidents of the comedy are too fragile and farcical to bear such elaborate scenic treatment as we endeavoured to depict of last-century life, when Beau Nash reigned in the pump-room at Bath."

Sheridan was temporarily, but not unduly elated by his triumph on the stage. What his feelings would have been can only be conjectured if he could have foreseen that, on the hundredth anniversary of its production, *The School for Scandal* would be played in the capital of Canada before his great-grandson, the Governor-General. The vigour and endurance of his dramatic fame are marvellous. The best explanation has been supplied to me by Sir Henry Irving. It will command the respect of the two worlds in which he moves and which he adorns, those of the stage and of society : " Sheridan brought the comedy of manners to the highest perfection, and *The School for Scandal* remains to this day the most popular comedy in the English language. Some of the characters both in this play and in *The Rivals* have become so closely associated with our current speech that we may fairly regard them as imperishable. No farce of our time has so excellent a chance of immortality as *The Critic*. A playwright of whom these things are commonplaces must have had brilliant qualities for his craft ; but the secret in this case, I think, lies in the pervading humanity of Sheridan's work. That is the only preservative against decay."

XI.

CHARACTERISTICS AS AN ORATOR.

No task is more difficult or more tantalizing than that which involves a critical judgment upon Parliamentary oratory at different periods. Francis Bacon was a telling speaker in the reigns of Elizabeth and James the First, and Pym in that of his son Charles; Walpole, Chesterfield, Pulteney and Bolingbroke were numbered among the great orators in Parliament during the reigns of Anne and the first George; while Chatham, William Pitt, Sheridan, Canning and Brougham occupied as high positions as they, and launched as powerful rhetorical thunderbolts during the reign of George the Third, yet if any of them could revisit the earth now and address either House of Parliament he might not maintain his historical reputation, because his audience had become accustomed to different modes of speech. Members of the last Parliament of Charles the First, who returned to public life in the first Parliament of his son, could not understand why their ancient jests were not accounted funny and why their impassioned appeals excited laughter. The orator who has entranced one generation may be termed a ranter by the next.

Since the Revolution of 1688 prepared the way for the establishment in England of Parliamentary supremacy, the most brilliant orators have often been at their best when members of the Opposition. The orator, like the stormy petrel, is at home amid the din and discord of warring elements. His ambition is to dominate the storm he or others may have raised. No Prime Minister has held high office for a longer time, or felt more secure in his place than Sir Robert Walpole ; but he was not a famous speaker. He could count with certainty, during twenty-one years, upon the venal votes of his obsequious followers, yet he quailed when that " terrible cornet of horse," as he styled the elder Pitt, denounced his policy, and Walpole ineffectually laboured for years to silence Pulteney, the leader of the Opposition, Pitt and Pulteney being convinced that each could fill Walpole's place with great satisfaction to himself.

No complete and trustworthy reports have survived of the speeches which helped to render Walpole's position untenable, and it requires a faith undistinguishable from childlike credulity to believe that a single authentic version of a speech by the elder Pitt is on record. One or two sentences he is said to have uttered, may have been handed down in the very words which he used, yet they serve as little to convey an adequate impression of the speech in which they occurred as the Pylons which have outlasted the ravages of centuries suffice to bring the Temple of Luxor before the mind of the spectator.

When the elder Pitt was in office, his reputation for oratory did not stand so high as it did during his career in Opposition, neither was it necessary for him to divert his mind from the business of administration while the Duke of Newcastle ensured him a majority by an unscrupulous distribution of patronage. Owing to the favour of George the Third and the influence of the King's friends, Lord North retained the office of Premier for twelve years. William Pitt's predominance was largely due to George the Third's fear that, if he parted with him, Charles James Fox, whom he hated without measure or reason, might take his place.

Perceval enjoyed the confidence of George the Third and his son, not on account of his oratory, which was alike fluent and contemptible, but because he was as subservient as Addington to the Sovereign, and sincerely believed that every abuse improved by being crusted with age, and that all changes must be bad because they altered the old order. The public had a liking for Perceval. He was a commonplace man who had attained to high office, and the commonplace Premier, like the slow-going horse, inspires confidence in his steadiness. Moreover, his private character was good and he had a very large family, all of whom he ostentatiously took to church every Sunday. Lord Liverpool was at the head of the Government for fifteen years, during which this country was misgoverned to an extent which appears incredible now ; neither he nor Perceval owed his promotion to oratory, and both were Ministers because such was the will of the Sovereign, and in the evil days before 1832 a majority could generally be formed in Parliament to support the Prime Minister who enjoyed the confidence of the Crown.

The true orator can influence his contemporaries, and the test of an orator's powers is the effect which he produces upon different bodies of his fellow-countrymen. Mr. Gladstone had been many years a member of Parliament before he addressed a public meeting, and his supremacy in the natural gift and acquired graces of speech was unquestioned after he had held a public meeting captive as completely as he had often done his fellow-members in the House. Pitt gave utterance to a very clever phrase at a banquet in the city of London, but there is no record of any speech being delivered by him at a public meeting of his fellow-countrymen. Burke spoke in Guildhall and at Bristol with great effect. Fox addressed the electors of Westminster from the hustings day after day while polling went on. Sheridan's first speech was delivered before a crowded meeting of the Westminster Association in Westminster Hall, and many others were delivered on the hustings at Stafford, yet the records of these speeches are lost; perhaps, indeed, none ever existed. Hence, in determining the character and rank of Sheridan as an orator, his reported speeches must be taken as a criterion.

He seldom spoke in the House of Commons without exciting pleasurable expectation; he sat down as seldom without gratifying it. But his speeches, when read now, do not fully explain the anticipated pleasure, neither do they enable the reader to realize the fulfilled desire. Most of them are imperfectly reported, yet the very words which he used fail to move the reader as they did his audience. This applies with equal truth to his plays; when they are adequately represented they fulfil their purpose. The best speech lacks in print the breath of life which the orator breathed into it. Half an orator's power lies in his personality. The virtue passes out of his speech in a report.

Yet I may affirm that the reason why Sheridan excelled as an orator was the geniality of his tone, the artistic arrangement of his material, the excellence of his voice and manner, the happiness with which he made points and his shrewdness in knowing how to make an end. Many a public speaker would rise to high rank among orators if he knew when to sit down. Such a man, having made a point, is seduced by applause into repeating the same thought till he wearies everyone but himself, and he resumes his seat thoroughly self-satisfied and an utter failure.

Sheridan had an eagle's eye for the ridiculous side of an opponent. The Duke of Richmond had been an advocate of universal suffrage till the French Revolution made some men think that they were about to live in perfect bliss on a regenerated earth, while others shrank aghast at the thought that old chaos was returning, and Sheridan thus referred to the Duke of Richmond, on the 4th of March, 1793, in a speech concerning seditious practices: "A noble Duke had formerly been of opinion that there was nothing to be seen but danger for want of a Parliamentary reform ; but he had so elevated himself of late on fortifications of his own creating, and availed himself of his great power of discernment, that he was now able to discover plots, conspiracies and treasons under the garb of a Parliamentary reform or any reform.

" The alarm had been brought forward in great pomp and form on Saturday morning. At night all the mail coaches were stopped ; the Duke of Richmond stationed himself, among other curiosities, at the Tower ; a great municipal officer, too, had made a discovery exceedingly beneficial to the people of this country—he meant the Lord Mayor of London —who had discovered that, at the King's Arms in Cornhill, was a debating society, where principles of the most dangerous tendency were propagated ; where people went to buy treason at sixpence a head, and where it was retailed to them by the glimmering of an inch of candle ; and five minutes, to be measured by the glass, were to be allowed to each traitor to perform his part in overturning the State."[1]

Another passage in the same vein occurs in a speech, delivered two years later, when Sheridan opposed the suspension of the Habeas Corpus Act, and said that, having been present at trials for sedition, he had heard Lord Chief Justice Eyre charge the jury, and added :—" It was an ostentatious and boastful conspiracy and it was much in favour of the accused that they had neither men, money, nor zeal to effect the

[1] " Speeches," vol. ii., p. 165.

purpose with which they were charged. On the first
trial one pike was produced, that was afterwards
withdrawn from mere shame. A formidable instrument was talked of to be employed against the
cavalry ; it appeared upon evidence to be a tee-totum
in a window at Sheffield. There was a camp in a
back shop, an arsenal provided with nine muskets,
and an exchequer containing nine pounds and one
bad shilling ; all to be directed against the whole
armed force and established Government of Great
Britain." As a piece of rhetoric the foregoing
passage could not be improved. The effect at
which Sheridan aimed is produced in the simplest
and most telling fashion, and if he invented the
"one bad shilling," as is not improbable, the stroke
was in the highest style of a master in the art of
putting things.

In 1800, when discussing the proposed negociation
with France, he placed before William Pitt's supporters a few facts which they had overlooked, but
would never forget again :—" It is strange, Sir, is it
not, that not a man on the Continent could be found
who would take part in a cause of such a nature
without being subsidized ! We have obliged them
to do their duty, to protect their property, to defend
their religion. We have been obliged to be the recruiting sergeants and paymasters-general to Europe.
. . . When you talk of a successful war, you must
mean one that has accomplished the objects for
which it was undertaken. Have you deterred other
countries from aggrandizement and rapine ? Have
you restored the Bourbons ? No ; but you have

taken Trincomalee. Have you re-established the *noblesse* of France? No; but you have taken Ceylon. Have you restored the [religious] orders of France? No; but you have taken the Cape."

What other member of the House when Addington, who had been Speaker, was appointed Premier and Chancellor of the Exchequer, could have defended him against attack with greater humour or point than Sheridan did when he asked: "What did these gentlemen expect from the present Chancellor of the Exchequer? We treated him, when in the Chair of this House, with the respect he merited. He has, I believe, Sir, over our present worthy Speaker [Abbot], the advantage in altitude; but did they expect that when he was Minister he was to stand up and call Europe to order? Was he to send Mr. Colman, the Sergeant-at-Arms, to the Baltic, and order the Northern Powers to the Bar of the House? Was he to see the Powers of Germany scrambling like members over the benches, and say, 'Gentlemen must take their places'? Was he expected to cast his eye to the Tuscan gallery, and exclaim that 'Strangers must withdraw'? Was he to stand across the Rhine and say, 'The Germans to the right, and the French to the left'?"[1]

The prevailing opinion of Sheridan as an orator has been formed after perusing the current version of his speech in Westminster Hall relative to Warren Hastings and the Begums of Oude. No accurate report was published in Sheridan's lifetime, and it was not till 1861 that the very words which

[1] "Speeches," vol. iii.; p. 426.

he used were printed, and could be compared with those which an incompetent reporter had put into his mouth. In the specimens of his oratory, the spurious version has a conspicuous place, and the reader whose taste is not utterly vitiated must think that Sheridan had given utterance to much inflated nonsense. This speech fills several pages. The reporter gives the larger part in the third person; but several passages which are printed within commas are in the first person, and these have been assumed to be transcripts of what was spoken. A comparison between what Sheridan is made to say, in a few passages which are given as if they had been spoken, with what he really uttered, is an instructive object lesson. The first passage within commas occurs in the exordium :

Concocted Report.

" The unfortunate gentleman at the bar is no mighty subject in my mind. Amidst the series of mischiefs, *to my sense*, seeming to surround him, what is he but a petty *nucleus*, involved in its *lamina*, scarcely see nor thought of?

" It is not the peering suspicion of apprehending guilt; it is not any popular abhorrence of its widespread consequences; it is not the secret consciousness in the bosom of the judge, which can excite the vengeance of the law and authorize its infliction! No. In this good

Verbatim Report.

"So far from it, that the unfortunate gentleman at your bar is scarcely in my contemplation when my mind is engaged in this business; that it then holds but two ideas—a sincere abhorrence of the crimes and a sanguine hope of the remedy.

"No, my Lords; we know well that it is the glory of this Constitution that not the general fame or character of any man—not the weight and power of any prosecutor, no plea of moral or political expediency—not even the secret consciousness of guilt which may live in the land, as high as it is happy, because as just as it is free, all is definite, equitable, and exact. The laws must be satisfied before infliction ensues. And ere a hair of the head can be plucked, LEGAL GUILT must be established by LEGAL PROOF."[1]

bosom of the judge—can justify any British court in passing any sentence, to touch a hair of the head or an atom in any respect of the property, of the fame, of the liberty, of the poorest or meanest subject that breathes the air of this just and free land. We know, my Lords, that there can be no legal guilt without legal proof; that the rule which defines the evidence is as much the law of the land as that which creates the crime. It is upon that ground we mean to stand."[2]

Attentive readers of the newspapers which instruct the public must be familiar with the following passage, as it appears in leading articles at short intervals :

[1] "Speeches," vol. i., pp. 368, 371
[2] "Warren Hastings's Trial," vol. i., pp. 483, 486.[a]

[a] Why were Sheridan's speeches often absurdly reported? Mr. Daniel Pultney, who sat for the Duke of Rutland's pocket Borough of Bramber, wrote to his patron, who was then Lord-Lieutenant of Ireland, on the 19th of March, 1788 : "Sheridan did not insinuate, or attempt to do it, that your Grace's representatives and the representatives of Ireland are in opposite interests. Nor did he say one half the nonsense Mr. [William] Woodfall has made him say on that subject ; but the case is that Mr. Sheridan is so connected with all these reporters as Manager, and [ex-] Secretary to the Treasury and author, that they are always determined to make him *pointed*, as they call it, in reply, and when they do not understand what he says, they give him any abuse of their own."[b]

[b] "The Rutland Manuscripts," vol. iii., p. 379.

Concocted Report.	*Verbatim Report.*
"He had sworn once—then again—and made nothing of it: then comes he with another, and swears a third time—and in *company* does better. *Single-handed* he can do nothing—but succeeds by *platoon swearing* and *volleys of oaths.*"[1]	"I imagine that your Lordships will now again think we have done with Doond Sing. No such thing. Here he is a third time swearing before Elijah Impey. But he is not to be trusted by himself; he is a bad one single-handed, and, as it was a military duty, he is coupled with somebody else; he is joined by Mir Ahmud Ali, subadar, and at last hits the mark."[2]

Though I gave to the public many years ago these examples of Sheridan's oratory, yet the false version is still current and will probably be remembered when the true is forgotten. One more specimen may be given to show, not only that the reporter wrote bombast, but also how slight an excuse he had for attributing it to Sheridan :

Concocted Report.	*Verbatim Report.*
"Oh Faith ; oh Justice !" exclaimed Mr. Sheridan, "I conjure you by your sacred names to depart for a moment from this place, though it be your peculiar residence ; nor hear your names profaned by such a sacrilegious combination as that which I am now compelled to repeat !—where all the fair forms of nature and art,	"Oh ! Justice, Faith, Policy ! fly from this spot—though your sanctuary—for a moment, and do not hear that human arrogance has charged you with such crimes ; for it is not in

[1] "Speeches," vol. i., p. 384.
[2] Shorthand Report, vol. i., p. 558.

truth and peace, policy and honour, shrank back aghast from the deleterious shade !— where all existences, nefarious and vile, had their sway !— where, amidst the black agents on one side, and Middleton and Impey on the other, the toughest head, the most unfeeling heart, the great figure of the piece, characteristic in his place, stood aloof and independent from the puny profligacy in his train !— but far from idle and inactive —turning a malignant eye on all mischief that awaited him ! the multiplied apparatus of temporizing expedients and intimidating instruments ! now cringing on his prey, and fawning on his vengeance ! now quickening the limpid (*sic*) pace of craft, and forcing every stand that retiring nature can make in the heart ! violating the attachments and decorums of life ! sacrificing every emotion of tenderness and honour ! and flagitiously levelling all the distinctions of national characteristics ! with a long catalogue of crimes and aggravations beyond the reach of thought for human malignity to perpetrate, or human vengeance to punish."[1]

the power of human vengeance to punish for such crimes."[2]

---

[1] "Speeches," vol. i., pp. 420, 421.
[2] Shorthand Report, vol. i., p. 702.

Since the facts connected with the Impeachment of Warren Hastings have been understood by the public, the interest in the speeches delivered in Westminster Hall has subsided, and it might have died out had not Macaulay made Hastings the subject of an article in which there is more rhetoric than truth, an article which is not more trustworthy as a whole than the passage in it where Macaulay vainly labours to demonstrate that Philip Francis wrote the "Letters" signed Junius. A correct version of Sheridan's speech in Westminster Hall was placed in Moore's hands. He stupidly dreaded an action for libel if he published it. Another reason had hindered its appearance immediately after the trial. Charles Brinsley Sheridan wrote to Moore that his father "considered this as the peculiar occasion on which he surpassed Fox, Burke, and Grey, and I remember his attributing the reluctance to publish the speeches at the time to Burke's sense of this."[1] The unpublished letter from which I quote these words, contains the following echo from the past : " I am aware that *reading* the speeches of my father and Burke, is not giving the former fair play ; his superiority being his success in what he said at the time, while I have understood that Burke's fine ideas and language, generally failed in producing

---

[1] Charles Brinsley, who was Sheridan's son by his second marriage, distinguished himself at Winchester and Cambridge. He was an enthusiast in the cause of Greek Independence and an active member of the English committee for promoting it. His "Thoughts on the Greek Revolution" were published in 1824 and his "Songs of Greece," from the Roumaic text, in 1825. He died unmarried in 1843.

conviction, or even securing attention ; *i.e.*, that, as speeches, like all other things, are good or bad, as they are calculated to attain their ends, Burke as a *debater* was inferior to my father, whatever he may have been as a composer of prose."[1]

The best oratory implies the perfect delivery of sentences couched in choice language, and the beauty of the phrases acquires a super-added charm from the grace of manner and appropriateness of intonation ; the same phrases in the mouth of an ineffective speaker are wanting in rhythmical balance and skilfully-timed pauses, and they degenerate into see-saw or sing-song. A great orator is also a great actor, and if nature has endowed the orator with a musical voice, he can captivate the hearers whom his reasoning might not convince.

During the eighteenth century, the best speakers in Parliament often wrote the worst prose. Wilkes styles Chatham the greatest orator and the worst letter-writer of his age. Cowper could not face the House of Lords when he had to answer a few easy questions, yet he wrote better letters than any contemporary. William Pitt was as great a speaker and as stiff a writer as his father. The letters of Fox have no literary finish, and few of Sheridan's

---

[1] Some of Lord Lytton's lines on Sheridan, in "St. Stephen's," may be quoted here :

> " If eloquence can find its surest test
> In the degree in which it thrills the breast,
> And not the enduring thought, which after-calm
> Retains, then thine the sceptre and the palm :
> For never fancy shot more georgeous ray,
> Nor left air duller when it died away."

letters repay perusal for their style. As an orator, however, Sheridan excelled every contemporary in casting his thoughts into the form of dialogue. I revert to his speech in Westminster Hall for an illustration from the verbatim report : " With regard to the first charge, which is a charge of direct actual rebellion, I do protest that, in order to satisfy my mind as much as I could, I have been hunting with all the industry at least, though not with the acuteness, of any antiquarian that ever belonged to the Antiquaries' Society, to find at what period this rebellion actually existed, and I have not found any one thing to guide me to the period of its existence. There never was a rebellion so concealed. We asked Mr. Middleton whether any battle was fought anywhere ? ' None,' he owns, ' that ever he heard of.' Did any one man, horse or foot, march to suppress this rebellion ? ' None.' Did you ever hear any orders for any troops to march to suppress it ? ' None.' The rebellion seems clearly to have died a natural death, though raised certainly for a most unnatural object."[1]

Many of Sheridan's colleagues in Parliament surpassed him in several departments of learning. The mathematical problem which Windham found a pleasant mental exercise would have puzzled Sheridan as greatly as a sentence in Sanscrit. William Pitt was far superior to him as a classical scholar, having enjoyed and profited by the University training which Sheridan's father could not afford to give him. Yet Sheridan had re-

[1] Shorthand Report, vol. i., p. 579.

membered much that he had been taught at Harrow, and could quote from the Latin classics with an aptness equal to any political rival. Fox knew more Greek than Sheridan had ever acquired, while Burke's knowledge was encyclopædic, yet neither Pitt nor Windham, Fox nor Burke could match Sheridan in representing in dramatic shape and with histrionic art any subject upon which he spoke.

A man may be a great orator and yet be unable to influence the House of Commons. It differs, as new members sometimes learn with surprise and to their cost, from a mere debating society. The House will not listen with patience to a speech, however fine, which is obviously designed to display the cleverness of the speaker. The man who becomes a power there is he who can play a leading part in debate, reply with crushing effect to statements put forward with a confidence bordering on effrontery, anticipate with something akin to intuition the objections which may be raised by those who are to follow him, and show beyond question that he has grasped all the essential facts and pressed them into the service of his argument. In this Pitt excelled, while Fox was on a par with him. Erskine, whose forensic triumphs were envied by every lawyer, was laughed at in Parliament; he could affirm but he could not discuss; he could put a case with point but he could not debate. Burke, whose intellect was marvellous in range and flexibility, whose memory was a treasure-house of the mental spoils of all the ages, was so miserable a debater that the House emptied when he

rose. Sheridan shone in debate, and those who had
the greatest aversion to his politics were ready to
acknowledge his pre-eminence in speech. Wilberforce said that " Sheridan avoided encountering Pitt
in unforeseen debating, but when forced to it usually
came off well." Those who are the best acquainted
with Wilberforce will rate this praise the most
highly.[1]

Readiness in debate, the knack of happy and
sparkling retort, the capacity for hitting the House
" between wind and water," understanding and
responding to its varying moods, and always commanding the respect of the most critical legislative
assembly in the world ; success in making a reputation and, what is far harder, preserving it unimpaired
during thirty-one years, are among the achievements
of Sheridan as a member of Parliament. He had
qualifications which heightened the effect of his
utterances. He possessed a fine and flexible voice ;
he used appropriate gestures ; his manner was in-
sinuating ; he was blessed with a temper which it
was difficult to ruffle and with a self-command which
was equal to every emergency ; he could say with
perfect truth of an opponent who tried to do him an
injury and who plumed himself upon his cleverness,
" I could laugh at his malice but not at his wit "; in
short, he was, what I have already stated a great
orator must be, a consummate actor also.

It is true that the member who has the misfortune to possess an execrable voice is not necessarily
debarred from succeeding in Parliament. That of

---

[1] " The Life of Wilberforce," vol. v., p. 259.

Pitt, "sounded as if he had worsted in his mouth";[1] when Fox was excited, he screeched. Dundas's voice reminded the hearer of the creaking of a rusty hinge. Dunning's bad habit of clearing his throat at very frequent intervals marred the effect of his polished sentences. Part of Burke's failure to obtain an attentive hearing was owing to his uncouth accent. Brougham, who rose to the first rank among Parliamentary speakers, did so in spite of his rasping voice. Lord Westbury was the ablest speaker in our day at the Bar, in Parliament and on the Bench, and no man of his fame ever minced his words so finically.

Sir James Graham and Sir John, afterwards Lord Coleridge used to enable members of the House of Commons to understand Pope's admiration for "silver-tongued Murray," for both had voices of bell-like clearness and sound. The mellow and measured tones in which John Bright delivered the argumentative or declamatory passages in his masterly speeches contributed as much as the stern simplicity of their diction to raise him to the first rank among orators. Mr. Gladstone was as superior to him in scholarship as Fox was to Sheridan, yet Mr. Gladstone's comprehensive attainments would not have sufficed to render him a greater Burke, if he had failed to obtain a musical voice from Nature, or to acquire a finely modulated intonation. If Disraeli had been equally gifted, he would have had an additional claim to a statue, and to the idolatry of female worshippers who never heard him speak.

[1] "Recollections of Rogers," p. 79.

Contemporaries who were the most hearty in acknowledging Sheridan's splendid and rare oratorical gifts were of opinion that the most elaborate passages in his speeches had been carefully written out. Wilberforce said the general impression was " that he came to the House with his flashes prepared and ready to let off."[1] Sir Gilbert Elliot wrote to his wife that Sheridan's speech in Westminster Hall " was strewed very thick with more brilliant periods of eloquence and poetical imagination, and more lively sallies of wit, than could be produced probably by more than one other man in the world [Burke], with whom, however, they spring up and shoot out with all the luxuriance and grace of spontaneous nature. This certainly cannot be said of Sheridan's flowers, which are produced by great pains, skill and preparation, and are delivered in perfect order, ready tied up in regular though *beautiful bouquets*, and very unlike Burke's wild and natural nosegays."[2] When dining in Bentham's house, Sir Samuel Romilly informed the company that " nothing could be more marked than the difference between the parts of Sheridan's speeches previously written out, and the extemporaneous parts. The audience could discover in a moment when he fell into the latter."[3]

His hearers were entirely mistaken in thinking that the finest passages had been carefully prepared. Both his private and public utterances were often very telling as well as clever and un-

[1] " Life," vol. v., p. 259.
[2] " Life and Letters," vol. i., p. 208.
[3] " Residence at the Court of London," by Mr. Rush, p. 290.

hackneyed. Lord Eldon noted one, and Madame D'Arblay another, the first being : " During the debate on the India Bill [Pitt's], at which period John Robinson was Secretary to the Treasury, Sheridan, one evening when Mr. Fox's majorities were decreasing, said, ' Mr. Speaker, this is not at all to be wondered at, when a member is employed to corrupt everybody in order to obtain votes.' Upon this there was a general outcry made by everybody in the House : ' Who is it ? Name him ! name him !' ' Sir,' said Sheridan to the Speaker, ' I shall not name the person. It is an unpleasant and invidious thing to do so, and therefore I shall not name him. But don't suppose, Sir, that I abstain because there is any difficulty in naming ; I could do that, Sir, as soon as you could say Jack Robinson.' "[1] The second was : " Mrs. Cholmondeley was making much sport by wishing for an acrostic on her name. ' An acrostic on your name,' said Mr. Sheridan, ' would be a formidable task ; it must be so long that I think it should be divided into cantos.' "[2]

Mr. Abbot, who was Speaker early in this century, and who became Lord Colchester, wrote in his *Diary* that Sheridan was " fluent in speech, shrewd in his conceptions, witty often when his subject required gravity, the most active and mischievous partisan of the Republican faction, playing off Fox as a constitutional opposer of the King's Ministers, and himself hand and heart with the most desperate

[1] " Life of Lord Eldon," vol. i., p. 161.
[2] " Diary of Madame D'Arblay," vol. i., p. 187.

Jacobins."[1]   The last words, which are at variance with facts, are those of a bigoted Tory, who could not deny, however, Sheridan's great oratorical merits.

Preparation of the kind with which Sheridan was credited is not that to which he was addicted.   He always gave his best to his audience.   He had a ready tongue.   Many men whose tongues wag easily are intolerable bores, pouring forth, as Castlereagh often did according to Moore, "a weak, washy everlasting flood."   Sheridan sometimes committed a few sentences, or parts of them, to paper ; but the passages in his speeches which are generally regarded as having been the most carefully elaborated, were not written beforehand.   He was industrious in collecting facts ; the margins of the parliamentary documents which were in his possession are covered with notes ; the extracts from the evidence concerning Warren Hastings were methodically marshalled, and they cover many pages, yet none of the flowery passages in that speech have been found in writing, and, seeing that he was as averse as a Turk to destroying a written paper, it is improbable that any ever existed.

The truth is that he composed his speeches in the same manner that he did the dialogue of his plays.   When he had settled the plot and the characters, he "could go on with the dialogue," as he told his second wife, "travelling, visiting, walking, anyhow, anywhere."   In like manner, he was able to cast in a literary form the parts in his speeches

[1] "Diary of Lord Colchester," vol. i., p. 23.

which he deemed the most important; he was an adept at mental composition, and he could rely upon his memory for the correct reproduction of what had been entrusted to it. [1]

Much of Sheridan's popularity without the walls of Parliament was due to the belief that he was a patriot to the core. The theatre in his hands was used to inculcate the greatness and glory of the nation, and the tirades in *Pizarro*, which jar upon the critic, helped to recruit the army in the season of trial.

I have set forth how nobly Sheridan acted when the Mutiny at the Nore had made his fellows despair of their country. He summed up his feelings as a patriot at a later day in the phrase, "defence not defiance"; he detested aggression and he was such a true friend of peace that he counselled any sacrifice in order to render an attack upon his country impossible or nugatory. Not sharing the prejudice against the French nation which was common in his day, he was hearty in sympathy and warm in his applause when that nation was battling for freedom. But when the sun of liberty which had dawned in France went down there in darkness and blood, and

---

[1] Sheil and Macaulay could do likewise. When Sheil undertook the defence of O'Connell, the reporters for the London Press desired a copy beforehand of what they supposed he had written. He informed him that "he had the speech in his head," and he dictated it to them. It was in print before it was delivered, and it was spoken in Court as it had been spoken in Sheil's room. Macaulay told the first Lord Lytton that he never wrote down his speeches lest they should acquire the character of formal essays. He, too, prepared and corrected them in his head.—Sheil's "Memoirs," vol. ii., p. 332, and "St. Stephen's," p. 108.

was succeeded by a night of despotism as crushing and cruel as that which had been overthrown, his voice was raised in denunciation of Bonaparte, who performed on the stage of Europe the part which Marlowe had made Tamburlaine act on the stage of the Play-house.

In 1803, when Great Britain was threatened with invasion, no voice was more eloquent that Sheridan's in counselling effective resistance ; not even Robert Hall's marvellous sermon, or William Cobbett's magnificent address to the people inspired fiercer feelings of patriotism than the language which Sheridan used in Parliament. He declared on the 10th of August, 1803, amid the loud applause of the House, that if a foreign soldier set foot on British soil, no peace should be made while he remained there. But he made another appeal as worthy of honour and one which should be remembered to his infinite credit. It was to the effect that members should suspend their political animosities for a season, refrain from disparaging the existing Government and that, instead of wasting time and energy in party contests and intrigue, they should devote all their efforts to performing the sublimer duties of patriotism. "This was a moment," he exclaimed, "which called on every honest man to unite heart and hand in support of all that is dear to us as a great and free people, against the greatest danger with which we were ever threatened. Let but this small sacrifice be made to patriotism, and when they once more assembled in that House, they might resume their favourite pursuits, under the pleasing consciousness, that they had contributed their efforts to the general safety."[1]

Sheridan was not a patriot of the common type who appears and acts upon the immoral maxim " my country right or wrong," or who in a London Music Hall, on a Paris pavement, or in a newspaper clamours for war, knowing well that he will not take part in it. The speech from which I have quoted was made in support of a motion that the Volunteers should be thanked for enrolling themselves in defence of the country. He stated at the outset that he appeared in the House as a Volunteer himself. No one who has written about him has mentioned the fact that he was Lieutenant Colonel of the St. James's Volunteer Corps and that he returned to the Secretary at War the thanks of the Corps for the compliment paid to it by the House of Commons.[2] His patriotism did not

[1] " Parliamentary Debates," vol. xxxvi., p. 1697.

[2] Charles Francis Sheridan, when visiting London, wrote to his wife in Dublin on the 10th of October, 1803 : " Richard [his brother] is Lieutenant-Colonel of the St. James's Volunteers, the Prince's Own, so he will be obliged to keep early hours in spite of himself." I have found among Sheridan's papers the draft, in his own hand, of a document which I print without comment : " My Lord, The thanks of the House of Commons having been communicated to the St. James's Volunteers which I have the honour to command, I am authorized by the whole Corps to express the ardent pride with which they have received at once the testimony and reward of the zeal which has called forth their exertions. The feelings of the Corps on this occasion are shortly and easily to be expressed. They are most grateful for the high honour conferred upon them. They consider it as a proof of the confidence which the representatives of the people repose in their

hinder him from giving the strongest support to Spain when struggling to shake off the yoke of the invader and regain her freedom. On the 15th of June, 1808, he urged the Government to send Sir Arthur Wellesley to represent " the enthusiasm of England in her cause " and used words which proved to be prophetic :—" Bonaparte has hitherto run a victorious race. Hitherto he has had to contend against Princes without dignity and Ministers without wisdom. He has fought against countries in which the people have been indifferent as to his success ; he has yet to learn what it is to fight against a country in which the people are animated with one spirit to resist him."

Opinions were divided as to the propriety of following the counsel which he gave, and his motion was withdrawn because, as he said, his object had been attained by the discussion. Castlereagh, then Minister-at-War, paid him a compliment which, coming from an irreconcilable political opponent, was no perfunctory eulogium :—" The motion had been brought forward by a Right Honourable Gentleman who, on all occasions of difficulty, in every crisis of the country, waving all political hostility, had uniformly come forward in support of the country."[1]

---

fixed resolution to make every sacrifice in support of their King, the Constitution and their country ; but they cherish the eager hope that the hour shall come in which they may have the more glorious opportunity of proving that this confidence has not been ill-placed."

[1] " Parliamentary Debates," vol. ii., pp. 880 and 885.

Sheridan's voice was heard in Parliament for the last time on the 21st of June, 1812. He then moved for certain papers relative to an overture for peace. His motion was carried without a division; but, before it was put, he replied to objections which had been raised to some of his statements, and ended with words which ought never to be forgotten :—" The immortality of nations was not consigned to mortal custody ; but to fight bravely and to perish gloriously was so. And such must be the example of Great Britain. Take the condition of this country with all its faults, and we should find it the best that ever existed in any nation. Take our Constitution, wanting certainly as it did many reforms, yet, practically, it afforded the best security that human wisdom had ever given to man. Yet with all this to contend for, we might not be able ultimately to command success. Even Great Britain, for her rights and her honour, might spend her treasure, shed more and more of her best and bravest blood, and at last might fall. Yet after the general subjugation and ruin of Europe, should there ever exist an independent historian to record the awful events that produced the universal calamity, let that historian, after describing the greatness and glory of Britain, have to say, 'She fell, and with her fell all the best securities for the charities of human life, for the power and honour, the fame, the glory and the liberties of herself and the whole civilized world.' "[1]

The most memorable mention of Sheridan in the

[1] "Parliamentary Debates," vol. xxiii., p. 1156.

House of Commons, during the life-time of the present generation, was made by John Bright in one of his finest speeches in support of Reform. Quoting what he styled ' the beautiful language of Sheridan,' he said that his ideal for the country was the advent of the time, depicted by him, when ' Content sits basking on the cheek of Toil,' and the House warmly responded to the invocation of the greatest of its past members by him whom it as fervently admired and as highly esteemed. Coleridge, who had heard Sheridan address the House, has indicated a stanza in Shakespeare's " Lover's Complaint " as being "almost prophetically characteristic " of him as an orator :—

> " So on the tip of his subduing tongue
> All kind of argument and question deep,
> All replication prompt and reason strong,
> For his advantage still did wake and sleep ;
> To make the weeper laugh, the laugher weep,
> He had the dialect and different skill,
> Catching all passions in his craft of will ;
> That he did in the general bosom reign
> Of young, of old."

XII.

THE VERDICT OF POSTERITY?

IF Sheridan could be made acquainted with all the stories written about him, he would find in them material for a farce as pungent and lively, as brilliant and comical as *The Critic*. In that event Sir Fretful Plagiary would be provided with companions in misfortune. Biographers have travestied his life and playwrights have parodied his career. The most amusing and successful attempt to represent him on the stage, as he was not in the flesh, was made by M. Langlé in 1863. His piece is entitled *Un Homme de Rien* and it had a long run at the Vaudeville Theatre, where Parisian playgoers applauded it. While differing from anything that has been written about him in English, it is not much more remote from truth and sense, and the French writer had the advantage over every English one in being utterly unconscious of misrepresenting the man whom he took for his hero.

The opening scene is in the garden of a tavern at Richmond near the favourite race-course on the bank of the Thames. A fashionable company has assembled, and the usual frequenters of races ply their usual trades, an Irishman offering game-cocks

for sale, and Susannah O'Donnor, lace cuffs. A
young man attired in an under-graduate's gown
and cap reels into the garden and calls for gin.
Susannah is attracted, and shows this by lecturing
him on the vice of intemperance. He displays his
gratitude by avowing that his name is Richard
Brinsley Sheridan ; that he has left the University
after having gained every honour and is starving ;
that, having written plays which are rejected because
he is unknown, and articles for newspapers which
have had the same fate because they were too long
and seditious, he has resolved to drown his sorrows
in the bowl. Susannah advises him to place himself
on the " waiting-seat " where jockeys remain till
they are engaged.

He does what she suggests and then over-hears
the Marquis de Champrosé tell Commodore Dunbar
that he can bring down not only a swallow, but also a
Mayfly on the wing, with a bullet. The Commodore
replies that he used to amuse himself by shooting
away the bowl of a pipe, the stem of which a
Polynesian chief held between his teeth, and that
he would back himself to do this for £40 if he
could find a man to undergo the ordeal. Sheridan
offers to stand with the pipe in his mouth, and he
never moves a muscle when the bowl is shot away
within an inch of his lips. The £40 are handed
over to him. The Commodore's jockey having
disappeared, Sheridan volunteers to act in his stead.
He wins the race and is rewarded with a valuable
diamond pin. The Duchess of Cardwell's sleeve
having been torn, she calls for a pin and Sheridan

hands her the one which he had received. She declines to take it on account of its great value, whereupon he pulls out the diamond, which he throws into the river, and then she consents to make use of the pin.

George, Prince of Wales, steps out of the tavern and graciously compliments Sheridan on his conduct. Having handed £2 to the Irish cock-fighter and £38 to the Clerk of the course, Sheridan is as poor at the end as he was at the beginning of the day, and he sleeps the sleep of the weary and the impecunious on the "waiting - stone." However, his fortune rapidly changes for the better, and he ascends at a bound to the first place among dramatists. The Duchess of Cardwell becomes his patroness and she introduces him to the Prince of Wales. Though famous, he is still poor, and the Duchess sends him £2,000 anonymously. He guesses that the money comes from her and returns it into her hands, where-upon she throws the bank-notes into the fire, saying as she does so, " You threw your diamond into the Thames ; now we are quits." Susannah is engaged as a lady's maid ; Paddy, the dealer in game-cocks, becomes Sheridan's valet, and, after several incidents as stirring and natural as all the others, the curtain falls upon Sheridan in the exalted position of Prime Minister, and the happy husband of the estimable Susannah O'Donnor.[1]

[1] A detailed account of this curious production appeared in *The Express*, an excellent evening Journal of bygone days, and was reproduced by *The Times* on the 29th of April, 1863.

M. Langlé had a master in absurdity in Villemain, a great

Sheridan deserves general pity for having lost in early youth the mother who loved him, and having had in his father the most unkind and unjust of parents, the most exacting and implacable of critics. His two sisters cherished an affection for him which was cordially and fully reciprocated; but they could neither aid him in his battle with the world, nor guide his steps amid the temptations which beset him. The intensity of their feelings was not lessened either by absence from each other's company, or the lapse of years. His elder sister told her niece, after being informed of her brother's death, that Mrs. Sheridan had sent a most kind letter,

---

authority in France respecting the literature of the eighteenth century, who states in the fourth volume, p. 179, of his *Littérature au Dix-huitième Siècle*, that Sheridan arrived in England from Ireland eager to distinguish himself and hardly pressed for money, while ready to lavish it, and filled with all youthful passions; that he began his career with a duel and an elopement and married a singer; that his second weakness was an unbridled love for gaming, and his third an equally unbridled love for wine. Few of Villemain's most intelligent readers may have known that Sheridan left Ireland at the age of eight, and that he never was a gamester.

A living writer emulates with complete success the reputation which M. Langlé and Villemain have acquired for blundering about Sheridan. M. Frederic Febre, having been sent to America with the view to instruct his countrymen, wrote that, shortly after landing, he went to Daly's Theatre in New York and saw " *The Critic* by Sheridan." He thus characterized it : "*La pièce est une adaptation d'un ouvrage Allemand—doux mélange de poudding et de choucroute.*" —" The piece is an adaptation from a German work, and is a sweet compound of pudding and sour-krout !"—*Le Gaulois*, 18 August, 1895.

in acknowledgment of one " I had written to my brother, when I heard he was ill, with the affection in which I always addressed him.   This is what she says : 'Sheridan shed many tears over your last letter (and it was a lovely one) saying as he always did that you were the most perfect of human beings.' Ah! my dear niece, far am I from meriting such a eulogy, but most grateful is it to my sad heart that such were his dying thoughts of me.   May the God of goodness look down upon us both and give us a meeting in a better world !"

Elizabeth, his second sister, was left almost penniless at her father's death.   Sheridan gave her a home and, when she married, he made her an annual allowance which was punctually paid so long as his means permitted.   He obtained a lucrative office for his elder brother, whose only return was to borrow money.   Sheridan's hand was never closed against an appeal for help ; he was more ready, as the Prince Regent acknowledged to Peter Moore, to confer than to accept favours, and when Fox was hard pressed for money wherewith to bet at Newmarket, he applied to Sheridan and received the sum required.[1]

His generosity and unselfishness elicited ingratitude or indifference.   If he had been niggardly he

---

[1] The following is one of Fox's unpublished notes: " Dear Sheridan, I have got the money that I wanted so much for the present, and therefore I should be sorry you gave yourself any more trouble about it ; but if you can get me 1000 or 1500 for me by the 15th of September, it would be a very great convenience to me."

would have been styled cautious and sensible. His reward during life was to be libelled by those who had preyed upon him ; his posthumous punishment has been to become the subject for moralizing by inconsiderate biographers. Professional money-lenders are said to have rightly suffered because Fox was their client, while humble tradesmen were cruelly wronged because Sheridan was their customer.[1] He was not a punctual paymaster ; but, as he wrote to his second wife, "the household bills did get paid somehow or other ;" it may be added that he was severely punished for his laxity in never keeping a key or taking a receipt. When his affairs were strictly investigated, it was found, as I have previously stated, that, for every twenty shillings which he owed, his creditors had received thirty.[2] Well might he write in 1806 to his second wife, " I am myself, I think, very much changed. I look back on the facility with which I have through my life been duped in every way and by everybody, and wonder whether I am possessed of common understanding."

He was a dutiful son, a most affectionate brother, and a husband who was devoted almost to uxorious-

---

[1] "Lives of the Sheridans," vol. ii., p. 52.

[2] The tradesmen's bills which have been preserved contain these items :—Wm. Smith charged him £3 15s. for pomatum and hair powder from May to December, while the charge for hair-cutting was 5s. each time and 2s. 6d. for dressing. In a bill of C. Weltje, dated 1784, three bottles of champagne are charged at the same fancy price as a novel in three volumes is now, that is £1 11s. 6d. ; " a Perigo Pie " is £3 3s. ; strawberries at the middle of July are charged 3s. a pottle, and cherries, when most plentiful, 5s. 6d. the pound.

ness.   His second wife had not the beautiful traits
of the first, yet her admiration for him was as intense, while her character appears in a very pleasing
light in the pathetic letter which she wrote to her
sister-in-law three months after his death : " I know
you will be glad to know that I am essentially better.
I will not say how often I have *wished* to write to
you.   I seldom think of Sheridan without associating
with those thoughts one who I am convinced would
understand my every feeling on that subject, and
had I been in health I am persuaded I should ere
this have found myself in Ireland in earnest conversation with you.   I never received till the other day
a letter of yours dated August by a private hand ;
it contained but a few lines.

   " Our dear Sheridan has left an incredible quantity
of private papers.   The effort I made to collect
them under the Bishop of London's roof in St.
James's Square (in which I have partially succeeded)
almost killed me, and after I had examined about
the 20th part of them and made the necessary
arrangements for the continuance of that examination in case of my death I was *ordered* out of Town.

   " I have taken a small house in Grosvenor Place,
number 27, where I shall be after the 5th of November, and as soon as I have got through the above
mentioned papers, I shall give my whole thoughts
to a biographical account and publishing his works.
It is a subject on which I am on fire, and I shall
have no peace till I see something given to the
public whether by the hand of one friend, or many
friends, simple, clear, just and eloquent, and it is to

you, my dear sister, that I would apply for the early
part of your loved brother's life, or for any memoirs
altogether that you may judge likely to be of use.
Nothing shall be *published* without your sanction
and strict review.

"I am wholly indifferent as to pecuniary considerations with respect to myself, nor will I ever
appropriate to myself anything arising from such a
publication. I believe his debts to be a mere trifle
compared with what they are reported to be, and
there is on my mind a never ceasing hope and wish
to pay them. Both Charles and myself would rather
see that day than secure a Dukedom. On this subject I would enter more fully, but writing is the one
thing that disagrees with me on account of being
compelled to leave the horizontal posture.

"Thank you a thousand times for your anxiety
respecting these matters. Charles will have plenty
of friends, and for myself I desire nothing. One
thing only I want, honour, glory and *truth* for
Sheridan. I could indeed make you adore the
Duke of Wellington! I should sooner have sent
you Lord Byron's Monody, but I knew you would
have seen it, and I had no opportunity of sending
so large a paquet free. I have been much pleased
with Mr. Phillip's verses. Some of them are *beautiful.* There is another Monody very good by
Mr. Gent, but I own there is a spirit and feeling in
Lord Byron's that blinds me to every fault.

"Lest you should mistake the nature of my illness, I will just tell you that I have now every
prospect of a recovery, and that I have been even

quite free from every symptom of a distressing or
dangerous nature. Repeated colds and utter neglect
of myself, united to constant anxiety of mind, have
been the real causes of my illness, which has now
lasted nearly four years. Great natural strength has
alone enabled me to cope with so many trials. I
have repeatedly during this illness given myself
over, and on that dreadful day I would gladly have
expired with him.

"You are much too kind to me. I am not handsome, I am full of faults and very ignorant. I have
a tolerable heart, and not a little mind, and I adore
merit in others, and that is all I can say for myself."[1]

A man may be a good son, a brother whose
sisters regard him with deep and true affection, the
husband of a wife who adores him, and yet he may
fail in the most difficult of all tasks, that of retaining

---

[1] This letter was written on the 24th of October, 1816 ; the writer,
who was happily unconscious of being afflicted with an incurable
disease, died at Frogmore on the 27th of October, 1817. Her
son Charles wrote from Trinity College, Cambridge, in November, 1817, to his cousin the Reverend T. P. Lefanu : "I have
again, alas, to address you on these sad and heart-rending subjects !
I have lost my brother too. A letter, which I have received to-
day from his unhappy widow, has brought the sad news. He
died on the 12th of September. She says he suffered little. She
is coming home immediately in the *Albion Transport*. Her life
has been a course of unparalleled devotion and attachment to my
poor brother. A thousand thanks for your kind, your very kind
letter. I only got it on my return here on Monday. How
sincerely I wish we were together ! I am sure you would teach
me better and more persuasively than anyone how all these things
coming in such sad succession *ought* to be borne."

the love and respect of his sons after they have
reached years of discretion, have become their own
masters and acquired the right to criticise him.
Both of Sheridan's sons vied with each other in
filial attachment and personal admiration ; they
were proud of his achievements ; they made due
allowance for his shortcomings.   Tom, his elder son,
had derived from his mother many beautiful mental
qualities, along with a delicacy of constitution which
caused him to descend, as she had done, into an
early grave.   The letters which he wrote to his
step-mother about his father, after his father had
ceased to be a member of Parliament, are as touching in tone, as they are practical in suggestion.

His son by a second marriage entertained an affection for his father which does him, and the parent
who inspired it, infinite credit.   He told Moore that
some of " his poor father's faults," which Moore had
unveiled, would have been kept in darkness by him.
The reverential attitude of both for their father
recalls what prevailed in the days of the Patriarchs.[1]

[1] All Sheridan's descendants have held him in high honour.
Miss Gore-Jones, his great-niece, favoured me with unpublished
letters concerning him.   Her sudden death at a very advanced
age, hinders me from learning whether what I have written, with
full knowledge and in good faith, would have been more welcome
than the work of a recent biographer of which she wrote immediately after perusing it :

I.

" Strive not with reckless hand to tear
        The garlands from his tomb ;
  Touch not the laurels springing there
        In everlasting bloom.

The families with which Sheridan became connected by marriage welcomed him as a brilliant
addition.   His father-in-law, Mr. Linley, exhibited
more affection for him than his own father had done ;
his sister-in-law, Mrs. Tickell, was warmly attached
to him ; Miss Ogle, his sister-in-law by his second
marriage, enlarged upon his merits to Moore who,
when recording this, added that she evidently desired him to be unstinted in his praise, a mistake
which he avoided with extreme, if not morbid care.[1]

Several of Sheridan's personal friends supplied
Moore with particulars which he did not publish.
Sir Richard Phillips is one of them.   He stated that,
meeting Sheridan on business and wishing to submit
to him certain information in writing, he remarked
that it would be useless to do so, as Sheridan had the
reputation of never opening or reading letters ; "he
replied, with great warmth, that the assertion was
'an infernal lie,' that he never [had] omitted to open

2.

"Not all the subtle art of man,
     His genius can debase,
Or cloud the star of Sheridan
     With shadows of disgrace.

3.

"Enough—He needs no hand to save
     His laurels or his fame,
The splendour flashing o'er his grave
     Reveals the spoiler's shame !"

[1] "Like a those of his friends or relatives I have met, [Miss
Ogle was] full of enthusiasm about his memory, his fame, etc.,
and trusting that I shall do him ample justice (*i.e.*, praise him
through thick and thin)."—"Diary" of Moore, vol. ii., p. 299.

a letter in his life, nor neglected to answer one, if it merited or required an answer ;[1] 'but,' said he, 'if you will not trust me with a letter, call upon me some morning and we will talk over the subject,' on which I replied that the difficulty seemed to increase, for it is generally understood 'that you never rise till evening,' on which he protested with great warmth : " That, Sir, is another of the lies of which I am the victim, and by which I am separated from the world, and my interests constantly thwarted ; I acknowledge I sometimes sit late and sometimes do not get up till the afternoon ; but I am apprized of calls, get up when necessary, and no person leaves my door about whom it is of importance that I should see . . ." He declared to Sir Richard that his life had been made miserable by calumnies, tales and stories, of one kind or another.

Disraeli made a like complaint, on the 23rd of September, 1870, in a letter to the late Baron Tauchnitz and said that he had invariably treated with utter indifference the infamous libels which had been written about him, adding, " Sometimes I ask myself what will Grub Street do after my departure, who will there be to abuse and caricature ?" I

---

[1] In its qualified form the statement may be accepted. Sheridan's habit was not to open or answer all letters on their receipt, but to put them into a bag with the intention of dealing with them at his leisure. I add his first wife's testimony in order that both sides should be represented. She wrote from Harrow to her sister-in-law in 1782 : " Poor Dick hardly ever reads his own letters, so that if ever a letter of mine finds it way into his pocket unopened, it might as well be in the bottomless pit for any good I am ever like to reap by it."

pointed out at the beginning of this work how Disraeli, by accepting a peerage during life, escaped being slandered after death, and said that Sheridan, if he had consented to wear a coronet, would have received fulsome adulation instead of foolish detraction.

That Sheridan was irregular in his hours of going to bed and getting up cannot be disputed ; but the stories about him in this matter, as in other matters, have been exaggerated. In a letter to his second wife, written on the 29th of December, 1806, a period of the year when the temptation to get up early is not irresistible in this country and climate, he says :—" I have changed my bad hours, and now constantly ring up the house before daylight, and Ma'am I mean this shall positively last notwithstanding the treachery of my former resolutions to the same effect." A fortnight afterwards he writes,— " I continue my early hours and industrious exertions. All connected with me will be the better for it, perhaps even myself."

The privilege of a public and popular personage is to have the minutest doings of his private life rigidly scrutinized and subjected to frivolous comment. As the reports on such matters generally differ, the momentous question as to whether Sheridan was a sluggard or an early riser, may be left for the idle and curious to discuss and settle. Probably the truth was that, suffering from insomnia for many years of his life, and finding his eyelids heavy in the morning, he may often have remained longer in bed than he would have done if refreshed with balmy sleep during the night. In assuring Sir Richard Phillips that he was particular in replying to all letters which required, or merited an answer, he affirmed what he believed to be the truth, yet many a correspondent may have deemed him negligent.   If alive now and occupied as he then was, he would employ a secretary to relieve him of the terrible burden of returning civil answers to the unsolicited and trumpery letters of unwelcome and exacting correspondents.

The calls upon Sheridan's time were more than he could meet ; the enterprises in which he embarked were more than he ought to have undertaken ; his society was courted by so many persons that the hours which he could devote to business were far too few, and it might be said of him, as of the Duke of Newcastle, whom Horace Walpole ridiculed, that he often lost an hour in the morning and spent the rest of the day in running after it.   His industry, at times, was exemplary ; but a hot fit of hard work was frequently followed by many hours of indolence. He could not sit down, with the punctuality and austere determination of Sir Walter Scott, and accomplish a stated task daily.

No one has ventured to charge Sheridan with being an insincere friend or an unpleasant companion.   He had the rare and admirable merit of attaching to himself everyone with whom he associated.   Indeed, his personal fascination was marvellous.   When very young, he twice fought a duel in vindication of his own honour and of Miss Linley's ; but, during thirty-one years of heated political rivalry, he never received a challenge nor ever had occasion to send one.   This was almost unprecedented in the case of an active and energetic member of Parliament. Wilkes fought with Martin and was dangerously wounded. Fox and Adam exchanged shots. Lord George Germain fought with Governor Johnstone; Lord Shelburne with Fullarton; Tierney with William Pitt; Canning with Castlereagh and the Duke of Wellington with the Earl of Winchilsea. Whitbread was hindered by the intervention of the Speaker from fighting with Hart Davies. Even Peel sent a challenge to O'Connell.

If not a more profound politician than many of his contemporaries who held high office and are honoured for having saved their country from imaginary perils, Sheridan was consistent in his views; he was most able and rational in giving expression to them and supreme among the members of his party as a patriot without bluster or blindness to signs of the times. The field of his knowledge was neither very wide nor laboriously cultivated, yet it produced choice fruit. Higher office than the ruling Whigs would accord to him was within his reach by joining Pitt in company with the Duke of Portland, Lord Spencer, Lord Fitzwilliam, Burke and Windham. When Addington was Prime Minister, either a peerage, or a pension larger than Burke's was at Sheridan's disposal. However. he preserved his independence at a great sacrifice and, while on minor matters he gave his vote for the Prince of Wales, he would not surrender his liberty of action on any question of principle. Even when a member of the Prince's household, he supported the emancipation of the Catholics, to which the Prince was strongly and irrationally hostile.

He had counted the cost of being true to his convictions, knowing well that to do so was a far greater trial than it would be to others with whom he was politically associated. He said to Byron, with perfect justice, and irrepressible emotion : " It is easy for my Lord G. or Earl G. or Marquess B. or Lord H., with thousands upon thousands a year, some of it either *presently* derived, or *inherited* in sinecure or acquisitions from the public money, to boast of their patriotism and keep aloof from temptation ; but they do not know from what temptation those have kept aloof, who had equal pride, or at least equal talents, and not unequal passions, and nevertheless knew not in the course of their lives what it was to have a shilling of their own."[1]

Horace Walpole took a like view when the Duke of Portland urged him to press Mr. Conway to resign :—" I said I could not take upon me to advise him to give up all he had. He laughed, and said it would not be for long ; everything came round in this country. I replied, ' Your Lordship with twenty thousand pounds a year, talks very much at your ease ; but Mr. Conway would have nothing in the world and would not go into Opposition to recover his fortune.' "[2] At a later day Thackeray crystallised the same idea when he made Becky Sharp declare that it was easy to be virtuous upon five thousand pounds a year. Yet the practice of virtue by either

[1] " Life of Byron," vol. ii., p. 202. Sheridan was the only Parliamentary orator whom Byron " ever wished to hear at greater length," p. 210.

[2] " Memoirs of the Reign of George III.," vol. ii., p. 383.

sex, whether in public or private life, depends less
upon the amount of one's income than upon the
ability for self-sacrifice when a principle is at stake.
Whether Sheridan would have been a greater honour
to his country if his fortune had been large cannot be
settled now ; yet it is unquestionable that he nobly
resisted inducements to swerve from the path of
honour, to which others succumbed, and, in an age
when venality was avowed and practised without
shame, he could truthfully write to his second wife
and say: " My price is not on this earth to do otherwise than what was right and go straight forward."

He may have taken too much claret during the
earlier and too much brandy during the later years
of his life, but whether he ever prepared himself for making a speech by swallowing a bottle of
brandy is open to question, even though Lord
Campbell be the authority for the statement.[1]   To
articulate after drinking so much brandy is a feat
of no common kind.   In Sheridan's day it was
a compliment " to be as drunk as a Lord."   Junius
ironically congratulated Lord Weymouth, when
Secretary of State, on having recovered from " the
bewitching smiles of Burgundy."[2]   Lord Mansfield
considered it his duty to remonstrate with the Duke
of Rutland, then Lord Lieutenant of Ireland, for
" drinking hard " and keeping irregular hours, while
the Duke's sister urged and implored him to be
abstemious " in eating as well as *drinking*."[3]   He
died at the age of thirty-three.   Yet some who were

---

[1] " Life " of Lord Campbell, vol. i., p. 108.
[2] " Letters," vol. i., p. 12.
[3] " Rutland Manuscripts," vol. iii., pp. 143 and 159.

the reverse of abstemious lived to a good old age.
Earl Grey was over eighty when he died.   Sir Gilbert
Elliot was present at an entertainment in 1788 where
"Grey drank more than any of them."[1]   At present,
few members of the Peerage are ever intemperate
except when addressing a public assembly.

Sheridan enjoyed very plain fare.   He wrote to
his second wife that he hoped she would provide for
him on arriving: "a boiled knuckle of veal and
bacon and greens."   Though simple in his tastes,
he was very fastidious, and he disliked, as much
as Byron did, the spectacle of women gorging themselves.   Lady Granville records, when at Bad-
minton in 1810, that "Sheridan says he sat by Lady
Catherine at supper, and that she munched and
munched platesful of salad, till he took her for an
old sow, and caught himself just going to say to the
servants, ' Pray change this lady's trough.' "[2]

One of his merits as a dramatist was to eschew
grossness.   This cost him no effort.   Mrs. Tickell
wrote to her sister, who was his first wife: "You
know that Sheridan hates indelicacies."   The failing of over-indulgence in stimulants was conquered
by him before his last illness.   His elder sister
informed her niece, a few days after his death,
that she had hoped: "the native strength of
his constitution [and] his habits, which for a long
time were extremely temperate, would have baffled
the disease."   Four months before her brother's
death, she gave the same niece a version of a story
which has often been told, but never in her words.

[1] "Life and Letters," vol. i., p. 189.
[2] "Letters of Countess Granville," vol. i., p. 5.

It proves that even when Sheridan had taken wine to excess his humour was unimpaired, while it may be doubted whether he was perfectly incapable when his mind was so active. The letter is dated the 25th of February, 1816 :—" I am tempted to tell you a story of Dick that will make you smile. It happened very lately. He was coming home from a very late dinner, a public one, at a very late hour. More wine than recollection [being] in his head he lost his way, and was found by a watchman in this dilemma ; the watchman offered to conduct his ' honour ' and his [services] were accepted. After other chat your Uncle asked him, did he know him ? The guardian of the night confessed ignorance of the name and quality of his *protégé*. ' Why,' said Dick, ' it is singular you should not know *me*. I am Mr. Wilberforce.' The watchman dropped his pole and lantern with astonishment at finding at 4 o'clock in the morning, in no very sober condition, the greatest saint in England." This was Sheridan's last practical joke.

He once learned the character which had been ascribed to him by the irresponsible concoctors of stories. William Pitt informed Dr. Burney when entertaining him at Walmer Castle that " Mrs. Lloyd, housekeeper at Kensington Palace, being in company with Mr. Sheridan without recollecting him, while *Pizarro* was the subject of discussion, she said to him, ' And so this fine " Pizarro " is printed ?' ' Yes, so I hear,' said Sherry. ' And did you ever in your life read such stuff!' cried she. ' Why! I believe it's bad enough,' quoth Sherry, ' but at least Madam, you must allow it's very loyal.'   ' Ah !' cried she, shaking her head, ' Loyal. You don't know its author so well as I do.' "[1]

Many who profess to understand Sheridan and have condemned him in strong language, know as much about him as Mrs. Lloyd.   Facts are far less attractive than fictions.   A fiction can be dressed in many fashions while truth requires no disguise, and has few admirers.   For this reason the following statement made in writing by Mr. Mulock to the late Honourable Caroline Norton, may appear much duller than the fables : " To extol Sheridan's unrivalled superiority over his great contemporaries (with the single exception of his countryman Burke) is needless. In variform power of mind he excelled them all, and also in independence of spirit.   Where he most failed as a public man was in his Irish yieldingness (not subserviency) to Anglo-Saxon assumption and arrogance.   Binding himself too implicitly to an ungrateful party, he became (unwittingly) a splendid drudge without permanent pay.   Much of what is called Sheridan's improvidence arose simply from the fact that his position was always higher than his pecuniary resources.   He contracted debt, not in anticipation of real income, but on the strength of contingent expectations, not often fulfilled ; and yet, his entire liabilities, if summed up, would have been wiped away by a tithe of the ostentatious bounty lavished on Fox and offered (by Lord Carrington and others) to Pitt.   No one, as you justly remark,

---

[1] " Memoirs of Dr. Burney," vol. iii., p. 279.

ever held out a helping hand to Sheridan.   In his
necessities, he walked alone.

"I knew him personally (for I am an old man)
and met him where his presence was always welcomed, particularly at the then Mr. Whitbread's.
In distinguished quarters I gleaned much of him, but
particularly from his sister, Mrs. Le Fanu, my
earliest lady friend, who was imbued with a rich
variety of her brother's talent, and who idolized him
under all his painful change of circumstances.   All
I heard (and verified) tended strongly to establish
the conclusion before stated.   Sheridan was *not* a
dishonest man, but his ' pride of place' (not however
with a placeman's certainties) involved him in engagements which he failed to keep, and those failures,
by constant recurrence, engendered a fatal familiarity
with promise-breaking.   The world past and present
overflows with such instances, but on a much larger
scale of indebtedness than poor Sheridan's.   I also
knew Mrs. Sheridan (*née* Ogle) and I am sorry to
say that she contributed to swell his embarrassments.

"Sheridan was going down hill when I first met
him, and it is evident that he had so accustomed
himself to stimulants that he required their impulse
before he could join in social converse.   But what
brilliancy shone forth when once he was excited!
I have spent evenings with Curran, with Walter
Scott and many other renowned conversationalists ;
but none of them had the graceful ease, the intellectual repartee, the sparkling pleasantry of
Sheridan.   He did not come into company with

SHERIDAN'S NAME CUT ON A PANEL IN THE FOURTH FORM
ROOM AT HARROW, REFERRED TO BY LORD BYRON.

prepared jokes for which occasion was to be sought, but his wit and jocularity out-flew as happy occasions offered themselves. He was the readiest of men, and yet Moore labours to sully him on this very point. But Moore was a memoir-monger."

It is unfortunate that Moore did not take, or, perhaps, was so circumstanced as to be unable to follow the shrewd advice of Byron: "In writing the *Life of Sheridan* never mind the angry lies of the humbug Whigs. Recollect that he was an Irishman and a clever fellow, and that we have had some very pleasant days with him. Don't forget that he was at school at Harrow, where, in my time, we used to show his name—R. B. Sheridan, 1765—as an honour to the walls. . . . Depend upon it that there were worse folks going, of that gang, than ever Sheridan was."[1]

The belief prevailed among those who knew them both that Moore was jealous of Sheridan. Each had access to the best society, but Sheridan moved therein on terms of equality, while Moore was welcomed as an entertainer.[2] There is not an instance on record of Sheridan truckling to, or

---

[1] "Life of Byron," vol. iv., p. 135.

[2] Moore could not help occupying a subordinate position, yet he might have felt as an indignity what he records as a compliment. He accompanied the Duke and Duchess of Bedford when they crossed the Channel to Calais in 1819 ; they parted there, as the Ducal couple were going to the Rhine and Moore was bound for Paris. He states that Lord John Russell told him afterwards the Duchess said she "wished they had someone with them, like Mr. Moore, to be agreeable when they got to their inn in the evenings."—Moore's *Diary*, vol. iii., p. 5.

fawning upon a soul. He resented patronage in any form and, if he manifested an exaggerated respect for the Prince of Wales, this was due to his loyalty rather than to his servility. He was misled, along with Burke and Fox, into thinking that the Prince was sincere in professing a personal liking for the principles of the Whig party. But he was undeceived before the end.

He died in charity with all men. He exemplified Schiller's ideal of displaying "the wisdom of grey hairs and retaining the heart of an innocent child." He had never intentionally made an enemy and of this he was justly proud. A few words hastily jotted down on paper, which he may have intended to use in an expanded form, afford a clue to his real sentiments in old age : " Yet the benefit of years is to abate political animosity, to learn that men attached to Pitt may be as honourable as Foxites. This, which I think experience would teach all, was early adopted in my mind, and never having had the arrogance, it is a pleasure to reflect that I never have forfeited a private friendship by political prejudice. Let us discuss our own differences with temper and reserve every angry feeling for etc."[1]

[1] The thought conveyed in these words closely resembles that which Lord Jeffrey has set forth in the following elaborate passage: " When the inordinate hopes of early youth, which provoke their own disappointment, have been sobered down by longer experience and more extended views; when the keen contentions and eager rivalries which employed our riper age, have expired or been abandoned; when we have seen year after year the objects of our fiercest hostility and of our fondest affection, lie down together in the hallowed peace of the grave; when ordinary pleasures and

His later years were over-shadowed with anxiety
for his elder son and rendered painful by struggles
with creditors. The health of his second wife gave
him as great concern as that of his son. He was
unaware of the nature of her illness. Both wives
had been doomed to die early and he was affected
by their sufferings while unconscious of their fate.
His own health had never been robust, though, as
his younger sister wrote, he often fancied himself
worse than the facts justified. None of his friends
suspected how much he suffered from ailments which
were not imaginary, the one being insomnia, the
other being swollen and ulcerated veins. That he
should have shown symptoms of early decrepitude
is less wonderful than that his vivacity should have
continued to be remarkable. Lady Granville dined
in his company at Holland House a year before his
death, when he has been depicted as a mental and
physical wreck. Her eyes were keen and her pen

---

amusements begin to be insipid, and the gay derision which
seasoned them to appear flat and importunate ; when we reflect
how often we have mourned and been comforted, what opposite
opinions we have successively maintained and abandoned, to what
inconsistent habits we have gradually been formed, and how frequently the objects of our pride have proved the sources of our
shame, we are naturally led to recur to the careless days of our
childhood, and from that distant starting place to retrace the
whole of our career and that of our contemporaries with feelings
of far greater humility and indulgence than those by which it had
actually been accompanied ; to think all vain but affection and
honour, the simplest and cheapest pleasures the truest and most
precious, and generosity of sentiment the only mental superiority
which ought either to be wished for or admired."—Contributions
to the *Edinburgh Review*, 2nd edition, vol. ii., pp. 392, 393.

was pointed, and she did not hesitate to tell her sister, Lady G. Morpeth, exactly what she thought of any person whom she met. On this occasion she wrote: " Mr. Sheridan was there at his best, discussing all the young women of his acquaintance with much praise and some little cuts. He says Silence [Lady Jersey] is a pretty, pushing [rushing ?] babbling stream, never stagnant. Lady Borino, his favourite, has hit the line between good-humoured frankness and vulgarity, just touch and run."[1]

When very young, he became known as the hero of a romance; at middle age he was chief among dramatists and parliamentary orators, and before his death he was the leading member of the first circles in the land and the founder of a family which has furnished society and the State with some of their brightest ornaments and most illustrious names. He may not have been a great statesman; but how many statesmen, who are styled great, really deserve the appellation and the compliment? Measures were advocated in his day which became law after his death, having the removal of abuses and the improvement of legislation for their object, and not a single one failed in receiving his approval and support. At the outset of his Parliamentary career he opposed the fatal policy which was pursued towards the American Colonies, and he received the thanks of those who represented them after they had become sovereign States. In 1794, when dis-

---

[1] "Letters" of Harriet, Countess Granville, vol. i., p. 80. Lady Granville was a daughter of the Duchess of Devonshire, and Sheridan's first wife was present at her birth.

cussing the relations between this country and France, he lauded the attitude and system of the United States, saying : "America remains neutral, prosperous and at peace ; America with a wisdom, prudence and magnanimity which we have disdained, thrives at this moment in a state of envied tranquillity, and is hourly clearing the paths to unbounded opulence. America has monopolized the commerce which we have abandoned. Oh! turn your eyes to her ; view her situation, her happiness, her content! Observe her trade and her manufactures adding daily to her general credit, to her private enjoyments, to her public resources ; her name and government rising above the nations of Europe with a simple but commanding dignity, which wins at once the respect, the confidence and the affection of the world."[1]

Sheridan supported the India Bill of Fox which William Pitt opposed and afterwards adopted, with insignificant changes, as his own. He was more ardent than Pitt in reforming the representation of the people in Parliament. It is now known that his great speeches concerning Warren Hastings were largely based on inaccurate reports and malicious misrepresentations, yet their oratorical merit subsists as that of Demosthenes and Cicero would do, even though it should be proved that Philip of Macedon and Verres were better men than had been imagined. He welcomed the triumph of the French people when they had burst the bonds of tyranny, and he was their heartiest opponent when

[1] "Speeches," vol. ii., p. 252.

they entered upon a crusade for the enslavement of the world. No man in Parliament was louder or more sincere in demanding that Ireland should receive full and absolute justice. Nor could a single member of Parliament vie with him as a consistent and eloquent advocate of the freedom of the Press. He took the Benchers of Lincoln's Inn to task in the House of Commons for conduct of which he made them ashamed. They had blundered by refusing to call to the Bar any member who wrote for the newspapers; and the publicity given to their foolish decision, and his comments thereon, led to its being rescinded. In his day the public Press was not perfect. The sanctity of private life was violated; the domestic sayings and doings of public persons were made the subjects of discussion, lampoons for which there was no excuse were circulated with an utter disregard for the pain which might be caused, the chief business of many newspapers in those bygone and unenlightened days being to print quack medicines and scandal in order to increase their circulation and their receipts.

Sheridan thought muzzling the Press a greater mischief than any which publicity could occasion, and he avowed the opinion in Parliament "that the Press should be unfettered, that its freedom should be, as indeed it was, commensurate with the freedom of the People and the well-being of a virtuous State; on that account he thought that even a hundred libels had better be ushered into the world than one prosecution be instituted which might en-

danger the liberty of the Press of this country."[1]
At a later day he uttered words which have become
historic : "Give them a corrupt House of Lords,
give them a venal House of Commons, give them a
tyrannical Prince, give them a truckling Court, and
let me have but an unfettered Press ; I will defy
them to encroach a hair's-breadth upon the liberties
of England."

Among the good measures which Sheridan supported with undissembled enthusiasm and genuine
sympathy those relating to the Slave Trade and
negro slavery deserve special mention. Moore
states that he was never "tempted to utter a
syllable on the subject of the Slave trade, except
once for a few minutes in the year 1787."[2] The
subject was not brought before Parliament in that
year. If Moore had read the Parliamentary Debates,
he would have found that Sheridan spoke with
great emphasis and effect upon the bill for abolishing the Slave Trade, declaring that he trusted the
present measure was but a preamble to one for the
abolition of slavery and that he had never given a
vote with more heartfelt satisfaction than he did in
support of the bill. He spoke on another occasion
in favour of abolishing slavery, and expressed his
exultation at the prospect of "so large a portion of
the human race being freed from the shackles of
tyranny ;" he indignantly asked "could man become
the property of man," and ended by quoting the

[1] "Speeches," vol. iii., p. 238.
[2] "Memoirs" of Sheridan, vol. ii., p. 185.

fine lines in which Cowper declared that no prospect
of wealth would induce him to have a slave to till
his ground.[1]

A public man, and one in particular who has
distanced his contemporaries, is a target for the
missiles of the envious and the disappointed. If
such a man displays sublime indifference, it is commonly supposed that he cannot deny the charges
brought against him, while those who make them
will be so annoyed as to redouble their attacks.
The supersensitive fare no better ; the more they
protest against false accusations the greater zest do
their enemies find in renewing and reiterating them.
A private station is the one which ought to be preferred by all, yet is the one which there is an incessant struggle to leave. Sheridan intimates in a
fragment which he left behind him what his personal attitude was in the face of envenomed attack :
" Whether my motive originally proceeded from
pride or negligence or both, it is a fact that I
have scarcely ever in my life contradicted any one
calumny against me. Finding myself in very early
days placed in a situation which necessarily exposed
me to the anger of dulness and disappointment, I
made an early resolution on this subject which I
afterwards applied to such calumny as my political
conduct and principles may have exposed me to.
. . . I have since on reflection ceased to approve
my own conduct in these respects. Were I to lead
my life over again I should act otherwise. No
man, not callous to all feeling, is really insensible

[1] " Parliamentary Debates," vol. x., pp. 137 and 145.

even to unmerited reproach. I have not been so. I have often felt in my bosom the sting which foul and false aspersion has planted there, although I have disdained to answer it, and, perhaps, have appeared not to feel it."

Thackeray amused himself by speculating about making the acquaintance of Shakespeare and Congreve, of Johnson, Goldsmith and Boswell. Another subject of ingenious speculation would be the reception which Sheridan would meet with, if it were possible for him to return to this lower world from that "Land of the Leal" where cold and care and sorrow are unknown, and where those who have lived together and loved each other are united for ever more. He would not have long to wait before being elected to Parliament, and Stafford, which rejected him in 1812, would account it a high honour to return him now without any payments for ale tickets or bribes to burgesses. The House of Commons would cheer him as an old favourite who has long been inscribed on the roll of its most honoured names. The audience of the theatre at which he appeared as a spectator would applaud him more enthusiastically than the greatest actor of the day. The street through which he was known to pass would be crowded with a shouting multitude, eager to gaze upon him and rejoicing over his presence, for a man who has established himself in the heart of the British nation, as Sheridan did, is enshrined there for all time. He would be importuned to appear at public meetings ; he would be overwhelmed with invitations to private houses, and the

living Prince of Wales, who is a contrast in all things
to George, Prince of Wales, who styled him friend,
would not be the least hearty in giving Sheridan a
welcome, alike sincere and cordial.   The Sovereign
who has displayed merits as a Constitutional head of
a free country which were alien to the mind and
spirit of the Sovereign whom he knew, would doubtless accord to him a most kindly greeting.   He would
soon find popularity too heavy a burden.   His own
words that there was " very snug lying in the
Abbey" would recur to his mind with the weight
and attraction of personal experience, and he would
gladly elect to return to the ineffable bliss of that
eternal repose which those who have enjoyed after
life's fitful fever must be the last to exchange for
any glory which this world can bestow.

The facts of Sheridan's diversified journey through
life have now been set forth without reticence or
partiality.   I have not written an apology for his
career : it requires none.   Moreover, the man whose
life needs an apology does not deserve to have it
written.   It is difficult to dismiss old illusions about
men or things ; they resemble the lichen which gives
colour and beauty to the old tree or the old rock.
The Sheridan of the romances which are styled
" Memoirs" is as mythical a personage as " Jack
the Giant-killer" or " Don Quixote."   The character
attributed to him is picturesque but untrue to life,
yet its very falseness and absurdity have attractions
for many persons.   In his fictitious career the most
discreditable incidents have been regarded as the

most natural. Delusions respecting notable public men have the vitality of the Great Sea Serpent. Moreover, there is a tendency in the public mind to be more receptive of scandal than of truth. Sheridan wrote some lines in an album containing advice which is too good to be willingly adopted and followed, but which deserved respect from those who have written about him :

> " Believe not each aspersing tongue,
>   As most weak persons do ;
> But still believe that story wrong
>   Which ought not to be true."

His worthiest contemporaries were more ready with their praise than their blame. Brougham wrote that, "with all his faults, all his failings, and all his defects, Sheridan was pre-eminent, among Fox's adherents, in Parliamentary genius and political power."[1] Byron was greater as a poet than a critic, yet he gave emphatic expression to what is incontrovertible when writing that whatever Sheridan did was perfect of its kind. Grattan said of him, with grace and truth, that his faults resembled those of men of genius in being " excesses of the generous virtues."[2] Leigh Hunt, who was bitter against him when alive, wrote after his death : "Sheridan's worst can affect but few ; his best will redound to the good of his country, and to the delight of thousands to come."[3]

[1] " Statement of the Reign of George III.," vol. i., p. 291.
[2] " Recollections " by Samuel Rogers, p. 104.
[3] *The Examiner* for July 14th, 1816.

Nothing is more futile than excessive eulogy couched in exaggerated phrase. I confine myself, then, to stating the simple fact that Sheridan is the greatest dramatist since Shakespeare and the greatest orator who ever addressed the House of Commons. Unaffected by detraction and indifferent to praise, he now moves among the Immortals, as he formerly did among the great ones of earth, an equal among his equals.

APPENDIX TO VOL. II.

SPEECH OF RICHARD BRINSLEY SHERIDAN, Esq.,

Manager for the House of Commons,

IN REPLY ON THE SECOND ARTICLE OF THE CHARGE AGAINST
WARREN HASTINGS, RELATING TO THE BEGUMS OF OUDE.

(May 14, 1794.)

MY LORDS,—In behalf of the Commons, I appear before your
Lordships to reply to the Counsel on the second Article of the
Charge of Impeachment preferred against Warren Hastings,
Esquire.

My Lords, there are many circumstances which induce the
Managers, as far as the great duty with which they are entrusted
will permit, to wish to trespass upon your Lordships' time as
shortly as possible, at the close of a trial already protracted to so
great a length, from circumstances which it is neither my duty nor
intention in this place to state or to discuss.

My Lords, I trust that I shall be able to compress what I have
to lay before your Lordships into a very short compass. I have
read attentively every word of the speeches of the learned Counsel;
I have compared them with every part of their evidence; and I
must first fairly say, my Lords, that what has puzzled and embarrassed me is, to discover any one point which they have so
pressed as to make it necessary, without disrespect to your Lordships' sagacity and discernment, to attempt to reply to or to refute
it. My Lords, when I say that I hope to compress what I have
to lay before you into a short compass, if I succeed in doing so, I

certainly shall claim no merit from it. The merit of it, my Lords, if any, belongs to the perspicuity, to the force, and to the weight of that evidence which, upon a former occasion, the Managers had the honour of submitting to your Lordships, and not one particle of which, I am bold to say, it has been in the power of the learned Counsel to overturn, nor any material part of it even within their courage to attempt to assail.

My Lords, the learned Counsel have on many occasions complained of the great delay of this trial: yet, my Lords, I really must take the freedom of saying that they seem to me to have considered that they should derive considerable advantage from delay; and they appear to me to have imagined, through the whole course of their speeches, that your Lordships must have forgotten every one of the arguments to which they were answering. And also, my Lords, I think—which is perhaps more extraordinary— that they seem entirely to have forgotten that the Managers have a right to reply to their answers.

My Lords, when I profess that it is my intention to be brief upon this subject, I am well aware that professions upon that subject in this trial are not likely, perhaps, to meet with any immediate credit from your Lordships. The learned Counsel themselves were not sparing in their remarks upon the prolixity with which they supposed the Managers conducted the business. When it came to their turn to speak, we certainly did conceive that they would have contrasted their conduct with ours. A learned Counsel, whose arguments I shall more particularly notice, introduced his speech with this observation:—he complained that the Article comprehended a great extent and variety of matter; "but," he says, "my Lords, I think, in examining it, the subject may be analysed and simplified, and reduced into that which is the plain subject of the principal part of the Charge, and it will be found to lie in a very narrow compass." With this observation, my Lords, the learned Counsel introduced a speech of four days!

My Lords, if this is the idea of brevity in the learned Counsel, I confess I must congratulate your Lordships that he was not disposed to be diffuse; for my imagination does not enable me to conceive what his prolixity would have been. But you certainly had the advantage of this determination of the Counsel, as it were, in a spirit of rebuke to his learned colleague, who had spoken only two days. This learned Counsel, possessing the power of analysing and simplifying, which I am to take for granted his learned brother did not possess—the learned Counsel, as it were, rebuking his learned brother for having spoken eight hours, did contrive to compress and squeeze the spirit and substance of his speech into the nutshell of a sixteen hours' oration.

My Lords, I say, after this example, it is not to be expected that a very ready credit will be given to professions of brevity upon this trial. And, my Lords, I am ready to confess, were I to follow the learned Counsel through speeches of infinite ability and ingenuity, through all the extraneous matter with which they have loaded their arguments, through all the laborious statements which they have employed upon self-evident propositions, through all their unnecessary amplifications, through all the mutual repetitions of each other's arguments and statements—I say, my Lords, if I was to attempt that, certainly there would be very little prospect of my fulfilling my promise. But such of your Lordships as have attended to and taken notes of the speeches of the learned Counsel—of which I assure you that I will strictly confine myself to such parts as are to the purpose—will not, I hope, despair that I shall be able to keep my word.

My Lords, in order to be brief, it is certainly necessary to avoid all attempts at superfluous ornament or decoration. Perhaps, in the commencement of this business, in order to win a little attention to something of a dry subject, the Managers did indulge themselves in something that might be called collateral matter, and also, perhaps, in some expressions of warm and fresh indignation, which they could not at the time but feel on account of the crimes which they arraigned. But, my Lords, I am ready to admit that now, approaching to the solemn hour of decision, those practices, perhaps, ought to be avoided. But when I admit this, my Lords, I here again cannot plead the example of the learned Counsel. They were extremely free in rebuking us for our proceeding on this sort of subject. A learned Counsel, who himself found great fault with the poetical flights—he particularly did me the honour to point at me, with some handsome compliments about imagination, poetry and eloquence, which I beg leave rather to decline, for I should have thought it a better compliment if he had admitted the authority with which I stated the facts in evidence—but the learned Counsel, having given this rebuke to the Managers, says:—" To a taste thus pampered, and, I had almost said, corrupted [with these luxurious delicacies we have nothing left to offer but the plain and simple food,] I had almost said the dry husk, of fact and argument."*

So that, my Lords, though the learned Counsel did reprobate such figurative way of proceeding, they certainly took care to show that it was not for want of means or talents to deal in something like the same sort of commodity. And I believe, if your Lordships will observe from your notes, through the whole of these speeches, you will for ever find them venting the most fanciful spleen against our indulgence in flights of imagination, and dealing in most figurative lamentation at our addiction to metaphor and ornament.

My Lords, I must mention one more circumstance upon the subject of brevity ; because your Lordships may naturally imagine that, if I do contrive to bring the matter into the compass which I hope to do, knowing the length and extent of the speeches to which I am replying, I am afraid your Lordships will imagine that I must necessarily have passed over a great mass of weighty and material fact or argument. In order to do away as early as possible that impression, I cannot but refer to a part of the speech of the learned gentleman who led in the business.

My Lords, in the Article, it so happened that the father of the elder Begum was mentioned by the name of Saadat ; and when it was mentioned that her father's name was Saadat that was the whole that was said upon that subject. In summing up upon that Charge, my Lords, I did not say one single word with respect to her ancestry or with respect to this Saadat. However, the learned Counsel, who had not, it seems, that talent of shortening, simplifying and analysing, finding the name Saadat mentioned, thought it an excellent opportunity to amuse us with a very pleasant story respecting this Saadat. Accordingly, I hold in my hand a note, at considerable length, of an extremely interesting and amusing Mogul tale, told in very pleasant though familiar language by this learned Counsel, the amount of which is that this Saadat was a man of extremely bad morals ; that he was a minister of Mohammed Shah and a rival of Nizam-ul-Mulk, and a rival also

* Mr. Law's speech in opening the defence.

of a more worthy man, one Condewar; that, about this time, Nadir Shah, vulgarly known by the name of Kuly Khan, invaded India, and that he carried on a treasonable correspondence with Nadir Shah; that at length Nadir Shah takes Delhi, and he then sends for these two traitors and rates them soundly on account of their treachery: he ends with sending them from his presence and spitting upon their beards. They meet in the other room, and to use the very words of the learned Counsel, " lay their heads together " upon this subject, and agree that it is utterly impossible for them to survive this disgrace. Upon which, they came to a resolution that they would both poison themselves. But, these being very immoral statesmen, they each suspected that the other would play him a trick. Accordingly, Saadat sends a spy to watch Nizam, to see whether he really poisons himself or not. But he, suspecting that he was suspected, took what he pretended to be poison, and feigning the agonies of death, fell down. The spy was deceived, and he returns to Saadat with horror in his countenance; and tells him that his friend had certainly poisoned himself. Upon which, says the learned Counsel, Saadat, in a perverse fit of honour, which then seized him for the first and last time of his life, really did poison himself; and thus he fell a victim, he says, to his own knavery. When he has finished the story, he says—" I will now return to the Article."*

Now, my Lords, that this is a very excellent story, and that, with the ingenuity of the learned Counsel, if they have time in the vacation and would introduce a little love into it, they might make an excellent tragedy of it or a pretty volume for a circulating library, I will not deny; but if your Lordships were to ask me— what on earth it has to do with the question—why it was introduced—or what colour of provocation there was—I confess I am utterly unable to answer. But I hope that to this part of the learned gentleman's speech, or to anything similar, it will not be expected that I should reply. If it was, I certainly should have put a volume of Mogul tales into my pocket before I came down; and, if this proceeding was to meet the grave countenance of your Lordships, unquestionably we should make this a place of very pretty Arabian mornings' entertainment; we should enliven the dry subject and make it much more amusing to many ladies that

* Mr. Law's speech in opening the defence on the second charge.

do us the honour to attend, but I do not think we should much edify your Lordships or advance much the real purposes of this trial.

Now my object in stating this a little more at length than, perhaps, might appear necessary at first to your Lordships is this : —that if I do, as I said before, compress what I have to say into a narrow compass, I beg your Lordships will not imagine that I must of necessity have passed over great, weighty and material, parts of the learned gentlemen's speeches ; for I believe that, if I were to pass over and take no notice of twenty such tales as these, or twenty of those strange amplifications on which they have dwelt, or their repetitions of the same argument, or a variety of irrelevant matter, your Lordships would· admit that I had passed over nothing that called for a reply, or that I had made any impression upon the Court to justify a reply ; and that your Lordships would be of opinion that the Counsel who informed you that the real point and substance of this question lay in a very narrow compass did give you a right opinion, though he unfortunately forgot to give it the sanction of his example.

My Lords, the arrangement which I shall propose to myself is —to follow the speech of the learned gentleman who spoke in the same situation in which I have the honour of addressing you ;—I mean the learned gentleman who summed up the evidence.* There is certainly very fair and clear arrangement in that speech, which the learned gentleman has not been able to disguise by all the irrelevant matter which his ingenuity has heaped upon it. What other passages relate really to the purpose in the other gentleman's speech I shall take notice of ; as they do, in fact, follow pretty nearly the same order which this learned gentleman has adopted.

My Lords, the first day's speech of the learned gentleman consisted entirely in endeavouring to establish two points which, if they had requested it or given an intimation that it was of any very material importance to them, and I had felt myself at liberty to act upon my own feeling and discretion, I would have tossed into the scale of their argument for nothing at all.   The point upon which he spent the whole of the first day was to establish the original right to the treasures in the Wazir, and to establish as

---

* The Hon. Manager refers to the speech of Mr. Plumer.

a principle that jagirs were in their nature resumable ;—two points which I contend would avail him nothing if he had established them. And I wish your Lordships now to observe the candour of the Counsel in the manner in which he has introduced it. The learned Counsel says :—"We will now consider, as the honourable Managers have occupied so much time upon discussing the sort of claim to these treasures, and have thought it essential to their case—as most essential it is on our part—to show the original right of the Wazir to those treasures, it is material," he says, "for us to establish that the original right was in the Wazir."

Now, my Lords, according to my apprehension of this subject, it is perfectly immaterial for either of us to dispute that point. If the learned gentleman means to say that he recurred to his original right, I wish him to point out what interpretation he gives to the treaty of 1775. I say, we might have stood upon the treaty of 1775 alone ; and that all discussion respecting the original right to the treasures is perfectly irrelevant and nugatory. The learned gentleman says that, upon the Begum's forfeiture of that treaty, he recurred to his original right. She certainly might have forfeited everything she possessed, but, when once that treaty was made, there was no other interpretation to be put upon it than that she was to retain these treasures *quamdiu se bene gesserit.* By one final partition upon the subject of the treasures, what the Nawab took he took as his portion ; what was left with the Begum was left with her as her acknowledged right. Unquestionably, by an act of treason she might forfeit these treasures to the Nawab, as she might forfeit every other right—her property or her life ; but to set up a plea that, the treaty being set aside, his original right recurred, shows a weakness in the argument of the Counsel and consciousness throughout that they cannot, in fact, prove the acts by which they say she did so forfeit that treaty.

But what I a little complain of here is, that the learned Counsel state as their reason for having argued this so much, that I had thought it particularly proper to lay so much stress upon it. Now if they had done me the honour to attend to my speech, they would have found that I went over that ground very lightly indeed, and that I prefaced and concluded what I said upon the subject with this remark :—I am glad the Counsel seem to have got my words under their eye :—that it was my original intention

not to have touched upon the subject of original right at all,
conceiving it to be a thing perfectly insignificant, but to have
taken up the matter from the treaty of 1775 ; but that I was
diverted from that intention by observing, in the course of the
cross-examination of the Counsel, that they meant to lay considerable stress upon the subject ; and even under that impression I
said, I was ashamed for having dwelt upon it at all or having
taken up any of your Lordships' time upon the subject. And
now the Counsel think it candid to state, that their reason for
having occupied such an infinite space of your attention and of
their own exertions upon it was—that the Managers were the
persons who seemed to lay stress upon that point.

Now, as so much has been said upon it, it is not for me to
assume that it is a matter perfectly insignificant. Therefore, my
Lords, I must notice what it is that they have proved or attempted
to prove upon that point. That which was laid before you by the
Managers was this :—that, by the general custom of the country,
persons in high situations, but above all persons in the situation
of Asoff-ud-Dowla, that is, the reigning prince of a great and
populous country—that, by the universal custom of the East, they
did hold it a matter most sacred, in the prospect of their death, to
provide independently for their wives, for their families, for all the
women in the Zanana, as it is called, and who were dependent on
and belonging to them.

Next, we showed to you the peculiar sacredness of the Zanana ;
and we did argue from that, my Lords, that, as it was the custom
to leave the treasures intended for the support of the women, and
for the portioning the offspring of those women in a place which
was considered [sacred], as we proved by most satisfactory evidence
and the admission of Mr. Hastings himself, and the sacredness of
which never has been violated, either by war, by rapine, by law,
or by any power on earth, till this instance given by the person
whom we now accuse, that that was in itself an argument of the
real destination, the use and purpose, of these treasures. And we
also proved, my Lords, that Suja-ud-Dowla had entertained a
peculiar respect for the Begum whom he left behind him ; that
she had shown him the greatest mark of fidelity and affection ;
that she had given him proof that whatever treasures he gave to her
were ready on any emergency for his own use ; that she had come

down to him, after the battle of Buxar when he was in distress, with all the money, all the jewels, and everything that she had possessed.

We also showed that Suja-ud-Dowla had no affection for his son, Asoff-ud-Dowla, who was to succeed him, but, on the contrary, that he had once even attempted his life, which had been preserved to him by his mother, the Begum. We also showed that, in Suja-ud-Dowla's lifetime, when he had drawn upon these treasures then kept in the Zanana, his draught was refused, but that, when the Begum drew upon them, then acknowledging them to be her property, the draught was accepted : a circumstance which, I believe, Mr. Middleton attempted—and no man but Mr. Middleton could have endeavoured—to show was a proof that the treasures were the Nawab's, and not the Begum's. But we also showed to your Lordships that the object to which we supposed these treasures were destined was of extent sufficient to require what was supposed to be their whole amount ; namely, that the family of Suja-ud-Dowla with the family of Suffdar Jung, his predecessor, consisted of above 2,000 women and children and their attendants.

We showed also, by the admission of the Counsel and of Mr. Hastings, that this treasure and the jagirs of the Begums were, in fact, the real resource for the maintenance of these women and children ; and we also showed to your Lordships that, when the jagirs were taken from them and when they were plundered of their treasures, these women were driven to famine, to desperation, and at last were turned, many of them, outcasts upon the world.

Now let us see what the learned Counsel oppose in reply to this mass of evidence. In the first place, they have not attempted to dispute that that posthumous jealousy with respect to their women was the feeling and the general sentiment of persons in the position of Asoff-ud-Dowla throughout the East. They have not attempted, for they could not do it, to deny the sacredness of the Zanana ; but they have denied that their being deposited there could be considered as any serious argument of the destination of the treasures.

I contended that the treasure being placed in a situation which no human power on earth can get at, but those who are themselves living in the Zanana, is a strong presumption that for their use alone that treasure can be intended. The learned Counsel, however, do not choose to trust that as a serious argument. And here they indulge a considerable degree of that pleasantry, which I must say has characterised their eloquence throughout all their speeches. The only difficulty I have sometimes found is—and I say it really without any affectation, but very seriously—to discover when they meant to be serious and when they were jocose. I really often admire much more their imagination than their arguments ; and I see frequently infinitely more fancy in their facts than in their jests. Sometimes, when one would imagine that they are going on in a fine vein of solemn irony, they are dealing in narrative and plain fact ; and very often, when I thought they were stating mere dry argument and fact, I found it was sheer drollery and humour. Now which this is, I must leave to your Lordships' judgment.

I beg your Lordships' pardon, but I am afraid I must quote this from memory, but I assure the Counsel I will do it very accurately. Perhaps the Counsel can point me out the place—I do not believe it could very easily have escaped the Counsel's memory, for it is one of the most laboured passages in the whole of his speech—I mean, where he ridicules my statement, that '' the title of these ladies to this treasure was the title of a saint to the relics on an altar, placed there by the hand of piety," I think, " guarded by holy superstition, and to be wrested thence only by the hand of sacrilege." That was the unfortunate statement which I happened to make, and which I maintain was a serious argument and not a flight of fancy. And the learned gentleman first laughs at the idea of this lady being a saint : he indulges a good deal of facetiousness upon that subject. He then says,—" placed there by the hand of piety ! they were placed there by the hand of rapine and bloodshed—by Suja-ud-Dowla." Then he says,— " placed upon an altar !"—and here the Counsel was extremely facetious : the whole is at great length : I regret I cannot lay my hand upon it :* he says :—" placed upon an altar ! how can that be ? for what were some of these treasures ?—camels and elephants." And then he gravely says ;—" how can you get a camel upon an altar ?" These are his words. I give you my

* The passage Mr. Sheridan refers to is in Mr. Plumer's speech of the 25th of April, 1793.

honour, my Lords, I really do not know how to reply to this. I am sure it is not law nor logic, and I shrewdly suspect it is not wit. He then says,—"guarded by holy superstition! why, they were guarded by two eunuchs." He says, whether they were very holy or not he will not pretend to say, but that they were perforce innocent:—a very decent allusion! But this really is the method in which the learned Counsel ran through this unfortunate simile of mine. And I do protest, if I had known that I could have drawn such a laborious effort of wit and ingenuity from them by any illustration of that sort, I certainly should have abstained from it. But I believe your Lordships will admit, that you never saw or heard of an unfortunate simile so hunted down before; that you never before saw special pleading employed upon such a purpose; that you never before saw a bill of indictment against a metaphor, or were present at the trial of a trope at *nisi prius*—for that is literally what the Counsel have done. But I must say, not attempting to decide whether they meant it as seriousness or as argument, that, if I was to reply to them in their way, I should deny their fact.

The learned Counsel has been so employed lately in researches in the Kuran that it is not surprising if he has a little forgot testimony of higher authority, at least, in the Christian volume. If he had, he would have recollected such a circumstance as the altar built by Solomon, the breadth whereof was twenty cubits, the height thereof was ten cubits, and the length thereof was twenty cubits; and that the multitudes of Israel assembled before it; that thereon they sacrificed oxen and sheep so that they could not be told or numbered. Therefore, in point of fact, if the learned gentleman meant it, and I was to reply to him in his own manner, whether he is serious or jocose upon this occasion he is equally unsuccessful; for, if serious, what he states is not a fact, and, if he is humourous, it is not a jest.

My Lords, however, I must do the learned Counsel the justice to say that they have not entirely built upon this laboured effort of wit of that very learned and facetious gentleman : they have also attempted to bring certainly other arguments and documents to prove the original right of the Wazir to these treasures. They have attempted, my Lords, to quote from books of high authority —from the Kuran, from the Hedaya—paragraphs which they have placed upon the evidence, which your Lordships may have observed, in which they endeavoured to show that by the Mohammedan law the [widow] is entitled only to an eighth, and so on ; and that there can be no property whatever claimed upon which there are any debts ; that the discharge of the debt is the first object to be looked to ; that the Company had a great debt upon this property, consequently that it could not belong to the widow. And they have shown that, whenever there is a will or property descends, there ought to be, according to the Hedaya, no partition of such [property] contrary to that will.

Now I must complain a little here that the learned gentlemen have, in a strange manner—I was almost going to say scandalous, but certainly it was not intentional upon their part—garbled and misquoted all the authorities to which they refer. We have since placed upon your Lordships' Minutes proof that, according to the Hedaya, whatever the title—by will or descent—if the parties choose to come to an agreement upon the property, that agreement is binding.

With respect to debts attaching in the first instance upon the property, I will not enter into that discussion or dispute the law with them ; because, if I did so, in point of fact, in 1775, the whole of the debt due from Suja-ud-Dowla to the Company was discharged, and by the means of the treasure given up by the Begums. Therefore their whole argument upon that goes for nothing at all.

The next thing they attempted to show, which they thought a pretty strong article of evidence, was the reason why the Nawab's draft was not answered and the Begum's was. They give the Begum a very high post and office : they say she was Lady High Treasurer; that it was not in a regular official manner of proceeding; that the Nawab should have drawn [upon] this High Treasurer, and that then the draft would have been answered. And they justify Mr. Middleton's inference that, when the Nawab drew, his draft was refused ; that, when she drew, her draft was answered ; and therefore that the treasures must be the Nawab's and not the Begum's :—they justify Mr. Middleton's inference and say, it was merely on account of an official mistake :—a pretty extraordinary circumstance, when we have shown that the Nawab was with the Begum at the time this transaction passed ! That he should be ignorant of the forms of his own office, and forget that it was necessary the Begum should sign the draft and not himself, is a circumstance very extraordinary and totally incredible.

With regard to the amount of the treasures, the gentlemen throughout the whole choose to assume that their amount was 170 lacs, and they speak really as if they had been in the Zanana and had counted every rupee of them. There is not a syllable of evidence before you to prove what the extent of the treasures was. There is nothing but a conjecture of Mr. Bristow's—a conjecture of a person employed, in fact, to extort money at the time from the Begum, and who of course would be likely to represent the treasures to be as extensive as possible. But the Counsel entirely pass over our endeavours to give a different turn to the admission of the Council at Calcutta, respecting a dispute which arose in the delivery of the sum which by agreement was to be paid to Asoff-ud-Dowla, according to the treaty of 1775. They have gone into the matter at considerable length ; which, I own, surprised me very much, because I thought I had made the thing so perfectly clear before that it really could not have admitted of a single doubt in the mind of any man whatever, that the dispute arose, not respecting the original right of the treasures, but respecting goods, camels and elephants, delivered by the Begum to the Nawab, and which he contended, not having been in the Zanana, ought not to be claimed as hers. The evidence adduced upon that and the direct inference which stands upon your Lordships' record is, that all the Council to a man admit that she was entitled to all the treasures within the Zanana ; which, I insist upon it, stands uncontradicted. There is a word or two of Mr. Francis' in one place that seems to doubt her original right to them ; but that, being in the Zanana, the treasures were hers and not the Nawab's, is the general admission of the whole Council, and Mr. Hastings most especially, who even calls the attempt of the Nawab to obtain any part of these treasures, an act of exaction ! I say, then, that, upon the whole either of the evidence or of the argument adduced by the learned Counsel, the question of the original right—unimportant as I contend it to be—stands exactly where I left it, when I had last the honour of addressing your Lordships.

The next point which the learned Counsel proceeded to is to

prove, first of all, that the jagirs are in their nature resumable :
and then, that the Begums' jagirs were not granted to them, but
during the pleasure of the Nawab. I am astonished how the
learned Counsel should quote so much authority upon the subject, which they certainly appear to have examined most carelessly ; for I need not enter into this matter but to answer them,
in one word, that their position—that jagirs are in their nature and
by the laws and customs of the East resumable—is directly
refuted by such a mass of evidence we have since brought in
reply as can leave not a shadow of a doubt upon the subject. We
have loaded your Lordships' table with copies of parwanas, of
grants of jagirs, having the sanction of Mr. Hastings himself to
almost every one of them, which prove in the general that the
prevailing custom of the East was, that the jagirs were granted
either in perpetuity or for life. Nay, we proved, in the case of
jagirs which contain an express clause of resumption at the will of
the grantor, yet that the practice had been so much the contrary
that even these were considered as jagirs of descent.

With regard to the particular jagirs of the Begums, we certainly
have it not in our power to give a direct proof that the parwanas
by which they were granted stated them to be in perpetuity or for
life ; but we have placed before your Lordships a considerable
mass of evidence, which shows that the Nawab himself admits
that they were not resumable by him, even previous to the treaty.
We have shown that the elder Begum states that one of her jagirs
was derived from Shah Alem, the King himself ; that she states
she had constantly left the collection of it in the hands of her son,
Suja-ud-Dowla ; that she was not the loser by so leaving it in his
hands. We have stated that the Nawab himself afterwards, in the
jagirs which he grants to the Bow Begum, in the manner and
tenor of his admission of the grant, seems to admit they were
granted for life to her ; and that, when he offers afterwards to
resume them, she so pleads the fact to be ; and also [of the] other
jagirs she says—" they were not granted by Asoff-ud-Dowla, and
therefore he had no right to resume them."

My Lords, I shall not dwell upon this, because it is a circumstance wholly unimportant ; for whether the jagirs were granted
for life or not, and whether it is the custom of the East that they
were resumable at pleasure or not, is exactly upon the same

ground as whether the treasures were by descent the Begums' or the Nawab's. It is a matter unimportant, not worth scarcely an argument ; because by the treaty of 1775, and afterwards of 1778, the jagirs were made over for life or in perpetuity to the Begums and the remaining part of the treasures was made and admitted to be their property. That ends the argument of the first day of the learned Counsel ; in which I affirm that he has completely failed in proving that which he has stated to be essential to his case ;— namely, the original right of the Nawab to the treasures, and consequently his right to recur to them, upon the forfeiture which is stated to have been committed by the Begum.

And now, my Lords, I come to the circumstance of the treaties, which is the real and more important part of this business. I am sure your Lordships recollect the circumstances of the treaty of 1775 particularly ; and your Lordships, I am sure, must have been surprised to find that, though each of the learned Counsel admits that that treaty was in the most solemn manner binding both upon the Nawab and upon the English nation, they had spent a very considerable portion of their time to prove that it was a treaty obtained by extortion, and—according to the terms of the learned gentleman—that it was, in fact, in itself null and void. And yet, my Lords, the learned Counsel, having spent one day in endeavouring to establish a point which, I contend, if he had established it, would have made nothing for his case, occupies nearly the whole of the second day in endeavouring to invalidate a treaty, when he concludes by admitting its validity in the utmost extent. It cannot be expected that I should feel the necessity of following the learned Counsel through all the various quantity of time which he has spent in endeavouring to prove that the treaty was a treaty of extortion ; that it ought not to have been made ; that it is in itself null and void ; when the Counsel himself, and each of them, concludes with saying that he admits it had the most sacred binding force, and that it was so considered by Mr. Hastings and by the Council. The learned Counsel, after having laboured to prove it to be a treaty which it was fit to consider as nugatory and void, and as obtained by extortion, proceeded in a detail of a variety of instances in which Mr. Hastings showed the most sacred regard and respect for this treaty. The Counsel did not perceive, perhaps, that it would have answered their argument

better to have endeavoured to have shown that it was always considered by Mr. Hastings as a treaty extorted, and which had
something in itself wrong and unfit to be much attended to ;
whereas, on the contrary, they labour the point extremely to show
that, upon various occasions, whenever the Nawab or his ministers
attempted to oppress the Begums and infringe this treaty, Mr.
Hastings always resented such conduct ; that he always upheld
the cause of the Begums ; that he always reproached them with
an attempt to violate so sacred a treaty, and that he always
himself considered it as binding.

There are a variety of cases in which it appears to me that the
Counsel, with a very perverse ingenuity, attempted to establish
points the very reverse of which it would have been their interest
to establish. It would have, in this case, been their interest to
establish the contrary of this proposition ; because what was the
effect of Mr. Hastings' maintaining so frequently the sacredness of
this treaty, but to infuse in the mind of the Begum the most
perfect reliance that Mr. Hastings would be the last man on earth
that could ever countenance the violation of it ? If it had
happened that at different times the Begum was aware that this
treaty was not considered as sacred by the British nation, it must
have been some caution to her in her conduct, supposing she was
capable of offending the British Government ; but, when she
found it treated in that manner by Mr. Hastings, she was en-
trapped into a notion that, at least, the manner in which that
treaty was obtained or the circumstances attending the guarantee
could never be a reproach to her, or be brought forward as a
pretence for the violation of that treaty.

In the same manner, the Counsel took infinite pains to prove
that, when Mr. Hastings left Calcutta and went into Oude, his
situation, previous to the attempt to seize the treasures of the
Begum, was so desperate, that it would have been ruinous to the
Company, and disgraceful and ruinous to himself, if he had not
obtained a large sum of money. The gentlemen had better have
proved that the Company was in prosperous circumstances, and
then they would have established that he had no temptation,
beyond what applies to the just punishment of treason, to look
out for resources. They took pains to prove that, throughout
Oude and in all India, there was not a single rupee to be acquired

but from the treasures in the Zanana belonging to the Begums. Here they had better have represented the Nawab's affairs in a more flourishing situation; that Mr. Hastings could have negotiated a loan from Gopal Doss or the Nawab's ministers; and that there was some other resource besides that of the Begums. For all those circumstances bring with them considerations of strong suspicion that, where the necessity was so great—where the supply existed only in one place—some means, foul or fair, would be used to obtain that supply. I said that, the binding force of this treaty of 1775 being so fully admitted by the Counsel, it would not be necessary for me to trace them through the insinuations which they have stated with regard to the manner of obtaining it. But, my Lords, there is another treaty—I mean the treaty of 1778—upon which again, to my surprise, I find an infinite deal of time wasted in a discussion, when they at last admit, in point of fact, the binding validity of that treaty also :—I mean the treaty with the elder Begum. The learned Counsel have stated, in their defence for Mr. Hastings, that they solemnly deny that the faith of the British nation ever was pledged to the elder Begum. I thought I had proved so forcibly to your Lordships that that was at least an erroneous assertion, that the learned Counsel would have had the discretion not again to meddle with the subject. However, they have again brought the matter forward. They have endeavoured to show you that that treaty never was sanctioned by the authority of the Board; that it was an act, if signed by Mr. Middleton, which they deny, of Mr. Middleton's own; and that the faith and guarantee of the British Government never were in any respect pledged to the elder Begum. They have not followed my argument upon the subject, or they would have seen that I have proved to your Lordships that the real construction of the letter of the 23d of May was what I have given it, namely, an application from Mr. Middleton stating two alternatives to the Council at Calcutta ;—first, that he conceived there would be no objection to his entering into a guarantee with the elder Begum, if he could obtain the Nawab's consent to it; but that, if he could not obtain the Nawab's consent, then he wished for permission in a manner to compel the Nawab to do her justice. The Council, receiving both these letters, answer, that they approve of his method of conciliating the differences, and of obtaining the security to the elder Begum, she having stated in this letter that the only security she could or would accept was the guarantee of the English. But then they negative the second proposition of Mr. Middleton, namely, that of compelling the Nawab, or of using any act of that sort towards him. They withheld their consent to that, but they fully approved the other mode proposed by Mr. Middleton.

Then what is the fact?—that the treaty is signed by Mr. Middleton. It appears afterwards that this treaty is [sent] down by Mr. Purling to the Council as a binding treaty; the elder Begum having pleaded that she had such a treaty under the signature and seal of Mr. Middleton, and that the Company were her guarantee. The Counsel here make a most extraordinary observation upon this. Because they found they could not easily get rid of the fact that we have proved—that, when this communication was made, Mr. Middleton was at that very moment in Calcutta; that he was not only in Calcutta, but that he was at that very time consulted by Mr. Hastings, and consulted respecting the affairs of Oude, so that there could be no pretence that he could not be examined upon this subject; that the result is that the Council return the treaty and desire that the jagirs may not be touched, because it is stated that they had the guarantee of the British nation;—the learned Counsel upon this say, it was a paper sent down to them, and the reference to this treaty was a mere marginal note; and one of them describes it to be a matter in a small hand: as if the printed Evidence before your Lordships was the exact type and counterpart of the communication to Mr. Purling, and that the circumstance of being a marginal note did not intitle it to the same degree of observation as if signed in a large broad hand! And the Counsel, although they made exactly the same answer upon that occasion, if they will look fairly into this letter, it is impossible that they can for an instant deny that the treaty of 1778 with the elder Begum had as fully the guarantee of the British nation as the treaty of 1775 with the younger Begum; and that, when Mr. Hastings left Calcutta, he left it as much bound by the terms of that treaty as the other. But I say again, this matter is not worth disputing with the Counsel, because they admit that, in another treaty made with the Bow Begum in 1778, all the essential parts of the treaty made with the elder

Begum are confirmed; by which I shall always contend that we guaranteed a provision to the Khourd Mahal as well as to the Begums.

There is one circumstance, however, attending the speech of the learned Counsel upon the treaty of 1778, which I must take something of a very particular notice of. My Lords, I have really looked carefully through the notes of the speeches which I had the honour before of making to your Lordships, to see if, in any one respect or on any one opportunity, I had been deficient in that respect to the learned Counsel, to which I certainly felt them intitled by their general character, and by everything that I had heard respecting them. I profess, I find that I have been guilty of no such disrespect; that, on the contrary, wherever I have mentioned them, I have mentioned them in terms which I am sure it would not be unflattering to them to have repeated. With this explanation, I must express a considerable degree of surprise at the manner in which one of the learned gentlemen has thought it decent and thought himself authorised to treat me—standing here as a Manager for the House of Commons—in a discussion respecting this treaty of 1778, which that learned Counsel bestowed infinite pains upon. He has this passage in his speech, to which I must humbly request the particular attention of your Lordships. He says :—

" I will now advert to another passage in the evidence before your Lordships, which I do think transcends anything I can say. It is enough to state the fact; [and if your Lordships recollect in history]—if any person who has been present at trials recollects—anybody having done these sort of things, I will admit the honourable Manager has fairly and honourably adopted that precedent."

He adds :—

" I am sure I do not wish to say anything improper and disrespectful, but, if this had been done by any of us in the ordinary lines of the profession, it would be considered as a species of judicial legerdemain. I do not know any other name to give it. I will show your Lordships how a question was asked about one treaty and a Clause read out of another, and the witness confounded and completely put out of countenance, and the credit of that witness most unjustly disposed of."

A grave and solemn charge, my Lords, I admit.

"God forbid anything should be taken on my assertion! But, if it is not as clear as the light of the sun that shines upon your Lordships [that this perversion has been made of the testimony, let all my observations] go for nothing, and let the honourable Manager be deemed one of the most fair, as he [certainly is one of the most eloquent, persons ever employed] upon such a subject."*

It is applied to Mr. Middleton, he says. He then states that, in page 517 of your Minutes, your Lordships will see the copy of this treaty. I need not read the extract from that part of the learned gentleman's speech: he goes on to require your Lordships to turn to page 520, and he says,—

"The honourable Manager puts this question to Mr. Middleton :—'whether there is not any clause whereby the Nawab binds himself to demand no loan of the elder Begum?' Mr. Middleton says, and he said very truly, 'No, I do not recollect.' Then the honourable Manager, for what purpose of truth or justice let him explain—read to him a passage out of the treaty with the younger Begum, as if it had been the treaty with the elder :—'Moreover his Highness shall not at any future period make demand of a loan or any other demands from her Highness ;' and he reads it to the witness as if it was a paragraph in the treaty with the elder Begum.' Mr. Middleton"—the Counsel says—"not having, as your Lordships must have observed, a great deal of presence of mind, was perfectly confounded. He sat down as convicted of the grossest falsehood, and the honourable Manager had a temporary triumph in that show of conviction. Now, at the distance of five years, the matter is set straight. Did Mr. Middleton"—mark this word—"impose upon your Lordships, or who did? I have no right to urge this against the honourable Manager : he is answerable to his own conscience."

My Lords, I am : and I should be ashamed to face this Court if I could not clear myself, at least, from the intention here imputed to me. My Lords, I believe the learned gentleman will admit, if this had been an act of inadvertence—if it had happened afterwards in the course of my speech and comment upon this part of the evidence—that I could not have intentionally endeavoured to entrap Mr. Middleton. I believe the gentleman will admit that he has urged this charge in terms in which he

* Speech of Mr. Plumer.

ought not to have urged it. The learned gentleman seems in-clined to afford me this grace and concession. But does the learned gentleman think I ask his favour upon this occasion? No, my Lords; the fact is that the whole of this charge is founded upon a complete, gross and scandalous, blunder of the learned gentleman's own! I say a blunder; for even the example of his total want of candour shall not make me stoop to retort the insinuation that the error was wilful. But it is unpardonable, I say, my Lords; for, in a case like this—in accusing the person he was accusing—for in my character in this [matter] the character of all the Managers and of the Commons of England would be implicated—he ought, and it was his duty, to have looked well to the grounds upon which he brought such a charge.

Now, my Lords, what was the fact? Was it a fact that such a question was put to Mr. Middleton and that the wrong treaty was so shown to him? My Lords, it was a fact. Was it a fact that that question and that proceeding did puzzle and confound Mr. Middleton? My Lords, so the fact was. But there is another little circumstance which that learned gentleman ought to have inquired into before he brought this charge against me, namely— was it I that did it? No, my Lords, it was not. It was one of your Lordship's Court : it was the late Earl Camden, whom we all regret, who put the question and directed the treaty to be shown the witness; and, what is more curious, I was the person who set Earl Camden right upon the subject! Now what will that Counsel say upon this matter? What did he see in any part of my conduct or character in this business that could make him think I could stoop to such a proceeding;—for it could not be error in me, and the Counsel more than insinuates that it could not be so; and for what purpose was the momentary triumph that I was to obtain? To disconcert Mr. Middleton? Good God! your Lordships remember Mr. Middleton at your bar. Could you imagine that I could have such an object; that I should try to mislead equivocation?—to intimidate servility?— to browbeat panic?—to make confusion worse confounded? It is impossible that your Lordships or any person could conceive that I could have had such an object, much less that I could stoop to such means to effect it.

But, I believe, Mr. Middleton would not thank the learned

gentleman for bringing him forward again in so conspicuous a situation to this House. Your Lordships, I am sure, remember his testimony when you saw him at your bar—as it were, prevarication personified,—when you saw me treating him with peculiar tenderness; for, if I had applied to your Lordships in some part of his testimony, you must and I am sure you would have committed that immaculate gentleman whom the learned Counsel were endeavouring to set up so high. It is not their interest, I say, to have endeavoured to have restored the credit of this testimony by the means which they have used. Remembering the whole of his evidence, I may say that that gentleman did certainly produce the exercise in others, in a very eminent degree, of that faculty of which he seemed totally dispossessed himself. I do believe there is nothing more memorable in the whole of this trial than Mr. Middleton's total want of all memory. I believe there is nothing which your Lordships forgot so little as his total oblivion of all the material passages of his life. This is the fact with respect to which the learned Counsel, I say again, should have well considered the subject before he had brought such a charge.

But it is not merely a charge against me: it is in some measure an accusation against himself. The learned gentleman says that I confounded and confused the presence of mind of Mr. Middleton; that he sat down confounded, and his credit disposed of. Why did not the learned gentleman take care of his credit, then? Was he so ignorant of the treaties as not to know that that which was secured by the younger Begum could not have been placed before the eyes of this Court as the treaty which the elder Begum had? Why did he suffer this witness, whose credit was so essential to the cause of his client, to be disposed of by such a mean and paltry trick? The learned gentleman was guilty of no such thing. If he had looked to the Minutes, which he ought to have consulted as well as to the printed Minutes, he would have found he assisted, as he ought to have done, to set your Lordships right, and that this confusion of Mr. Middleton's did not last for an instant; for the matter was instantly explained, and the Counsel himself assisted in doing it. But the gentleman, in undertaking the defence of the presence of mind of Mr. Middleton, seems to be affected with the memory of Mr. Middleton; for it is a little extraordinary that he should have remembered the fact of the confusion and the ill consequences of a total disposal of the credit of the witness, and yet entirely have forgotten by whom that was effected.

But I have taken Mr. Middleton's part in a degree upon this subject: I have taken also the learned Counsel's part: but there is another person whose cause I also must take upon me to support. The learned Counsel ends his imprecation by saying, that, if he does not prove that I have been guilty of a thing worse than anything that Mr. Hastings has been guilty of, he implores your Lordships' condemnation of him. I implore your Lordships not to grant that request to him! I must take Mr. Hastings under my protection, and save him from the peril into which his defender has brought him. I must implore your Lordships not to visit the sins of the Counsel upon the client! I must intreat your Lordships not to take for granted that I have proved every charge against Mr. Hastings, because Mr. Law has failed in proving this single charge against me!

But it is not the only penalty which the Counsel wishes to follow his failure upon this instance. He says that, if he does not make it as clear to your Lordships as the sun—which I suppose then shone upon the Court—"let all my observations go for nothing!"

But does the learned Counsel think that I will enforce this penalty? No; I will not let him off so. On the contrary, if your Lordships think me intitled to any atonement upon this matter, as I am sure you do, my revenge shall be to entreat your Lordships to remember every word the Counsel has said, from the beginning of his speech. If time would permit, I would endeavour to remind you with the most vindictive accuracy of every argument, of every reasoning, of every statement, of every jargon, of the Counsel, from the beginning of his speeches to the end of them. And, if I could, and they were to live in your Lordships' memory, and you were to be at the trouble to recollect them, I am sure you would find that all his facts—that all his reasonings—that all his arguments—have precisely as good a foundation as the charge which he has now brought against me, and are equally worthy of your Lordships' notice and approbation.

My Lords, if this matter related to myself only, I should have done with the learned 'Counsel here, but, feeling as I do the character of the Managers for the Commons implicated in the matter, I must say a graver word or two still to that learned Counsel. My Lords, that learned Counsel says of this trick of *legerdemain*—this scandalous imposition; for such it would have been—this mean, dirty shift—that it would have been called by these names in the ordinary lines of the profession. I must tell that learned gentleman, that, if he judges of us, in the character in which we stand here, by the rules which are to regulate him in the ordinary lines of his profession, he neither understands our situation nor his own. I tell him that we stand here upon different and higher ground than that learned Counsel can do.

My Lords, I do not mean to assume an arrogance from my situation. I trust I am the last man on earth that would wish to presume on a little brief authority, or to state an unfair inequality between men in your Lordships' judgment. In many respects we are equal, but I say that we do stand here in a different and in a higher character; that upon this account your Lordships have a right to expect from us a superior degree of purity and fairness, if I may say so, in our proceedings—a greater abhorrence of anything like shift or indirect proceeding in the course of this trial; that you have a right to expect from us a conscious conviction of the rectitude of the measures which we are pursuing; that it is our business and object, not merely to convict the person accused, but to bring the whole truth before your Lordships. And for this reason I say, my Lords, the learned Counsel cannot claim that that is their situation. It is not the duty or the business of a Counsel to be conscientiously convinced—much less to profess it—of the justice of the cause which he is supporting. It is a happiness enjoyed under a constitution like this, that the merciful generosity of the law considers every man as innocent till he is convicted. It is legal evidence alone by which he can be convicted. Every person is equally entitled to the assistance of Counsel learned in the law. Confessed, detected, guilt even is equally entitled to that assistance. He is entitled, not merely to his abilities and to his arguments, but that he should take every advantage that is not absolutely unfair; that he should produce his acquittal by any irregularity even in the proceedings against him—by any flaw in the indictment: and, though a guilty person by such proceedings may sometimes escape, yet, in matter of advantage, the strictly adhering to these forms is the true security of English justice and the basis of true British jurisprudence. Therefore a Counsel is not to profess that he thinks in his conscience his client is innocent. If he does profess it, undoubtedly he thinks so, and it may produce some momentary effect upon the judge and jury; but, when he abstains from professing it, does not that Counsel see that his silence becomes the most damning evidence against the client whose cause he is bound to support; and that he himself, who ought to defend him, may be the means of his condemnation?

My Lords, we do not stand upon that ground. I say that the Managers for the Commons were bound, before they appeared here, to be convinced of the justice of the cause which was committed to their care. And I do protest, for one, that, entering into this cause with a peremptory conviction of the guilt of the person whom we were bound to arraign, and regretting as I do that that impression has not been diminished but strengthened by the defence which I have heard, if, in the course of it, I had found by reasoning or by evidence that I had embarked in error and that the person was innocent—if that previous conviction in my own mind had been removed—I would have returned to the Commons and said that it was my duty to decline the office, and that some other person ought to be appointed in my place. This I hold to be the duty of a Manager; and that it is his duty, even if he saw, by some error or mistake, your Lordships misconceiving any matter of testimony which was given at your bar, and that it made by error and mistake an impression against the criminal— that it would be as much the duty of the Managers for the Commons to remove that impression from your Lordships' minds as it would have been for the Defendant's own Counsel; for that we stand here not foully to procure a conviction of the person, but, respecting our situations in proportion to the weight and authority with which we act, that we are bound to act with an additional purity, and to omit no methods that your Lordships' judgments may be formed upon a full view of the whole truth,— whether it tends to convict or acquit the person accused. This I take to be the distinction between the Managers and any feed Counsel in any Court whatever—that they have different duties, and that a superior degree of rectitude ought to be expected from them. And therefore I say, that if the gentleman had understood the character in which we stand, that if the gentleman had understood his own professional character, it should have given him a tenfold degree of caution before he had brought such a charge as the present. My Lords, there I shall leave it; and I trust it will be a warning to that learned Counsel, when next he accuses any Manager or any other person, either to be a little more cautious in his charge or a little surer of his fact.

My Lords, I have thought it my duty to dwell a good deal upon this matter. It may be also proper to state to your Lordships that the error, as I conceive it, into which the learned Counsel fell, was his looking simply at the printed Evidence, and not giving himself the trouble to compare it with the notes of the shorthand writer, which, I believe, would be admitted, even by the clerk at your Lordships' table, to be more correct upon the subject than his notes even affect or attempt to be. But what makes it more extraordinary is, that, if the learned gentleman had taken the trouble to have cast his eye a little above the passage he has quoted, he would have seen that the examination on the part of the Managers had ended, and that the question following had been put by a noble Lord, and that according to the order of the testimony it had not been again interrupted, and that the inference ought to have been—that the examination had continued from that break by the Court, and had not been resumed by any of the Managers. Earl Camden says :—

"I should be glad to know from the witness "—I have before stated I had done my examination—" for what reason it was that he did not send an account of this material transaction either to the Governor or to the Board?'—" I could have had no other reason than not considering it as any new transaction, but merely a confirmation of the former."

Earl Camden. " I should be glad to know whether, now the treaty has been read to him, he is ready upon his own observation to say that they are precisely the same?"—" They are not precisely the same. There are some exchange of conditions proposed and agreed to by the Nabob and the Begum mutually."

Earl Camden. " Whether there is not a clause whereby the Nawab binds himself to demand no loan from the elder Begum?"

Lord Chancellor. " Do you recollect that clause by which the Nawab binds himself to demand no loan from the elder Begum ?" —"No : I don't recollect it."

Lord Chancellor. " Read that passage again, then. I think there is such a clause."

The clerk read ; and then it was, I presume, that Mr. Middleton is stated to have sat down confounded. Mr. Law afterwards himself states—" That relates to the younger Begum." And there the whole matter was cleared up : and therefore the confusion of the witness continuing in that manner was matter of imagination of the learned gentleman.

My Lords, the Counsel now are certainly come, at the end of the second day's speaking, to where, in my opinion, they ought to have commenced the first day's speaking : they are come to the point, whether or not—the guarantee and treaty having been admitted by us all, and the original right either to the treasures or guarantees being totally out of the question upon any other [ground] than as settled by that treaty — they come now to whether the Begum did, or not, do anything to violate that guarantee. They seem to come to that very slowly and with considerable reluctance ; and now they have got closely to it they touch it with great caution.

The learned Counsel says, that Mr. Hastings conceived by the law of nations that every treaty is upon an implied, if not an express, condition of mutual friendship. He then quotes a passage from Grotius, to show you that a treaty is always binding upon both parties, and he refers to another quotation to the same purpose, made by his learned friend from Puffendorf : he adds— " I find Vattel in his second book states the same doctrine." Then he says,—" If mutual friendship be an implied condition of a treaty of guarantee, the violation of that treaty dissolves the whole." He then quotes Puffendorf again, as quoted by his learned friend, upon which I will not tire your Lordships ; but it is stated that all the articles of a public treaty are in the nature of conditions, and that if one of them be not fully performed, it dissolves the whole.

He also assures you from the same high authorities—and all the way through it is very observable the caution which the gentlemen use whenever there is no occasion ; whenever they want to establish any self-evident proposition — any palpable truism—they proceed with the utmost degree of diffidence ; when anything very silly is going to be produced, it is countenanced by a quotation from Puffendorf! I am certain, if the Counsel had occasion to risk the assertion that two and two make four, they would quote Cocker's Arithmetic. It is not a want of art; for they want to impress upon your Lordships' minds that they will risk nothing—hazard no assertion ; that they will bring their authority with them every step they take : and when they have established, as they think, that sort of character for diffidence and caution, under the mask of that assumed caution, whenever they come to facts or to real important matter, they make no scruple of assuming the whole—not only without any proof or evidence, but in the very teeth of proof, evidence and fact. They say— without going into more authorities upon this subject, it seems to be a self-evident proposition—that one party who is guarantee for another ought not to leave the other party in the enjoyment of the means which that other is employing for the destruction of the protecting party. I would have admitted all their propositions, all their doctrines upon this head, which may be very edifying to other parts of the [audience], without giving them the trouble of quoting a single authority. As the courtesy of this House allots a box even for foreign ambassadors, I hope when the gentleman made this speech there were a number of these ministers present ; that they understood the language ; and, if they did, that they re- ceived all these undoubted diplomatic truths with all the respect and reverence they deserve.

This being established, we come to the question, whether or not the Begum did violate this guarantee. And here, my Lords, the learned Counsel go into a considerable mass of evidence which, I confess, it was my idea they never would at all have re- sorted to. I did myself take a considerable degree of pains with respect to that part of the evidence upon which the Begums were accused ; I mean the affidavits taken by Sir Elijah Impey. The learned Counsel, however, dissatisfied with my statement of them, which upon reviewing I really think perfectly fair and candid, have gone over the whole of these affidavits again. My Lords, I will not follow them again through that subject. I have winnowed that chaff before, and I insist upon it that there is not, throughout the whole, a single grain of anything like testimony upon which the slightest presumption even can be founded. I give full credit to all that is sworn by the British officers, though not exactly corroborated—certainly from failure of memory—by the parol testimony at your Lordships' bar ; but I will give full credit to it ; and the amount of the whole is, that there were a great number of foolish and idle rumours respecting both the Wazir himself and Saadat Ali, all of which, certainly, with respect to the Nawab and Saadat Ali, turned out perfectly groundless and ill-founded.

I will now come to that part of the learned Counsel's argument in which he states the extent of the report respecting the infidelity or supposed disaffection of the Begum. And the learned Counsel states the number of persons who had given evidence at your Lordship's bar, and whose testimony was taken in India, with respect to the fact of their having heard the report of the insurrection or disaffection of the Begums. And the learned Counsel says, it is very extraordinary to consider the number of persons who must have been engaged in this conspiracy : I have contended and do contend that the whole was a plot—a conspiracy—on the part of Mr. Hastings, Mr. Middleton, Sir Elijah Impey and Colonel Hannay, to bring this accusation, for the purpose I have stated and proved, against the Begums. The Counsel argue it in this manner :—then, if this is a plot and a conspiracy, here is Mr. Wheler, Mr. Macpherson, Colonel Popham, Captain this and Lieutenant so-and-so, and all the persons, amounting in all, I think, to forty-seven, who, he says, must have been parties in this conspiracy.

My Lords, this is the most singular mode of arguing that ever was attempted in any court of justice. Our accusation is this— that Mr. Hastings, having a foul purpose to answer, did plot and conspire with certain persons to accuse the Begums of treason, in order that he might have a pretence to confiscate their treasures. The learned gentleman's argument is, to bring as proof of the existence of the treason the success of the imposition which charged them with that treason ! Why, has the learned gentleman never heard of persons being convicted of crimes in consequence of a conspiracy, with a general prevailing belief, at the time, that they were guilty, till afterwards facts have come out to prove the contrary ? The learned gentleman must have heard of numberless instances which I could refer him to in illustration of that. But if there is positive proof brought to you, and we let you, as it were, into the closet where you hear these people con-spiring, and settling and agreeing that they will bring this accusa-tion against the Begums—if we bring before your Lordships, under their very hands, confession that they were not in possession of any proof and had not even a suspicion that they really were guilty, but that they were waiting for opportunities to charge them with the guilt—can there be anything on earth so preposterous as to bring us the number of persons who are the dupes of this imposition, as positive proof that the imposture never existed ? That is the fair state of the argument. For instance, in the case of Mr. Wheler and Mr. Macpherson, they believed what ? What they signed their names to, I suppose, in the account they sent to the Directors. What was that account ? That the Begums were suspected by Mr. Hastings, and therefore he thought it proper to resume their jagirs ; that, upon the first attempt to resume their jagirs, they raised a second rebellion and opposed the Company's troops, making a new insurrection ; that Mr. Hastings, having intelligence of this second rebellion, sends a body of troops, and afterwards, in concert with the Nawab, in order to punish them for it, con-fiscates their treasures. This is the account sent home ;—sent by whom ? By Sir John Macpherson, Mr. Wheler, and by Mr. Hastings himself ! Why is this a proof that the fact was so ? Have we not direct evidence upon your Lordships' table—the evidence of Sir Elijah Impey, of Mr. Middleton himself, of every one of their witnesses—that that account was totally false in every particular ?

My Lords, Sir Elijah Impey is examined at your Lordships' bar upon a letter signed by Mr. Hastings, Mr. Wheler and Mr. Macpherson : it is in page 1638 of the printed Evidence. The account is this :—he states the just grounds of suspicion which had been given to the Nawab by the Begums and other principal jagirdars in his country, by the symptoms of disaffection and so on which they had offered. He then says—this letter, I should tell your Lordships, is dated in February, 1782—he says :—

"On the first attempt made by the Nabob to carry this plan into execution against the Begum, she determined to resist his authority, and raised a revolt by means of her eunuchs, Jewar Ali Khan and Behar Ali Khan, who had collected a force of about five thousand men in order to set the Nabob at defiance."

Now mind :—

" Notice of this second insurrection having been transmitted by the Resident without loss of time to the Governor-General at Benares, he immediately ordered a large detachment to march from Cawnpore, and the Nabob resolved to go in person to Fyzabad. On his arrival there, by the assistance of our troops he took possession of the Kella, and the eunuchs, seeing it would be in vain to make a stand when superior forces were expected, surrendered themselves prisoners to the Nabob, and their followers dispersed."

Now mind, my Lords :—

" In order to punish the Begum for this daring ill conduct, and to put it out of her power to apply the treasures which she had amassed to the purpose of raising further commotion, the Nabob resolved to seize her wealth, which by the Mahomedan laws he was entitled to as an inheritance from his father, who in the latter years of his life had committed his treasury wholly to her charge."

This is signed—" Warren Hastings, Edward Wheler, John Macpherson." Then the witness—and this your Lordships will remember is Sir Elijah Impey—was asked—" whether this account, of your own certain knowledge, is not wholly false ?" He says :—

" I know this, that the reason assigned to me for seizing the treasures was the rebellion of the Begums. Whether any other causes mixed in Mr. Hastings' mind I cannot tell, but he did not communicate more to me." " Did you not carry Mr. Hastings' pleasure respecting the seizing of these treasures, in November, 1782, to Lucknow ?"—" I certainly did." " Then could anything that happened in January have been the reason for the determination of Mr. Hastings, which you carried to Lucknow in November ?"—" No ; certainly not."

In another place you will find proof upon proof of the whole manner in which this conspiracy was conducted.

Here you have an instance of the Council having been completely imposed upon. They could never have signed wilfully a falsehood. Mr. Wheler and Mr. Macpherson must have believed the statement made by Mr. Hastings, namely, that he had no charge against her for disaffection or rebellion previous to the attempt to resume her jagirs; which is stated in this very letter to have been a measure which ought not to have been excepted to by her, because, being uncharged and unaccused, a full equivalent was provided for her; that, notwithstanding this equivalent, she endeavoured to levy war and create a second rebellion;—

"And then," says Mr. Hastings, "in order to punish her for that ill conduct, the Nawab and I resolved to seize her treasures."

They believe it. But is their belief of this fact a proof that the fact was true? Is it anything more than a proof that the imposture and imposition were successful? So it is throughout the whole of this business. And, if I was to go into the whole of the evidence again, the Counsel would draw me into this situation— that I should be only making the same speech I made before, and be reading over and over again all the evidence by which I did prove, in a manner which admits not of a doubt, the existence of this conspiracy, and the absolute innocence of the Begums.

The witness is, in another place, asked:—

"What do you mean by this passage in a letter dated the 1st of December, 1781, from Chunargur:—'What we talked of concerning the Begums he highly approves and would have himself advised. He wishes it to be done immediately. I need not mention the necessity of taking care that the money be applied to the Company's use.'—Do you remember this passage?"— "I do." "What was the object of it?"—"The object of that passage I take to be the seizing the treasures of the Begums." "Did you not understand that, when the Nabob consented to the seizing of the treasure, it was an alternative in lieu of seizing the jagirs?"—"I have not the least recollection of such an alternative." "Was it upon account of the supposed rebellion of the Begums that the treasures were to be seized?"—"I understood so." "When did you hear of any attempt made to resume the jagirs?"—"I cannot ascertain the dates and times: I have no memorandum concerning it." "Do you remember this passage in a letter from Mr. Middleton to you, dated Lucknow, the 19th of December, 1781:—'I think the opposition the Begum has given to the measure of resuming the jagir'—this was before the resuming the jagirs was effected, when it was expected she would make opposition—'which, as far as it concerns her, bears not the shadow of exception, as she is to receive the value in ready money, will be a full justification of the further demands his Excellency has to make upon her.'—Do you know anything of that passage ?"—" I believe there is such a passage in a letter from Mr. Middleton to me." " Do you not see it is here admitted that the ground of seizing the treasures was the supposed resistance to giving up the jagirs when she was to be no sufferer by it, and there was no mention of a rebellion ?"—" In the passage read there is certainly no mention of any rebellion, and from that passage it would certainly so appear ; but that is Mr. Middleton's sense and not mine." " Then did you understand that Mr. Middleton was ignorant of the rebellion when he was at Lucknow ?"—" I apprehend not, because Mr. Middleton had mentioned the rebellion to me ; but I apprehend by this Mr. Middleton was pointing out two causes for seizing the treasures— a cause in addition to the rebellion." " Whether you did think the rebellion a sufficient justification by itself for seizing the treasures, without any second cause ?"—" I did not think the second cause had anything to do with it : I thought only of the rebellion." " Did you, in point of fact, know there had been no attempt to resume the jagirs, and consequently no resistance to it, on the 19th of December ?"—" I know nothing but what I have received by information from Mr. Middleton. I thought his letters contained the truth, and that there had been an attempt to resume the jagirs. I now learn it for the first time."

Now, my Lords, in another letter, in page 637 of the printed Minutes—this is the parol evidence of Sir Elijah Impey—he is examined on another passage. Mr. Middleton says to him :—

" ' Do not, my dear Sir Elijah Impey, suffer this delay to be urged or considered as an imputation of blame upon me. I entered on the business the very day after you left me, and went so far as to look upon the matter as finally agreed upon ; the actual execution only suspended until I could receive either yours or the Governor's sentiments upon the further proposal ' "— which was the seizure of the treasury,—" which is certainly of far greater consequence than the resumption of the jagirs, as it will do at one stroke, if we are not all grossly mistaken, what the jagirs will be at least two years in doing."—" What did you understand was to be done *at one stroke?*"—"I understood that to be the seizing of the treasures of the Begums; and Mr. Middleton represents that it would raise a greater sum:"—He, Sir Elijah Impey, having himself carried this proposition and this order in November to Mr. Middleton—"Did you not carry Mr. Hastings' pleasure respecting the seizure of the treasures, in November, 1782, to Lucknow?"—"I certainly did."

In another place, it appears that Sir Elijah Impey, in his answer to Mr. Middleton, says that:—

" If the Begum does resist the resumption of the jagirs,"—no accusation whatever having been then brought against her,— " then "—he says—" I think our friend . . . ."*

You afterwards have letter upon letter from Mr. Middleton, acknowledging the time on which he received the first orders to seize the treasure. You have a statement from him of the situation of the Nawab's mind; of the extreme reluctance with which he came into the measure; of his refusing absolutely to issue his parwanas to resume the jagirs, so that Mr. Middleton says, he issued his parwanas in despite of him. At last, there is a letter which states, that the Nawab, sooner than have it appear not to be his own act and his authority, consents that it shall appear his own act, though it is, in fact, an act of compulsion. I should really be fatiguing your Lordships, and going over precisely the same ground as I troubled your Lordships upon on a former occasion, if I were to trouble your Lordships with the whole of the evidence upon this case—with the private correspondence between Sir Elijah Impey, Mr. Hastings and Mr. Middleton. But in that private correspondence does lie the real gist and point of the whole of this foul mystery; and all the other letters which were written by the Nawab or Mr. Middleton, after you have detected the manner in which these letters were suborned, ought to go for nothing, and your Lordship should blot them out of your recollection.

I do not know how to meet the Counsel upon this subject. If this private correspondence had never been produced, I confess, I should have had a strong suspicion that the Begums must have been innocent, and the accusation against them the effect of a

* The letter quoted from has not been found.

conspiracy and plot, but could not have stood in this place pledged to bring the guilt home to Mr. Hastings. I should have thought, in the first place, that, from the extreme improbability of their making such an attempt, from the impossibility of succeeding in it, from the notorious fact of their great dependence upon the British Government for security against the ill will of the Nawab's ministers, it was a degree of infatuation which could not easily be suspected of them. I should have taken for granted, when I looked into what they call a mass of legal evidence, which I found nothing but a collection of trash—of rumours—when I found that called perfectly legal evidence which contained nothing like fact or proof—I should have thought that they showed great weakness in their case, when they produced nothing but such evidence. When I found also that, by the admission of Mr. Hastings himself, he was in such a situation that his character was destroyed and the affairs of his master ruined—but certainly his own ruin involved in it, unless somewhere or other he procured treasure to this amount—I should have thought that a suspicious circumstance; and upon the whole should found a strong impression— if anything short of absolute conviction—that the Begums were innocent, and that this was a plot and conspiracy of Mr. Hastings': but I could have gone no further. But we come and bring proof which the Counsel have endeavoured to slip from in every instance, but which they have never once dared or attempted to grapple with ;—I mean, the private correspondence which was afterwards providentially produced by Mr. Hastings, when Mr. Hastings returned to Calcutta—when he endeavoured to destroy and ruin Mr. Middleton—when his anger outwent his discretion—and when his revenge turned King's evidence, as it were, against corruption. Then, in a happy providential hour for the punishment of guilt, Mr. Hastings produces this private correspondence. Look at that correspondence, and, I say, the case is proved; unless the Counsel are able to show that they are forgeries—that the letter was not written. Because, what is the story which is there told? It is a complete admission that, upon the 19th of September, when Mr. Hastings signed the treaty of Chunar, though he says he had suspicions respecting the Begums, yet that he had no proof or demonstration upon the subject.

You afterwards find Sir Elijah Impey join with him, after his failure in seizing the treasures at Bidjey Gur. You see Sir Elijah Impey's description of him—that he seemed in a desperate situation ; that he had but two resources—that of Benares and that of Oude ; that of Benares had failed ;—that he dare not return without the great object of his journey. Then he found Sir Elijah Impey, the Chief Justice, going upon that scandalous errand to Lucknow, in order to collect evidence against the Begums ; their destruction and the seizure of their property having been previously determined upon ; and Sir Elijah Impey bearing in his pocket the warrant for that seizure to Mr. Middleton.

You find in these private letters that Sir Elijah Impey is not stated to have a direct order or commission from Mr. Hastings, but that he expects that Mr. Middleton should return the proposition to him in the shape and form of a proposition from the Nawab. You find the correspondence upon this subject between Mr. Middleton and Sir Elijah Impey. He states in this familiar correspondence the agonies that he has felt himself throughout this business ; the difficulty he has had to persuade the Nawab to come into it ; the unconquerable reluctance the Nawab has shown. He states that the desperate situation this has brought the Nawab to is such that his health was wasted and impaired ; that this is a direct compulsion upon the Nawab, and, as far as accusation of treason on the part of the Begums, an imposition on the public in general.

Your Lordships find at last the event is accomplished ; that the Nawab is dragged to plunder his mother ; that the object of gaining the treasure is obtained. And, when all that is complete, Mr. Hastings returns to Calcutta ; and then he signs with his colleagues the letter I have just read, falsifying the whole of the fact ; not daring to tell the directors even that the Begums had any hand in the rebellion of Cheyt Sing, or any hand in the insurrections in Baraitch or Goruckpore, he says simply, that it was a general measure, salutary to the province of Oude, that all the jagirs should be resumed ; the Begums were not to suffer anything by this measure, because they were to have an equivalent secured to them ; they took arms, encouraged other jagirdars to resist ; and then, in order to punish them, he encouraged the Nawab to seize their treasures.

When you hear the secret whispers of these conspirators, and have the admission under their hands that they never had the least ground of accusation, but that they fabricated the charge as well as encouraged the plunder, it is something farcical and idle in the Counsel afterwards to heap upon your Lordships' Minutes, as they have done, extracts of an ostensible letter from Mr. Middleton, saying—the Nawab proposes to seize his mother's treasures. The private letter says before—Sir Elijah Impey brings you Mr. Hastings' pleasure that you should desire the Nawab to write such a letter you afterwards find the Nawab writing—that the treasure was unjustly held from him. In the preceding private letter he says :—

" I have with great difficulty prevailed upon the Nabob to write such a letter to Mr. Hastings."

When you are detecting and tracing this through every instance, I say, it does not show respect in the Counsel to have wasted your Lordships' time in commenting upon the letter in the public correspondence of the Nawab and Mr. Middleton, when the real gist upon which the whole turns is contained in the private correspondence.

Instead of disputing with them that a number of people did believe this impostor; that all the officers who had given the testimony have really somewhere or other heard that the Begum had justly forfeited the protection of this Government; I admit—and admit it as aggravation of the guilt of Mr. Hastings—what the parties charge ! I say that he was as successful in his calumny against these princesses as in his plunder and oppression ; that he deprived them, not of their treasure only, but of their good name ; that he took from them " the immediate jewel of their soul," as the very means and instrument to rob them of that which he certainly did not consider as " trash "! Therefore, instead of flying from or evading this part of the argument upon which the Counsel laid so much stress, I admit it in its fullest force, and contend that, instead of extenuation, it is an aggravation of the guilt of their client.

Having stated very shortly—more from memory than from the paper which I have under my eye, but I presume it must be in your Lordships' recollection—the circumstances with respect to the plot itself, and the effect it produced of something like a general belief—if they will have it—that the Begums merited their fate, I will shortly allude to what the Counsel have introduced with a considerable degree of parade, namely, the actual circumstances of the Begums' guilt. These were stated formally in three heads ; namely, that they principally encouraged the disturbances in Baraitch and Goruckpore ; that they gave actual assistance to Cheyt Sing ; and that they excited the jagirdars to insurrection, in order to oppose the resumption of the jagirs. Fortunately, my trouble upon this occasion, and your Lordships', is shortened by one of these charges having been completely abandoned, though stated and solemnly signed by Mr. Hastings—that they principally excited the jagirdars to resistance ; because no attempt has been made to disprove what we fully established, namely, that resistance to the resumption of the jagirs there never was any. Therefore it is confined to the other two circumstances.

The learned Counsel say, with regard to the disturbances in Baraitch and Goruckpore, that they admit they have not attempted to disprove what we have affirmed to be the causes of these disturbances, namely, that they were the consequences of British oppression and rapacity, exercised in a degree beyond anything that, I believe, ever has disgraced human nature before. We have shown to your Lordship, and traced the origin and progress of, all these oppressions and all these disturbances. We have shown you, and [they have] admitted, the calamity of one year. We have marked the progress of a Hannay the next year—more fell than famine and war joined. We have shown the abhorrence and detestation in which he was held by all the country : we have shown the abhorrence in which the Nawab held him.

We have shown the admission of Mr. Hastings himself upon that subject. We have shown that, when Colonel Hannay had attacked some of these poor wretches in the province where they lived, their abhorrence and detestation of him was such, that, while they were bleeding upon the ground, they refused life and quarter from hands they detested so much ; that afterwards, when Major Naylor succeeded and used some little kindness to these people, they even brought him food in the night. We traced all the consequences of Salim Sing, Futteh Shah, Pertipal Sing, etc., —that they all came to rescue their zamindar from the hand of oppression, or to revenge former injuries. These facts the Counsel have not attempted to disprove. But then come the Counsel and say,—" We admit these causes might exist ; but it does not follow that there might not have been a co-existing cause with them "; and might not the exertions of the Begum have operated with these " causes to produce the effect ?"

I admit that, when I state the existence of one cause, it does not exclude the co-existence of another cause which might have produced the same effect ; but if I state a cause fully adequate to produce a certain effect, and which must of necessity have produced that effect, then it is incumbent upon the Counsel not to take any evidence from the existence of that effect to prove the existence of their cause : it behoves them either to disprove the existence of the cause I state, which they have not attempted to do, or to prove the existence of their own cause, which they have attempted, but in which attempt they have totally failed.

Now, with regard to the assistance given to Cheyt Sing ; much stress is laid by the Counsel upon a circumstance that I did not at the time think deserved much weight—I mean, the supposition that a certain number of horse and foot had marched from Fyzabad to the assistance of Cheyt Sing. The Counsel laid particular stress upon a circumstance that is come out since by parol evidence at your Lordships' bar, namely, that there were some wounded najibs taken prisoners in the battle of Pateeta, and that they confessed that they were sent from Fyzabad. The evidence of one is, that they were there but two days and had received two wounds —it rises a little afterwards—that they had received two rupees. This facetious wounded najib says, he had been there two days ; he had received two wounds, and had got but two rupees for them.

How did they prove that they were sent there by the Begums ? What is their proof upon the subject ? I believe every word and syllable that these respectable officers say—namely, that they did hear that rumour, and that this wounded najib gave this account of himself. But it is to be observed, in the first place, and it is quoted and stress is laid upon it by the Counsel who summed up the character which Mr. Hastings gives of the situation of the Nawab himself—that the Nawab, though he believes him inclined to the English Government, yet was surrounded by persons who had his power entirely in their hands, and who were actuated by the utmost hate for the English nation. There is, throughout the

whole of this evidence, every ground and reason to suspect that
this description of Mr. Hastings is just and accurate, and that
the persons principally surrounding the Nawab, and who could
make use of his power, did wish, at the first breaking out of the
insurrection of Cheyt Sing, to have employed that power in a
manner hostile to the English.   Accordingly, we find in an intercepted paper—to which, however, Mr. Hastings gives considerable
authority—an account of Cheyt Sing's force, signed by the second
in command—we find it is there stated that 1,000 najibs came
from Lucknow.   Mr. Hastings' comment upon that is, that it is a
palpable mistake—that it means Fyzabad ; and afterwards, in the
course of the evidence of these wounded najibs, his Counsel
argue that it must have been a mistake.   But at what time was
this evidence respecting the wounded najibs given, and when
could it come to the ear of Mr. Hastings ?   It does not appear
from Colonel Popham, or any other that conversed with them,
that they had ever communicated the circumstance to Mr.
Hastings.   If it was not communicated to him, it was not a fact
upon which he could have acted in any proceeding against the
Begums.   If it was communicated to him, then it is a fact he did
not believe ; because subsequent to that communication it is that
Mr. Hastings gives the most solemn authenticity to this paper,
which states that these najibs came from Lucknow, and not from
Fyzabad.   He does this with the utmost solemnity, and gives
every authority in referring to the paper, which he could not have
given, if this circumstance of the najibs had come to his recollection, without certifying that that must have been a mistake.   But
this testimony respecting the wounded najib is the only scrap of
evidence offered to be produced by the learned Counsel.

The next circumstance they lay considerable stress upon is the
affair of Captain Gordon.   And, to my astonishment, I now find
that this circumstance, which I conceived to be the most decisive
proof, and which I so argued, of the Begums' innocence, and of
the foul conspiracy which had been commenced against them,
has been found out by the Counsel to make strongly against the
Begums and much in favour of Mr. Hastings !   What is the fact ?
The Begum is charged, not only with giving actually assistance to
Cheyt Sing, but with preventing a British officer from bringing his
force to join Colonel Hannay, and by that means leaving Colonel

Hannay in a considerable degree of peril. The fact is proved to be that Captain Gordon marches to a river, the fort on the opposite side being under the command of a person named Shumshire Khan, connected with the Begum's eunuch. There then comes an extraordinary circumstance. Captain Gordon, who was not then in the Begum's country, but had been assisted by the country people through the whole of his march, is desirous to pass over, and is not very readily accommodated with a boat in order that he might pass over into the Begum's territories.

There is this remarkable circumstance attending the transaction: —it is stated that these country people detested the English; and the Counsel, all through their speeches, choose to assume that they were set on by the Begums, though not in their territories; that his detachment desert and leave him with only nine or ten people; that then the country people, who before were more than a match for him, leave him, and he is carried over in safety to Tanda and placed under the protection of Shumshire Khan.

Now we produce—as all our material evidence has consisted in papers which have accidentally come to light—we produce a letter of thanks from Captain Gordon and Colonel Hannay addressed to the Begum, who, the moment she hears of their situation, sends an escort to them, and brings Captain Gordon up to Fyzabad, and afterwards places him in safety with Colonel Hannay. He writes a letter full of gratitude, confessing that he owes his life entirely to the Begum. Captain Gordon says, in terms of glowing gratitude—"that their safety and life are entirely the gift of her Highness."

Your Lordships are to observe that these letters were for a considerable time suppressed. You are to observe this most remarkable and strikingly suspicious circumstance—that, when Sir Elijah Impey went to Lucknow, in order to take depositions upon which afterwards charge and proof were to be founded against the Begums, in swearing Mr. Middleton, who knew the fact of this transaction of the Begum's having rescued and saved Captain Gordon—in swearing Colonel Hannay—in swearing Captain Gordon himself—they all three, bound as they were to swear and tell the whole truth, swear to the circumstance of the delay of Behar Ali Khan's adopted son-in-law, Shumshire Khan, in sending over the boat for the rescue of Captain Gordon: they all state that as a suspicious circumstance, and they all three suppress the fact of the Begum having saved their lives, and of their having returned their thanks in this letter of gratitude to her.

Does the matter rest there? When Mr. Middleton was examined upon the subject at your bar, here, I am sure your Lordships recollect that most disgraceful transaction, which ought indeed to have confounded and set aside, and did, I believe, for ever dispose of all credit with respect to that witness—that, when his books of correspondence were produced at your bar, I showed to your Lordships that, in the very place and very time when Major Gilpin states that he afterwards sent down these proofs of the Begum's innocence to Mr. Middleton at Lucknow—I proved to your Lordships that they had been upon his book and were torn out. Your Lordships—some of you—examined the threads of the book, compared the dates, numbered the pages. I could have shown afterwards and proved, if it had been necessary, that part of the paper which followed that is a paper not of Indian manufacture, and could not have existed at the time Mr. Middleton states the subsequent proof to have arisen. But we did prove a letter to be received at the time Mr. Middleton must have received this letter from Major Gilpin; that these papers were torn out, which evidently, upon the face of them, contained copies of this letter. We also proved in his book, from the copies of the letter sent, that there were a similar number of leaves torn out.

Lord Kenyon.—Refer to the page on the Minutes.

Mr. Sheridan.—It is in page 746 of the Minutes. There is an examination :—

" Look at these loose leaves, and say when those loose leaves were put into that book, when they were copied."—" Those were certainly copied at Calcutta ; I know it from the handwriting of the letters." " Do you know when they were copied ?"—" No ; I cannot say when." " Do you know when they were put into the book ?"—" No ; I do not indeed."

This is a part of the evidence which I very seriously recommend to your Lordships' attention. It is in pages 746 and 747 of your Minutes.

But the suspicious circumstances of this transaction do not rest here. We examined Mr. Middleton further on the subject. He admits that he had knowledge himself of the transaction at the time. And here the learned Counsel have endeavoured to give a motive for their having suppressed this letter, upon which, I find, the Counsel in their answer have laid considerable stress.

My Lords, the learned Counsel have quoted the letters of Colonel Hannay and Captain Gordon, as in themselves proof that they could not have believed the Begum sincerely well affected to us; and the reason they give is, that they say, if you advert to these letters you will find that they are not written in the style in which a British officer would write to or address any person of the Begum's rank. He even says, they are written with a humility and in a style which he seems to think was beneath Colonel Hannay or Captain Gordon to use, in addressing themselves to the mother of the reigning prince. Now, that they can infer an argument that, a person whose life was just saved by an act of bounty and humanity of a person of character, sex and rank—the Princess of Oude—there was something [so] unbecoming a British officer to address her with any degree of honour, any expressions of gratitude, that that was internal evidence that it must be the effect of fear and not grateful feeling towards the Begum, is an argument that, I think, does not do much respect to the feeling or sensibility of the learned gentleman who has used it.

They have endeavoured to establish the fact, that, at the time the Begum did this act of benevolence with respect to Captain Gordon, she could not have had a disinterested motive, but that it was at a time, in point of fact, when the British affairs had taken a favourable turn, that she tried to wipe off former imputation by this act of good will. I am astonished the Counsel can have had the hardiness to resort to this kind of argument. At first, it was on account of the letter being undated; but we did prove it a dated letter—that it was on the 7th of April; and we established upon the Minutes the most unanswerable testimony that this was not a period when a favourable turn in Mr. Hastings' situation had taken place; that it was not when a rumour of such a turn had taken place at Oude; but that it was at a time when the rumour of the danger of his situation was even exaggerated; that it was at a time when Major Macdonald states to Mr. Middleton, whose letter was subsequent, that their situation was so desperate and their suspicion so strong even of the Nawab himself, that he thinks that he and his friend Middleton—whom he called "dear Nat." upon that occasion—would never meet again upon this earth;—that it was at this moment of the extremest danger and distress of Mr. Hastings in these provinces that they do this generous act, which is attempted now to be turned against them, and is argued gravely by the Counsel as a proof that they had ill will to this country, and is denied by him to be any negative against the imputations alleged against their conduct.

There are no other actual circumstances whatever, alleged or pretended by the learned Counsel as any overt acts or any facts done, beyond the two which I have stated, by the Begums; I mean, the imputation of their having excited or assisted the disturbances in Baraitch and Goruckpore, and of their having sent some actual aid to Cheyt Sing in the persons of these najibs. And it is pretty remarkable, the manner in which the learned Counsel have proved that the Begums had najibs. For they thought it a part of their case to show the probability of these najibs having come from Fyzabad and not Lucknow, to prove that the Begums had najibs in their service. And the instance they take to prove it is, her acknowledgment and Captain Gordon's confession that she sent a party of najibs to rescue him from the peril he conceived himself to be in at Tanda. So that this circumstance of her interposing to save a British officer is the instance they bring to prove her persecution of them; and [they infer] the probability of her having najibs, because by najibs she saved Captain Gordon and restored him to Colonel Hannay! But I say that anything like a fact or overt act beyond this the Counsel have not attempted even to state.

Then your Lordships are to put the testimony—give it what weight you will—of these wounded najibs, and the circumstance of Captain Gordon's and Mr. Middleton's idea—that when she saved his life she did it upon a suspicion that a favourable turn had been taken in the affairs of Mr. Hastings—you are to put whatever inferences can arise from these two circumstances against the whole weight and mass of evidence which we have brought before you upon this occasion—against the original utter improbability of their having ever attempted any such design—against the actual impossibility of their having ever accomplished it—

against the fact, proved again and again, that the English were their only protectors, and that they would have destroyed themselves if they could have destroyed the English—against the positive fact of having saved and not attempted to destroy Captain Gordon—against the suspicious circumstance that all those who swore respecting that transaction suppressed the main circumstance of it—against the fact of the record of it having been torn from Mr. Middleton's book ;—against all those circumstances together you are to put—and I leave it in your Lordships' breasts to give what weight to it you can—the inference the Counsel have attempted to draw from the testimony of these two wounded najibs and the conduct of Shumshire Khan at Tanda.

I believe I said wrong when I said they have not attempted to state any other thing in the shape of a fact. I think they have attempted to lay some stress upon a certain intercepted letter; but I really did not think it worth while to trouble your Lordships upon that head—though I have had it suggested since—because the Counsel did himself completely abandon every inference from that intercepted letter. It is a letter of Captain Williams, found in an old trunk, without any direction or any signature. We examined Mr. Halhed, a very intelligent gentleman, and Mr. Brome had been examined before, to know if they could draw any inference from the letter or make any guess whom it was addressed to, or from whom it came ; and they candidly acknowledged that they could form no surmise from whom it came, or whom it was addressed to.

Then the only argument to be drawn from it is from the purport of it. And I think it clearly shows it could not have come from the Begums or any agent of the Begums, and could not be addressed to any person as an encouragement for him to come forward and assist Cheyt Sing's rebellion. But, on the contrary, the internal evidence of the letter goes to show that it must have been written by some power friendly to the English—the Nawab, who had in his pay sepoys. There are other circumstances which describe the situation generally of the zamindars who are attached to the Nawab and the English, namely, that the person to whom it was addressed should have his sepoys in a state of mutiny ; and by calling them to the presence it is clear that that meant the court of the Nawab—that it could not apply to the court of the

Begums at Fyzabad.   It was certainly one of those summonses which it is stated upon the evidence that the Nawab issued, when Captain Gordon was near Fyzabad and mustered his forces from all parts, before he attempted to march towards Mr. Hastings at Chunar.   I will say no more upon that letter, because, if anything is to be inferred from that, it makes against the cause it is brought to support ; and more so, because the Counsel had the candour at last to say, they did not attempt to draw any inference from it and did not place the least reliance upon it.

I cannot find any circumstance much dwelt upon by the Counsel as a proof of the guilt of the Begums, beyond what I have stated, except in one very extraordinary circumstance and mode of argument indeed.   The learned Counsel state the violent words and expressions used by the Begum, at the time when Mr. Middleton first announced to her the determination of her son, abetted by Mr. Hastings, to seize her treasures.   I was astonished at the unmanliness, almost, I may say, of the learned Counsel, to lay so much stress upon any such matter.   They describe the words which she uses when she says—" if you seize my jagirs extremity shall be the consequence ;"—" if I am driven from the country," she says, " God grant that every soul in it may perish !"   When she found she was deceived and defrauded by both Mr. Middleton and Mr. Hastings she says—" infamy upon you !"   They quote and lay stress for a considerable length of time upon all those passages and all those expressions.   They argue upon them, and press them upon your Lordships' attention, as proof of the rebellious, inflammatory, diabolical, temper and nature of this woman, which made her likely to attempt such a thing as the extirpation of the English, and rendered her an unfit object either of the favour or forbearance of Mr. Hastings.

I have read their argument upon the subject and the stress they laid upon it with astonishment.   It is not an imputation of guilt which the Counsel attempt to fix upon those persons, circumstanced as they were.   It is not a proof of an ill, or a bad, or a depraved nature, that a woman is capable of a strong degree of anger.   My Lords, a lofty spirit may be seated in the gentlest bosom and accompanied by the gentlest nature : I had almost said that a woman ought to be a passionate creature.   I do not mean to say that a violent temper is any part of their moral duty ;

I agree with your Lordships that it is certainly not ; but this much I say, that temper and patience, like all other qualities of the mind or improvements of the understanding, are things in themselves artificial, and to be acquired by experience ; that patience is the fruit of suffering ; that a forbearing temper is to be learned by conversing with injury—by having been in the habit and in the way of insult ; that it does suit the nature of a man born to bustle and struggle with difficulty in the world, to meet with injury, to meet with ingratitude, to meet with reproach—that it does suit him to have a forbearing and patient temper ; but it is a school in which a woman ought not to be practised. If this was the case in days of chivalry formerly and days of modern gallantry here, then ought not it to be the case in India ? There within their reverenced walls is homage and adoration. It is not surprising then that a person of the Princess of Oude's rank, who never could have been in the way of meeting the slightest degree of insult or of injury, when she was looking towards her protectors— when looking towards Mr. Hastings, the person to whose care she was consigned on the deathbed of her husband—when she said, holding up her hands—" they are attempting on me this injury, though you, the English, are at hand "—when she applied to Mr. Middleton for protection—when she stated the confidence she had in Mr. Hastings, that he was her guide, her counsel, that she looked to him for everything—it is not astonishing that, when she found all her hopes fail, and that they were to be her persecutors and not her protectors—it is not astonishing that, lashed into madness by her wrongs, she might have broken out into most vehement expressions. It is the nature of disappointment, when you find persecution where you expect gratitude, to feel in this manner :—" for it was not an enemy that reproached me ; for then I could have borne it : neither was it he that hated me that did magnify himself against me ; then I would have hid myself from him ; but it was thou, a man mine equal, my guide and mine acquaintance. We took sweet counsel together." These were her feelings. She had every right to depend upon the protection of Mr. Hastings : he had professed to be her guide, her counsellor. It was to him she looked for protection against injury ; and it is not to be wondered at, if she had been even moved to madness, when she experienced such treatment from such a quarter.

Excepting the inference which the Counsel had, as I said before, given so much weight to, I do not find any other material circumstance, throughout the whole of their very able, ingenious and laborious speeches, that applies really to the point which is more immediately under your Lordships' discussion. But there is one circumstance with which the learned Counsel, whose speech I have been last quoting, has summed up the whole of his arguments and his efforts, which I think still more surprising than any one which I have hitherto alluded to.

My Lords, I was accidentally, I believe, not attending my duty in this House when the learned gentleman came to this part of his speech ; and I really exceedingly regret my absence, for I should like to have been present. I am sorry that I missed the exhibition of the astonishing power of face which, I think, the learned Counsel must have exhibited, when we come to this part of his speech. For, my Lords, finding himself baffled in every attempt to prove the innocence of Mr. Hastings—finding himself weak and unsupported in every endeavour to fasten guilt upon the Begums—finding himself, with all his ability and ingenuity, compelled to slip away and to pass by, as I stated before to your Lordships, the real pinching part of the question, namely, the whole of that private correspondence which is in itself completely irrefragable—finding himself in this situation, he comes forward in the face of day—he comes forward in the face of this Court— he comes forward in the face of the Commons of England—he comes forward in the face of the people of England—he boldly and courageously offers you a bribe of half a million if you will acquit his client ! That is literally what the gentleman has con- cluded the whole of his argument with !

He says :—" Has any one person ever thought of doing that which in the result must be done ; namely, to restore all the money that was taken from them, with interest ?" He says :—" I am happy to find that the honour of Mr. Hastings and the honour of the nation must stand or fall together." He says, the people of India are mercenary people ; they are hunting after [money] ; money is their god ; that you have a right to say to them, " see what a virtuous and generous disinterested people we are : we pay with impeachment—we punish the individual ; we keep the money!" Upon that idea he proceeds to argue, and states his perfect conviction that his client must be acquitted—be the evidence what it may—because, he says:—"I know, neither your Lordships, nor the Commons, nor the Company, nor the people of England, will ever think of refunding the money with interest." "It is impossible," says he:—"so, thank God! the honour of Mr. Hastings and the honour of the nation have a common cause here." That is, they make a common cash purse; and he thinks himself completely secure, knowing that the word *refund* has not a very musical sound in the economical ears of a British House of Commons; knowing the Company will not hear of it, he thinks it impossible you can dare to convict him. But, if you do it, it is not in this instance only that you must refund; but, if he confesses more unsuspected and un-detected frauds, you must refund the whole; so that he may, in one hour of prodigal contrition, confess and bankrupt his masters, the Company. This the gentleman thinks an utter impossibility. Therefore he says—"Thank God! my client is completely safe."

I answer the gentleman's question :—"Has any one person thought of doing that which in the result must be done—to restore all the money taken from them, with interest?" I answer—"Yes! for one, I have." And I am glad to see the gentleman thinks I am right in the assertion; but I am astonished he should seem to put any surprise in his countenance upon the declaration. Does any person think it were dishonourable of the British nation, if we found this an act of plunder and robbery—the effect of conspiracy—that it was never merited by the Begums—that it would do any discredit to the British nation that they should refund the money? "Will you refund it with interest?" Yes! with interest. I would seek out Cheyt Sing. The gentleman seems to assume that, if Mr. Hastings is acquitted, Cheyt Sing will be a convicted rebel, and that Mr. Hastings is to be called to no account for that transaction. I say that, if Mr. Hastings is condemned upon that Article, it will become the dignity of the British nation to seek him out, in the camp of Madaji Scindia, or wherever he is—it will become their justice, dignity and humanity, to seek him out and make him compensation. So I say with respect to the Begums. I would search out all those miserable victims of rapacity, all those wretched children that were beat back, all those women and children who were proved to be considered by the reigning Nawab to have been the same as his mother, brother and sister; in whatever degraded situation they are, I would search them out through India. I would humiliate the British nation at their feet in atonement, and think the British character more honoured and possessing more dignity in that posture than in the proudest situation in which their oppressor ever placed that country, or himself as representing it! The honourable gentleman therefore, as far as my opinion goes, is answered upon that subject; and I trust that this last desperate attempt to win your Lordships' favour to the prisoner, by offering, as it were, a bribe in the face of the world, will certainly fail.

The gentleman says—" will you after such a lapse of time do it ?" I regret that so much time has elapsed. The delay of this trial is a thing much, deeply, to be regretted, but not to be argued upon by me now. But justice is not less a debt for having been delayed. We know that sometimes the judgments and visitations of Providence fall quickly and instantly upon those that have offended ; that, when they do, it is an awful and striking example. But, sometimes also, these judgments are long delayed ; and perhaps the consequence and the effect of the awfulness of that judgment is rather increased than weakened, when, after long protraction, it at last overtakes the guilty. Such, my Lords, may be the effect of your judgment, which is now looked to upon this great question by all India :—such will be the effect and consequence of that judgment.

I trust, my Lords, that you will not be either corrupted or intimidated by this last, most indecent and desperate, expedient of the Counsel. He tells us that the people of India love money; that money is their god. The learned Counsel shows that he thinks it is we who are so passionately attached to lucre ; that it is we who make money our god ;—nay, he comes himself, like the god of money, like Mammon, to tempt us here ! He addresses us as Mammon does—that if we will do this foul deed, see what a shining heap of money we shall have ! But I trust I speak the sentiments of the Commons and people of England

when I may be permitted to reply, in the language of Sir **Guyon**
to **Mammon** :—

[" ' Certes,' sayd he, ' I n'ill thine offred grace,
    Ne to be made so happy doe intend !
Another blis before mine eyes I place,
    Another happiness, another end.
To them that list these base regardes I lend ;
    But I, in armes and in atchievements brave,
Do rather choose my flitting houres to spend,
    And to be lord of them that riches have,
Than them to have my selfe, and be their servile slave.' "]*

These I trust will be the feelings of the British Government ;—
that upon no occasion will they be corrupted from their duty ;
that they will never be bribed from the integrity of their situation ;
while they hold this language—which I trust they ever will do—
that they will feel as strongly as can be felt in the heart that
which is expressed in the language of poetry—that Great Britain
and its Government will be—

" Lord of those that riches have,"

and will deserve and obtain the respect and homage of the
world !

My Lords, I may have omitted a great many circumstances which
the Counsel may have laid more stress upon than I think they
deserved, but, as they have avoided closing with me upon what I
think really the main point of the whole business—the point most
worthy of your Lordships' attention and consideration, and upon
which the guilt or innocence of Mr. Hastings entirely depends—
I mean, the history of the transaction given in that private correspondence—as they have not attempted to invalidate any part of
that, I should hold it perfectly nugatory and a waste of your
Lordships' time to pursue them further in any of the quotations
either of letters or evidence which they have adduced.

If I have treated any part of this subject with more levity than,
perhaps, seemed to belong to it, I confess I have done it under an
impression that, through most of their speeches, which I assure
your Lordships I have read very carefully, the Counsel themselves
could not really mean to be serious.   They use such arguments—

* " Faerie Queene," Book II., Canto VII.

such repetition of things so palpably detected and so contrary to the evidence before your Lordships—that I almost felt that they themselves could not be in earnest.

I shall trouble your lordships no further. I think the case sufficiently clear and proved. The learned Counsel, I hope, will not think, except in the transaction of one learned gentleman, that I meant to treat them in any manner unhandsomely. I am sure they have done their best for their client. They exerted great talents and ability, but the cause was against them. It was a cause which, on this part, called for no exertion and could yield no triumph.

Upon the whole of the case the second Article is now closed. The decision remains with your Lordships. Whatever that decision is, it certainly will be received by me with respectful submission ; but I must say that, till that decision is known, I entertain the same opinion with which I entered into this cause, strengthened and confirmed—that an acquittal upon this Article is absolutely impossible.

INDEX.

ABBOT, Charles. See Colchester, Lord
Aberdour, Right Hon. Sholtoe, Lord, i. 35
Abington, Mrs., i. 319 ; ii. 320
Adair, Sir Robert, ii. 223
Adam, i. 377 ; ii. 188, 245, 364
Adams, i. 170, 213 ; ii. 113
Addington, Henry. See Sidmouth, Lord
Addison, Joseph, i. 6, 269, 361 ; ii. 6
Adolphus, John, i. 337 ; ii. 194
Aikenhead, i. 72
Alcock, ii. 261
Alem Shah, ii. 396
Alen, James, i. 254
Alexander, The Emperor, ii. 269
Almon, John, i. 91
Althorp, Lord, i. 396. See Spencer
Andrews, Miles Peter, i. 139, 141, 142, 189
Angelo, Henry, i. 77, 78
Angelo, i. 77
Anne, Queen, i. 7 ; ii. 323
Anstey, Christopher, i. 85, 142
Anstruther, Sir John, ii. 188
Arblay, 'Madame d'. See Burney, Frances
Arcot, The Naboh of, i. 353
Arden, Pepper, ii. 52, 53
Aristænetus, i. 111, 112, 120
Arnold, Matthew, ii. 72
Ashburton, Lord, ii. 48, 340, 370
Assof-ud-Dowla, ii. 390, 391, 395, 396
Auckland, Lord, ii. 73, 89, 102
Austen, Cassandra, i. 86
Austen, Edward, i. 86
Austen, Jane, i. 57, 81, 84, 86, 87, 89
Aylesbury, Lady, i. 92
Ayscough, Captain G. E., i. 315

Bacon, Francis, ii. 323
Bagehot, i. 394, 400
Bailie, Dr., ii. 286, 290

Bain, Dr., ii. 146, 148, 150, 281, 284, 290
Bancrofts, The, i. xx ; ii. 320
Barber, Alderman, i. 12, 14
Barnard, i. 198, 199
Barnave, Antoine, ii. 108
Barnett, i. 198, 199
Barré, Isaac, i. 365
Barrington, Sir Jonah, ii. 261
Barry, Mrs., i. 136
Barry, Spranger, i. 30, 136
Barsanti, Miss, i. 287
Bath, William Pulteney, Earl of, i. 88
Bearcroft, ii. 50, 52
Beauclerc, Topham, i. 76
Beaufort, Duke of, ii. 265
Beaumarchais, Peter Augustin Caron de, i. 305 ; ii. 20
Bedford, Fourth Duke of, i. 353 ; ii. 130, 143, 173, 223, 371
Bedford, Duchess of, ii. 371
Begums of Oude, The, ii. 58, 67, 188, 330, 383-434
Behar, Ali Khan, ii. 412, 423
Belgrave, Lord, i. 71 ; ii. 107
Bell, Dr., ii. 35
Bellamy, Miss, i. 20
Bembridge, i. 380
Bentham, Jeremy, i. 363 ; ii. 341
Bergerac, Cyrano de, i. 324
Berry, Miss, ii. 166, 209
Berwick, i. 214
Bessborough, Earl of, i. 356-358
Betty, W. H. W., ii. 181
Bickerstaffe, Isaac, i. 99
Birch, Mr. and Mrs., ii. 18
Bismarck, Prince, i. 368
Blackburne, Archdeacon, ii. 5
Blessington, Marguerite, Lady, i. 94
Boaden, John, ii. 13, 185
Bolingbroke, Henry St. John, Viscount, i. 88 ; ii. 323
Bonaparte, Napoleon, ii. 253, 269, 345, 347

Booth, Barton, i. 26
Borino, Lady, ii. 374
Boswell, James, i. 35, 40, 76, 370 ; ii. 178, 213
Bouverie, John, ii. 157
Bouverie, Mrs., ii. 42, 117, 128, 140, 154, 157
Bowers, i. 215
Bowers, Mrs., i. 215
Boyle, Miss, ii. 131
Brereton, G., i. 245
Brereton, William, i. 91, 171, 178
Bright, John, ii. 340, 349
Bristow, ii. 395
Brome, ii. 427
Brothers, Richard, i. 118
Brougham, Henry, Lord, ii. 323, 340, 381
Brown, Miss, i. 302
Browne, Sir Thomas, ii. 294
Brummell, ii. 6
Brunton, Miss, ii. 12
Buchanan, ii. 272
Buckingham and Chandos, Duke of, i. 393, 403
Buckingham, George Villiers, second Duke of, 100, 108, 336, 337
Buckingham, Marquess of. See Grenville, Thomas
Bulkley, Mrs., i. 288
Bunyan, John, i 344
Burdett, Sir Francis, ii. 228
Burges, Sir Jas. B., ii. 72, 73, 179
Burgoyne, Lieut.-General, i. 383, 390 ; ii. 2, 8, 19, 22-24, 124, 185, 188
Burke, Edmund, x, i. 88, 309, 344, 352, 353, 360, 363, 365-367, 370, 379, 380, 396, 401, 407, 415, 416 ; ii. 40, 42, 54-60, 68, 69, 71-74, 76-79, 91, 92, 108, 188, 192, 193, 236, 237, 240, 265, 269, 293, 326, 335, 338, 340, 341, 364, 369, 372
Burnand, F. C., i. 102
Burnet, Bishop, i. 283
Burney, Dr., i. 49 ; ii. 368, 369
Burney, Frances, i. 38, 57, 84-86, 89, 94, 289, 342, 343 ; ii. 90, 203, 342
Burns, Robert, i. 368
Bute, John Stuart, Earl of, i. 33
Butler, A. J., i 265 ; ii. 146
Butler, Charles, i. 315 ; ii. 1, 181, 204
Byron, Lord, i. 68 ; ii. 180, 210, 300, 307, 317, 357, 365, 367, 371, 381

Cahir, Lady, ii. 225
Callender, Caroline. See Sheridan, Caroline
Camden, Earl, ii. 122, 191, 403, 408
Campbell, John, Lord, ii. 178, 181, 366
Canning, George, ii. 100, 175, 230, 257, 364
Canning, Hon. Louisa, i. 357 ; ii. 113
Canning, Miss, ii. 146, 153, 160

Canning, Mrs. Stratford, i. 265, 287, 357 ; ii. 16, 17, 111, 113, 121, 127, 138, 145, 149, 150, 152, 153, 156, 160, 162, 165-170, 183, 287
Canning, Stratford, ii. 145, 295
Canning, William, ii. 157
Canterbury, C. M. Sutton, Archbishop of, ii. 89, 102
Carlisle, Lord, i. 93, 383
Carlyle, Mrs., i. 309
Carlyle, Thomas, i. 309
Carrington, Lord, ii. 369
Carteret, John, Earl of Granville, i. 5
Castlereagh, Robert Stuart, Lord, i. 405 ; ii. 175, 293, 343, 347, 364
Cavendish, John, Lord, i. 376, 393, 395, 396, 398, 400, 407, 410 ; ii. 89
Caxton, ii. 319
Cazotte, i. 61
Chamberlaine, Frances. See Sheridan, Frances
Chamberlaine, Dr. Philip, i. 37
Chamberlaine, Richard, i. 37, 60, 71-73, 182, 203, 214
Chamberlaine, Rev. Walter, i. 37, 39
Charlemont, ii. 89
Charlemont, Lord, i. 384
Charles I., ii. 323
Charles II., ii. 83, 173
Charlotte, Queen, i. 262, 269 ; ii. 20, 75, 82, 91, 102, 222, 283
Chasles, Philarète, ii. 318
Chatham, William Pitt, Earl of, i. 88, 363, 366 ; ii. 60, 323-325, 336
Chatham, Lady, i. 379
Chatterton, Thomas, i. 269 ; ii. 181
Cheit Singh. See Cheyt Singh
Chesterfield, Philip Dormer Stanhope, Earl of, i. 88 ; ii. 323
Cheyt Singh, ii. 58, 418, 420-422, 427, 431
Cholmondeley, Mrs., i. 342 ; ii. 342
Churchill, Rev. Charles, i. 27, 28
Cibber, Colley, i. 26
Clarence, William, Duke of, i. 195 ; ii. 75, 136
Clarges, Sir T., i. 242, 243, 256
Cleaver, Bishop, i. 209, 210, 220, 236
Clements, Dr., i. 32
Cleveland, Duchess of, ii. 203
Clinch, i. 292
Cline, Dr., ii. 214, 279
Clive, Kitty, i. 314
Clive, Mrs., i. 47
Cobb, James, ii. 1, 18, 19
Cobbett, William, ii 345
Cochrane, Thomas, Lord, ii. 232
Cocker, Edward, ii. 410
Colchester, Charles Abbot, Lord, ii. 330, 343
Colclough, John, ii. 261
Coleridge, John, Lord, ii. 340, 349
Collier, Jeremy, ii. 315
Colman, ii. 330

Colman, George, the younger, i. 125, 260 ; ii. 21
Condewar, ii. 387
Congreve, William, i. 289, 314 ; ii. 316
Conway, i. 393 ; ii. 365
Coombe, Dr., ii. 186
Coote, i. 279
Corbett, Thomas, ii. 49
Cork, Lady, i. 280, 287
Cornwall, Charles W , ii. 98
Cornwallis, Charles, Lord, i. 387
Cosway, Richard, ii. 33
Cotton, ii. 157
Court, i. 112
Courtenay i. 366
Courtney, ii. 188
Courtney, W. P., i. 165
Cowley, Abraham, ii. 307
Cowley, Mrs., ii. 19
Cowper, William, i. 56 ; ii. 336
Cox, G. V., ii. 266
Crabbe, George, i. 140
Cramer, ii. 20
Crawford, ii. 65
Creevy, ii. 196
Crewe, ii. 125, 129
Crewe, Miss, ii. 35
Crewe, Mrs., i. 343 ; ii. 35, 75, 76, 103, 117, 125, 128, 132, 140, 154, 159, 183
Croker, John Wilson, ii. 232, 283, 284, 286, 291
Crooke, i. 135
Cruger, ii. 240
Crutwell, i. 176, 177
Cumberland, Richard, i. 158, 290, 366 ; ii. 315
Curran, ii. 370
Cyrano de Bergerac, i. 324

Daly, Augustin, i. xix ; ii. 318
Dante, i. 339
Davenport, Dr., 191
Davies, Hart, ii. 364
Debrett, ii. 23
Delany, Mrs., i. 29, 32, 274
Delap, Dr., ii. 19
De Morgan, Mrs., ii. 5
Dempster, George, ii. 238
Derby, Countess of. See Farren, Miss
De Redcliffe, Lord Stratford, ii. 16, 113, 121, 145
Devonshire, Duke of, i. xvii ; ii. 223
Devonshire, Georgina, Duchess of, i. 279, 354 ; ii. 17, 36, 48, 117, 153, 154, 374
Dewes, Mrs., i. 29
Dickens, Charles, i. 89
Digges, i. 22
Dignam, Brown, i. 350
Disraeli, Benjamin, i. 3, 102, 348, 362, 405 ; ii. 257, 340, 361
Ditcher, Dr., i. 199
Dixon, Mrs., ii. 76

Doddington, Bubb, ii. 241
Dodsley, ii. 44
D'Oily, Miss, i. 215
Dolman, Dr. R. i. 168, 169
Dolman, Mrs., i. 169
Doond Sing, ii. 333
Dorset, Duke of, i. 22
Douglas, David, i. 35
Drake, ii. 106
Drax, Mrs., i. 141
Dryden, John, ii. 313
Dubellamy, i. 301
Duckett, ii. 197, 198
Dufferin and Ava, Marquess of, Introduction by, vii
Dufferin, Lady, i. 296
Duncomb, i. 43
Dundas, Lord Advocate, i. 386, 409, 414 ; ii. 137, 198, 213, 238-240, 244, 340
Dundonald, Earl. See Cochrane, Lord
Dunning, John. See Ashburton, Lord
Dyer, i. 20
Dyer, Mrs., i. 20

Earle, William, i. 67 ; ii. 80, 149, 180
Eastlake, Lady, ii. 283
Ebrington, i. 20
Eden. See Auckland, Lord
Edgworth, Maria, ii. 200
Edgworth, Richard Lovell, ii. 200
Edward, ii. 57
Edwards, Sutherland, i. xx, 304
Egerton, Lady Louisa, i. xvii
Eldon, John Scott, Earl of, ii. 182, 265, 342
Elizabeth, Queen, ii. 323
Ellenborough, Lord, ii. 75, 188, 191, 253, 295, 386, 387, 405, 409
Elliot, Lord, ii. 243
Elliot, Sir Gilbert, ii. 25, 35, 59, 69-71, 72, 136, 159, 188, 341, 367
Elphin, Bishop of, i. 6
Erskine, Sir James, ii. 188
Erskine, Thomas, Lord, i. 361 ; ii. 94, 178, 223, 338
Espinasse, Francis, i. 309
Evill, i. 215
Ewart, Simon, i. 131, 135, 166, 178, 203, 259, 261
Ewart, S., jun., i. 126, 131, 202
Eyre, Lord Chief Justice, ii. 328

Farren, Miss, i. 319 ; ii. 130, 174
Faulkener, E., ii. 223
Febre, Frederic, ii. 353
Fielding, Henry, i. 235 ; ii. 27
Fisher, i. 297
Fitzgerald, Percy, i. xx, 52, 59, 167, 261, 318, 356 ; ii. 137, 168, 169, 172, 204, 355
Fitz-Henry, Mrs., i. 136
Fitzherbert, Mrs., ii. 85, 102, 246

Fitzmaurice, Edmond, Lord, i. 379, 385, 395

Fitzpatrick, Colonel, i. 383, 393, 396 ; ii. 188

Fitzpatrick, i. 338, 357 ; ii. 12, 198, 223

Fitzwilliam, Lord, ii. 364

Flood, Henry, i. 361

Foine, i. 383

Foote, Samuel, i. 76, 99, 101, 127, 158, 290

Ford, Dr., i. 310, 311 ; ii. 14, 37

Fordyce, i. 309

Fordyce, Hon. Lady Margaret, i. 139

Fosbrook, ii. 14

Fox, Charles James, i. x, 44, 71, 88, 209, 299, 309, 351-353, 359, 364, 365, 367, 369, 370, 372, 379, 381, 383-388, 391-393, 395-398, 400-402, 404-412, 415, 416 ; ii. 40-42, 45-50, 52, 53, 57, 58, 60, 68, 76, 79, 85-87, 89-91, 98, 99, 106-108, 128, 130, 188, 192, 193, 213, 221, 223, 229, 233, 238, 243, 247, 249, 252-257, 263, 272, 293, 294, 325, 326, 335, 336, 338, 340, 342, 343, 354, 364, 369, 372, 375, 381

Francis, Lady, ii. 178

Francis, Sir Philip, i. 221 ; ii. 54, 61, 78, 79, 178, 188, 193, 223, 335, 395

Franklin, Benjamin, i. 384, 385, 390

Fraser, Sir W., i. 348

Frederick, Prince of Wales, ii. 241

Froude, i., 350

Fullarton, Colonel, ii. 107, 364

Futteh Shah, i. 420

Gainsborough, Thomas, i. 144, 284

Garrick, David, i. 28, 45-47, 52, 54, 57, 94, 101, 108, 158, 261, 298, 309-312, 314-318, 320, 326, 337, 338, 340-342 ; ii. 4, 12, 115, 172, 319

Garrick, Mrs., ii. 25

Gay, John, i. 297

Geary, Sir William, ii. 204

Gent, ii. 357

George I., i. 323

George III., i. 262, 351, 370, 378, 385, 393-395, 400, 402-404, 408, 410 ; ii. 19, 20, 39, 47, 53, 75, 82, 85, 87, 90, 95, 97, 100-105, 107, 203, 222, 247, 251-253, 271, 323, 325

George IV., i. 195, 356, 357 ; ii. 36, 76, 80, 84, 87, 90, 96, 97, 100, 123, 194, 219, 231, 232, 240-248, 255, 258, 271, 273, 274, 283-285, 288, 291, 325, 354, 364, 372, 380

Germain, Lord George, i. 350, 376 ; ii. 364

Gervinus, ii. 317

Gibbon, Edward, i. 309, 365 ; ii. 68, 69, 71, 72, 87

Gilbert, i. 26

Gilpin, ii. 57

Gilpin, Major, ii. 424

Gilray, ii. 213

Gladstone, W. E., i. xx, 353 ; ii. 326, 340

Goethe, John Wolfgang von, i. 325, 339

Goldsmith, Oliver, i. 289 ; ii. 299, 306

Gopal Doss, ii. 399

Gordon, Captain, ii. 420, 421, 423, 425-428

Gore-Jones, Miss, ii. 359

Grafton, Duke of, i. 68, 349, 364, 395

Graham, Sir James, ii. 340

Grantley, Lord, ii. 98

Granville, Bernard, i. 274

Granville, Harriet, Countess, ii. 367, 373

Granville, John, Earl of, i. 5

Grasse, Count de, i. 387, 391

Grattan, Right Hon. Henry, i. 1, 362, 383, 384 ; ii. 250, 268, 381

Grenville, Thomas, i. xiii, 163, 200, 209, 210, 216, 217, 220, 221, 224, 229, 232, 236, 238, 243-245, 249, 266, 351, 384, 385, 387, 388, 392, 402, 403, 410 ; ii. 90, 94, 95, 175, 208, 210, 264, 293

Grenville, William Wyndham, Lord, i. 402 ; ii. 96, 97, 246, 253, 254, 257, 265, 267, 272

Grétry, André E. M., ii. 24

Greville, H., ii. 134

Grey, Earl, i. 352, 369 ; ii. 79, 86, 169, 188, 205, 229, 238, 255, 256, 272, 335, 367

Grey, Sir George, ii. 198

Grote, George, i. 362

Grotius, Hugo, i. 325, 409

Halford, Sir Henry, ii. 282, 290

Halhed, Nathaniel Brassey, i. 95-129, 134, 149-156, 159, 169, 220, 268, 339 ; ii. 427

Halhed, W. B., i. 96

Hall, Robert, ii. 345

Hammersley, ii. 204

Hampden, Lady, ii. 131

Hannay, Colonel, ii. 411, 420, 423, 425, 426

Hardy, Thomas, i. 80, 258

Hare, i. 205

Hare, James, ii. 153, 223

Harness, Rev. W., i. 342

Harpe, La, i. 61

Harris, i. 297 ; ii. 130, 178

Haseltine, Mrs., ii. 225

Hastings, Warren, i. 116, 117 ; ii. 54, 55, 58, 60, 61, 63, 67, 71, 74-77-79, 187-197, 330, 335, 343, 375, 382-434

Hemin, Miss, i. 50

Henderson, ii. 7

Herbert, ii. 175

Hernan's Miscellany, i. 121

Hertford, Lord, i. 320

Hill, G. B., i. 93, 370

Hobart, Mrs., ii., 132
Hodges, Captain, i. 191
Holland, Henry, third Lord, ii. 86, 223, 282
Holt, ii. 57
Home, John, i. 35
Hood, Samuel, Lord, ii. 53, 58, 257
Hopkins, i. 320, 327
Horne, John (Horne Tooke), i. 51, 214
Howe, Admiral Lord, i. 386, 390
Howick, Lord. See Grey, Earl
Howley, Bishop, ii. 282, 286, 287, 288, 290, 356
Hunt, James Henry Leigh, ii. 248, 381
Hurst, Thomas, ii. 281

Impeh, Sir Elijah, ii. 333, 410-419
Inchbald, Mrs., ii. 13
Ireland, Samuel, ii. 178, 180
Ireland, W. H., ii. 178, 180, 181
Irving, Sir Henry, i. xx ; ii. 322

Jackson, William, ii. 151
James I., ii. 272, 323
James, C., ii. 20
Jaques, ii. 57
Jarvis, Dr., ii. 29
Jeffrey, Francis, i. 362
Jeffrey, Lord, ii. 372
Jekyll, i. 279, 401
Jenkinson, ii. 125
Jennings, Louis J., ii. 283
Jersey, Lady, ii. 234, 374
Jewar Ali Khan, ii. 412
Johnson, Dr., i. 29, 32-34, 36, 40, 44, 93, 134, 263, 274, 308, 340, 344, 356, 361, 370 ; ii. 182, 213
Johnson, Miss Esther, i. 4
Johnstone, George, i. 390 ; ii. 364
Jones, Dr., i. 3
Jones, T. Tyrwhitt, ii. 229
Jones, Sir William, i. 148
Jordan, ii. 185
Jordan, Mrs., ii. 1, 12-15, 25, 95, 130, 180
Joy, i. 359
"Junius," i. 221, 364, 368, 369 ; ii. 335, 366

Kean, Edmund, ii. 143
Keats, John, ii. 121, 150
Kelly, Hugh, i. 20
Kelly, Michael, ii. 143, 183, 185, 186, 201, 281, 297
Kemble, John, ii. 1, 12, 19, 25, 174, 179, 181
Kenyon, Sir Lloyd, ii. 49, 50, 189, 424
Keppel, Augustus, Admiral Viscount, i. 378, 393
Keppel, Mrs., ii. 156
Ker, Dr. Lewis, i. 77, 125-134, 139, 264
Khourd Mahal, ii. 401

Killigrew, ii. 173
King, Thomas, ii. 8, 9, 11, 18, 38, 320
Kingsley, Charles, i. 321
Kinloss, the Baroness, i. xviii, 217
Knight, Captain, 178, 214
Knight, Major, ii. 260
Kotzebue, August F. F. von, ii. 176
Kuly Khan, ii. 387

La Croix, ii. 197
Lacy, i. 310, 311, 315
Lafayette, Gilbert Mortier, Marquis de, 390
Lake, Gerard, General Viscount, ii. 244
Lamb, Charles, 321
Lamb, W. See Melbourne, Lord
Lambton, ii. 238
Lane, Mrs., ii. 125
Lane-Poole, Stanley, ii. 145, 295
Lanesborough, Viscount, i. 60
Langlé, ii. 350
Lannell, ii. 206
Lansdowne, Marquess of. See Shelburne, Earl
Lansdowne, Henry Petty Fitzmaurice, third Marquess of, 353
Lauderdale, Lord, ii. 290-292, 294
Laurie, Gilbert, i. 35
Law, Edward. See Ellenborough, Lord
Lawrence, Dr. French, ii. 193
Lawson, Sir Charles, ii. 194
Lecky, W. E. H., ii. 250
Lee, i. 292, 396 ; ii. 50
Leeds, Duke of, ii. 108
Lefanu, Alicia. See Sheridan, Alicia
Lefanu, Elizabeth. See Sheridan, Elizabeth
Lefanu, Henry, i. 162 ; ii. 33, 95
Lefanu, Joseph, ii. 33, 65, 95
Lefanu, Miss, i. 47, 325
Lefanu, Rev. T. P., ii. 358
Le Fanu, Miss, ii. 6
Le Fanu, W. R., ii. 6
Le Fanu, Mrs. W. R., ii. 6
Lefevre, Right Hon. G. Shaw, ii. 205
Leigh, The Rev., ii. 161
Leigh, Mrs., ii. 156
Leigh-Hunt. See Hunt
Lenox, Colonel, ii. 75
Leoni, i. 299, 301
Lessing, i. xxi
Lewis the XIV., ii. 270
Lewis, Charles, ii. 7
Lewis, Sir Watkin, ii. 278
Leyden, i. 98
Lind, George, Lord Provost of Edinburgh, i. 35
Linley, Elizabeth Anne. See Sheridan, Mrs. Richard Brinsley
Linley, Jane, ii. 34, 161
Linley, Maria, ii. 7, 168

Linley, Mary (Mrs. Tickell), i. 90, 91, 166, 194, 262, 284-286, 343, 357, 401 ; ii. 7-15, 17, 21, 22, 24-27, 36, 41, 83, 119, 126, 156, 159, 160, 168, 287, 360, 367
Linley, Rev. Ozias, ii. 8, 128, 161, 256
Linley, Thomas, senr., i. 49, 138, 162, 163, 166, 171, 172, 175, 177, 191, 192, 200, 207, 259, 260, 262. 268, 277, 278, 296, 309-314, 317, 341 ; ii. 7, 10, 11, 18, 24, 161, 167, 360 See also letters from Sheridan to, under Sheridan, R. B.
Linley, Mrs. Thomas, i. 194, 207 ; ii. 2, 7, 10, 168
Linley, Thomas, junr., i. 49, 201, 262, 268, 296, 298 ; ii. 7, 167
Linley, William, ii. 8
Liverpool, Lord, ii. 325
Lloyd, Mrs., ii. 368, 369
Lockhart, John Gibson, i. 177, 420 ; ii. 235, 249, 283, 299
Loménie, Louis de, 281
London, Bishop of. See Howley
Londonderry, Marquess of. See Castlereagh
Long, i. 157-163, 260, 261
Long, Dudley, ii. 60, 69, 188
Longford, i. 316
Lothian, Lord, ii. 96
Loughborough, Lord, ii. 88, 90, 91, 93
Louis XIV., ii. 270
Louis XVI., ii. 108
Lowell, James Russell, ii. 156
Lowther, Sir James, i. 352
Lucian, i. 112
Luttrel, i. 138
Luyster, Mrs. Mary, i. 253-255, 259
Lyn, Mrs., i. 191
Lynedoch, Lord, ii. 224
Lynn, Mrs., i. 182, 191
Lytton, Bulwer, i. 362 ; ii. 336, 344

Macaulay, Thomas Babington, Lord, i. 281, 353, 362, 369, 387 ; ii. 71, 283, 335, 344
Macclesfield, Lord, ii. 79
Macdonald, Major, ii. 425
Macfadden, Charles, i. 3
Macfadden, Elizabeth, i. 3, 31
Mackintosh, Sir James, i. 362
MacMahon, ii. 246
MacNally, Leonard, ii. 24
Macpherson, James, i. 365 ; ii. 91
Macpherson, Sir John, ii. 411-413
Madan, F., i. 151
Mahan, Captain, ii. 199
Mainaduc, Dr. See Marmaduke
Maintenon, Madame de, i. 269
Maitland, Viscount, ii. 188
Malleson, Colonel, ii. 194
Malmesbury, James Harris, Earl of, ii. 249

Malone, Edmund, ii. 19, 89, 178, 193
Mann, Sir Horace, i. 391
Mansfield, William Murray, Earl of, ii. 183, 340, 366
Marck, Comte de la, ii. 109
Marie Antoinette, ii. 108
Marlowe, Christopher, i. 325 ; ii. 345
Marmaduke, Dr., ii. 35, 36
Martial, Marcus Valerius, i. 119
Martin, ii. 364
Mathew, General, ii. 175
Mathews, Brander, i. 310, 311 ; ii. 319
Mathews, Charles, i. 338
Mathews, Major Thomas, i. 158, 161, 164, 165, 170-184, 193, 197, 198, 200, 202-207, 242, 243, 250, 257
Mattocks, Mrs., 300-302
Maxwell, Rev. Dr., 36
McHenry, i. vii
Meath, The Bishop of, ii. 81
Melbourne, William Lamb, Viscount, ii. 230, 283
Melcombe, Lord, i. 195
Melville, Lord, ii. 79
Mercy-Argenteau, Count, ii. 109
Merry, "Della Cruscan," i. 322
Merry, Robert, ii. 180
Meynell, Mrs., ii. 131
Middleton, Nathaniel, ii. 69, 337, 391, 394, 399, 400, 402-405, 409, 411, 412, 414-419, 423-429
Mill, John Stuart, i. 362
Millar, i. 48
Miller, Lady Calliope, i. 91-94
Miller, Captain, i. 92
Milton, John, ii. 300
Minto, Earl of. See Elliot, Sir Gilbert
Mirabeau, Count, ii. 109
Mir Ahmed Ali, ii. 333
Mohammed Shah, ii. 387
Moira, Lord, ii. 219
Molière, Jean Baptiste, i. 324
Monckton, i. 354, 358 ; ii. 133
Montagu, F., i. 396 ; ii. 188
Montague, Matthew, ii. 274
Montesquieu, Charles de Secondat, Baron de, ii. 225
Moore, Peter, ii. 274, 284, 294, 295, 354
Moore, Thomas, i. vi, vii, viii, xi, 59, 64-66, 68, 70, 95, 101, 108, 112, 124, 151, 157, 162, 168, 177, 187, 201, 212, 216, 231, 252, 259, 261, 279, 280, 287, 302, 304, 306, 311, 318, 324-327, 330, 359, 367, 380, 381, 385, 420 ; ii. 29, 68, 104, 134, 136, 137, 150, 164, 167, 177, 187, 189, 195, 198, 206, 208, 224, 231, 237, 242, 272, 278, 282, 288, 295, 299, 335, 343, 359, 360, 371, 377
More, Hannah, i. 48, 49, 87, 88, 338
Morpeth, Lady G., ii. 374
Morris, ii. 275
Morris, Dr., ii. 28, 29
Morris, Malcolm, ii. 203

Motley, John L., i. xviii
Mulock, ii. 208, 369
Mulock, Miss, ii. 209
Mundy, ii. 136
Murphy, Arthur, i. 290
Murray, Dr. J. A. H., ii. 120
Murray, John, i. 177
Murray, William. See Mansfield, Earl

Nadir Shah, ii. 387
Nash, Richard ("Beau"), ii. 321
Naylor, Major, ii. 420
Nesbitt, Dr., i. 135
Newcastle, Duke of, i. 353; ii. 325, 363
Nizam-ul-Mulk, ii. 386, 387
Norfolk, Duke of, ii. 34, 37, 136, 231, 232
Norris, i. 148
North, Christopher, ii. 299
North, Dudley, ii. 223
North, E. A., ii. 188
North, Francis, Lord, i. 44, 279, 351, 364, 372, 377, 378, 394, 396, 398, 400-406, 410-412; ii. 6, 41, 47, 50, 83, 91, 245, 325
Northumberland, Hugh, Duke of, ii. 184, 185, 257
Northumberland, Duchess of, i. 93
Norton, Hon. Caroline, i. 177, 296, 420; ii. 209, 369
Norton, Sir Fletcher, i. 376
Nugent, Mrs., ii. 120

O'Brien, Denis, ii. 281
O'Connell, Daniel, i. 362; ii. 344, 364
Ogle, Dean, ii. 202, 203, 222
Ogle, Esther Jane. See Sheridan, Esther Jane
Ogle, Miss, ii. 360
Ogle, Mrs., ii. 203, 263, 264
Ogle, Nathaniel, ii. 206
Ogle, ii. 264, 265, 290
O'Hara, Kane, i. 99
Oliphant, Mrs. Margaret, i. 177
O'Reilly, ii. 131
Orleans, Duke of, ii. 83, 84
Orrery, John, Earl of, i. 4, 14, 15
Ossory, The Countess of, i. 278; ii. 23
Oswald, Richard, i. 384-386, 388
Oude, Begums of. See Begums of Oude.
Oxford, Robert Harley, Earl of, i. 9

Pacchierotti, i. 343
Paisiello, Giovanni, i. 305
Palliser, Sir Hugh, i. 351
Palmer, John, ii. 320
Palmerston, Lord, i. 68, 93; ii. 183
Palmerston, Lady, ii. 35, 133
Panton, Rev. Mr., i. 201, 206
Paoli, General, i. 76
Papendiek, ii. 101, 103

Papendiek, Mrs., ii. 101, 103
Parker, i. 210, 214
Parker, Mrs., i. 210, 214, 216
Parker, Richard, ii. 197, 198
Parkhurst, Mrs., ii. 289
Parr, Dr. Samuel, i. 35, 36, 55, 67, 68, 69, 70, 71, 97, 98; ii. 148, 158, 162, 178
Parr, Mrs., ii. 126
Patmore, P. G., i. 107
Patrick, Elizabeth, ii. 153
Patrick, Mehetabel. See Canning, Mrs. Stratford
Paumier, Captain, i. 199, 206, 214, 215, 243, 245, 246
Peake, Mrs., i. 214, 216
Peake, Miss, i. 214, 216
Peckard, Rev. Peter, ii. 5
Peel, Sir Robert, i. 69; ii. 364
Pelham, ii. 188
Pellenc, ii. 109
Pembroke Lady, ii. 103
Pennecuik, Alexander, ii. 239
Perceval, Spencer, ii. 175, 271-274, 325
Percy, Lord, ii. 257
Perkins, ii. 259
Pertipal Sing, ii. 420
Petty, William. See Shelburne, Earl
Phillips, ii. 357
Phillips, Sir Richard, ii. 360, 363
Philostratus, i. 112
Pigott, i. 386, 390
Pigott, Sir Arthur, ii. 216
Piron, Alexis, ii. 307
Pitt, George, i. 93
Pitt, William, the elder. See Chatham, Earl
Pitt, William, i. x, 71, 88, 352, 353, 366, 367, 369, 378-380, 386, 391-393, 395, 398, 400, 401, 406-411, 413, 414, 416; ii. 10, 20, 22, 39-43, 45-48, 49, 52-54, 58-61, 68, 79, 83, 85, 90-92, 97, 105, 108, 136, 137, 177, 179, 192, 193, 196, 213, 228, 229, 238, 244, 249, 251-253, 255, 293, 294, 323, 325, 326, 329, 336-339, 342, 364, 368, 369, 372, 375
Plato, i. 112
Pleydell, Mrs., i. 156
Plumer, ii. 189, 388, 392, 402
Plunket, William Conyngham, Lord, ii. 249
Plutarch, i. 112
Ponsonby, ii. 175
Pope, Alexander, i. 328; ii. 340
Popham, Colonel, ii. 411, 422
Porson, Richard, ii. 179
Portland, Duke of, i. 351, 383, 393, 395, 396, 401, 406, 410; ii. 83, 87, 89, 90, 93, 106, 133, 265, 364, 365
Powell, i. 380
Prescott, Miss, i. 43
Prévost, Abbé, i. 44

Priestley, Dr., i. 177
Puffendorf, Samuel de, ii. 409
Pultney, Daniel, ii. 59, 332
Pulteney, William, Earl of Bath, i. 88 ; ii. 323, 324
Purdie, Mrs., i. 215
Purling, ii. 400
Pye, Henry James, ii. 179
Pym, John, ii. 323

Quesnel, Father, i. 133
Quick, i. 300

Rae, John, i. 35
Raleigh, Sir Walter, i. 321
Ram, Colonel, ii. 261
Reed, Isaac, i. 323
Reid, ii. 104, 131
Reid, Mrs., ii. 131
Reynolds, Frederick, ii. 1
Reynolds, Sir Joshua, i. 279, 284, 309 ; ii. 154
Ribaut, Helena (Mrs. Halhed), i. 157
Rich, Miss, i. 92
Richardson, Joseph, ii. 32, 94, 99, 104, 133, 178, 183-186, 191, 223
Richardson, Samuel, i. 33, 40, 41-43, 45, 66
Richmond, Duke of, i. 351, 363, 369, 393 ; ii. 46, 327, 328
Ridgway, i. 332
Rigby, i. 358, 376, 377
Riggs, Madam, i. 92
Rivarol, Anthony de, ii. 82
Robarts, C. H., i. 357
Robertson, Dr. William, i. 34
Robinson, John, ii. 342
Robinson, Mrs., i. 319 ; ii. 83
Rockambeau, i. 387
Rockingham, Charles, Marquess of, i. 352, 363, 364, 378, 379, 392-395 ; ii. 106
Rodney, Admiral Sir G., i. 386, 387, 390, 391
Roeckel, J. L., i. 305
Roger, i. 332
Rogers, Samuel, i. 1 ; ii. 29, 183, 234, 237, 282, 340, 381
Rolle, i. 390, 407
Romilly, Sir Samuel, ii. 294, 341
" Roscius." See Betty, W. H. W.
Roscoe, Miss, i. 192
Rossini, Gioacchino, i. 305
Roupell, i. 390
Rückert, i. xxi
Rush, Benjamin, ii. 341
Russell, Archdeacon, i. 7, 9
Russell, Lord John, i. 352, 353, 369 ; ii. 69, 223, 371
Rutland, Duchess of, ii. 154
Rutland, Duke of, i. 408 ; ii. 49, 59-61, 293, 332, 366

Saadat Ali, ii. 386, 387, 411
St. John, Andrew, ii. 188
St. John, Mrs., ii. 131
St. Vincent, John Jervis, Lord, ii. 242
Sainte-Beuve, i. 61
Salim Singh, ii. 420
Salisbury, Lady, ii. 36
Salisbury, Lord, ii. 131
Sambucus, i. 112
Sandwich, Lord, i. 358
Saunders, Miss, i. 420, 421
Savage, Richard, ii. 182
Sawbridge, Alderman, i. 351 ; ii. 52, 53
Schiller, Frederick, ii. 372
Schomberg, Dr., i. 122
Scott, Captain Robert, i. 89
Scott, Sir Walter, i. 4, 13, 16, 81, 88, 420 ; ii. 80, 204, 234, 249, 370
Selwyn, George, i. 356, 358
Shah Alem, ii. 396
Shakespeare, William, i. 325 ; ii. 177, 316-318, 349
Sharp, Dr., i. 199
Sheffield, Lord, ii. 69, 71
Sheil, Richard Lalor, ii. 344
Shelburne, William Petty, Earl of, i. 33, 363, 369, 379, 384-386, 392-398, 400, 402, 410 ; ii. 29, 92, 364
Sheridan, Algernon, i. xii, xviii
Sheridan, Alicia (Mrs. Joseph Lefanu), i. 38, 42, 49, 60, 65, 73-76, 165, 175-177, 206, 215, 216, 230, 244 ; ii. 3, 5, 29, 64, 65, 140, 152, 155, 162, 165, 240, 251, 289, 353, 367, 370
Sheridan, Caroline (Mrs. Tom), ii. 225, 227, 260, 289, 358
Sheridan, Charles Brinsley, i. xv., 70, 252 ; ii. 204, 206, 223, 224, 234, 272, 278, 286, 290, 292, 293, 335, 357-359
Sheridan, Charles Francis, i. 50, 60, 74, 76, 78, 90, 128, 130, 138, 147, 148, 162, 164, 169, 173, 175, 176, 178, 179, 182-186, 190, 197, 202, 205, 258, 268, 381 ; ii. 2, 3, 16, 28, 64, 65, 155, 165, 346
Sheridan, Mrs. Charles, ii. 16, 155
Sheridan, Elizabeth Hume Crawford (Mrs. Henry Lefanu), i. 49, 50, 60, 74-76, 139, 147, 148, 161-165, 168, 171, 173, 174, 177, 182, 195, 197, 205, 209, 210-212, 214, 230, 245, 259, 325 ; ii. 3-8, 10, 15, 25, 28, 32, 36, 37, 75, 93, 96, 98, 99, 101-104, 138, 140, 141, 158, 167, 168, 240, 251, 353, 354
Sheridan, Elizabeth, *née* Linley, first wife of Richard Brinsley :
   " a mistress of harmony," i. 141
   announces her marriage with Sheridan, i. 201
   appeals to Sheridan for protection against Mathews, i. 165
   applications for her services as an actress, i. 260

Sheridan, Elizabeth—*continued*
assists her husband in his Parliamentary work, ii. 73
attends a ball given by the Duke of Clarence, ii. 75
attends a masquerade, i. 194, 195
begs Sheridan to return her letters, i. 255
birth of her daughter Mary, ii. 144
Charles Francis Sheridan's feelings towards, i. 149
comedy concerning (*The Maid of Bath*), i. 158
confides in Sheridan's sisters, i. 165
commits her infant daughter to the care of Mrs. Canning, ii. 150
Gainsborough's picture of, with her sister, ii. 156
George III.'s admiration of, i. 278
Halhed's admiration of, i. 148, 149, 151-157
Halhed's and Sheridan's letters regarding, i. 151
her acquaintance with the Duchess of Devonshire, i. 279
her acquaintance with Sir Joshua Reynolds, i. 279
her agitation at the impeachment of Warren Hastings, ii. 73
her agitation on hearing of Sheridan's second duel, i. 201
her amiability, ii. 154
her anxiety regarding her father, ii. 10
her appearance at Oxford, i. 150, 279
her beauty, i. 343
her burial in Wells Cathedral, ii. 160
her cheerful disposition, ii. 142
her comic song, i. 150
her death, ii. 149-151
her delicate health, ii. 142-146, 363
her description of Lord and Lady Palmerston, ii. 183
her dislike of Tickell, ii. 164
her domestic abilities, ii. 156
her early married life, i. 265
her education, ii. 154
her elopement with Sheridan, i. 166, 255
her emotion on hearing Pacchierotti sing, i. 343
her epitaph on her sister Mary, ii. 27
her experiences of "animal magnetism," ii. 35
her fondness for entertaining company, ii. 141
her good sense as a mother, ii. 158
her home life, ii. 32, 33
her honeymoon at East Burnham, i. 261, 266

Sheridan, Elizabeth—*continued*
"her husband's good genius," i. 341
her illness on hearing of Sheridan's duel with Mathews, i. 177
her last letter, ii. 148
her letter from Alicia Sheridan, ii. 67
her letter from Burke, ii. 55
her letter from her sister Mary, ii. 367
her letter from the Prince of Wales, ii. 80
her letter to her father, ii. 18
her letter to Dr. Parr, ii. 158
her letters to her sister, ii. 117
her letter to her sister-in-law, ii. 74
her letters to Mrs. Stratford Canning, i. 265 ; ii. 16. 121, 156
her letters to Mrs. Lefanu, ii. 15, 29, 127, 136, 155
her letters to Miss Saunders, i. 420, 421
her letters to Sheridan, i. 189, 191, 193-197, 206-210, 227, 243, 252, 253, 255 ; ii. 112, 118, 119, 122-126, 128-136, 142, 144. 148
her many suitors, i. 148, 149, 156, 157
her marriage with Sheridan, i. 167, 261, 263 ; ii. 111
her meetings with Sheridan, i. 90, 210
her modesty, i. 263 ; ii. 155
her musical powers, i. 279, 342 ; ii. 34
her personal appearance, i. 262, 342, 343 ; ii. 111, 149, 154, 155
her portrait by Reynolds, i. 284
her record of her sister's closing years, ii. 26
her talent for verse-writing, i. 284
her verses to Sheridan, i. 196 ; ii. 138
her voice, i. 149, 262 ; ii. 159
her wish to live in the country, ii. 122, 136
influence of Mrs. L. and Miss C. on her courtship with Sheridan, i. 253
is present at the birth of Harriet, Countess Granville, ii. 374
is taken to Hotwells, Bristol, ii. 145
keeps accounts of Drury Lane Theatre, i. 341
Kitty Clive's admiration of, i. 314
letters concerning, i. 219, 223, 230, 232, 242, 250, 251
Long's offer of marriage to, i. 157
Major Mathews' persecution of, i. 164
reads manuscripts of plays, i. 342 ; ii. 8

Sheridan, Elizabeth—*continued*
report of her engagement to Sir T. Clarges, i. 242, 243
returns to England with her father and husband, i. 171
Sheridan's verses to, i. 187
sings before the King and Queen at Buckingham Palace, i. 262
sings in Oxford, i. 192, 200
sings with the Prince of Wales (George IV.), i. 195
sits as the Virgin in Reynolds' "Nativity," i. 284
The School for Scandal attributed to her, i. 323
verses by, ii. 8, 115, 135
visits her father-in-law, ii. 28
visits Mrs. Bouverie at Delapré Abbey, ii. 42
Wilkes' (John) description of, i. 91
Sheridan, Esther Jane, *née* Ogle, second wife of Richard Brinsley
Berry's (Miss) description of, ii. 209
collects Sheridan's papers, ii. 356
dances at Mrs. Villiers', ii. 209
her admiration for Sheridan, ii. 208, 356
her affection for her step-son Tom, ii. 208, 243
her attendance at Sheridan's death-bed, ii. 288, 290
her contributions to Sheridan's embarrassments, ii. 370
her death, ii. 288, 358
her delicate health, ii. 279, 373
her dislike of politics, ii. 208
her extravagance, ii. 209
her first meeting with Sheridan, ii. 202
her letters to Sheridan, ii. 211, 212
her life at Fulham Palace, ii. 286, 288
her marriage, ii. 187, 202
letters from Sheridan. See Sheridan's letters to
letters to Elizabeth Sheridan, ii. 353-356
Sheridan's pet name for, ii. 210
takes a house in Grosvenor Place, ii. 356
Tom Sheridan's letters to, ii. 359
Sheridan (Frances), Mrs. Thomas
her birth, i. 37
her characteristics, i. 39, 40, 55
her comedy *The Discovery*, i. 320
her death, i. 55, 73
her first meeting with Thomas Sheridan, i. 38
her life in France, i. 49-55
her literary reputation, i. 56, 57
her marriage to Thomas Sheridan, i. 39
her "Memoirs," i. 23, 34, 46, 72, 76, 78, 326 ; ii. 170

Sheridan, Frances—*continued*
her personal appearance, i. 56
Kitty Clive's affection for, i. 314
the original of "Mrs. Malaprop," ii. 304
works, i. 38, 43-45, 47, 48, 51, 52, 54
writes in praise of Thomas Sheridan, i. 22, 38
Sheridan, Mary, ii. 166, 169, 170, 234
Sheridan, Mr. and Mrs. Algernon, i. xviii
SHERIDAN, RICHARD BRINSLEY
appears before the Privy Council, ii. 275
as confidential adviser to George IV., ii. 248
as Lieutenant-Colonel of a volunteer corps, ii. 346
as manager of Drury Lane, i. 340 ; ii. 9
as proxy for Fox, ii. 42
asks Fanny Burney to write a comedy, i. 57, 343
asks James Cobb to write an opera, ii. 18
at a ball given by the Duke of Clarence, ii. 75
at his father's funeral, ii. 32
at Joseph Richardson's funeral, ii. 186
at the Levée, ii. 222
Bancroft's description of, ii. 52
Bancroft's remarks on his plays, ii. 320
becomes a householder, i. 277
becomes a proprietor of Drury Lane Theatre, i. 310, 311
birth of his first child, i. 296
birth of his daughter Mary, ii. 144
brings his wife back to England, i. 175
Brougham's statement regarding, ii. 381
Burney's (Fanny) description of, i. 344
buys Dr. Ford's share in Drury Lane Theatre, ii. 37
Byron's advice to Moore concerning, ii. 371
Byron's Monody on, ii. 357
Byron's statement regarding, ii. 381
calumnies concerning, ii. 361
comes to England, i. 67
comparison with Disraeli, i. 348
conduct of his creditors, ii. 277, 280, 373
contests the borough of Stafford, i. 354
contributes to Bath newspapers, i. 90, 268
cost of his election, 355
criticises Shelburne's Ministry, i. 398

Sheridan, Richard Brinsley—*continued*
  Croker's lampoons on, ii. 283
  Cumberland's jealousy of, ii. 315
  death of his daughter Mary, ii. 170
  death of his father, ii. 27, 28
  death of his first wife, i. 151-162, 171
  declines a Peerage, ii. 362, 364
  dines at Holland House, ii. 374
  dines at Lord Lynedoch's, ii. 224
  discovers his vocation as a playwright, i. 281
  drinks the King's health, ii. 104
  Drury Lane under his management, i. 314
  elopes with Miss Linley to Dunkirk, i. 166, 255
  enters the Middle Temple, i. 210
  essays by, i. 146, 349, 350
  expurgates Vanbrugh's *Relapse*, and renames it *A Trip to Scarborough*, i. 318
  final breakdown of his health, ii. 280
  Fitzgerald's "Lives of the Sheridans." See under Fitzgerald.
  forces an apology from Major Mathews, i. 177
  founds *Hernan's Miscellany*, i. 121
  Francis' (Philip) feelings towards, ii. 61
  fulfilment of his early anticipations, i. 340
  Garrick's opinion of his plays, ii. 319
  George IV.'s esteem for, ii. 240
  Gent's Monody on, ii. 357
  Gore-Jones's (Miss) verses on, ii. 359
  Granville's (Lady) description of, ii. 374
  Grattan's statement regarding, ii. 381
  Halhed's letters to, i. 95, 96, 101-115, 122, 128, 148, 149, 151-156.
  his ability as a debater, ii. 237-339
  his acquaintance with the Linley family, i. 90, 161
  his acquaintance with Mrs. Lloyd, ii. 367
  his acquaintance with Sir Joshua Reynolds, i. 279
  his account of Mathews' conduct, i. 179-182
  his action regarding the mutiny at the Nore, ii. 198
  his action regarding the mutiny at Portsmouth, ii. 197
  his action regarding the Regency, ii. 91-93, 97, 104, 107
  his activity, ii. 88
  his affection for Earl Gray, ii. 229
  his affection for his children, ii. 169

Sheridan, Richard Brinsley—*continued*
  his ambition, ii. 88
  his ambition to be buried in Westminster, ii. 294
  his anxiety concerning his son Tom, ii. 226
  his appearance in the Court of Chancery, ii. 181
  his appointment as Privy Councillor, ii. 253
  his appointment as Receiver of the Duchy of Cornwall, ii. 243
  his appointment as Secretary to the Treasury, i. 401
  his appointment as Treasurer to the Navy, ii. 253
  his appointment as Under-Secretary for Foreign Affairs, i. 380
  his arrangement with Beaumarchais, ii. 20
  his arrest for debt, ii. 277
  his attachment to Lord Holland, ii. 223
  his attitude towards his subordinates, ii. 8, 9
  his aversion from gaming, i. 348
  his belief in his own powers, i. 313
  his birth, i. 59
  his championship of the Scottish burgesses, ii. 237-239
  his character, i. 317
  his characteristics as a dramatist, ii. 298
  his characteristics as an orator, ii. 323
  his collaboration with Halhed, i. 97-113, 120
  his "Commentary on Lord Chesterfield's Letters," i. 274
  his comparison of *The Critic* and *The Rehearsal*, i. 337
  his comparative statement of Pitt's and Fox's proposals for administration of India, i. 409 ; ii. 375
  his conduct during the burning of Drury Lane, ii. 175
  his conduct towards his wife, ii. 136
  his confidence in himself, i. 346
  his connections by marriage, ii. 7, 360
  his connection with Mrs. L. and Miss C., i. 253
  his conversational talents, i. 279, 280 ; ii 370
  his correspondence with Thos. Granville, i. xiii
  his criticism of "Letters to the Catholics," ii. 233
  his criticisms on Pitt's India Bill, ii. 42, 43
  his dealings with his creditors, ii. 37

Sheridan, Richard Brinsley—*continued*
his dealings with Lacy, i. 315-317
his dealings with Whitbread, i. 276-279
his death, i. xv., ii. 285, 286
his debts, ii. 221, 293, 355
his defence of the Prince of Wales, ii. 82, 241
his devotion to his Parliamentary duties, i. 370 ; ii. 227
his devotion to his second wife, ii. 210
his dislike of strangers, ii. 224
his disposition, i. 264
his dramatic works, i. 53, 54, 97-134. See also his Plays
his duels with Major Mathews, i. 75, 78, 178-186, 193-206 ; ii. 363
his ear for music, i. 299
his early difficulties, i. 265
his early experiences used as materials in playwriting, i. 327
his early married life, i. 265
his education, i. 64, 65, 67-70, 77, 213, 252, ; ii. 337, 371
his election for Ilchester, ii. 257
his election for Stafford, i. 355, 413 ; ii. 133
his election for Westminster, ii. 257
his election to Brooks's Club, i. 355, 356
his election to the Literary Club, i. 309
his epigrams and "Crazy Tales," i. 121
his epilogue to *Semiramis*, i. 315
his extravagance, i. 342
his facility of composition, i. 146
his fame as a dramatist, i. 339
his father's attitude towards. See under Thomas Sheridan
his final retirement from Parliament, ii. 259
his financial difficulties, ii. 181
his first comedy, i. 278
his first meeting with the Duchess of Devonshire, i. 279
his first sketch for *The School for Scandal*, i. 327
his first speech in the House of Commons, i. 358 ; ii. 326
his fondness for practical jokes, ii. 183, 368
his friendship with Halhed, i. 95, 268
his friendship with Lewis Ker, i. 125
his friendship with the Prince of Wales, ii. 76, 80-82
his funeral, i. xvi. ; ii. 284, 291, 294-296
his generosity, ii. 293, 296, 354
his good-nature, ii. 36, 354
his grief for the loss of his wife, ii. 161, 162, 201

Sheridan, Richard Brinsley—*continued*
his grief on account of his wife's illness, ii. 147
his health, ii. 373
his honeymoon at East Burnham, i. 261, 266
his hospitality, i. 342 ; ii. 293
his inability to save money, i. 342
his income at the time of his second marriage, ii. 216
his independence, ii. 372
his independence in Parliament, ii. 53
his industry, ii. 237
his infancy, i. 60-66
his interest in enclosure of commons, ii. 205
his interview with General Gordon, ii. 226
his intimacy with Major Mathews, i. 165
his jealousy, ii. 136
his journalistic work, i. 269
his kindness to his sister Elizabeth, ii. 354
his knowledge of the classics, i. 70, 71, 97
his last moments, ii. 286.
his last practical joke, ii. 368
his last speech in the House of Commons, ii. 236, 348
his life at Bath, i. 80, 90, 95, 135, 146
his literary schemes, i. 120, 268
his letters, i. 72, 73, 214-220, 224-229, 232, 236, 238, 239, 242, 244, 245, 249, 266
his letters from Burke, ii. 56
his letter from Fox, ii. 88, 354
his letter from his brother Charles Francis, i. 381 ; ii. 65
his letters from and to his father, i. 135, 212
his letter from his sister Alicia, ii. 65
his letters from his first wife. See her letters to him
his letter from the Duke of Portland, ii. 84
his letters from the Prince of Wales, ii. 241-243, 245-248
his letter to Fox, ii. 254
his letters to Halhed, i. 95, 96, 151, 153
his letter to his brother Charles Frances, i. 169, 382 ; ii. 28
his letters to his first wife, i. 205 ; ii. 112, 126
his letters to his second wife, ii. 202, 204, 205, 209, 211, 212, 214, 215, 235, 249, 255, 272, 275-277, 294, 355, 362

Sheridan, Richard Brinsley—*continued*

his letter to his son Charles Brinsley, ii. 279

his letters to his son Tom, ii. 258, 273, 280

his letters to Mr. Linley, i. 277, 279, 297, 303, 309, 310, 314, 315, 317, 318

his letter to Mrs. Ogle, ii. 263

his letter to Mr. Perkins, ii. 259

his letter to the Duchess of Devonshire, i. 355

his letter to the Vice-Chancellor at Oxford, ii. 267

his loss by the burning of Drury Lane, ii. 176

his marriage settlements on his second wife, ii. 204

his marriage to Elizabeth Linley, i. 75, 168, 261, 263 ; ii. 111

his marriage to Esther Ogle, ii. 187, 200

his meetings with Miss Linley, i. 90, 162, 210

his memorandum concerning remuneration of authors, ii. 2

his memory, i. 91 ; ii. 344

his merits as a financier, ii. 45

his method of dealing with his letters, ii. 360

his monody on Garrick, i. 338

his notes written to Richard Tickell, i. 399

his nomination for the County of Wexford, ii. 261, 263

his observations on the Westminster Scrutiny, ii. 49, 50

his official despatches, i. 385, 388, 392

his opinion of James Cobb, ii. 19

his opinion of the French Revolution, ii. 107-109

his opinion of gaming, ii. 40

his opinion of the Game Laws, ii. 40

his opinion of Lady Miller's parties at Bath-Easton, i. 94

his opposition to Pitt, ii. 40

his oratorical achievements, ii. 61, 67-69, 73, 192, 323, 341

his pride in his son Tom, i. 296, 318 ; ii. 226

his productivity, i. 339

his proposal to speak in Paris on behalf of Louis XVI., ii. 109

his prosperity, i. 287, 342, 344

his provisions for his family, ii. 293

his parents, ii. 353

his Parliamentary career, i. xvi, 68, 71, 118, 307, 348 *et seq.* ; ii. 11, 41, 89, 99, 102, 227, 336, 374

his parody on *The Rehearsal*, i. 337

Sheridan, Richard Brinsley—*continued*

his part in the impeachment of Warren Hastings, i. 54, 55, 61-73, 77, 79, 330

his patriotism, ii. 345

his personal appearance, i. 75

his personal fascination, ii. 363

his physical training, i. 77

his plans for advancement, i. 95, 120

his plans for going to France, i. 210

his plays, ii. 298

his plays, adaptation of *Pizarro*, ii. 176

his plays, adaptation of *The Stranger*, ii. 176

his plays, *The Critic*, i. 336, 337

his plays, *The Duenna*, i. 296-304

his plays, *The Rivals*, i. 281-288

his plays, *St. Patrick's Day*, i. 292-295

his plays, *The School for Scandal*, i. 319, 320-327

his political career. See his Parliamentary career

his political opinions, ii. 230, 364, 372

his popularity, i. xvi, 146, 342 344 ; ii. 227, 237, 344

his popularity in America, ii. 318

his posthumous papers, ii. 356

his powers of observation, i. 91

his qualities as son, brother, and husband, ii. 355

his reception at the Guildhall, ii. 224

his reconciliation to his father, i. 291, 302, 309

his recklessness, i. 288 313 ; ii. 36

his religious opinions, ii. 287

his remarks on the tax on race-horses, ii. 41

his re-election for Stafford, i. 413 ; ii. 133

his sanguine temperament, i. 313

his satire on Grantley and Cornwall, ii. 98

second duel with Mathews, i. 193, 198-209

his second wife, ii. 355

his self-confidence, ii. 9

his self-control, i. 347 ; ii. 236

his settlement upon his sister Elizabeth, i. 75

his sisters' affection for him, ii. 353

his sons' admiration of him, ii. 359

his speeches in Parliament, ii. 40, 42, 43-47, 58, 105, 236, 326, 375. See also particular speeches indexed separately

his speeches in the trial of Warren Hastings, ii. 58-73, 77, 188, 189, 190-194, 330, 375, 383

Sheridan, Richard Brinsley—*continued*
his speeches in Warren Hastings'
  trial :
    Burke's praise of, ii. 72
    Sir G. Elliot's praise of, ii. 59,
      69, 70
    Philip Francis' praise of, ii. 61
    Gibbons' praise of, ii. 68
    Lord Sheffield's praise of, ii. 69
    Wilkes' praise of, ii. 58
    Wraxall's praise of, ii. 59
his speech on Cold - Bath Fields
  Prison, ii. 228
his speech on Ireland, ii. 268
his speech on Pitt, ii. 255
his speech on the police, 371-375
his speeches on the Union with
  Ireland, ii. 250
his speech regarding Mrs. Fitzherbert, ii. 87
his style of writing, i. 293
his superiority over his contemporaries, i. 290
his supreme ambition, ii. 1
his tastes, ii. 367
his tenderness towards his wife, ii.
  147, 152
his translation of Aristænetus'
  works, i. 112-133
his treatment of his father-in-law,
  ii. 10
his verses to his wife, i. 187, 231 ;
  ii. 112, 113
his views of life, i. 229
his visit to Oxford in 1810, ii. 265,
  266
his visit to Scotland, ii. 263-265
his visit to the Marquess of Buckingham at Stowe, ii. 264
hopes to become an author, i. 95
inaccuracy in the reports of his
  speeches, ii. 331
illness of, i. 42
influence of his speech on Pitt, ii. 61
is excluded from Parliament, ii. 231
is seized with giddiness in the
  House of Commons, ii. 229
is sent to Waltham Abbey, i. 210,
  212
Ker's letters to, i. 125, 126-128,
  132-134
Langlé's attempt to represent him,
  ii. 350
last mention of, in the House of
  Commons ii 348
last years of his life, ii. 279-373
Leigh Hunt's statement regarding,
  ii. 381
lends money to Fox, ii. 354
makes his father stage-manager at
  Drury Lane, i. 302
manager of Drury Lane Theatre,
  i. 116

Sheridan, Richard Brinsley—*continued*
meets Fanny Burney, i. 343
meets Thomas Grenville, i. 209
meets Richard Tickell at Bath, ii. 6
" monarch of the Stage," i. 344
Moore's jealousy of, ii. 371
Moore's " Memoirs of." See under
  Moore.
Moore's, Peter, description of, ii.
  284
Mulock's statement regarding, ii.
  369
North, Christopher, on, ii. 299
obituary notices of, ii. 297. 299
obtains a Government appointment
  for his brother Charles Francis,
  i. 381
offers of pecuniary aid to, ii. 281,
  284
opposes proposal for a rival theatre,
  ii. 275
Parkhurst's (Mrs.) account of, ii.
  289
Phillips' verses on, ii. 357
Pitt's opinion of, i. 367 .
preparation of his speeches, ii. 343
prevailing impression concerning
  him in 1784, i. 414
produces *Douglas*, ii. 181
produces *Vortigern and Rowena*,
  ii. 178
proposes to retire to the country,
  ii. 122
purchases the Polesden Estate, ii.
  204
puts his affairs in order, ii. 219,
  276
rebuilds Drury Lane Theatre, ii.
  172
refuses to live by his wife's singing,
  i. 263
removes to Wanstead, ii. 168
rents Mrs. Keppel's house at Isleworth, ii. 166
representation of him in a French
  play, ii. 351
resigns Under - Secretaryship of
  State for Foreign Affairs, i. 396
Scott's eulogy of, ii. 235
sees *The Rivals* acted by amateurs,
  ii. 225
Smyth's accounts of. See Smyth,
  Professor
strike of actors at Drury Lane,
  i. 317
suffers from insomnia, ii. 214
swears not to marry Miss Linley,
  i. 206
takes his wife to Hotwells, Bristol,
  ii. 145
takes to farming, ii. 205
Thursby's opinion of, ii. 128
translations of his works, ii. 318

Sheridan, Richard Brinsley—*continued*
undertakes not to claim Miss Linley's fortune, 261
verses by, i. 130, 139-144, 146, 187, 231 ; ii. 112-115, 121, 201, 210, 381
Villemain's account of, ii. 353
visits at Woburn, ii. 223
wins a place in the ranks of fame, i. 287
writes *The Royal Sanctuary*, i. 269
writes a puff in the *Public Advertiser*, ii. 6
writ served upon him, ii. 281
Sheridan, Richard, jun., ii. 165
Sheridan, Sackville, i. 24
Sheridan, Rev. Thomas (Grandfather of Richard Brinsley), i. 1
becomes owner of Drumlane, Co. Cavan, i. 9
declines appointment to the Royal School at Armagh, i. 5
his birth, i. 3
his career at Trinity College, Dublin, i. 3
his characteristics, i. 13, 16
his death, i. 13
his literary works, i. 13-15, 19
his marriage, i. 3
his school in Dublin, i. 4
removes to Cavan Free School, i. 10
removes to Cork, i. 6
removes to Dublin, i. 12
removes to Dunboyne, i. 10
rupture of his friendship with Swift, i. 13
the bosom friend of Swift, i. 1
Sheridan, Thomas (Father of Richard Brinsley)
a pension offered to, i. 25
destruction of his theatre, i. 21, 24, 64
enters Trinity College, Dublin, i. 18
forgives Sheridan for his marriage, i. 302
his account of Richard Brinsley's second duel with Mathews, i. 203
his acquaintance with Dr. Sumner, i. 67
his appearance in *Cato*, i. 302
his appointment as stage-manager at Drury Lane, i. 302, 341
his attitude towards Richard Brinsley, i. 72, 75-77, 205, 268, 291, 302, 309, 313, 340, 341 ; ii. 2-4, 29, 31, 32, 64, 66, 353
his birth, i. 17.
his career on the stage, i. 18-24, 28, 29, 35, 36, 46, 47, 210
his characteristics, i. 18, 78
his criticism of *The School for Scandal*, i. 322

Sheridan, Thomas—*continued*
his death, i. 36, 75 ; ii. 27, 29
his edition of Swift's works, i. 7, 11, 13, 16
his education at Westminster School, i. 9, 17
his favourite toast, i. 78
his letters, i. 10
his letter regarding Richard Brinsley's affair with Mathews, i. 185
his letters to and from Richard Brinsley. See R. B. Sheridan's letters to and from his father
his letters to Charles Francis, i. 258 ; ii. 2, 3
his life in France, i. 49
his life in London, i. 27, 64, 76
his literary works, i. 18
his London residence, i. 32
his marriage, i. 22, 39
his opposition to Richard Brinsley's marriage. See his attitude towards Richard Brinsley.
his position among actors, i. 28
his wishes regarding his children, i. 76
his preference for Charles Francis, i. 198
receives the freedom of the City of Edinburgh, i. 34
removes to Bath, i. 79
removes to England, i. 25, 30
returns to Dublin, i. 30, 163
snubs Garrick, 341
Scott's mention of, ii. 235
teaches the Marquess of Buckingham, i. 163
Sheridan, Thomas (son of Richard Brinsley), i. 296, 318, xv. : ii. 17, 33, 80, 123, 126, 142, 144, 148, 157, 161, 162, 166, 168, 169, 205, 208, 218, 219, 226, 232, 243, 254, 258-260, 273, 276, 280, 286, 291, 293, 294, 358, 359, 373
Sheridan, Thomas (infant), i. 60
Shumshire Khan, ii. 423, 427
Siddons, Mrs., i. 36 ; ii. 1, 11, 13, 14, 73, 143, 174, 181
Sidmouth, Henry, Lord, ii. 98, 242-244, 252, 253, 325, 330, 364
Sidney, Sir Philip, i. 234
Simpson, ii. 20
Skelton, Dr., i. 350
Smith, i. 178 ; ii. 320
Smith, Adam, i. 35, 309 ; ii. 45
Smith, Sydney, i. 328, 371 ; ii. 233
Smollet, Tobias, i. 80, 84, 235
Smyth, Professor, i. viii. ; ii. 138, 168, 169, 190-192, 281
Somerset, the Duchess of (Sheridan's grand-daughter), i. 296
Southampton, Lord, ii. 241
Southey, Robert, ii. 276
Spencer, Lady, i. 354 ; ii. 283

Spencer, Lord, i. 354 ; ii. 364
Spencer, Lord R., ii. 223
Spenser, Edmund, i. 321
Stanhope, Earl, i. 378, 379 ; ii. 49, 53, 92
Steele, Sir Richard, i. 269, 361
" Stella," Swift's (Miss Esther Johnson),
    i. 4
Stevens, George Alexander, i. 103
Stoker, Matilda, i. xix
Storace, Stephen, i. 277
Sturt, Mrs., i. 195
Suckling, Sir John, i. 322
Suffdar Jung, ii. 391
Suja-ud-Dowla, ii. 390-392, 394
Sumner, ii. 206
Sumner, Dr., of Harrow, i. 55, 67, 68,
    72, 74
Surrey, Earl of, ii. 41
Sutton, Charles Manners.   See Canter-
    bury, Archbishop of
Swift, Jonathan, Dean, i. 1-8, 10, 11,
    13-15, 19, 31, 339 ; ii. 6, 171, 235
Sydney, Lord, ii. 94

Taine, H. A., i. 281
Tamburlaine, ii. 345
Tarleton, General, ii. 275
Tauchnitz, Baron, ii. 361
Taylor, ii. 37
Taylor, John, i. 28; ii. 131, 186, 187, 280
Taylor, Michael Angelo, ii. 50, 188, 257
Taylor, William, ii. 279
Temple, Earl.   See Grenville, Thomas
Thackeray, William Makepeace, i. 89 ;
    ii. 365, 379
Thanet, Lord, i. 205 ; ii. 294
Thiers, Louis Adolphe, ii. 212
Thompson, Benjamin, ii. 176
Thompson, Captain, i. 316
Thornbery, i. 244
Thrale, Mrs., i. 40
Thurlow, Lord, i. 364 ; ii. 48, 88, 91,
    185, 223, 256, 293
Thursby, ii. 128
Thwaites, i. 215
Tickell, Elizabeth, ii. 147, 161
Tickell, Mary.   See Linley, Mary
Tickell, Richard, i. 357, 358, 399, 401 ;
    ii. 6, 8, 11, 13, 25, 26, 32, 38, 42, 82,
    94, 99, 104, 156, 163, 183-185, 287
Tickell, Thomas, i. 6
Tierney, i. 367 ; ii. 272, 273, 364
Tighe, Richard, i. 7
Tone, Wolfe, ii. 197
Tooke, Horne, i. 51
Townshend, John, Lord, i. 205, 240,
    250, 351 ; ii. 129, 223
Trollope, Anthony, ii. 185
Truguet, ii. 197
Turner, ii. 198

Unwin, Mrs., i. 56

Vaillant, Le, ii. 144
Vanbrugh, Sir John, i. 289
Vattel, Emmerick, ii. 409
Vaughan, Taylor, ii. 284
Vawkes, i. 97
Verelst, Governor, i. 112
Vergennes, Count de, i. 384
Victor, Mrs., i. 52
Villemain, Abel François, ii. 319, 353
Villiers, Mrs., ii. 209
Vogler, Abbé, ii. 132
Voltaire, i. 133, 315

Wade, i. 214, 245
Waldegrave, The Ladies, ii. 154
Wales, Albert Edward, Prince of, ii.
    380
Wake, Sir William, i. 214
Waller, Miss, i. 141, 189
Wallis, i. 311 ; ii. 123, 221
Walpole, Horace, i. 80, 92-94, 262, 278,
    314, 321, 338, 391, 394 ; ii. 23, 48, 68,
    166, 174, 365
Walpole, Sir Robert, ii. 324
Ward, Mrs. (Jane Linley), ii. 294
Ward, Plumer, ii. 272
Warren, Dr., ii. 88, 100
Washington, George, i. 387 ; ii. 318
Watkins, Dr., i. vii, 59, 65, 263, 311,
    322-325, 338 ; ii. 58, 149, 263, 295
Watts, i. 149
Wedderburn, i. 33, 76, 364
Wellesley, Sir Arthur.   See Wellington,
    Duke of
Wellesley, The Marquess of, ii. 292
Wellington, Duke of, i. 378 ; ii. 291,
    347, 357, 364
Wendover, Lord, i. 352
Westbury, Lord, ii. 340
Weymouth, Lord, ii. 366
Wharton, Dr., ii. 178
Wheatley, Mr., i. 197
Wheeler, Edward, ii. 411-413
Whitbread, ii. 204, 256, 258, 273, 276-
    279, 364, 369
White, Anastasia, i. 37
Whiteway, Mrs. (Swift's housekeeper),
    i. 12
Whitfield, ii. 179
Whitney, Sam, ii. 82
Whitworth, Benjamin, i. 358
Whyte, Samuel, i. 32, 50, 55, 64, 65,
    359
Wilberforce, William, i. 88 ; ii. 40, 48,
    159, 171, 175, 238, 339, 341
Wilbraham, R., ii. 127, 189
Wilding, i. 148
Wilkes, John, i. 51, 88, 91, 320, 351,
    358, 365, 372 ; ii. 58, 154, 336, 364
Wilkie, i. 127, 129, 135
Wilks, ' Jack,' i. 26
William IV.   See Clarence, Duke of
William of Orange, i. 3

Williams, ii. 225
Williams, Captain, ii. 427
Williams, Mrs., i. 194
Williams, Sir Watkin, i. 244
Willis, Dr., ii. 100, 105
Wilson, ii. 246
Wilson, Professor. See North, Christopher
Wilson, Richard, i. 300; ii. 186
Winchester, Dean of. See Ogle, Dean
Winchilsea, Earl of, ii. 364
Windham, William, i. 138, 352; ii. 14, 42, 145, 175, 188, 337, 338, 364
Wombell, ii. 56
Woodfall, Henry Sampson, i. 368
Woodfall, William, i. 221, 359; ii. 44, 332

Wordsworth, William, ii. 300
Wraxall, Sir Nathaniel, i. 355-359, 408, 416; ii. 59, 63, 67, 69, 73, 91, 92, 278
Wray, Sir Cecil, ii. 48
Wycherley, William, i. 289; ii. 203
Wyndham (? William Windham), i. 138
Wynn, Lady Watkin Williams, ii. 117
Wynn, Sir Watkin Williams, ii. 19, 95

Yates, Mrs., i. 315
York and Albany, Frederick, Duke of, ii. 75, 92, 93, 96, 100, 242, 291
Young, Dr., i. 33
Young, Miss, ii. 7

Zimmerman, ii. 215

ERRATA.

Vol. i., p. 325, l. 2, *for* Marlow *read* Marlowe.
Vol. i., p. 357, l. 29, *for* gvien *read* given.
Vol. i., p. 396, l. 1, *for* Althorpe *read* Althorp.
Vol. ii., p. 53, l. 8, *for* sticker *read* stickler.
Vol. ii., p. 240, l. 3, *for* incorrctly *read* incorrectly.

THE END.

BILLING AND SONS, PRINTERS, GUILDFORD.
J. D. & Co.

CPSIA information can be obtained at www.ICGtesting.com
Printed in the USA
BVOW07s1147200514

354052BV00014B/372/P